WOMEN AND POLITICS IN EARLY MODERN ENGLAND, 1450-1700

For Karen Robertson, Sara Jayne Steen and Susan Frye

Women and Politics in Early Modern England, 1450-1700

Edited by

JAMES DAYBELL
Central Michigan University, USA

ASHGATE

Published by
Ashgate Publishing Limited
Gower House
Croft Road
Aldershot
Hampshire GU11 3HR
England

Ashgate Publishing Company
Suite 420
101 Cherry Street
Burlington, VT 05401-4405
USA

Ashgate website: http://www.ashgate.com

British Library Cataloguing in Publication Data
Women and politics in early modern England, 1450-1700
1. Women in politics – England – History – 16th century
2. Women in politics – England – History – 17th century
3. Women – England – Attitudes – History – 16th century
4. Women – England – Attitudes – History – 17th century
5. Great Britain – Politics and government – 1558-1603
6. Great Britain – Politics and government – 1603-1704
I. Daybell, James
320' .082'0942'0903

Library of Congress Cataloging-in-Publication Data
Women and politics in early modern England, 1450-1700 / edited by James Daybell.
p. cm.
Includes bibliographical references and index.
ISBN 0-7546-0988-X (alk. paper)
1. Women in politics–England–History. 2. Women–History–Renaissance, 1450-1600. 3. Women–History–Modern period, 1600- 4. Great Britain–Politics and government–To 1485. 5. Great Britain–Politics and governement–1485- I. Daybell, James, 1972-

HQ1236.5.G7W65 2004
306.2'082'0942–dc21

2003048926

ISBN 0 7546 0988 X

Printed and bound by TJ International Ltd, Padstow, Cornwall

Contents

List of Figures

Notes on Contributors

Tricia Bracher completed her PhD on 'Representations of Intimacy and the Historiography of Early Modern Private Life' (University of London, 2000), is the holder of research fellowships at the Folger Shakespeare and Henry E. Huntington Libraries, and is currently writing the first full-length study of the life and works of Esther Inglis.

Elizabeth Clarke is Reader in English at Warwick University, where she is Director of the Perdita Project. She is the author of *Theory and Theology in George Herbert's Poetry* (Oxford UP, 1997) and co-editor of *This Double Voice: Gendered Writing in Early Modern England* (Palgrave, 2000). She is currently completing a monograph entitled *Re-writing the Bride: Authorship, Politics and the Song of Songs in Early Modern England.*

James Daybell, formerly a Research Fellow in History at the University of Reading, is Assistant Professor in Medieval and Early Modern History at Central Michigan University. He is author of numerous articles, editor of *Early Modern Women's Letter-Writing, 1450-1700* (Palgrave, 2001; winner of the Society for the Study of Early Modern Women award for best collaborative project, 2002), and is currently completing a monograph entitled *Women Letter-Writers in Tudor England* (forthcoming, Oxford UP, 2005).

Jerome de Groot is Lecturer in English at Keele University. He is the author of a number of articles on Royalist culture during the 1640s. He is currently working on a book on Royalist politics and identity during the period 1640 to 1660.

Susan Frye, Professor of English at the University of Wyoming, is the author of *Elizabeth I* (Oxford UP, 1993; 1997) and co-editor with Karen Robertson of *Maids and Mistresses, Cousins and Queens: Women's Alliances in Early Modern Europe* (Oxford UP, 1999).

Barbara J. Harris is Professor of History and Women's Studies at the University of North Carolina at Chapel Hill. In addition to numerous articles, her publications include *Edward Stafford, Third Duke of Buckingham* (Stanford UP, 1986) and the recently published *English Aristocratic Women, 1450-1550: Marriage and Family, Property and Careers* (Oxford UP, 2002).

Lynne Magnusson, Professor of English at the University of Toronto, is the author of *Shakespeare and Social Dialogue: Dramatic Language and Elizabethan Letters* (Cambridge UP, 1999) and a co-author and co-editor of *Reading Shakespeare's Dramatic Language* (Arden Shakespeare, 2001). Currently she is working on a book on early modern women's letters.

Natalie Mears is a Lecturer in Early Modern History at the University of Durham. She has published several articles and is currently working on a monograph entitled *Counselling Elizabeth I: Queenship, Politics and Political Discourse* (forthcoming, Cambridge UP, 2004/2005).

Helen Payne gained her University of London PhD in 2001 for a thesis on 'Aristocratic Women and the Jacobean Court, 1603-1625'. She is currently a Visiting Research Fellow in the Discipline of History, School of History and Politics, University of Adelaide, South Australia.

Karen Robertson, Associate Professor of English and Women's Studies at Vassar College, is author of numerous articles on early modern women and Renaissance drama, and co-editor with Susan Frye of *Maids and Mistresses, Cousins and Queens: Women's Alliances in Early Modern Europe* (Oxford UP, 1999), and of *Sexuality and Politics in Renaissance Drama* (1991) with Carole Levin. She is currently working on a book on Pocahontas among the Jacobeans.

Sara Jayne Steen, Dean of the College of Letters and Science and Professor of English at Montana State University, is the author of books and articles on early modern theatre and women writers and the editor of *The Letters of Lady Arbella Stuart* (Oxford UP, 1994).

Alan Stewart is Professor of English and Comparative Literature at Columbia University, and Associate Director of the AHRB Centre for Editing Lives and Letters in London. His publications include *Close Readers: Humanism and Sodomy in Early Modern England* (1997), *Hostage to Fortune: The Troubled Life of Francis Bacon* (with Lisa Jardine, 1998), *Philip Sidney: A Double Life* (2000) and *The Cradle King: A Life of James VI and I* (2003).

Claire Walker lectures in early modern European History in the School of Liberal Arts at the University of Newcastle, Australia. She researches early modern women's religious houses, and she is author of *Gender and Politics in Early Modern Europe: English Convents in France and the Low Countries* (Palgrave, 2003).

Valerie Wayne is Professor of English at the University of Hawaii. She has edited Edmund Tilney's *The Flower of Friendship* (Cornell UP, 1992), Thomas Middleton's *A Trick to Catch the Old One* for *The Collected Works of Thomas Middleton* (forthcoming), the translations of Anne Cooke Bacon in facsimile (Ashgate, 2000), and is preparing an edition of *Cymbeline* for the Arden Shakespeare, third series.

Acknowledgements

This collection of essays grew out of several lengthy conversations that I enjoyed with Karen Robertson over the course of the summer of 2000 in and around the Thames Valley. It was our shared belief that a decade after the publication of Barbara Harris's seminal article 'Women and Politics in Early Tudor England' *HJ* (1990), the topic of women and politics in early modern England was ripe for renewed and further exploration. The upshot of our discussions was a conference organised at the University of Reading in July 2001, entitled 'Rethinking Women and Politics in Early Modern England', from which this collection at least partly derives. In the months after this event, many participants developed and enhanced their papers, in light of discussion at the conference. Other participants including Susan Frye, Barbara Harris, Lynne Magnusson, Claire Walker and Valerie Wayne produced new essays allied to the book's central themes, and further new contributions were sought in order to broaden and strengthen the scope of the volume, which produced the present essays by Tricia Bracher, Jerome de Groot and Natalie Mears. While individual essays express their own acknowledgements, as editor I would like to thank the various contributors for their commitment and enthusiasm to this project from the outset.

I would like to register my gratitude to the following, for their help, insight and input at different times and in different ways in the transformation from conference to book: Stanley Chojnacki, Elizabeth Heale, Ralph Houlbrooke, David Norbrook and Alan Stewart. At Ashgate I would like to thank Erika Gaffney, Ann Donahue and Sarah Charters for all their kind help and assistance, and I am grateful to the anonymous reader for his or her useful comments. I also owe a huge debt of gratitude to my students at the University of Reading for patiently allowing me to rehearse many of the ideas in this book in a course I taught on 'Women and Politics in Early Modern England'. For generous funding towards the organisation of the conference, I would like to thank The British Academy, The Royal Historical Society, and Professor Anne Curry and the School of History at the University of Reading, who also contributed towards the cost of illustrations. For her continual support and devotion I would also like to thank Julia Fox. Finally and above all, I would like to thank Karen Robertson, Sara Jayne Steen and Susan Frye, who over the last four or five years, and throughout the course of this project, have been a constant source of support, encouragement, counsel, inspiration and friendship. It is probably not customary to dedicate a book to someone who has contributed an essay to it (let alone to three such people). Convention aside, however, it is to these three inspiring women that this book is dedicated, with deepest affection and thanks, as scholars, friends and feminists.

J.R.T.D
Holland Park

List of Abbreviations

APC	*Acts of the Privy Council of England*, John Roche Dasent, *et al.* (eds), 46 vols, London: HMSO, 1890-
BIHR	*Bulletin of the Institute of Historical Research*
BL	British Library
BL Add. MS	British Library, Additional MS
BL Cott. MS	British Library, Cottonian MS
BL Eg. MS	British Library, Egerton MS
BL Harl. MS	British Library, Harleian MS
BL Lansd. MS	British Library, Lansdowne MS
Bodl.	Bodleian Library, Oxford
CKS	Centre for Kentish Studies, Maidstone
CSPDom	*Calendar of State Papers, Domestic*
CSPSpanish	*Calendar of Letters, Despatches and State Papers Relating to Negotiations Between England and Spain: Preserved in the Archives at Simancas and Elsewhere*, G.A. Bergenroth, *et al.* (eds), 13 vols in 20, London: HMSO, 1864-1954
CSPVenice	*Calendar of State Papers and Manuscripts, Relating to English Affairs, Existing in the Archives and Collections of Venice, and in Other Libraries of Northern Italy*, Allen B. Hinds (ed.), London: HMSO, 1911
CUL	Cambridge University Library
CUP	Cambridge University Press
DNB	*Dictionary of National Biography*
DWL	Dr Williams's Library, London
EcHR	*Economic History Review*
EETS	*Early English Text Society*
EHR	*English Historical Review*
ELH	*English Literary History*
ELR	*English Literary Renaissance*
Folger	Folger Shakespeare Library, Washington, D.C.
GEC	George E. Cokayne *et al.*, *The Complete Peerage of England, Scotland, Ireland, Great Britain and the United Kingdom, Extant, Extinct or Dormant*, 13 vols

	in 14, London: St Catherine's Press, 1910-59 [reprint, Gloucester: Alan Sutton, 1982-98]
GLRO	Greater London Record Office
HC 1509-58	*The House of Commons 1509-1558*, S.T. Bindoff (ed.), 3 vols, London: History of Parliament Trust, 1982
HC 1558-1603	*The House of Commons 1558-1603*, P.W. Hasler (ed.), 3 vols, London: History of Parliament Trust, 1981
HEH	Henry E. Huntington Library, San Marino, California
HJ	*Historical Journal*
HMC	Historical Manuscripts Commission
HMSO	Her Majesty's Stationery Office
IHR	Institute of Historical Research
InqPM	*Calendar of the Inquisitions Post Mortem, Henry VII*, London: HMSO, 1898
Kendal RO	Kendal Record Office, Cumbria
LP	*Letters and Papers, Foreign and Domestic, of the Reign of Henry VIII*, J. S. Brewer, *et al.* (eds), 21 vols and *Addenda*, London: HMSO, 1862-1932
LPL	Lambeth Palace Library
LSE	*Leeds Studies in English*
MSS	Manuscripts
NLS	National Library of Scotland, Edinburgh
N&Q	*Notes and Queries*
NRA	National Register of Archives
NRO	Norfolk Record Office, Norwich
NUL	Nottingham University Library
OED	*Oxford English Dictionary*
OUP	Oxford University Press
P&P	*Past and Present*
PMLA	*Publications of the Modern Language Association of America*
PRO	Public Record Office, Kew
PRO SP 10	Public Record Office, State Papers, Domestic, Edward VI
PRO SP 12	Public Record Office, State Papers, Domestic, Elizabeth I
PRO SP 15	Public Record Office, State Papers, Domestic, Addenda

PRO SP 46	Public Record Office, State Papers, Domestic, Supplementary
RES	*Review of English Studies*
RH	*Recusant History*
RO	Record Office
RQ	*Renaissance Quarterly*
SQ	*Shakespeare Quarterly*
Staffs. RO	Staffordshire Record Office
STC	*A Short Title Catalogue of Books Printed in England, Scotland and Ireland and of English Books Printed Abroad, 1475-1640*, W. A. Jackson, F.S. Ferguson and Katharine F. Pantzer (eds), 3 vols, 2nd ed., London: Bibliographical Society, 1976-91
TE	*Testamenta Eboracensia, A Selection of Wills From the Registry at York*, J. Raine (ed.), vol. 4, *Surtees Society*, vol. 53, 1868
TJHSE	*Transactions of the Jewish Historical Society of England*
TRHS	*Transactions of the Royal Historical Society*
TV	*Testamenta Vetusta*, Nicholas H. Nicolas (ed.), London, 1826
WCRO	Warwickshire County Record Office
YAS	Yorkshire Archaeological Society, Leeds

Original spelling and punctuation has been retained throughout in quotations from manuscripts. Contractions and abbreviations of words are extended by the use of italics, while square brackets supply apparently omitted words, provide explanations, and gloss archaic terms and unusual spellings. Contractions appearing in superscript in the original are modernised silently. The letters 'i' and 'j' and 'u' and 'v' are distinguished, and 'th' substituted for the medieval thorn ('γ'). Dates appear in the Old Style, but the year is assumed to have begun on 1 January rather than on 25 March. Women are referred to by the name or title used of them at the particular point in time written about.

Chapter 1

Introduction: Rethinking Women and Politics in Early Modern England

James Daybell

Women's involvement in *politics* – the narratives of kings and queens, and colourful stories of women's participation in court plots and intrigues – has always been the domain of biographers and historians interested in old-fashioned high political history. Writing in the nineteenth-century Rankean tradition, for example, Agnes and Elizabeth Strickland published their twelve-volume *Lives of the Queens of England* (1840-48), a survey of some 40 queens regnant and consort from Matilda to Queen Victoria.[1] Women connected to male monarchs – wives, mistresses, mothers, daughters and kin – have long been the subject of repeated historical enquiry for the kinds of power that they could wield from behind the throne.[2] Controversies over the religious influence, alleged adultery and fall of Anne Boleyn have produced some of the most heated and entrenched debate in recent Tudor historiography; historians colonise Anne Boleyn because she represents a lens through which to scrutinise the very nature of Henry VIII's monarchy.[3] Yet, despite this occasional focus on exceptional female protagonists, present-day historians are often deeply hesitant of attributing too much power, influence and agency to women: to Steven Gunn, 'there is no sign that' women at the court of Henry VII 'were regarded as important figures in their own right'; to George Bernard, Anne Boleyn was little more than a flirt and 'a loose-living lady'; to Robert Ashton, Anne of Denmark was 'incurably frivolous'; and to Malcolm Smuts, Henrietta Maria was similarly 'a frivolous young woman, temperamentally ill-equipped for serious statecraft'.[4]

In traditional political narratives, women are marginal figures: their domain, the household or 'domestic' sphere, rather than the public, male world of business and politics; the roles they played often consigned to footnotes. M.L. Bush, for example, in his analysis of the Lisle-Seymour land disputes only briefly mentions the part played by Honor Lady Lisle, a woman at the very centre of Calais politics and her husband's matters of business; Sara Lopez usually receives scarcely more than a footnote in historical accounts of her husband, Dr Roderigo Lopez.[5] Likewise, Steven Gunn in his superb essay on the 'Structures of Politics in Early Tudor England' excludes from his analysis the ways in which politics might have been shaped by structures of gender, relegating to his footnotes recent pioneering work in that area.[6]

In particular, Dr Gunn footnoted Barbara Harris's seminal essay 'Women and Politics in Early Tudor England', an essay that has provided an important framework – both conceptual and historical – for subsequent studies of women's political roles. By broadening the definition of what constituted early modern *politics*, Professor Harris has questioned traditional conceptualisations of influence and power.[7] These are themes very much at the heart of the present book of essays. A blend of traditional Tudor history and insights from modern feminist theory, the article stands as an exemplary model of how to practise women's history. Influenced by the work of Tudor historians such as David Starkey whose studies of patronage, the great household and the court argue for the personal nature of political relationships, Professor Harris moved away from a model of politics that was narrowly viewed through male-dominated state institutions, such as Parliament, the Privy Council and the law courts, in order better to facilitate the incorporation of women into the study of politics. Political goals and aspirations for the landed elite extended beyond mere influence over state government and policy, to include dynastic and family concerns, which were shared by both men and women: accumulation of land and wealth, maintenance of status and reputation, and advancement of family members' interests, in terms of careers and marriage. A constant theme of Professor Harris's research has been to show that in a very real sense, the 'domestic' and the 'political', and the 'private' and the 'public' are hard to separate during the early modern period.[8] Indeed, the family was the basic political unit through which women operated; female roles of wives and mothers were 'careers' imbued with political significance. In a patronage society where interpersonal relationships counted for so much, women were intimately involved in building and maintaining patronage and kinship networks through various social activities – marriage-arranging, placing children in other households, gift-giving, hospitality and letter-writing. By rethinking as political these social activities readily associated with the household, Professor Harris aligns herself with feminist theorists who have sought to re-conceptualise the 'domestic' as 'political'.

This book makes no claim to offer a definitive study of women and politics in early modern England. Most of the essays are concerned with socially elite women: well-connected aristocrats and literate women of the 'middling sort' operating within sophisticated manuscript cultures or urban and mercantile environments. This book does not (with the possible exception of Elizabeth Clarke's essay) deal with female involvement in popular politics – for example, protests about religious and political issues, and direct action over food prices and common rights – a field of investigation already represented by a substantial body of work. Such work defines politics broadly to encompass the political activities of ordinary men and women and highlights the ways in which the actions of rulers were influenced by perceptions of their behaviour.[9] Social status did affect the lives and experiences of women; as a group they were united less by ties of gender, than divided by differences of rank. While it was possible for women of the nobility and gentry to keep abreast of the affairs of court, parliament and foreign policy, for the majority of women their political involvement and actions were more localised, and often the action they took was direct. Indeed, Elizabeth Clarke identifies a mode of female intervention in politics (often evidenced by letters) based on rank, family, property and contacts that is distinct to women of the aristocracy: Mary Rich, countess of Warwick's influence was based on her relationships with powerful government politicians and churchmen. Yet the ability of noblewomen to intervene in politics in this manner was at its height in England during the Tudor and early Stuart period when, as Barbara Harris has argued, aristocratic women 'benefited from the evolution of the late medieval, and early modern English monarchy ... when the growth of the crown occurred in a context in which the king lacked the financial resources to create a royal army or bureaucracy' and 'depended on the unpaid service of the aristocracy whom he rewarded with the limited patronage at his disposal, and developed the court as the political and symbolic center of the monarchy'.[10] This centralisation of government though may have reduced the role of great noble households as political institutions, which performed many of the functions – administrative, judicial, patronage and military – later assumed by the State, a process that limited the opportunities for women as members of aristocratic households to achieve political influence.[11] The circumstances that allowed women significant political influence were relatively short-lived: by the late seventeenth century the growth of Parliament and new bureaucratic institutions, and the emergence of political parties 'drained power and resources from king, court, and patronage networks, the institutions that facilitated aristocratic women's political activity'.[12] The early modern period, therefore, marked an epoch of women's political influence.

While upper-class women achieved influence through social position, relationships and powerful contacts, many of the modes by which they operated shared similar traits with those identified as being used by women lower down the social scale. The deferential tropes described by Lynne Magnusson in female suitors' letters, and the language of female submission found in such letters of petition, is mirrored in the petitions of women to Parliament during the Civil War.[13] The degree of linguistic facility among literate women is matched by the ordinary female deponents studied by Laura Gowing, who manipulated language and narratives for political ends.[14] Throughout society, gifts attained a political significance. New Year gifts presented to the monarch and manuscript books as diplomatic gifts worked in much the same way as did love tokens in the economy of courtship, and gifts of food and home-made medicines as forms of sociable and neighbourly exchange in everyday life.[15] The underlying similarities of these political activities, which functioned at all levels of society, attest the intersection of literate, oral and material cultures. Nevertheless, more widespread incorporation of women into 'popular politics' (although clearly not as part of the electorate) resulted at least partly from increased female literacy – perhaps especially the ability to read – which gave greater access to a range of news, information and ideas.[16]

The essays in this book are organised largely chronologically rather than thematically, covering the years from the early Tudor period through to the beginning of the eighteenth century. While clear themes emerge from the volume – female alliances and networks, the politics of letter-writing, manuscript and material culture, women and the court, the family as a political unit, the political significance of marriage, queenship and female royalty, religion and political culture and ideology – on the whole they span individual essays, which resists a rigid interpretational or compartmentalised structure. One of the main aims of this introduction, however, is to highlight and examine some of this book's broader themes. Its overall approach is necessarily interdisciplinary. Thus, the work of social, cultural and political historians sits side-by-side literary critics; that of scholars of linguistics and manuscript experts resides by feminists and gender specialists; and social theory rests with historical empiricism. Many of the individual contributions straddle these different disciplines or approaches. Only through this kind of multi-focal inquiry can scholarship best recover and re-conceptualise in the broadest possible way women's political lives and experiences in early modern England. By no means does this book represent a unified viewpoint on women's political roles; read as a whole, tensions or 'ruptures' do appear, some of which this introduction has attempted to draw out, but a part of the collection's strength lies in its variety and the disjunctures it exposes.

This book, as with much work on women's history and women's writing, represents an act of archival recovery as well as a re-conceptualising of the ways in which we think about and study early modern women. Alan Stewart's essay, for example, recovers an interconnected group of mercantile Jewish women seemingly erased from official archives; Sara Jayne Steen uncovers the political activities of the Cavendish/Talbot women; and Lynne Magnusson engages in the important process of recovering women's writings by looking at female suitors' letters. Many of the essays combine recovery of archival material with a rethinking of traditional social categories. Elizabeth Clarke catalogues women's manuscript spiritual journals, interpreting as political this seemingly 'private' written form; my own essay argues for the *politicisation* of gossip, and the need to rethink the gendered ways in which we employ terms such as 'gossip', 'news', and 'intelligence'; Tricia Bracher details for the first time the political context of Esther Inglis's 1599 calligraphic manuscripts, and reads them as diplomatic. Scholars interested in material culture have extended the range of texts available for studying women who were largely excluded from traditional printed and literary forms. In this way, scholars including Susan Frye, Peter Stallybrass and Ann Rosalind Jones have approached women's embroidery and needlework – a mode of production probably most clearly associated as 'feminine' or 'domestic' – as a site of women's engagement in politics.[17]

The essay by Natalie Mears on 'Politics in the Elizabethan Privy Chamber' approaches the task of rethinking women and politics differently from many of the other contributions to this book; it therefore offers a useful and important contrast in terms of perspective and methodology. Whereas many essays take as their starting point the re-conceptualising of women's activities in order to place them in a wider political milieu, Dr Mears begins by re-examining the political culture of Elizabethan England as a way of reinterpreting the roles that Privy Chamber women could play. Challenging Eltonian perceptions of Elizabethan policy-making as institutional, and downplaying the role and influence of the Privy Council, she emphasises the personal nature of politics based upon face-to-face relationships. By way of two detailed case studies – Lady Mary Sidney's involvement in Elizabeth's marriage negotiations with the Spanish ambassador for Archduke Charles in 1559, and the support of Eric XIV of Sweden's suit in 1562 by Katherine Ashley and Dorothy Broadbelte – the essay reconsiders the extent to which Privy Chamber women through ad hoc counsel were involved in the central issues of Elizabeth's reign:

marriage, succession and Catholic conspiracy. Her analysis of Robert Beale's 'Instructions for a Principall Secretarie' builds on the view that women were 'barometers of the queen's moods', arguing not only that Chamberers functioned as 'information brokers', but also explicitly linking their activities as intermediaries with Elizabeth to policy-making. As such, the essay acts as an important corrective to the influential work of Pam Wright, and the subsequent reappraisals of her work by Charlotte Merton and Joan Greenbaum Goldsmith, which argue that Privy Chamber women were prevented from taking independent initiatives on key political issues, and that their activities were restricted to working for personal, family or friends' interests.

The role and influence of Privy Chamber women as 'information brokers' is further explored in my own essay on the news and intelligence networks of Elizabeth Talbot, countess of Shrewsbury (c.1527-1608). Female courtiers numbered among the countess's sixty or so correspondents, and their letters impart the kinds of privy and personal information to which only those women who attended upon the queen had ready access: the countess's favour with the queen, her standing at court, the monarch's reactions to her gifts, and the progress of her suits. Information of this nature – so often dismissed as ephemeral 'gossip' – was necessary to successful operation at court, where status, reputation and favour formed important political capital. These intimate first-hand accounts from the Privy Chamber differed from the generalised rumours of St Paul's and the court that characterise the letters of her male correspondents. More broadly, the essay attempts to integrate women into manuscript news and information networks, which scholars have largely viewed as the preserve of men. The countess of Shrewsbury was herself at the centre of a web of news and information networks; she cultivated useful correspondents and gathered intelligence for utilitarian purposes. During the period 1569-74, for example, when her husband the earl of Shrewsbury acted as keeper to Mary, queen of Scots, the countess was independently kept abreast of European and court politics by regular letters from a range of correspondents. The letters she received throughout her life illustrate her interest in areas of news traditionally viewed as 'male', such as parliamentary business, war, armed rebellions and naval preparations. The assassination of Henri III, for example, was reported to the countess in all its gruesome detail. In this sense, news was not gendered according to environment – women reading and writing about household, family and locality, men about affairs in London, the court or abroad. Aristocratic women had access through correspondence (as well as through oral and printed news forms) to a wide range of news from beyond their immediate locale.

Similar intelligence services, as Claire Walker shows, were performed during the Interregnum by nuns on the Continent. Mary Knatchbull, Abbess of the Ghent Benedictines, put her reliable mail networks at the disposal of Royalists; her convent effectively acted as a sorting house for Royalist correspondence, and she was familiar with the aliases and ciphers they used. The abbess also passed on pamphlets, newsletters and information of political events in England and the whereabouts of the king's supporters to Sir Edward Hyde. Ingenious ways of concealing or transporting letters were part and parcel of successful intelligencing. Letters to Mary, queen of Scots, for example, were sometimes concealed in staffs or hidden under stones; Bridget Sherland wrote on behalf of Arbella Stuart, when her mistress's letters were intercepted and read, because letters in her own hand would go unsuspected. Sara Jayne Steen identifies that Arbella Stuart, as a potential heir to the throne, used to her own political advantage the fact that her letters were confiscated, inventing for herself a fictional lover.

The Anglo-Scottish intelligence activities surrounding the English succession crisis of 1599 frame Tricia Bracher's detailed contextual reading of three of Esther Inglis's manuscript books that were presented as gifts to Elizabeth I, Robert Devereux, earl of Essex and Anthony Bacon. In asserting the diplomatic importance of Inglis's manuscripts in the context of relations between James VI of Scotland and the Essex faction, Dr Bracher's essay offers a complementary reading to scholarship that has praised the calligraphic skill of Inglis's work, and treated her more generally as a woman writer. Her approach, however, is antagonistic to Jonathan Goldberg's reductive analysis of Inglis which stresses her 'limited empowerment' and subordinates her to an *a priori* model of a culture that sought to regulate the act of writing and to control the extent of women's education. While Inglis's gifts to Elizabeth I have been viewed as representative of a female gift-exchange community, the essay's analysis of Inglis' *Livre des Pseaumes* (dedicated to Elizabeth in March 1599) renders deeply problematic the concept of a purely feminine alliance in this precise context. Based on textual, marginal and contextual analysis of the book and the letters of Inglis's husband, Bartholomew Kello, the essay argues that *Livre des Pseaumes* functioned both as a gift and a 'profound political threat', which works to destabilise the 'unity and beauty' of this book, and to expose the uneasiness of Elizabeth and James's political partnership. Read in conjunction with Karen Robertson's essay on Lady Ralegh, the activities of Inglis are viewed within the context of women's political involvement in the factional struggles over the succession: both Inglis and Elizabeth Ralegh highlight the fragility of Elizabeth's position.

The process of recovering women's roles in the past facilitates the better integration of women into traditional political narratives. In this way, Helen Payne's essay documents the careers of three aristocratic women at the Jacobean court – Elizabeth, Lady Carey, Lucy, countess of Bedford and Jane Drummond – showing their intimate involvement in matters of patronage. The essay, as it seeks to integrate these three women into the study of patronage, offers two very different, yet complementary models of power and influence at court. The first is a highly *roi*-centric and patriarchal conceptualisation of power which understands that significant *formal* and *direct* power was only conferred by institutional position and office – official posts from which women were excluded – and that women were forced to work through powerful men. Approached from this perspective which privileges direct and tangible rewards of patronage (offices, titles, land and annuities), it is easy to emphasise the restrictions on female agency, the limited extent of women's patronage and political activities, and thus, to perpetuate early modern as well as modern patriarchal assumptions of female incapacity. Competing with this restrictive standpoint is a model of power that borrows from the work of Sharon Kettering and Barbara Harris, and emphasises the plurality, fluidity and non-institutional nature of early modern patronage relations, where influence was exerted indirectly through personal connections.[18] At the heart of Dr Payne's essay is women's operation through family court networks, of which they were an integral part. Such an approach, stressing the importance of marital alliances, kinship and wider social contacts, is more akin to the socio-political studies of patronage undertaken by historians of early modern Europe.[19] Unlike historians of Tudor and Stuart patronage, Europeanists are not stymied by the very top-down model of politics viewed from the perspective of key men such as Thomas Cromwell, the earls of Essex and Leicester, Lord Burghley, Robert Cecil and the duke of Buckingham. By the accumulation of detailed studies of individual women and families – for example, Lucy, countess of Bedford, Mary Sidney, countess of Pembroke, the Newdigates, Harleys or the women surrounding the Cecils – scholars have redressed this imbalance of perspective, and exposed the complex political roles that women played both at local and national levels.[20]

Yet the impulses behind writing women's history do not stop with recovering women's pasts, nor is the ultimate goal simply the better integration of women into traditional historical narratives. Indeed, one of the central purposes of this book of essays on women and politics was not only to show women's contribution to what is traditionally considered a male arena, but also to facilitate a rethinking of the nature of politics altogether. Thus, Dr Payne's essay contributes to a reconsideration of the dynamics of patronage relations, in which the personal, flexible and informal nature of patronage is emphasised, a situation perhaps well suited to female modes of operation. In this sense, strands within this book follow Lisa Jardine's prescriptions that women's history should be 'rupturing' as well as 'accumulative', in other words that women's history should not merely comprise men's history with that of women tacked on, but rather that approaching a subject through the lens of women and gender should be a way of 'unpicking' traditional historical narratives.[21] Echoes of this notion are found in Tricia Bracher's essay in which 'marital rupture' – the partnership of Esther Inglis and her husband Bartholomew Kello in presenting a gift manuscript to queen Elizabeth – is cited to critique interpretations of Inglis's work as achieving currency within the context of female gift exchange. In so doing, Dr Bracher's work – as with Elizabeth Clarke's reference to the 'unsisterly' act of the midwife who abandoned Elizabeth Turner during labour – 'unpicks' the concept of female community, which itself now forms a dominant feminist interpretive framework.

A sophisticated and nuanced study of female alliances is provided by Barbara Harris's contribution to this book, which comprehensively details the contours of female friendships and networks among aristocratic women in Yorkist and early Tudor England. Stemming from major long-term research in this area, the essay effectively historicises a range of female relationships (familial and extra-familial) barely visible in historical records, and carries out the archival spadework, preparing the groundwork for future generations of scholars to theorise about all-female connections.[22] Professor Harris's focus solely on women's alliances – in particular, on the emotional and material support provided by female groups – is necessary to offer a plausible alternative to the narrative of women 'identified with and serving men and male interests'; yet she readily maintains that female networks 'coexisted' and were compatible with primary loyalties to the patrilineages of women's marital families. Using a wide range of primary documentary material – wills and court documents, and sources of sociability, such as letters and accounts – the essay uncovers a dense network of female relationships. While natal kin dominated women's networks, similar patterns of friendship and mutual support did develop with mothers- and sisters-in-law, as well as with distant relatives. Women's neighbourhood networks overlapped (though not exclusively) with ties to collateral marital kin due to the patrilocal nature of aristocratic intermarriage during the fifteenth and early sixteenth centuries. These positive emotional or affective bonds could be drawn upon for diverse purposes, though negative bonds also existed.[23] Female contacts offered emotional and material support during pregnancy and childbirth; were useful in placing girls either at court or in aristocratic households, and in arranging marriages; and provided material support during legal disputes, and through benefactions in their wills. After marriage, women maintained links through letters, visits, and the exchange of favours and gifts. By sustaining and drawing on these 'horizontal ties', aristocratic women enhanced their careers as wives, mothers and widows and increased the political power of both their natal and marital families.

The theme of female alliances receives substantive treatment in two further essays, both of which, working in very different ways, broaden our understanding of how other groups of women outside of the aristocracy – namely English nuns and Jewish (or 'Portingale') mercantile women – fitted into early modern networks. Claire Walker's study of the links between English nuns on the Continent and royalty during the mid to late seventeenth century explores the reciprocal nature of women's alliances. The benefits from the relationships between convents and Stuart royals – often based on kinship, patronage and tradition – ran both ways. Royal patrons, such as Henrietta Maria and Mary of Modena, Charles II and James II, provided support for monastic establishments in economic and political terms, preserving the houses' rights and privileges in the face of challenges from civic or ecclesiastical authorities; while royal and elite nuns acted in the interests of secular kin, and engaged actively in the politics of both Church and State, that went beyond the realms of hospitality, prayer and dispensing spiritual alms. This dual relationship may have been strengthened by the fact that the two parties were united by the shared experience of exile. The essay further argues that Catholic women who took religious vows, though less publicly confrontational than Catholic priests who made pastoral ministrations to a recusant minority, through their existence, work and prayer were arguably as subversive as many of their confrères, but that their exile abroad ensured they did not directly clash with the English ecclesiastical and civic establishment.

In most cases, connections between women (usually through family) are rendered visible by a re-reading of traditional documents and texts. Thus, female suitors' letters expose enforced ties of kinship; widows' wills signal connections through benefactions; and household accounts record transactions of sociability. Here, historical imagination allied to a different set of questions, problems and, assumptions relating to women's roles, has led to important new ways of looking at old texts. In this way,

Jane Lawson in her important forthcoming work on New Year gift-exchanges of the sixteenth-century English court has identified networks of women who grouped together to present queen Elizabeth coordinated outfits of clothing.[24] Nevertheless, other factors work to erase women from the archives, to render them 'hidden from history'. Social transactions such as women's reading of their husbands' correspondence pass unrecorded because their names are not on the address leaves of letters; and the fact that women changed their names upon marriage also works to obstruct their survival in historical records.

Alan Stewart's essay works to recover early modern women erased from the archive, while simultaneously arguing that in fact this very invisibility may not always have been an entirely negative phenomenon, but could be exploited by women in various ways to commercial and political ends. In his study of Portingale women in Elizabethan London – which forms a part of a large-scale project on Dr Rodrigo Lopez – Professor Stewart explores the loopholes created by the nature of the English legal system, and the laws governing English marriage that allowed women to operate more or less undetectably. We hear very little of married women, until they become widows, and this situation is exacerbated, he argues, by the fact that in the Jewish mode a woman's name was associated with her father rather than with her husband. By use of two case studies – those of the Freire sisters and of Sara Lopez – the essay shows how Portingale women, because of their invisibility, provided a cover for a resourceful, commercially successful and politically influential Jewish family business. It identifies a covert form of female operation, different from the kinds of subversive or carnivalesque activities described by Natalie Zemon Davis in her landmark essay 'Women on Top' in which women could legitimately and visibly engage by hiding behind their sex.[25] Building on Christiane Klapisch-Zuber's model of female relations in Renaissance Florence, Professor Stewart shows that the Freire women were more than 'passing guests' in their husbands' houses, both in terms of lineage and physical buildings; marriage not only cemented alliances between men, but also actively produced trade agreements and an international trading venture, with women providing the continuity. His critique of Klapisch-Zuber's study as historically and culturally specific, more broadly corroborates Barbara Harris's work on the relative importance of marriage for women in which she argues that aristocratic women as they remarried accrued 'support and retained resources from each of their families as they moved from one to another'.[26]

The erasure of women from the archives is also a recurring theme of Elizabeth Clarke's essay on women's political manuscripts. She argues here, that in Nonconformist women's spiritual journals, the personalities and circumstances of individual women are erased – quite literally in the case of Mary Love (then Bradshaw) who erased her own name; personal identities are subsumed by rhetorical tropes of providential deliverance and the author as Bride of Christ, which minimises the value of such journals as autobiographical sources. The persuasive or political currency of these manuscripts lay not in identifying their female authors as influential or powerful – which was typical of elite women writings – but in the feminine Protestant proto-democratic ideals that they expounded, ideals that achieved moral potency in the later seventeenth century. The essay also interrogates the categorisation of journals as an essentially private, inward-looking form, suggesting that women's spiritual writing was often written for public circulation with a wider significance than that of recording a woman's spiritual progress. That many manuscript journals exist in copies or fair copies prompts the possibilities of editing and female involvement in circulating these texts within manuscript communities. In several cases women's texts were apparently manipulated by men with political ambition, which itself problematises the very concept of *women's* writing, as a uniquely female preserve (in the same way, women's letters were often written in collaboration with men).[27] Elizabeth Jekyll's diary, for example – a document that had 'all the hallmarks of vindicatory Protestant rhetoric', extolling the godliness of her husband, John Jekyll – was 'scribally published' and circulated in 1685 at the time of John Jekyll's imprisonment, perhaps at his instigation, and when his illegal printing press was shut down. During this period, and at other times, women's writings could avoid censorship when men's received harsh suppression: thus, civil war women often addressed the outside of letters because correspondence in female hands was less likely to incur suspicion and be opened. Given the strictures against female publication, more 'personal' types of writing were deemed acceptable for women. In this manner, Mary Love's correspondence to her husband Christopher Love – which functioned as a martyrology for Love, the leader of the 1651 Presbyterian Plot – was printed and scribally published because letter-writing as a genre was considered appropriate for women, in that it was ostensibly private and unrhetorical.

In contrast to the ways in which spiritual journals worked, the power of correspondence lay in the political influence of individual women, as is demonstrated by several contributions to this book; and indeed, the early modern letter represents the dominant written form by which women exerted power and influence.[28] Sara Jayne Steen, for example, examines the ways in which three generations of women from the Cavendish-Talbot family – Bess of Hardwick, Mary Talbot and Arbella Stuart – through letter-writing operated in high court politics. In her analysis of these three women's lives and letters, Professor Steen illuminates the skilful use of correspondence to political ends by female writers well versed in the epistolary medium. All three wrote with great facility, drafting and redrafting letters, even at times forging and fabricating correspondences; they were aware of the linguistic subtleties of court decorum, and employed a range of strategies in their letters, including a language of submission in letters to King James; they maintained a network of correspondents at court and beyond; they were able to outwit early modern surveillance, and to use postal delivery systems to their advantage. In short, they had all the requisite skills of courtiership for a successful career in Elizabethan and Jacobean England.

Similarly, Karen Robertson's essay examines the epistolary strategies employed by Lady Elizabeth Ralegh in negotiating court favour for both herself and her husband, after the discovery of their clandestine marriage led to their fall into disfavour. During a period of shifting political alliances at court during the 1590s, and the increased polarisation of the Essex and Cecil factions, the essay illustrates the way in which Lady Ralegh was able to maintain Cecil-Ralegh connections through her correspondence. Her suits to Sir Robert Cecil are viewed as one part of the political manoeuvrings that led to Sir Walter's reinstatement as Captain of the Guards in 1597. In the matter of her own return to the Privy Chamber, however, her efforts came to nothing; yet despite this she continued to write to Cecil on her husband's behalf during his voyages, imprisonment for treason and eventual death sentence. For Lady Ralegh, who was denied the access to the queen that she had enjoyed as a Maid-of-Honour, letter-writing represented an important means of redress: it was one of the only ways for her to mobilise allies and supporters. Her letters to Robert Cecil, which form the essay's main focus, capitalise on an earlier friendship forged at court, an alliance that led the then Secretary of State to place his son in her household. A mixture of rhetorical humility, informality and playfulness, her correspondence contrasts with the more formal letters of petition that Cecil received from other women. Indeed, the intimacy of her letters to Robert Cecil echoes the easy confidence with which Katherine, duchess of Suffolk corresponded with his father, her long-time friend William Cecil.[29] More generally, the essay itself acts as an exercise of reinstatement. While my own essay repackages Bess of Hardwick as a woman at the heart of a complex intelligence network, so too Karen Robertson reclaims Lady Ralegh from the shadows cast by her flamboyant husband, by the male luminaries contemporary with her at court, and by Henry Howard's savage denunciation of her as 'furious' Proserpina.

Whereas Sara Jayne Steen and Karen Robertson concentrate on individual female writers, Lynne Magnusson approaches the *politics* of women's letter-writing by concentrating on a particular epistolary genre: the suitor's letter or letter of petition. In her essay, she sensitively reads these texts against sixteenth-century epistolographies and modern-day linguistic analysis, notably discourse pragmatics and Pierre Bordieu's economic model for linguistic exchange. She explores the genre of the suitors' letters with attention to recurring linguistic strategies and the subject positions that the act of petitioning constructs for participants, thus, complementing work that argues for women's mastery of rhetorical tropes and sophisticated epistolary forms. In a patronage society, women frequently wrote on behalf of husbands, children, servants and kinsfolk in order to secure offices, titles, land and monopolies, as well as for themselves in response to imprisonment, to secure royal favour, and to recover income and property. Adapting Angel Day's prescriptions for petitioning letters in his *The English Secretorie* (1586), Professor Magnusson identifies two different 'social scripts' that were used in female suitors' letters: those of 'humility and entreaty' and 'supposal and assurance'. Letters of humility and entreaty, which Professor Magnusson terms 'trouble-taking', are marked by tropes of deference and self-deprecation; in contrast, letters of supposal and assurance ('trouble-taking' letters) are characterised by authority, confidence and assertions of social expectation to be met. While these scripts are often highly formulaic and conventional, it is in the choice of script (given that this could be influenced by secretaries and advisers) that Professor Magnusson discerns elements of female individuality. She argues, along with Bordieu, that a woman's choice of trope – whether bold or timid – was reflective of linguistic habitus ('the set of dispositions acquired in learning to speak or write in particular contexts') which was modulated more by class (or social status) than by gender. In this sense, there is a correlation between a woman's language and her self-perception of her power.

In this analysis, women suitors' letters differ very little from the letters of male writers, which followed similar social hierarchies based on rank and social position. The importance of this reading lies in the confidence and self-assurance that it attributes to women dealing with patronage matters; indeed, many women adopted much of the language of patronage and political friendship utilised in men's letters. However, what emerges as distinct to women suitors' letters as opposed to men's is the use of negative female gender assumptions in letters of deference: female 'weakness' and 'frailty' was a standard deferential trope.[30] Thus, Mary Throckmorton informed her father of her reply to a letter from Sir Thomas Jerningham: 'I haue answered his letter like a woman very submissively if that will serve for I perceive that they do not indure to be tolde of theyr faults'.[31] That it was culturally understood that women were able to manipulate male assumptions of female incapacity – 'pretending ignorance' as a 'cultural script' – is apparent in Valerie Wayne's reading of Middleton's *A Trick to Catch the Old One* and *The Case of Mary Carleton.* Such readings further expose the ways in which women could work within the limitations and constraints imposed by early modern patriarchy; and the mapping of the kinds of space and freedoms that women could carve out for themselves within a dominant repressive and authoritarian culture has formed a significant strand of recent feminist scholarship.[32]

In the same way that language or social scripts attained political significance as markers of rank and status, so too did clothing, jewels and apparel, as is observable in Valerie Wayne's essay. Clothing during the early modern period was a site for ornament, public display of wealth, opulence and status. Sumptuary laws attempted to enforce strict standards of clothing which were inflected by gender and social status: women were exhorted to avoid sumptuous clothing and not to dress above their station. Influenced by the work of Peter Stallybrass and Ann Rosalind Jones, which argues for the 'transnaturing power' of clothing, that clothes 'work as inscriptions upon us', the essay looks at three seventeenth-century texts – Thomas Middleton's *A Trick to Catch the Old One*; Aphra Behn's *The City-Heiress*; and the autobiographical narrative *The Case of Mary Carleton* – each of which deal with women assuming gentle status (by adopting the clothes, personal effects and manners suitable to women of that social status) that they were not born to as a means of duping potential husbands and marrying well. In the example of Mary Carleton, her duplicity extends to pretending to write and receive letters from the continent about money from her estate as a means to preserve external belief in her assumed status. Professor Wayne argues that Aphra Behn likewise performed above her social status by aligning herself through her writing with Tory politics, and showing her allegiance to royalty. In itself, Behn's engagement with Royalist politics, as with Bess of Hardwick's interest in contemporary events, supports Danielle Clarke's argument in her book *The Politics of Early Modern Women's Writing* that women writers did not merely work from the 'margins' of early modern culture, but that they engaged centrally 'with matters of state, culture, religion and subjecthood'.[33]

While many of the essays in this book examine the ways in which women controlled their self-presentation, Jerome de Groot's essay acts as a sanguine reminder of the ways in which early modern *representations* of women, whether negative or positive, were always political. As with

Elizabeth Clarke's essay, female stereotypes are employed by men for propagandist purposes (the incidence of negative female imagery is also touched upon by Karen Robertson and Sara Jayne Steen). Throughout, Dr de Groot depicts the kinds of patriarchal injunctions on women's activities and roles as he discusses Royalist caricatures of Parliamentarian women and representations of Henrietta Maria. The promotion of Roundhead women – such as Lady Waller – to 'abnormal' public roles was portrayed by Royalist polemic as dangerous, transgressive and socially disruptive. This situation was troubling for a regime which invested in maintaining the existing social order and power relations predicated on rigid social and gender hierarchies. Parliamentarian women were attacked on grounds of sexual licentiousness and hypocrisy; female petitioners were satirised as 'Shee Committees'. Royalist women, on the other hand (at least to Royalists) did not blur these boundaries: even women who took on non-traditional roles, such as the countess of Derby who defended Latham House during a long siege, were seen to be defending social norms, circumstances forcing them to act in the absence of husbands in a manner that they would not otherwise do. The doyenne of Royalist image makers, however, was Henrietta Maria, and the essay considers the ways in which the queen was represented in an extended reading of the panegyric collection *Musarum Oxoniensum Serenissimæ*, produced by Oxford University and published in 1643 to 'celebrate the queen's return from Holland'.[34] Henrietta Maria was in many ways viewed as a transformative, healing or uniting figure (a role that she could achieve independent of the king). A potentially disruptive figure, the essay argues that Henrietta Maria becomes a seventeenth-century Royalist equivalent of a 'pin-up' or 'cover girl', that in fact she was fetishised by Royalists. She represents a Royalist ideal, a mother-figure whose return from exile promised to repair the chaos, heal the wounds of the country, and knit together the nation.

The essay by Susan Frye reads Shakespeare and Fletcher's *Henry VIII* as a play partly concerned with the political importance of historical queens – Katherine of Aragon, Anne Boleyn and the future queen, Elizabeth I – and considers the application of such a theme at a time when Anne of Denmark was queen consort. It argues that the interconnections between Henry VIII and Katherine, and James and Anne, both historically and as staged in the play – the 'discarded' queens, opposition to male favourites, court rivalries, Catholicism, and the homosocial (perhaps homoerotic) relations at court – must have registered with seventeenth-century audiences. Katherine's repeated conflicts with Wolsey are seen explicitly to mirror Anne's opposition to Robert Carr during the period 1612-13. Building on Leeds Barroll's reinstatement and recovery of Anne's cultural and political significance, Professor Frye's treatment of *Henry VIII* prompts a wider reconsideration of Anne's political function. While acknowledging that male favourites and institutions such as the Privy Council effectively worked to marginalise Anne's role in political decision making, Professor Frye argues that James and Anne formed a 'loose partnership'. In foreign policy, Anne was able indirectly to influence her husband, and as part of a regal 'team' she shared responsibility in dealing with ambassadors. On the domestic policy front, Anne maintained links with the landed elites through royal progresses, attendance at baptisms and as a recipient of suitors' requests. In emphasising the collegiality of Anne's interventions, the essay usefully counters Barbara Lewalski's oppositional model of women's political interventions.[35]

Rethinking female involvement in politics in early modern England is a task that forces scholars to move beyond a process of recovery and reincorporation of women into traditional political structures and narratives. As the essays in this book demonstrate, attending to early modern women and politics necessitates redefining what actually constituted politics, as well as recognition of women's roles and activities as 'political'. Taken as a whole, this book offers several different, perhaps competing models, cross-disciplinary approaches and ways of thinking about and conceptualising female political activities, at least to some of which this introduction has attempted to draw attention. While it is hoped that this book will enhance understanding of the broader significance of women's roles in Tudor and Stuart England, a range of issues nonetheless require further examination. How well, for example, do women fit into factional, oppositional, collegial and social status based models of politics? Did women operate in significantly different ways from men, perhaps complementing their efforts? In what ways did women's power and influence change or develop over time? Could women operate beyond the family? How far were women's political actions motivated by ideology? To what extent were women involved in the formation of political opinion within the public sphere? How far could female gender be manipulated as a political strategy? Many of these are in fact questions to which scholars have already begun to offer answers; however, much remains to be written and researched. Finally, in drawing attention to these and other issues, one of the main intentions of this book is to contribute towards stimulating new areas of research by opening up new debates and controversies relating to the lives and experiences of early modern women.

Notes

I would like to thank Roger Dalrymple and Alan Stewart for commenting on earlier drafts of this introductory essay.

1 Agnes [and Elizabeth] Strickland, *Lives of the Queens of England, from the Norman Conquest*, 12 vols, London, 1840-48. This biographical tradition can be traced back to Plutarch's *Lives* and to the saints' lives of the early Church.

2 For a recent survey of this scholarship see Sara Mendelson and Patricia Crawford, *Women in Early Modern England, 1550-1720*, Oxford: Clarendon Press, 1998, pp. 365-80. For an earlier period, scholars have attributed key roles during the Wars of the Roses to Margaret of Anjou, Cecily Neville, dowager duchess of York and Lady Margaret Beaufort in defending their families' political interests: M. Jones and M. Underwood, *The King's Mother: Lady Margaret Beaufort, Countess of Richmond and Derby*, Cambridge: CUP, 1992.

3 The academic trench-warfare that represents the Anne Boleyn debate has been fought chiefly among E.W. Ives, G.W. Bernard and R.M. Warnicke in the pages of *HJ* and *EHR*. For a recent bibliographical survey of this debate see, S.J. Gunn, 'The Structures of Politics in Early Tudor England', *TRHS*, 6th series, V (1995), 59-90 (pp. 59-60).

4 S.J. Gunn, 'The Courtiers of Henry VII', *EHR*, 108 (1993), 23-49 (pp. 35-36); G.W. Bernard, 'The Fall of Anne Boleyn', *EHR*, 106 (1991), 584-610 (p. 609); Robert Ashton, *James I By His Contemporaries*, London: Hutchinson & Company, 1969, p. 86; R.M. Smuts, 'The Puritan Followers of Henrietta Maria in the 1630s', *EHR*, 93 (1978), 26-45 (p. 31).

5 M.L. Bush, 'The Lisle-Seymour Land Disputes: a Study of Power and Influence in the 1530s', *HJ*, 9 (1966), 255-74 (pp. 260, 269-70, 273). Muriel St Clare Byrne (ed.), *The Lisle Letters*, 6 vols, Chicago and London: The University of Chicago Press, 1981; on Sara Lopez see Alan Stewart's essay in this volume (ch. 5, p. 83).

6 S.J. Gunn, 'The Structures of Politics', p. 63, n.13.

7 Barbara J. Harris, 'Women and Politics in Early Tudor England', *HJ*, 33 (1990), 259-81. The approaches pioneered by Professor Harris in this essay have been further developed in a large number of important essays including 'Aristocratic Women and the State in Early Tudor England', in Charles Carlton, Robert L. Woods, Mary C. Robertson and Joseph S. Block (eds), *State, Sovereigns and Society in Early Modern England: Essays in Honour of A.J. Slavin*, Stroud: Sutton Publishing, 1998, pp. 3-24; 'Property, Power and Personal Relations: Elite Mothers and Sons in Yorkist and Early Tudor England', *Signs*, 15, 3 (1990), 606-32; 'The View From My Lady's Chamber: New Perspectives on the Early Tudor Monarchy', *Huntington Library Quarterly*, 60, 3 (Spring 1999), 215-47; and in her book-length study, *English Aristocratic Women, 1450-1550: Marriage and Family, Property and Careers*, New York and Oxford: OUP, 2002.

8 Harris, 'Women and Politics', pp. 260, 281; *eadem*, 'Property, Power and Personal Relations', p. 632.

9 See, for example, Ralph A. Houlbrooke, 'Women's Social Life and Common Actions in England From the Fifteenth Century to the Eve of the Civil War', *Continuity and Change*, 1, 2 (1986), 171-89; A. Hughes, 'Gender and Politics in Leveller Literature', in S. Amussen and M. Kishlansky (eds), *Political Culture and Cultural Politics in Early Modern Europe*, Manchester: Manchester UP, 1995; J. Walter, 'Grain Riots and Popular Attitudes to the Law: Maldon and the Crisis of 1629', in J. Brewer and J. Styles (eds), *An Ungovernable People*, London: Hutchinson, 1979; Keith Thomas, 'Women and Civil War Sects', *P&P*, 13 (1958), 42-62.

[10] Harris, *English Aristocratic Women*, p.13.
[11] Joan Kelly, 'Did Women Have a Renaissance?', in Joan Kelly, *Women, History and Theory*, Chicago: University of Chicago Press, 1984, pp. 19-50 (p. 35); Mary Erler and Maryanne Kowaleski (eds), *Women and Power in the Middle Ages*, Athens, Georgia: University of Georgia Press, 1988, pp. 1-13; Mary Beth Rose, *Women in the Middle Ages and the Renaissance: Literary and Historical Perspectives*, Syracuse: Syracuse UP, 1988, pp. xvi-xvii; James Daybell, 'The Political Role of Upper-Class Women in Early Tudor Noblewomen as Evidenced Through their Letters', unpublished MA dissertation, University of Reading, 1996.
[12] Harris, *English Aristocratic Women*, p.13.
[13] Patricia Higgins, 'The Reactions of Women, With Special Reference to Women Petitioners', in B. Manning (ed.), *Politics, Religion and the English Civil War*, London: Edward Arnold, 1973, pp. 177-222; James Daybell, 'Women's Letters and Letter-Writing in England, 1540-1603', unpublished PhD thesis, University of Reading, 1999, ch. 5.
[14] Laura Gowing, *Domestic Dangers: Women, Words and Sex in Early Modern London*, Oxford: Clarendon Press, 1996, pp. 201, 235-39.
[15] Diana O'Hara, *Courtship and Constraint: Rethinking the Making of Marriage in Tudor England*, Manchester: MUP, 2000, pp. 57-98; Sara Mendelson and Patricia Crawford, *Women in Early Modern England*, Oxford: Clarendon Press, 1998, p. 225.
[16] On increased female involvement in popular politics see Marcus Nevitt, 'Women in the Business of Revolutionary News: Elizabeth Alkin, "Parliament Joan", and the Commonwealth Newsbook' in Joad Raymond (ed.), *News, Newspapers, and Society in Early Modern Britain*, London: Frank Cass, 1999, pp. 84-108. See also, Lois G. Schwoerer, 'Women's Public Political Voice in England: 1640-1740', in Hilda L. Smith (ed.), *Women Writers and the Early Modern British Political Tradition* (Cambridge: CUP, 1998), pp. 56-74.
[17] Susan Frye, 'Sewing Connections: Elizabeth Tudor, Mary Stuart, Elizabeth Talbot, and Seventeenth-Century Anonymous Needleworkers', in Susan Frye and Karen Robertson (eds), *Maids and Mistresses, Cousins and Queens: Women's Alliances in Early Modern England*, New York and Oxford: OUP, 1999, pp. 165-82; Peter Stallybrass and Ann Rosalind Jones, 'The Needle and the Pen: Needlework and the Appropriation of Printed Texts', in *Renaissance Clothing and the Materials of Memory*, Cambridge: CUP, 2000, pp. 134-71.
[18] Sharon Kettering, 'The Patronage Power of Early Modern French Noblewomen', *HJ*, 32 (1989), 817-41; *eadem*, *Patrons, Brokers, and Clients in Seventeenth-Century France*, New York and Oxford: OUP, 1986; *eadem*, *Patronage in Sixteenth- and Seventeenth-Century France*, Aldershot: Ashgate, 2002; Harris, 'Women and Politics'; *eadem*, *English Aristocratic Women*.
[19] Most notably see Roland Mousnier, *Les Institutions de la France Sous la Monarchie Absolue, 1598-1789*, 2 vols, Paris: Presses Universitaires, 1974-80.
[20] See, for example, Barbara Lewalski, 'Lucy, countess of Bedford: Images of a Jacobean Courtier and Patroness', in Kevin Sharpe and Steven Zwicker (eds), *The Politics of Discourse*, Berkeley and Los Angeles, CA: University of California Press, 1987, pp. 52-77; *eadem*, 'Exercising Power: the countess of Bedford as Courtier, Patron and Coeterie Poet', in *Writing Women in Jacobean England*, Harvard: Harvard UP, 1993; pp. 95-123; Margaret M. Byard, 'The Trade of Courtiership: the Countess of Bedford and the Bedford Memorials', *History Today* (Jan. 1979), 20-28; Mary Ellen Lamb, 'The Countess of Pembroke's Patronage', *ELR* (1982), 162-79; Vivienne Larminie, *Wealth, Kinship and Culture: the Seventeenth-Century Newdigates of Arbury and Their World*, Woodbridge: The

Boydell Press, 1995; Jacqueline Eales, *Puritans and Roundheads: the Harleys of Brampton Bryan and the Outbreak of the English Civil War*, Cambridge: CUP, 1990; Helen Payne, 'The Cecil Women at Court', in Pauline Croft (ed.), *Patronage, Culture and Power: the Early Cecils 1558-1612*, New Haven & London: Yale UP, 2002, pp. 265-81.

[21] Lisa Jardine, 'Unpicking the Tapestry: the Scholar of Women's History as Penelope Among her Suitors', in Lisa Jardine, *Reading Shakespeare Historically*, London and New York: Routledge, 1996, pp. 132-47.

[22] Professor Harris's work complements that of other feminist scholars who have studied women's alliances. See, for example, Frye and Robertson (eds), *Maids and Mistresses, Cousins and Queens*.

[23] For an example of negative bonds between a mother- and daughter-in-law see Alison D. Wall, 'Deference and Defiance in Women's Letters of the Thynne Family: the Rhetoric of Relationships', in James Daybell (ed.), *Women's Letters and Letter Writing in England, 1400-1700*, Basingstoke: Palgrave, 2001, pp. 77-93 (pp. 85-89); *eadem*, 'Elizabethan Precept and Feminine Practice: the Thynne Family of Longleat', *History*, 75 (1990), 23-38.

[24] I am grateful to Jane Lawson for discussion on this point. Her research has identified groupings of embroidery motifs and fabric colours for pieces of outfits presented by groups of women. This kind of collaboration also extends to gifts from husband and wife, and brother and sister, as well as to gifts given by the queen to married couples.

[25] Natalie Zemon Davis, 'Women on Top', in *Society and Culture in Early Modern France*, London: Polity Press, 1965, pp. 124-51.

[26] Harris, *English Aristocratic Women*, p. 10.

[27] James Daybell, 'Women's Letters and Letter Writing in England, 1540-1603: an Introduction to the Issues of Authorship and Construction', *Shakespeare Studies*, 27 (1999), 161-86.

[28] On women's letter-writing see James Daybell (ed.), *Early Modern Women's Letter Writing, 1450-1700*, Basingstoke: Palgrave, 2001.

[29] See, for example, PRO SP 10/10/39: Katherine, duchess of Suffolk to William Cecil, 2 Oct. 1550.

[30] Daybell, Thesis, pp. 159-64.

[31] WCRO, Throckmorton Papers, CR 1998/Box 60/Folder 3/11^{v}: Mary Throckmorton to Thomas Throckmorton, 25 Dec. n.y.

[32] See, for example, Laura Gowing, *Domestic Dangers*; Tim Stretton, *Women Waging Law in Elizabethan England*, Cambridge: CUP, 1998; Maria L. Cioni, 'The Elizabethan Chancery and Women's Rights', in D. J. Guth and J. W. McKenna (eds), *Tudor Rule and Revolution: Essays for G.R. Elton From His American Friends*, Cambridge: CUP, 1982, pp. 159-82.

[33] Danielle Clarke, *The Politics of Early Modern Women's Writing*, Harlow: Longman, 2001, p. 1. For further analysis of the historical and political nature of Behn's plays see Melinda Zook, 'Contextualizing Aphra Behn: Plays, Politics and Party, 1679-1689', in Smith (ed.), *Women Writers*, pp. 75-93.

[34] While Dr de Groot is concerned with representations of Henrietta Maria, the queen was also involved in presentations of herself: see, for example, Erica Veevers, *Images of Love and Religion: Queen Henrietta Maria and Court Entertainments*, Cambridge: CUP, 1989, pp. 10-11, *passim*.

[35] See especially Barbara Kiefer Lewalski, 'Enacting Opposition: Queen Anne and the Subversions of Masquing', in *Writing Women in Jacobean England*, Cambridge: Harvard UP, 1993, pp. 15-43. The model of female opposition to male authority, however, is applied wholesale throughout the book.

Chapter 2

Sisterhood, Friendship and the Power of English Aristocratic Women, 1450-1550

Barbara J. Harris

In late medieval and early modern England, marriage was the gateway that opened lifelong careers to aristocratic women. As wives, they devoted most of their time and energy to reproductive, managerial, political and social functions essential to the survival and prosperity of their husbands' patrilineages, focusing particularly on advancing their husbands' and sons' careers, arranging their daughters' marriages, and managing their estates and households. Wives who carried out these responsibilities successfully were rewarded materially and earned the love and respect of their husbands and admiration of their family and friends. When they were widowed, as most of them were, they continued to perform these functions with increased independence and authority. Well over three-quarters of them also assumed new responsibilities as administrators of their husbands' estates and guardians of their non-inheriting, unmarried children. The high female marriage rate – just under 94 per cent of the daughters of knights and noblemen married at least once – and the large proportion of wives who survived their husbands – around 70 per cent – meant that aristocratic women played a crucial role in the social reproduction of their families and class.[1]

Contemporary sources about Yorkist and early Tudor aristocratic women performing these functions highlight their relations with men, particularly their most powerful male kin – their husbands, adult sons, fathers and brothers. In conjunction with their devotion to promoting the interests of their marital patrilineages, this evidence creates a plausible narrative of women identified with and serving men and male interests. There is, however, another less visible story of emotional and material relationships between women – mothers and daughters, sisters, aunts and nieces, mothers-, daughters- and sisters-in-law – embedded in the documents.[2] This essay presents some of the evidence of this easily neglected dimension of aristocratic women's lives. It argues that their relationships with each other were often as emotionally important to them as their relationships with men and that their control of property as wives and widows enabled them to play a significant role in ensuring each other's material well-being. Childless aristocratic women often had particularly strong bonds with their sisters and nieces and chose them as major beneficiaries of their estates. It is in their care for their female kin that aristocratic women revealed values and perspectives that contrasted with those that dominated the culture in which they lived. For women who spent most of their lives serving patriarchal families and institutions, their female networks may well have provided them with the emotional and material cushion that enabled them to accept, even flourish in, their subordinated positions.

However significant they were personally to individual aristocratic women, female networks were equally significant in their contribution to their families' political power. Throughout the Yorkist and Tudor periods, the monarchy lacked the military and bureaucratic resources necessary to govern England and Wales on its own. At the same time, the crown was steadily absorbing the land, offices, and fees on which members of the aristocracy depended to reward their clients and servants and maintain their social and political status. In these circumstances, the central government relied on noblemen, knights and their families to mobilise their neighbours, clients, and servants to implement its policies and maintain law and order in the countryside, and rewarded them for their service with grants from the growing stock of land, offices and fees at its disposal. Nothing was more important, therefore, to members of the aristocracy than maintaining and strengthening the networks of kin, clients, neighbours and servants that gave them a claim on the bounty of the crown.

This essay demonstrates that female networks played an important role in this informal, but essential, dimension of Yorkist and Tudor politics. Women's ongoing relationships with their mothers, sisters, aunts and nieces preserved and strengthened the bond that their marriages initially created between their natal and marital families, expanding the networks and regional power of both. Most wives also developed friendships and patronage relations with their husbands' non-resident collateral kin and aristocratic and gentle neighbours. These connections further extended the women's networks and reinforced their spouses' political position in their neighbourhoods and counties. Collectively, therefore, aristocratic women's horizontal ties enhanced their careers as wives, mothers and widows and increased the political power of both their natal and marital families.

I

Female networks played an important role in aristocratic women's lives from the earliest years of their marriages. During and after their child-bearing years, they participated in each others' lyings-in, a period of a month or more that began in the last stages of their pregnancies and ended two to four weeks after their babies were born. During this period, pregnant mothers withdrew from their households into specially designated chambers where they were attended exclusively by women.[3] Women's mothers and mothers-in-law often travelled long distances to attend them during this period. The countess of Westmorland journeyed from the Lake Country to Belvoir Castle, Lincolnshire, when her son and heir's wife, who was very young and still living with her parents, gave birth for the first time.[4] The countess of Bath made the shorter journey from Hengrave, Suffolk to London to help one of her daughters until she was successfully 'brought to bed'.[5] In a variation on this pattern one of William, Lord Paget's, daughters returned to her natal home in London to give birth. Her married sister, Jane Kitson, also came home to participate in her confinement.[6]

Other women gave birth in the homes of their in-laws, where their mothers-in-law supervised their lyings-in. Lady Ursula Stafford's first child was born at the castle of her father-in-law, the duke of Buckingham, in 1520.[7] When Lady Anne Lestrange gave birth to her third or fourth child in her marital home in 1519, her mother was dead and her mother-in-law had remarried and lived elsewhere. In these circumstances, two of her husband's aunts who lived in the neighbourhood, Lady Elizabeth Woodhouse and Mrs Banyard, attended her for three weeks.[8]

The female networks that played such an important part in the rituals surrounding childbirth were equally important when parents chose their daughters' godparents. The custom was to give each infant three godparents, two of its own sex, one of the other. Grandmothers frequently served as spiritual parents to their granddaughters. One of the same-sex godparents named the child, often christening it with her own name.[9] Aristocratic women apparently attached great importance to having at least one granddaughter/goddaughter bearing their name, for Dame Joyce Percy bequeathed the considerable sum of 20 marks to her daughter 'if god send her a daughter it to have my name'.[10] The choice of a girl's godmothers both reaffirmed her mother's female network and functioned as the first step in creating her own.

Women's wills provide evidence of their attachment to and material support of their spiritual daughters. In fact, goddaughters were among the most common legatees outside the circle of close relatives who received the great majority of women's benefactions. Fifty-four (20.3 per cent) of the testators in a sample of 266 made bequests to at least one goddaughter. In comparison, only seventeen women (6.3 per cent of the testators) made bequests to godsons. Of the total of ninety-five goddaughters who received benefactions in these wills, sixty-one (64 per cent) had the same first name as their godmothers. Twenty-two (23 per cent) were their godmothers' granddaughters; two, their step-granddaughters; and five their nieces. In addition, twenty-three of the testators left gifts to granddaughters with their name; many of them were probably their goddaughters although they were not identified as such.

While some of the legacies to their goddaughters were as small as 3s. 4d. and 6s. 8d.,[11] many of the godmothers' bequests were considerably larger. Margery Copuldyke had apparently assumed all or a significant part of the financial responsibility for her goddaughter Margaret, whose father, her son, was apparently already dead. In her will, she asked her eldest son to take charge of Margaret until she was 20, married, or became a nun. She purchased land to support her until that time in addition to leaving her £20 and a large amount of furniture and household goods for her dowry.[12]

Some godmothers made their bequests in the form of jewellery or plate that they themselves had used while they were alive. Jewellery and plate were common stores of value in this period and were frequently included in women's dowries. But legacies of this sort did more than enrich the recipients. They also expressed the donors' attachment to their goddaughters in a more personal, even intimate, way than cash and embodied the ties between them in carefully chosen objects the girls could use for the rest of their lives. Margery Waldegrave, who left both her goddaughters a number of pieces of gold jewellery decorated with precious stones, commented that she had already given one of the girls a gold heart decorated with rubies 'to wear at convenient times about her neck', which she was now bequeathing to her.[13] She had obviously received great pleasure from the thought of her goddaughter wearing it during her lifetime and wanted her to continue to do so after her death. Another godmother, Margaret Leynham, had intended to leave three heavy silver goblets to her sister, but when her sister unexpectedly died, left them instead to her sister's daughter, her niece and godchild. Her decision suggests the way in which valuable personal items circulated among women and perpetuated their relationships with their natal female kin.[14]

Women's networks were also crucial when their daughters reached adolescence and needed to be placed in other aristocratic households to complete their educations, expand their social circles and, hopefully, secure the assistance of another well-connected family in arranging their marriages. The girls' placement had considerable political importance because of its impact on the younger women's prospects of marrying advantageously and creating valuable patronage connections of their own. A woman's voice in the process was crucial because the senior woman in the household receiving the young woman had to agree to accept custodial responsibility for her. Thus, when Lady Lisle discussed the possibility of placing her daughter in the earl of Hertford's household in 1539, he responded that 'I have since my coming home not only pondered the same with myself but also declared it unto my wife, who is no less desirous to have her'.[15] Aristocratic women were much more likely to respond positively to girls from their natal than from their marital families. Often, in fact, they took their younger sisters into their homes, a pattern which strengthened their ties to their parents by assisting them to find appropriate places for their daughters. Sir Robert Plumpton's daughter Eleanor lived with her sister Margaret after the latter's marriage to Germain Pole.[16] Two of Eleanor, countess of Rutland's sisters, Elizabeth and Margaret, lived with her at different times after her marriage.[17] Elizabeth Gresham, daughter of Sir Richard, died at the London home of her sister, Lady Christian Thynne, wife of Sir John, in 1552. On her deathbed, she bequeathed all her goods to them because they 'hath been very good unto me this four years'.[18] Edith, Lady Darcy, and her husband Thomas not only negotiated a marriage for her younger sister while she was living in their household, but also agreed to pay 100 marks toward her dowry.[19] A quarter of a century later, the dowager countess of Westmorland thanked her daughter Margaret, wife of the second earl of Rutland, for 'furthering' her sister's marriage. Her letter implied that the ceremony was going to take place in Margaret's household.[20] That same year, Jane Leche was living at Chatsworth with her half-sister, Elizabeth, then married to Sir William Cavendish. On one occasion, Lady Cavendish wrote angrily from London to one of her servants because word had reached her that Jane

> ...cane not have thynges that ys nedefoulle for hare to haue amoungste you yf yet be trewe you lacke agreat of honyste as well as dyscrescyon to deny hare any thynge that she hathe a mynde to beynge yn case as she hathe bene. I wolde be lothe to have any stranger so yoused yn my howse and then assure your selfe I cane not lyke ytt to have my syster so yousede.[21]

Grandmothers and aunts frequently provided places for girls in the next generation. In her 1496 will, for example, Dame Margery Salvin remarked on her 'niece Langton being with me'.[22] Decades later, two of the duchess of Norfolk's nieces lived with her.[23] The countess of Salisbury's willingness to take her granddaughter, Margaret Stafford, one of her daughter Ursula's thirteen children, into her household must have been a great relief to Ursula and her financially beleaguered husband, Henry, Lord Stafford. Three of Margaret's female first cousins, daughters of her uncles Arthur and Geoffrey Pole, also lived with the countess, which had the additional advantage of facilitating the creation of a network among the next generation of Pole women.[24] Similarly, Katherine, Lady Daubney's three daughters lived with their grandmother, Agnes, duchess of Norfolk; their first cousin, Catherine Howard, Henry VIII's future wife, was also a member of the household.[25] Occasionally aristocratic women found places for the daughters of their more distant kin in their households. In the 1460s, for example, the countess of Oxford helped her cousin, John Howard, place two of his daughters, one in her household, the other in her daughter's.[26] Margaret Paston's daughter Anne lived with her distant cousins, the Calthorps, after her father's death. When the Calthorps could no longer keep her, Margaret asked her younger son, John III, to inquire about placing her with their equally distant relatives, the Cleres.[27]

A parallel to aristocratic women's control over the admission of adolescent girls to their households existed at court, where the appointment of the Queen's Maids-of-Honour depended on the patronage of her Ladies-in-Waiting and the Gentlewomen of her Privy Chamber. By and large, these women favoured the daughters of their friends and kin when they recommended new maids to the Queen, a pattern that reinforced the tendency of established court families to perpetuate their position at court. This method of recruitment gave the Queen's senior ladies control over a crucial area of royal patronage and considerable power within the inner circle of court families.

Competition for the positions was keen because the maids gained privileged access to the King and his favourites and were well placed to secure patronage for themselves, their families and friends. The short supply of places compared to the demand accorded enormous power to the networks of women from court families. When Lady Lisle began her campaign to place two daughters from her first marriage, Anne and Katherine Basset, in Jane Seymour's household, for example, John Husee, her agent in London, told her firmly it was 'no meet suit for any man to move such matters, but only for such Ladies and women as be your friends'.[28] Lord Montague's response to her request for assistance was that he would ask his mother, the countess of Salisbury, 'to do her best' in the matter; he also advised Lord Lisle that 'it will sooner take effect' if he wrote to his mother directly.[29] As Lady Lisle discovered, parents who wanted their daughters to become the Queen's maids had to cultivate and reward the senior members of her entourage. To forward her suit, Lady Lisle obtained the active assistance of two relatives at court, the countesses of Rutland and Sussex, two other members of the Queen's Privy Chamber, Mistresses Horsman and Coffin, the Queen's sister-in-law, Anne, Lady Beauchamp, and two other influential noblewomen, the countess of Salisbury and marchioness of Exeter. In the end, her two kinswomen, the countess of Rutland and Sussex, intervened with Queen Jane at a crucial moment and secured her agreement to appoint one of Lady Lisle's daughters to her service.[30]

Lady Lisle's success in using her connections to secure her daughter Anne's appointment in the Queen's household dramatically increased her ties to the court and her indirect access to Henry VIII. Anne became her mother's regular intermediary with the King within a few years of her arrival at court, justifying the financial investment she had made to secure her selection. On one occasion, Anne reported that she had 'declared unto the King's Highness all things, as your ladyship willed me to do, so that his Grace took the same in right good part, accepting your good will and toward mind therein'.[31] On another, she wrote that she did not dare ask the King to send her mother a token 'for fear lest how his Grace would take it' and that despite her efforts, he had once again refused to appoint her sister Katherine to the Queen's household.[32] Anne's judgment about approaching and responding to Henry was obviously sound. By 1542, she stood so high in his favour that a Spanish observer attributed her stepfather's release from the Tower of London to his affection for her, a clear example of the fact that the maids could gain influence with the King and use it effectively on behalf of their families.[33]

Mothers, grandmothers and aunts also played an important role in assuring the futures of their favourite daughters, granddaughters and nieces by supplementing the dowries the girls received from their fathers, who had primary responsibility for financing their first marriages. Adding to their dowries was the most important material contribution they could make to the young women's futures since the size of their portions was a crucial factor in determining the financial, social and political desirability of the matches that could be negotiated for them. Widows with unmarried daughters often increased their daughters' marriage portions, even if their fathers had already provided for them generously. When Sir Thomas Delamere died in 1490, for example, he left 200 marks for the marriages of his daughter Jane and younger son George. Four years later his widow, Dame Elizabeth, added 100 marks to Jane's portion.[34] Mabel Parr left her daughter Anne 400 marks worth of plate 'over and besides' the 400 marks her father had given her twelve years earlier, effectively doubling her marriage portion.[35] Dame Joan Denny added 500 marks apiece to the dowries of 600 marks her husband had already left each of their five daughters, raising their portions to a size adequate for the daughters of barons.[36] In all, half of the mothers in a group of forty-six who had unmarried daughters when they wrote their wills added to their dowries.

Grandmothers and aunts also contributed to their nieces' and granddaughters' marriage portions when their own children were satisfactorily settled or they had no children of their own. In a group of 266 female wills, 24 grandmothers and 7 aunts included bequests of this kind. Sometimes their gifts were large enough to affect the recipients' futures significantly. For example, Joan, Lady Dynham left one of her granddaughters 100 marks and two others 50 marks each, while Dame Anne Weston left her niece and namesake £100.[37] In some cases the testators had evidently arranged the girls' marriages since their bequests were conditional on completion of the matches. Joan, Lady Clinton, left her granddaughter Margaret 200 marks if she married Robert Wele, but only 100 marks if she married someone else; Dame Constance Ferrers's gift of 100 marks was conditional on her granddaughter marrying William Sheperde.[38] Elizabeth Scrope, Lady Scrope of Upsall and Masham, who had no surviving children, made her niece Lucy Brown her heir if she married John Cutte.[39]

Occasionally, in unusual circumstances, grandmothers and aunts assumed guardianship and financial responsibility for their granddaughters and nieces, as we have already seen in the case of Margery Copuldyke. When Robert, earl of Sussex, died in 1542, he gave his mother-in-law, Anne, countess of Derby, custody of his daughter Jane and his ward, Lord Berkeley. He left Lord Berkeley's marriage to Jane in the hope they would marry, but if the marriage did not take place, the countess and his other executors were to give her a dowry equal to or double the value of the wardship. The earl had remarried after the death of Jane's mother, but he apparently thought the countess would take better care of and provide more generously for her than his wife, the girl's stepmother.[40] Three years later, the countess sold Berkeley's wardship to his widowed mother for £1000, almost certainly because the young pair were no longer expected to marry. The countess carefully bequeathed the profits of the sale to Jane for her dowry when she died in 1550. She also left Jane some expensive clothing and furniture, a sign of affection for her granddaughter that went beyond the obligation she had assumed for her marriage.[41]

Although women usually accepted responsibility for their natal kin, they occasionally did so for their marital relatives, as the example of the Frowick family indicates. When Sir Henry Frowick wrote his will in April

1505, he appointed his brother, Sir Thomas, as one of his co-executors. Since he assumed Sir Thomas would acquire his sons' wardships and rear his unmarried daughters, he left his sister-in-law, Lady Elizabeth, 100s. 'to be good lady and aunt' to them.[42] Within the year, in anticipation of his own death, Sir Thomas assigned the boys' wardships and marriages and administration of his brother's remaining goods to his wife.[43] In accordance with his wishes, she took her husband's place as guardian of Sir Henry's two sons and three daughters.

A decade later, Dame Frowick's own will indicated that she had developed a close relationship with one of the girls, Elizabeth, by then married to Sir John Spelman and the only one of Sir Henry's children included among her beneficiaries. Elizabeth Spelman's daughter, her great-niece, was her goddaughter and namesake. Dame Frowick bequeathed the bed she slept in, some clothing, and a gold chain with a cross to Lady Spelman and a silver and gilt cup with a cover, two tablecloths, a ring and £20 to her goddaughter. Since Lady Spelman had twenty children, thirteen of whom were boys, Dame Frowick's decision to single out her goddaughter as her beneficiary reflected a conscious decision in favour of a female network that extended through three generations. As an heiress, Dame Frowick also had land to bequeath. She gave most of it to her only daughter Frideswide, as we would expect, but left the residue to Sir John Spelman, whom she appointed one of her co-executors, another indication of the close ties between the two families that resulted from her initial responsibility for raising his wife.[44]

II

As Dame Frowick's long-term relations with Lady Spelman and her family demonstrate, women's ties to each other continued long after their marriages. They perpetuated their relationships through letters, visiting, and the exchange of favours and gifts. The relationships between mothers and their married daughters were often quite close. As we have seen, women often travelled long distances to assist at their daughters' lyings-in. But these were not the only reasons they visited each other. In 1488, for example, Alice, Lady Fitzhugh, told John Paston III that even though it meant foregoing an advantageous business deal, she could not leave her daughter, whose husband, Francis, Lord Lovell, had disappeared the year before after the Battle of Stoke.[45] Decades later, in a more ordinary situation, Dame Maud Parr journeyed from Hertfordshire to Lincolnshire to visit her daughter Katherine, recently married to Edward Burgh.[46] Lady

Elizabeth Cavendish's mother spent four days with her in London in 1552.[47]

When they could not travel to see each other, mothers and daughters expressed their mutual affection by exchanging gifts. Margaret Paston and her mother sent each other tokens after her marriage to John Paston I in 1440.[48] A century later, Frances, Lady Burgavenny, gave her mother, Eleanor, dowager countess of Rutland, some 'gear', a word used generically for clothing. The countess thanked her in 'gentle letters' and reciprocated with a white linen cap called a creppyn. Frances then requested some green silk for a shirt for her husband.[49] Their contemporary, Lady Dorothy Packington, received a cup, almost certainly made of silver or silver gilt, from her mother, Margaret, countess of Bath, whom she thanked verbally through a servant.[50] Many mothers – 94 or 35 per cent of 266 – remembered their married daughters in their wills. Not only were they generous to them, but also often gave them personal, emotionally charged items that embodied their mutual love and signified their daughters' continued membership in their natal families. Agnes Say gave her daughter, Margaret Leynham, a cup she had originally received from Margaret's father, while Margaret Capell bequeathed to her daughter, Elizabeth Paulet, a diamond ring 'which was the first ring her father gave me' and a gold collar and gold heart 'which were both my lady my mother's'.[51]

Aristocratic mothers also expressed their affection for their married daughters by assisting them in practical matters. On the everyday level, Margaret, countess of Bath, recommended a servant to her daughter Catherine, wife of Sir John Spencer.[52] In a more serious situation, her daughter Dorothy begged her to answer a letter from her husband, Sir Thomas Packington. 'For she sayeth', the countess's servant reported, 'at his coming he will blame her and say she did never remember the same and she cared not'.[53] Packington clearly assumed that if she took the trouble, his wife would be able to prevail upon her mother to grant him the favour he had requested. Mothers were particularly solicitous and generous when their sons-in-law's improvidence, insecure inheritances, or political misfortunes jeopardized their daughters' comfort and security. Shortly after her daughter Isabel's marriage to Sir Robert Plumpton, who was being ruined by the feud over his inheritance, Lady Edith Nevill returned a bond he had given her husband to relieve them of one of his debts.[54] Dorothy Codrington received legal assistance from her mother and stepfather when her husband died without assuring her jointure.[55] As we have already seen, mothers also helped their daughters by helping them to prefer *their* daughters, either by taking them into their households when they reached the age to be put out or by contributing to their dowries.

Widows frequently went to court or left conditional bequests in their wills to protect their daughters' inheritances, dowries and jointures. Elizabeth Tailboys sued her brother for her daughter's dowry in a petition that exposed the complicated agreements and transactions that often accompanied aristocratic marriages. According to Lady Tailboys, the contested money was part of her own unpaid marriage portion.[56] Anne Bourchier offered to cancel her son-in-law's debt to her, if he would assure her daughter's jointure according to the marriage contract she had signed with his father.[57] Ursula Hynde relied on a similar strategy and bequeathed her son-in-law a considerable amount of plate, a number of farm animals and the featherbed in her chamber 'with all that goes with it' if he gave his wife a particular manor as her jointure.[58] In more desperate situations, mothers – Elizabeth, Lady Latimer, Cecily, dowager marchioness of Dorset, and Dame Jane Corbet are examples – arranged livings for their daughters from their own property.[59] Lady Margaret Bryan, who spoke tenderly of her daughter Elizabeth 'being so kind a child to me', spared no trouble petitioning Thomas Cromwell for Elizabeth after her husband, Sir Nicholas Carew, was attainted for treason.[60]

Unlike Anne Bouchier, Ursula Hynde and Lady Latimer, who needed to provide for daughters facing financially insecure futures, most aristocratic widows writing their wills had daughters who were well settled in their marriages. Nonetheless, many of them were exceedingly generous to these daughters as well, bequeathing them large portions of their luxury goods – plate, jewellery, expensive beds and clothing. Their bequests were the last expression of the strong mother-daughter relationships that survived the younger women's marriages. When Sir Henry Heydon died in 1503, for example, he divided most of his movable goods between his widow and heir. Seven years later, she carefully distributed most of her jewellery, plate and many of her household goods to her surviving married daughters, their husbands and their children. She left a relatively small legacy, some household goods and my 'worser' silver basin and ewer, to a younger son and the household goods at 'my place in Kent', but no plate or jewels, to the Heydon heir.[61] Mabel Parr left her daughter Katherine, then married to Edward Borough, the heir of Thomas, Lord Borough, an enormous amount of jewellery and a purple satin bed 'panyd with cloth of gold' over and above her marriage portion, a gift that substantially reduced the movables that would descend to her only son. The jewels included two items that would usually have gone to the eldest son as heirlooms: a tablet with pictures of the King and Queen and beads 'dressed with gold which the said

Queen's grace gave me'.[62] Legacies on this scale enriched women's married daughters at the expense of their eldest sons, who might have been expected to inherit these goods and is one way mothers deviated from the commitment to the patrilineage characteristic of so much of their adult activity.

The relations between mothers and their married daughters were not, of course, always conflict free. Cecily, marchioness of Dorset, was extremely slow about paying her daughters' dowries, although she subsequently provided a living for the neediest of them, Cecily, Lady Dudley.[63] Dame Dorothy Verney tried unsuccessfully to use a fraudulent will to gain possession of her only daughter's inheritance.[64] John Holcroft accused his daughter-in-law's mother, Dame Margaret Bolde, of defrauding her of her dowry.[65] But cases of this kind were relatively rare. Of 551 suits involving aristocratic women in the courts of Chancery, Requests, and Star Chamber, mothers and daughters litigated against each other less than a dozen times. Women were much more likely to protect their daughters than to withhold their dowries and inheritances.

The interaction between adult married sisters resembled their relations with their mothers, mixing affection and practical mutual support. In this context, they do not appear to have distinguished between full- and half-siblings, evidence of the success of families created by successive marriages. Sisters often visited each other when they were ill and supplied each other with game for their households. In 1538, when Elizabeth, Lady Dacre, fell ill after her churching, her husband summoned her sister, the countess of Northumberland, because her presence would be a 'consolation and comfort' to her.[66] A few years later Anne, Lady Powis, visited her half-sister, Eleanor, countess of Cumberland, who was ill with 'jaundice and the ague'.[67]

Honor, Lady Lisle, who had three sisters, was closest to Mary, wife of Thomas St Aubyn. By far the richer of the two, Lady Lisle sent Mary a variety of gifts, including a doe for her daughter's wedding and beads that Thomas described as 'fair and goodly' and 'like none that could be found in Cornwall'.[68] In addition, Lady Lisle supplemented the St Aubyns' income by appointing Thomas overseer of her property in Cornwall.[69] Both the Lisles, who needed trustworthy estate officials while they were in Calais, and the St Aubyns benefited from the arrangement, which strengthened the links between Lady Lisle's natal and marital families.[70] Although another of Lady Lisle's sisters, Philippa, was dead by the time she moved to Calais, she continued to take an interest in Philippa's children. Between 1533 and 1535, she mobilised her court connections on behalf of Philippa's daughter, Elizabeth Staynings, whose husband was in prison for debt and whose creditors were threatening to foreclose on land he had mortgaged. Her efforts saved Staynings's inheritance and secured his release from prison. A few years later, when he died of the plague, Lady Lisle invited his widow to live with her at Calais.[71] Lady Lisle's relations with the St Aubyns and Staynings demonstrate how important a woman who married upward could be to her female natal kin.

Despite these kinds of warm, mutually supportive relations, few widows, only twenty-nine (11 per cent) of 266, remembered their sisters in their wills. They were even less likely to include them among their executors and then only when they had no children.[72] Women's legacies to their sisters usually consisted of specific pieces of clothing or jewellery or treasured books, the same kinds of objects mothers gave their daughters, but in smaller quantities. The gold ring with a sapphire that Bridget, Lady Marney, left her sister and co-executor, Dame Dorothy Spring; the gold flower with a ruby and two half-pearls that Dame Jane Nevill gave her sister Elizabeth, Lady Welles; and the £10 that Dame Elizabeth Hussey left to each of her sisters were typical of such bequests.[73]

Aristocratic women were no more likely to leave property to their siblings' children than to their sisters. Thirty-one (12 per cent) of 266 female testators left legacies to their siblings' children, about the same frequency with which they remembered their sisters. Their bequests to them also usually consisted of the same kind of gifts – small amounts of cash, jewellery, single pieces of plate and luxury clothing.[74] The contrast between aristocratic women's legacies and their warm relations with their sisters underscores the fact that knightly and noble families defined themselves first and foremost in patrilineal terms and distributed most of their property accordingly – to their children and grandchildren – when they died.

The major exception to this bequest pattern occurred when aristocratic women had no children of their own. In these cases, they were likely to prefer their sisters and their sisters' children as their beneficiaries, illustrating the way that female networks created alternative bonds for the minority of aristocratic wives who were not also mothers.[75] Thus the childless Elizabeth Pechey left her sister, Agnes Redman, whom she named as one of her co-executors, a huge amount of plate, pewter, household goods and furniture, including 'the bed that I lie in wholely as it standeth'.[76] Margaret Leynham, who had five sisters and no children, divided her property among her surviving sisters and the offspring of those who predeceased her. Since her husband, Sir John, had left her almost all his goods, chattels, debts and land, she had considerable property to distribute.[77] Most important was the disposition of her land. She left manors with rights of inheritance to her sisters Elizabeth and Katherine, and life rights in a manor to one of her nephews, John Brown, and his wife Agnes. The beneficiaries of her plate, jewellery and other luxury goods included her sisters Elizabeth and Katherine, her half-sister Alice, Alice's two sons, Elizabeth's son and three daughters, and her deceased sister Agnes's sons. When her sister Katherine died, she transferred her legacy to her daughters.[78]

Ursula Knightley, the childless coheir of the fourteenth earl of Oxford, also divided her estate between her sister and her sister's children. She appointed her sister's widowed daughter, Elizabeth Naunton, sole executor of her will and gave her use of some of her land for twenty years to perform it. She recorded that she had already given Dame Naunton movables, chattels and plate 'for many considerations me moving'. In addition, she assigned life rights in her estates in Suffolk and Essex to her sister, Dame Elizabeth Wingfield, and directed that they should descend to her eldest son, Sir Robert, when she died. She also provided pensions for her sister's four younger sons for twenty years.[79]

In a variation on this pattern, Elizabeth, Lady Scrope of Upsall and Masham, the childless coheir of John Nevill, marquess of Montague, adopted her sister's daughter Lucy as her heir if she agreed to the match her aunt had arranged for her. A year after she wrote her will, Lady Scrope added a codicil that showed the wedding had already taken place. Accordingly, in addition to inheriting her aunt's land, Lucy was named residual heir of her movable goods. Since Lucy had two brothers, neither of whom were mentioned in Lady Scrope's will at all, her arrangements clearly indicated her preference for promoting a female over two males who stood in the same relationship to her.[80]

Childless aunts who were not heiresses also made substantial contributions to their nieces' and nephews' futures. A number of them left their siblings' sons land they had acquired from their husbands or purchased during their widowhoods.[81] Another aunt, Elizabeth Tailboys Greystock, contributed 20 marks and a gold collar to one of her nieces' dowries.[82] Dame Mary Gates gave enough cash to her sister Martha Carew's younger sons to increase their livings substantially.[83]

The most extensive female network involving the circulation of goods among sisters, some of whom died without children, centred on the eight daughters of Sir Richard Scrope of Bentley, a younger son of Henry, Lord Scrope of Bolton and Masham.[84] When Sir Richard wrote his will, he directed that if he had no son and his wife remarried (both of which happened), the manor of Bentley, his main property, should be sold for his daughters' benefit. Presumably he intended the profits to be used for the dowries of those who were still single, since he made no other provision for them. His only other legacy to the girls was a piece of plate for Anne, who became a nun.[85] Of the seven sisters who married, one, Elizabeth, viscountess Beaumont and then countess of Oxford, died childless and another, Margaret, duchess of Suffolk, had an only daughter, Elizabeth, who became a nun at the Minories.

Sir Richard's widow, Eleanor, married Sir John Wyndham as her second husband. Like many aristocratic women in her situation, she arranged a marriage between a daughter by her first husband, Eleanor, and her second husband's heir, Thomas. Her second husband assisted her first family by purchasing Bentley and two other Scrope manors and bequeathing the sale price, £1000, to three of her Scrope daughters, Katherine, Mary and Jane, for their marriages.[86] When Dame Wyndham died twenty years after her first husband, her Scrope daughters were among her main beneficiaries. She left much smaller legacies to her children by Wyndham.[87]

The surviving wills of three of the Scrope sisters, Margaret, duchess of Suffolk, Elizabeth, countess of Oxford, and Lady Mary Jerningham Kingston, document their continuing ties to each other and their respective children over the next four decades.[88] The duchess, the first to die, lived with her childless niece, Lady Elizabeth Pechey, and her husband, Sir John, at Lullingstone, Kent, and made her largest bequests to them.[89] But she also remembered five of her sisters, giving the countess of Oxford her image of St Michael with pearls and precious stones, Jane Brews, a standing cup of silver, all gilt, Frances St Clere all her pearls, Mary Jerningham some table linen, and Anne, a nun at Barking, a silver pot.[90]

Two decades later, when another sister, Elizabeth, countess of Oxford, wrote her will, the connections among them were still strong. Indeed, the countess, whose main residences were at Castle Hedingham and Wivenhoe in Essex, regularly visited at Felbrigg and Norwich in Norfolk in order to see her sisters and other members of the Scrope family.[91] The countess bequeathed a silver basin and ewer, chaced with gilt, 'of the newest making', a gold goblet engraved with two of her husbands' badges and a gold book set with pearl to her sister, Lady Mary Kingston. She was even more generous to another sister, Jane Brews, whom she gave a silver basin and ewer chaced with gilt 'of the oldest sort … having my Lord of Oxford's arms in the bottom', a great goblet with a silver cover, partially gilt 'which she lately gave me', a gold cross that had belonged to their father, a bed and counterpoint of black velvet and scarlet cloth embroidered with gold letters, and some bed clothing and accessories. She divided her samplers equally between Mary and Jane. She was somewhat less generous to a third sister, Lady Frances Clere, who received a silver and gilt cup, £4 in cash, a bed of black velvet and satin, a counterpoint, and some bed clothing and accessories. The countess also bequeathed plate or jewellery to two of her brothers-in-law, Mary's second husband, Sir William Kingston, and Sir John St Clere, and eleven nieces and nephews, her sisters' children. She was particularly generous to Elizabeth St Clere, who bore her name and was probably her goddaughter. In addition to leaving her some plate, she contributed £100 to her dowry.[92]

Unlike the countess of Oxford, Dame Mary Kingston, the third Scrope sister whose will has survived, had both children and grandchildren. When she died in 1549, her major beneficiaries were her son by her first marriage, Henry Jerningham, and his daughter Mary, who was probably her goddaughter and namesake. Nonetheless, her legacies also perpetuated her ties to her natal family. She gave one of her surviving sisters, Jane Brews, a gold hoop and a book covered with purple velvet, and Lady Frances St Clere, the other, a black velvet gown, a tawney satin kirtle and a pair of beads. She also bequeathed a black velvet kirtle to Frances's daughter Elizabeth, and a gold brooch to Jane's son John.[93]

III

Women's natal kin dominated their female networks whether they had children or not. Nonetheless, many of them did develop similar patterns of friendship and mutual support with their mothers- and sisters-in-law although they were less intense and less evident in surviving documents. They established many of these relationships in the early years of their marriages when they resided with their husbands' parents, a situation that could last for decades, since it often ended only when both their fathers- and mothers-in-law died or their widowed mothers-in-law remarried.[94] Co-residence gave young wives an opportunity to develop warm relationships with their mothers-in-law and those of their sisters-in-law still living at home. The long periods they spent together in their husbands' absences and during the younger women's pregnancies and lyings-in encouraged intimacy between them. In addition, the early years of women's first marriages functioned like apprenticeships in which their mothers-in-law taught them how to manage their large households and oversee their estates. Lady Anne Lestrange's accounts indicate, for example, that she was beginning to involve her daughter-in-law Ellen, who had married her eldest son Nicholas in 1528, in agricultural activities at Hunstanton.[95]

Aristocratic women's wills reflected the affection they felt for their daughters-in-law. Forty-nine of 266 testators left them bequests, eight times the comparable figure for fathers- and daughters-in-law in 763 male wills. The difference reflects the bonding that occurred between the women when they co-resided, the frequent absence of men from their households, and women's somewhat weaker commitment to their husbands' patrilineages. Women's legacies to their daughters-in-law consisted of the same kinds of objects – jewellery, clothes, small amounts of cash and plate – they gave their sisters and nieces. Occasionally they noted that they thought the bequests would have special emotional significance to them. In 1487, for example, Dame Elizabeth Uvedale left her son Robert's wife 'a hoop of gold with which I was wedded to the said Sir Thomas Uvedale his father'.[96] One mother-in-law, Dame Elizabeth Fitzjames, even included her son's wife among her executors.[97] In two cases, widows who predeceased their mothers-in-law left remembrances to the older women.[98]

Aristocratic wives' relations with their mothers-in-law were their most important connections with the women in their marital families in the early years of their marriages. But they become increasingly involved in the lives of their brothers- and sisters-in-law when their husbands inherited their estates and took over as heads of their natal families, and they themselves grew into their mature roles as managers of their households. Their husbands' younger siblings often lived with them until they were married or otherwise settled. Many wives also helped to arrange their sisters-in-law's matches. Although her husband's sister, Elizabeth, resided elsewhere, for example, Margaret Paston was intimately involved in the long-drawn out, frustrating process of arranging her marriage. In 1453, after speaking with Elizabeth herself, she wrote to her husband exhorting him to pursue a possible match. A year later she raised the subject again.[99] Most importantly, as supervisors of their husbands' affairs, wives made payments of all kinds to their sisters- and brothers-in-law whatever the latter's ages.

Three generations later, Margaret Paston's great-granddaughter Eleanor married Thomas, first earl of Rutland. During the period the countess kept the Rutland household accounts, one of her husband's unmarried sisters, Anne, resided with them. The earl also had a dependent younger brother, Richard, who lived elsewhere, and two married sisters, Catherine, wife of Sir Robert Constable of Everingham, and Elizabeth, wife of Thomas Sandys, who became second Lord Sandys in 1540. The countess was closely involved in all their lives and made numerous payments to them, sometimes at her husband's direction, sometimes on her own initiative. In 1528, for example, she paid the quarterly instalment on

Richard's annuity and 20s to his married sister, Elizabeth Sandys, at 'my Lord's commandment'.[100] Two years later, her husband directed her to pay for a velvet bonnet for Elizabeth. But there were no notations of this sort when she spent £3 15s for some goldsmith's work for his sister Anne, bought her eight ounces of pearls for a frontlet, gave Elizabeth Sandys another 23s, or gave the earl's sister, Catherine Constable, 20s for her travel expenses after she visited the Rutlands.[101] Nor were the countess's expenditures for her sisters-in-law limited to small sums of this sort. She also paid Anne's and Margaret's dowries, which involved transferring huge sums of cash.[102]

When they were adults and lived apart, sisters-in-law expressed their friendship and concern for each other by replicating the patterns of visiting and mutual assistance characteristic of sisters. Grace, countess of Shrewsbury, wife of Francis, the fifth earl, visited his sister, Elizabeth, Lady Dacre, and her daughter Anne, countess of Cumberland, at Skipton Castle in the 1550s, probably during one of Anne's lyings-in. Lady Dacre thanked her for the 'great pains' she had taken with her daughter. Shortly afterwards, Lady Dacre wanted to borrow £10 from her brother, but instead of writing to him directly, asked the countess 'to be a mean' to him for the loan.[103] Lady Shrewsbury intervened successfully and a week later Lady Dacre wrote to thank her 'very good brother' for the money.[104] During her years at Calais, Honor, Lady Lisle, and Margaret, widow of her brother, Sir Roger, exchanged friendly letters and tokens.[105] In 1533, she took a distant relative, John Worth, into her service at Margaret's request.[106]

The similarity between aristocratic women's relations with their sisters-in-law and sisters also appeared in the small number of sisters-in-law – only 19 or 7 per cent of 266 female testators – who mentioned each other in their wills. Their legacies to each other were generally smaller than those they left to their sisters, but consisted of the same kinds of objects – single pieces of jewellery or plate, clothing, books and small amounts of money. Again, the largest bequests were from childless women. Anne, Lady Scrope, an only daughter who married three times but had no children, remembered the sisters of all her husbands when she died. She left some land to her sister-in-law, Dame Elizabeth Chamberlain, widow of her first husband's brother Sir Robert, and their son 'for the good love, will and confidence' she had in them.[107] She made smaller gifts from among her movables to four of her other sisters-in-law. Two were the sisters of her second husband, Sir Robert Wingfield, and two the sisters of her third.[108] Another childless widow, Dame Jane Talbot, left her sister-in-law, Elizabeth, duchess of Norfolk, £40 and all the household stuff, including her hangings and bedding, at her home in London. She also named the duchess her chief executor.[109] Dame Elizabeth Frowick, an heiress with an only daughter, left luxury clothing to her sister-in-law, Dame Isabel Haute, in return for her prayers. She also remembered Dame Isabel's daughter.[110]

IV

In addition to the comparatively narrow group of natal and marital relatives who formed the core of their female networks, most married aristocratic women maintained ties with at least some of their distant relatives – aunts, great-aunts, great-nieces and a host of others whom they called cousin. Some of the latter were first and second cousins, but in other cases the term applied to such distant kin it is impossible to reconstruct the connections today. Contemporaries often referred to these more distant relatives collectively as their friends, a term that also included neighbours with whom they exchanged visits, favours and patronage. Like the men of their class, aristocratic wives and widows favoured their distant kin when they took adolescents into their households, and responded to requests for their intervention at court. In turn, they called on these connections when they themselves needed assistance. From the point of view of aristocratic women's primary commitment to their spouses, children and grandchildren, these networks constituted valuable resources and contributed to their success as wives, mothers and widows. At some junctures they could even have a major effect on their families. On the other hand, women with children rarely remembered relatives of this kind in their wills. In the totality of their lives and conception of their families, these horizontal connections could not compete with their devotion to their husbands and immediate lineal descendants.

Margaret Paston's letters provide an unusually vivid and detailed picture of such a network in their record of her life-long relations with her distant cousins, the Mountfords, Cleres and Calthorps.[111] The Pastons regularly turned to the Calthorps and Cleres for assistance as they struggled to protect their property and continue their social ascent. Margaret Paston's great-aunt, Eleanor Mautby, had married the Sir William Calthorp who died in 1421. Eleanor's grandson, another Sir William, was heir of the Mautby lands after Margaret's own children.[112] The relationship between the families was warm and mutually supportive: Anne Paston, Margaret's daughter, lived in the Calthorp household after her father's death, while Margaret and Lady Elizabeth exchanged herbal remedies.[113] Even more importantly, Lady Calthorp helped Margaret's younger son, John III, to settle his feud over his inheritance with his uncle, William II.[114]

The Cleres, to whom the Pastons were connected through Sir John Fastolf, played an even larger role in the Pastons' affairs, although their relationship was still more removed.[115] Margaret, her husband John I, and their children were particularly close to Elizabeth Clere and her son, Robert, who was knighted in 1494. The two families were in constant contact and regularly supplied each other with news.[116] They also assisted each other in a myriad of practical matters. In the 1440s, Elizabeth Clere, wife of Robert, esq. of Ormesby, actively promoted a match between Stephen Scrope and Elizabeth Paston, Margaret's sister-in-law. Drawing on her considerable knowledge of the law, she reminded Elizabeth's brother, John I, to examine the indentures for the marriage of Scrope's daughter by his first wife and advised him to support the match only if a son by Elizabeth would inherit his land. She also expressed alarm about Agnes Paston's mistreatment of Elizabeth and her refusal to permit her to see or speak to any of her potential suitors.[117]

Relations of this kind between the two families continued for the rest of the century. In 1453, Margaret borrowed a necklace from Elizabeth Clere when she was presented to the Queen because she was ashamed to wear her own jewellery 'among so many fresh gentlewomen'.[118] Ten years later, the Cleres sold the manor of Horninghall or Caister Clere to William Paston II; Mistress Clere served as one of his feoffees.[119] In 1474, when the Calthorps could no longer keep Margaret's daughter, Anne, she asked her younger son, John III, to inquire about placing her with the Cleres.[120] The Cleres also lent the Pastons money on a number of occasions.[121] While the wealthier Cleres assisted the Pastons financially, John I reciprocated by acting as his cousin Elizabeth's lawyer and business agent.[122] At the end of the century, the two families crowned their long friendship with a marriage between John III's daughter, Elizabeth, and Sir Robert Clere's son William.[123]

Margaret Paston's relations with the Cleres and Calthorps served as a resource in her family's relentless struggle to rise socially and defend its property. Connections of this kind functioned differently for high-ranking women from established families. In contrast to the Pastons, they incorporated distant kin of lower rank into their patronage networks. Thus the Pastons' contemporary, Elizabeth Mowbray, duchess of Norfolk, extended her favour to her first cousin, Richard Roos, esq., in return for his service.[124] On one occasion, she agreed to arrange (and presumably finance) the marriages of two of his daughters.[125] Her assistance was probably responsible for Mary Roos's advantageous match with Hugh Denys, a member of Henry VII's Privy Chamber.[126] High-ranking women often appointed kin from more modest families as their household servants or estate officials. Joan, Lady Clinton, daughter of Sir Ralph Mignell, employed her goddaughter Joan Mignell,[127] and Elizabeth Mowbray, duchess of Norfolk, took her distant relative, Anne Montgomery, a childless widow, into her service.[128] The duchess lived in Essex much of the time and was powerful enough around Malden, the family seat of Anne Montgomery's natal family, the Darcys, to intervene in a parliamentary election there in 1472.[129] In 1488, Anne moved with her patron to the Minories in London and remained there until she died ten years later.[130]

Since aristocratic families tended to intermarry and most marriages in the fifteenth and early sixteenth centuries were patrilocal, women's neighbourhood networks overlapped with their ties to their collateral marital kin, but were not limited to them. What is distinctive about these networks is that they were based on geographical proximity and often drew their members into the affinities of noblemen who dominated the region. As mistress of Hunstanton, located in the northwest corner of Norfolk, for example, Lady Anne Lestrange, wife of Sir Thomas, lived within easy travelling distance of many of her husband's relatives. Some were close connections like his sister, Katherine, wife of Sir Hugh Hastings; others were like Edmund Wyndham, son of Sir Thomas, whom the Lestranges called cousin because they had marital relatives in common. Lady Lestrange's husband also had marital relatives in common with the third duke of Norfolk and belonged to his affinity. Within this extensive circle, Lady Lestrange developed her own relationships with women such as her husband's sister, Katherine Hastings, and two of his aunts of the half-blood, Lady Elizabeth Woodhouse and Mistress Anne Banyard, who visited Hunstanton regularly and participated in her lyings-in.[131] Her connections with these women reinforced her husband's relations with their spouses, which strengthened his local political significance and enhanced his value as a member of the duke of Norfolk's affinity.

Lady Lestrange's contemporary, Eleanor, countess of Rutland, also cultivated her ties to women from the knightly and gentry families residing in the area around her main residence, Belvoir Castle, Lincolnshire. As one of the Queen's ladies-in-waiting, she divided her time between Belvoir and the court and developed some of her most important relationships within the royal household. Nonetheless, she maintained ties to a number of knightly families, the Strelleys and Markhams, for example, from the nearby area of Nottinghamshire. The countess appointed Isabell Strelley, probably a daughter of Sir Nicholas, one of her gentlewoman servants. Her eldest son, Henry, and her son-in-law, George Talbot, attended Henry Strelley's wedding in 1539.[132] Members of the Markham of Cottam family also appear frequently in the Rutland accounts. Lady Markham sent the countess numerous gifts during the summer and fall of 1539.[133] The following January, Lady Markham also sent presents to Lady Anne, the countess's daughter-in-law, when she gave birth to her first child at Belvoir.[134] The wives of Sir John Byron and Sir Brian Stapleton, two other Nottinghamshire knights, also visited Belvoir or sent gifts that year.[135] Many of the heads of these families were the earl's clients and served in his retinue during the wars in Scotland in 1541.[136] The countess's relations with their wives reinforced the bonds between their families and cemented loyalties that were indispensable to maintaining the earl's political and military power.

The countess of Rutland's relationships with the Strelleys and Markhams were based not on kinship but rather on their geographical proximity to her husband's chief residence. Other women of her class who were not related by blood or marriage also developed friendships because they lived in the same localities and occasionally remembered each other in their wills. Thus, Dame Constance Culpepper left her Kentish neighbour and friend, Lady Anne Grey, gold beads, rings and a gold button for a partlett,[137] while Sir John Porte's second wife, Dorothy, frequently visited her Derbyshire neighbour, Lady Cavendish.[138] While such relationships did not make a major contribution to aristocratic women's careers as wives, mothers and widows, their existence provides further evidence of their integration into their neighbourhoods. In a broad sense such friendships almost certainly contributed to their husbands' local position.

Extended networks of collateral relatives, neighbours and friends also functioned as additional resources for aristocratic widows and wives in trouble. Lady Margaret Beaufort opened her great household at Collyweston to numerous women of this kind. Lady Anne Clifford, her half-brother's daughter, and her two daughters found refuge with her when she separated from her husband, Henry, Lord Clifford.[139] Elizabeth, Lady Scrope, lived at Collyweston after the death of her second husband, Sir Henry Wentworth, in 1501. When her stepson, Sir Richard, disputed the terms of her marriage contract with his father, Lady Margaret intervened and forced him to sign heavy bonds in which he promised to accept the findings of an arbitration panel headed by her chamberlain. At some point Lady Margaret gave Lady Scrope a valuable primer and psalter; Lady Scrope bequeathed it in turn to her sister when she died.[140] Another of Lady Margaret's widowed friends, Cecily, Viscountess Welles, visited Collyweston frequently. When she died in 1506, Lady Margaret arranged for prayers to be said for her in her private chapel. Three years later, she bequeathed 'a heart of gold with a fair sapphire' to Lady Powis's daughter in her own will.[141]

A similar circle gathered around Elizabeth Mowbray, duchess of Norfolk, who retired to the Minories in London in 1488. In addition to Anne Montgomery, whom we have already mentioned, the group included her sister-in-law, Dame Jane Talbot, widow of Sir Humphrey, Elizabeth Brackenbury, coheir of Sir Robert, a follower of Richard III who died at Bosworth, and Mary Tyrell, Anne Montgomery's niece.[142] Anne Montgomery died and was buried at the Minories in 1498. Subsequently, both the duchess and Dame Talbot asked to be buried near her, a final tribute to the strength of their mutual ties.[143]

Decades later, two high-ranking noblewomen, Eleanor, countess of Rutland, and Catherine, countess of Westmorland, who were connected by the marriage of their children, retired together to Halliwell, the London home of the Rutland heir, Henry, the second earl. When they died in the early 1550s, they were both buried in the nearby church of St Leonard Shoreditch.[144] Margaret, the second earl's wife and the countess of Westmorland's daughter, was also buried there in 1559.[145] The interment of the three countesses at St Leonard's turned it into a mausoleum for members of the earl of Rutland's family. Eventually, two of Eleanor, countess of Rutland's sons, Oliver and Sir Thomas, her daughter, Anne, and her granddaughter, Catherine Nevill, wife of Sir John Constable, were also buried there. Lady Constable's sister, Lady Adeline Nevill, built a monument in the church marking their tombs.[146]

Aristocratic women who chose to be buried with each other rather than their husbands were making a particularly strong, public statement about the intensity of their mutual ties since the great majority of widows directed their executors to bury them with their husbands.[147] Yet they were unusual only in departing from a normative custom, not in their strong ties to one another. Female friendships and networks coexisted with their primary loyalty to the patrilineages of their marital families and played an important part in most aristocratic women's lives. They constituted a source of emotional support for women outside their marriages and marital families and expanded the circle on which they could draw for material and political assistance as they promoted and defended the careers and interests of their husbands, sons, and daughters. Since the family was the ultimate source of power among the aristocracy, their activities inevitably affected the political influence and effectiveness of their spouses and children. In the larger context outside their households, women's networks enhanced the power of both their natal and marital families by cementing the bonds between them and encouraging them to include each other in the circle of their friends, clients and patrons. In this respect they played a key role in turning the political potential of their marriages into reality. Similarly, they reinforced their husbands' local position as they developed friendships and habits of mutual assistance with other noble- and gentlewomen residing in their neighbourhoods. Throughout the Yorkist and early Tudor periods, therefore, female networks were an important, if generally neglected, component in the complex chains of patronage and clientage that empowered aristocratic families on the local and regional levels and enabled them to rule England in partnership with the crown.

Notes

[1] Barbara J. Harris, *English Aristocratic Women, 1450-1550: Marriage and Family, Property and Careers*, New York: OUP, 2002, pp. 18, 127, 129.

[2] Ibid., pp. 62-3.

[3] Ibid., pp. 103-6.

[4] *HMC, The Manuscripts of His Grace the Duke of Rutland, K.G. preserved at Belvoir Castle*, London: HMSO, 1888-1905, 4, pp. 295, 296, 302, 305. The young mother was Anne Manners Nevill, daughter of the first earl of Rutland and wife of Henry Nevill, the earl of Westmorland's heir (1540).

[5] CUL, Hengrave MS 88, vol.1, fol. 19.

[6] Barrett L. Beer and Sybil J. Jack (eds), 'The Letters of William Lord Paget of Beaudesert, 1547-63', *Camden Miscellany XXV*, Camden Society, 4th ser., 13 (1974), p. 122.

[7] *LP*, 3 (1): 1285, pp. 499-500.

[8] Daniel Guerney, 'Extracts from the Household and Privy Purse Accounts of the LeStranges of Hunstanton', *Archaeologia*, 25 (1834), pp. 428-29; p. 448 for identification of Mr Banyard; the other aunt was Elizabeth, née Radcliffe, daughter of Sir Thomas's grandmother by her second husband, Sir Robert Radcliffe of Hunstanton; she was married to Sir Roger Woodhouse.

[9] For example, Dame Jane Strangeways (d. 1502) and Dame Anne Bourchier (d. 1519) each had five goddaughters bearing their names; Dame Constance Culpepper had four; Dame Elizabeth Fitzwilliam (d. 1502) and Dame Dorothy Hungerford (d. 1551), three; Prob11/19/32 (Bourchier); Prob11/29/12 (Culpepper); *TE*, 4: 133, p. 211 (Fitzwilliam); 4: 97, p. 186 (Strangeways); BL, Add. MS 33412, fol. 40 (Hungerford).

[10] Prob11/19/26 (1519).

[11] For example, Dame Anne Bourchier, Prob11/19/32 (1519); Dame Philippa Brudenell, Prob11/24/16 (1531); Dame Margaret Darcy, Prob11/8/20 (1489).

[12] There is no way of knowing if her bequest constituted Margaret's entire dowry or supplemented one provided by her father. The furniture she left Margaret included such expensive items as a featherbed with the hangings and everything else that went with it; a wainscot chair; and a long settle. Prob11/22/32 (1526).

[13] Prob11/28/6 (1540); see also Prob11/14/38, Dame Jane Talbot (1505).

[14] Prob11/7/6 (1482).

[15] Muriel St. Clare Byrne (ed.), *The Lisle Letters*, Chicago and London: Chicago UP, 1981, 5: 1379 (p. 432) [hereafter cited as *Lisle Letters*].

[16] Thomas Stapleton (ed.), *The Plumpton Correspondence*, Camden Society, old ser., IV, 1839 [Reprint, Wolfeboro Falls, N.H., 1990], p. 132.

[17] M. A. E. Wood Green, *Letters of Royal and Illustrious Ladies of Great Britain*, London: Henry Colburn, 1846, 3, pp. 169-70; *HMC, Rutland*, 4, pp. 296, 315.

[18] *Miscellanea Genealogica and Heraldica*, new series, 2, p. 431 (1549); Thynne Papers, vol. 48, fol. 165 (microfilm at IHR).

[19] PRO, SP1/232, fol. 94 (1518).

[20] *HMC, Rutland*, 1, p. 56.

[21] Folger, X.d.428 (82): Lady Elizabeth Cavendish to Francis Whitfield, 14 Nov. [1552]; Maud Stepney Rawson, *Bess of Hardwick and Her Circle*, London: 1910, p. 9.

[22] *TE*, 4: 57 (116 and n.).

[23] BL, Titus B1, fol. 162 (orig. 152). Elizabeth, wife of the third duke of Norfolk.

[24] PRO, SP1/139, fol. 97.

[25] *LP*, 16: 1320, 1321, 1385, 1440.

[26] Anne Crawford, *The Career of John Howard, Duke of Norfolk, 1420-1485*, unpublished M. Phil. thesis, University of London, 1975, pp. 95-6. The countess's daughter was Lady Jane Norris, wife of Sir William.

[27] Norman Davis (ed.), *The Paston Letters and Papers of the Fifteenth Century*, Oxford: Clarendon Press, 1971-76, 1, pp. lxii-xiii, 206, 220, 371.

[28] *Lisle Letters*, 4: 896 (p. 167).

[29] Ibid., 4: 850 (ii) (p. 109), 876; despite this, Sir John Wallop apparently assisted Anne by approaching the King directly on her behalf, 880.

[30] For a detailed account of the appointment of Maids-of-Honour, see Harris, *English Aristocratic Women*, pp. 219-20; on their political importance, pp. 210-14, 226-7, 236.

[31] *Lisle Letters*, 5: 1620 (p. 730).

[32] Ibid., 6: 1653 (p. 34); 5: 1513.

[33] *CSPSpanish*, 6 (1): 230 (1542).

[34] Prob11/ 9/22; Prob11/ 10/10.

[35] J. W. Clay (ed.), *North Country Wills, 1338-1558*, Surtees Society, vol. 116, 1908, no. 67 (1517), p. 88; no. 68 (1531), p. 92.

[36] Prob11/32/37 (1545); Prob11/36/11 (1545).

[37] Prob11/11/10 (1496); Prob11/32/19 (1548).

[38] *TV*, vol. 1, p. 285 (1485); Prob11/ 34/29 (1551).

[39] Prob11/ 20/19 (1521).

[40] Prob11/31/1 (1542). Jane's mother was the earl's second wife, Margaret Stanley, daughter of the second earl of Derby; her stepmother was his third, Mary Arundell, daughter of Sir John of Lanherne. GEC, XII (pt. 1), pp. 519-20.

[41] Prob11/34/7 (1550); HEH, Hastings Collection, HAP Box 8, folder (actually a roll) 11.

[42] Prob11/14/41 (1505).

[43] Prob11/15/15 (1505, codicil 1506).

[44] Prob11/18/13 (1515).

[45] N. Davis, *Paston Letters and Papers*, 2: 813 (p. 456); on Lovel, GEC, 8, p. 225.

[46] Susan E. James, *Kateryn Parr, The Making of a Queen*, Brookfield, Vt: Ashgate, 1999, pp. 15, 62.

[47] David N. Durant, *Bess of Hardwick: Portrait of an Elizabethan Dynast*, London: Weidenfield and Nicolson, 1977, p. 21.

[48] N. Davis, *Paston Letters and Papers*, 1: 126 (p. 218).

[49] *HMC, Rutland*, 1, p. 56.

[50] CUL, Hengrave MS 88, vol. 1, fol. 119.

[51] Prob11/6/34, Say (1478); Prob11/19/2, Capell (1516).

[52] CUL, Hengrave MS 88, vol. 1, fol. 8.

[53] CUL, Hengrave MS 88, vol. 1, fol. 157.

[54] GEC, 4, pp. 73-4; Stapleton (ed.), *Plumpton Correspondence*, 160 (196), and genealogy facing, pp. v-viii.

[55] PRO, C1/405/29 (1517-29).

[56] C1/1074/5-9 (1533-44). Her claim that her father-in-law, Sir Robert Tailboys, had bequeathed the unpaid part of her dowry to her daughter, his granddaughter, is not sustained by his will, Prob11/10/24.

[57] Prob11/19/32 (1519).

[58] Prob11/37/35 (1555 or 56).

[59] *TV*, 1, p. 359 (1480); InqPM, vol. 1, pp. 905, 906 (1494). GEC, 4, p. 480, note a. on Latimer; SP1/141, fol. 212 (1538); LP, 12 (1): 1263; GEC, 4, p. 481 on Dorset (fns 105-107); Prob11/33/14 (1544); C1/1205/66 and C24/24 on Corbet.

[60] PRO, SP1/156, fol. 147 (1539).

[61] Prob11/14/23 (1503); Prob11/16/28 (1510); by this time the Heydons' two other married daughters, Anne or Amy Lestrange, wife of Sir Roger and Elizabeth, wife of Sir Walter Herbert, had died without children; Cord Oestmann, *Lordship and Community, The Lestrange Family and the Village of Hunstanton, Norfolk, in the First Half of the Sixteenth Century*, Woodbridge, Suffolk: Boydell Press, 1994, p. 13; Herbert married the third duke of Buckingham's sister as his second wife in 1500; Barbara Harris, *Edward Stafford, Third Duke of Buckingham, 1478-1521*, Stanford, CA.: Stanford UP, 1986, p. 49; Dame Heydon's will also mentioned a deceased son, William.

[62] *North Country Wills*, no. 68 (93).

[63] BL, Titus B1. XI, fol. 362, Elizabeth, countess of Kildare, 1523; PRO, SP1/26, fol. 184, Lady Cecily Dudley, 1522.

[64] PRO, C1/1080/61 (1540); Req 2/4/3; Prob11/32/4; C1/1080/61 (1540); Req 2/4/3; Prob11/32/4; John Bruce (ed.), *Letters and Papers of the Verney Family Down to the End of the Year 1639*, Camden Society, old ser., 56 (1853), p. 49.

[65] Henry Fishwick (ed.), 'Pleadings and Depositions in the Duchy Court of Lancashire', *Lancashire and Cheshire Record Society*, 35 (1897), p. 192.

[66] LPL, Shrewsbury MS 695, fol. 89.

[67] A.G. Dickens (ed.), *Clifford Letters of the Sixteenth Century*, Surtees Society, 172 (1957), p. 44.

[68] *Lisle Letters*, 1: xxviii, xxxvi, 80 (5); 2: 278; 5: 1095.

[69] Ibid., 1: xxix, 80; 2: 277.

[70] Ibid., 4: 971.

[71] Ibid., 1: xxxviii (1533), p. 342; 2: 202, pp. 164-7, 170-71; 201, 202, 202a (1534), 312, 429 (1535); 4: 825 (1535), 904 (1537).

[72] For example, Prob11/6/5, Lady Anne Vere (1472); Rev. Charles Moor, 'The Bygods, Earls of Norfolk: Bigod of Settrington etc.', *Yorkshire Archaeological Journal*, 32 (1936), 172-213 (p. 195), Katherine Bigod (1506); Prob11/33/11, Bridget, Lady Marney (1549).

[73] Prob11/33/11, Bridget, Lady Marney (1549); Prob11/14/22, Hussey (1503); Prob11/5/31, Nevill (1470).

[74] For example, Prob11/7/6, Margaret Leynham (1482); Prob11/14/38, Jane Talbot (1505); J.W. Clay (ed.), *North Country Wills, 1338-1558*, Surtees Society, 116 (1908), p. 77, Katherine Babington (1537).

[75] Of the 94 per cent of aristocratic women who married, 91 per cent bore at least one child: Harris, *English Aristocratic Women*, pp. 99 and 276n.

[76] Prob11/30/21 (1541).

[77] Prob11/6/37 (1479).

[78] Prob11/7/6 (1482); most likely, John Brown was the son of her sister Agnes, by her first husband, William Brown; Agnes subsequently married Sir Geoffrey Gates (d. 1478), and appears by this name in her mother, Agnes Say's, will; Sir John Maclean and W.C. Heane (eds), *Visitation of Gloucestershire...1623*, Harleian Society, 21 (1886), p. 65.

[79] Prob11/42A/1 (1558); A. Luders *et al.* (eds), *Statutes of the Realm*, 11 vols, London, 1810-28, 3: 412-13, 23 Hen VIII, c. 32; Rev. Henry Isham (ed.), *Visitation of the County of Northampton...1681*, Harleian Society, 87 (1935), p.103; *HC 1509-1558*, 2, p. 476 states incorrectly that Ursula Knightley had six daughters.

[80] Prob11/20/19 (1514); Lucy was the daughter of her sister Lucy Brown and her second husband, Sir Anthony. Her sister had a son by her first husband, Sir William Fitzwilliam, and another by Brown: *HC 1509-1558*, 1, p. 518, 2, p. 142.

[81] For example, Prob11/7/6, Margaret Leynham (1476); Lieut. Col. John Pilkington, *History of the Pilkington Family, 1066-1600*, Liverpool: privately printed, 1910, p. 264, Dame Joan Pilkington (1498); Prob11/17/2, Sibill Danvers (1511).

[82] Prob11/16/16, Elizabeth Tailboys Greystock (1505).

[83] Prob11/26/28 (1582); Mary and Martha were daughters of Sir Edmund Denny; Martha was married to Sir Wymond Carew; her eldest son was Thomas, *HC 1509-1558*, 1, p. 581, 2, p. 198.

[84] Scrope's only son died without children; he also had a daughter, Dorothy, who died unmarried.

[85] *TE*, 3: 122 (297; 1485).

[86] Prob11/21/3, Sir Thomas Wyndham (1522), Sir John's heir, mentioned the transaction in his will; H.A. Wyndham, *A Family History, 1410-1688, vol. 1, The Wyndhams of Norfolk, Somerset, Sussex*, London: OUP, 1939, p. 26.

[87] Prob11/15/1 (1505).

[88] Of the daughters for whom we do not have wills, the last mention of Katherine is in her mother's 1505 will (Prob11/15/1); Anne, the nun, was still alive in 1515 (Prob11/18/6); Eleanor died by 1509 since her husband's son by his second wife was born c. 1510, Wyndham, *Family History, 1410-1688*, p. 53; (Prob11/21/3); Frances, wife of Sir John St Clere, and Jane, wife of Thomas Brews (Bruce), were living in 1546 (Prob11/32/33).
[89] Joseph Foster, *Pedigrees of the County Families of Yorkshire*, 3 vols, London, 1874, vol. 2, *North and East Riding*, Scrope pedigree, no pagination; Elizabeth Pechy was the daughter of Robert Scrope, her father's brother; GEC, 12 (1):453; Edward Hasted, *The History and Topographical Survey of the County of Kent*, 4 vols, Canterbury: W. Bristow, 1778-99, 1, p. 311.
[90] Prob11/18/6 (1515).
[91] Verily Anderson, *The DeVeres of Castle Hedingham*, Lavenham: Terence Dalton, 1993, p. 137.
[92] Prob11/18/6 (1515).
[93] Prob11/32/22 (1546); *HC 1509-1558*, 2, p. 443.
[94] On the pattern of patrilocality, see Harris, *English Aristocratic Women*, pp. 62-3.
[95] Guerney, 'Accounts of the LeStranges', p. 517.
[96] Prob11/8/15 (1487).
[97] *Somerset Medieval Wills (1531-1558)*, p. 87; *HC 1509-1558*, 2, pp. 418-19; her son was one of her overseers.
[98] Prob11/10/4, Katherine Hawte; *TE*, 4: 75 (152), Anne, Lady Scrope (1498).
[99] N. Davis, *Paston Letters and Papers*, 1, pp. 145, 150.
[100] *HMC, Rutland*, 4, p. 268.
[101] Ibid., pp. 269, 270, 275, 277.
[102] Ibid., pp. 273, 276.
[103] LPL, Shrewsbury Papers, MS 3205, fol. 10 (Dec. 22).
[104] Green, *Letters of Royal and Illustrious Ladies*, 3, p. 272 (Dec. 29); GEC, 3, p. 567, 4, p. 22; neither date indicates the year.
[105] *Lisle Letters*, 2: 450; 4: 1014.
[106] Ibid., 1: 32 (511).
[107] InqPM, Hen VII, 2:114 (75).
[108] *TE*, 4: 75, 152 (1498).
[109] Prob11/14/38 (1505).
[110] Prob11/18/18 (1515).
[111] See Karen Robertson, 'Tracing Women's Connections From a Letter of Elizabeth Lady Ralegh', in Susan Frye and Karen Robertson (eds), *Maids and Mistresses, Cousins and Queens: Women's Alliances in Early Modern England*, New York and Oxford: OUP, 1999, pp. 149-64 for an extended female network from the late Elizabethan/early Stuart period; like Margaret Paston's network, many of the connections were through Ralegh's mother.
[112] Colin Richmond, *The Paston Family in the Fifteenth Century: the First Phase*, Cambridge: CUP, 1990, p. 149; the younger Sir William died in 1495.
[113] N. Davis, *Paston Letters and Papers*, 1, pp. lxii-xiii, 206, 220 (p. 371).

[114] Ibid., 1: 417, 418.
[115] Richmond, *Paston Family ... The First Phase*, p. 168n; N. Davis, *Paston Letters and Papers*, 1: 24 (p. 37), 54 (Fastolf calls John Paston cousin in his will).
[116] For example, N. Davis, *Paston Letters and Papers*, 1: 133 (1449), 320 (1462), p. 630.
[117] Ibid., 1: 18; 2: 446 (1449).
[118] Ibid., 1: 146 (p. 250).
[119] Richmond, *Paston Family ... The First Phase*, p. 183, n. 82; 188 (1464).
[120] N. Davis, *Paston Letters and Papers*, 1: 206 ([1470]); Richmond, *Paston Family ... The First Phase*, p. 188, p. 168, n. 4, p. 190, n. 126.
[121] Ibid., 1: 95 (1474), 209 (1471); 221-3 (1475).
[122] For example, ibid., 2: 500, 594, 600 (before 1459-60).
[123] Ibid., 1: p. 630.
[124] Ibid., 1: 108-9 (1479).
[125] *HMC, Rutland*, 4: 188; Ethel Seaton, *Sir Richard Roos, c. 1410-1482: Lancastrian Poet*, London: Rupert Hart-Davis, 1961, p. 40.
[126] Mary Roos's sister, Elizabeth, seems to have died unmarried.
[127] *TV*, 1: 284 (1457); I have not been able to work out their precise relationship.
[128] N. Davis, *Paston Letters and Papers*, 1: 383 (p. 618); Martha Carlin, 'Holy Trinity Minories: Abbey of St. Clare, 1293/4-1539', in Derek Keene (ed.), *St. Botolph Aldgate Gazetteer, Historical Gazetteer of London Before the Great Fire*, London: Centre for Metropolitan History: 1987, p. 41. (Typescript available at IHR).
[129] Roger Virgoe, 'The Recovery of the Howards in East Anglia, 1485-1529', in E.W. Ives, R.J. Knecht and J.J. Scarisbrick (eds), *Wealth and Power in Tudor England: Essays Presented to S.T. Bindoff*, London: Athlone Press, 1978, pp. 1-20 (p. 15); N. Davis, *Paston Letters and Papers*, 1: 354, 354a.
[130] Carlin, 'Holy Trinity Minories', p. 41.
[131] Guerney, 'Accounts of the LeStranges', pp. 425, 428-9, 436, 437, 448, 452-4, 467n, 484-5, 488-9, 494, 527-8, 537, 539, 550.
[132] *HMC, Rutland*, 4, pp. 296, 304, 335, 337.
[133] Ibid., pp. 290, 293-94; also 313-14, 319.
[134] Ibid., pp. 295, 302, 311.
[135] Ibid., pp. 292, 311; *HC 1509-1558*, 1, p. 562.
[136] *HMC, Rutland*, 4, pp. 332, 335-6; *HC 1509-1558*, 2, pp. 569-70.
[137] Prob11/29/12 (1541).
[138] Durant, *Bess of Hardwick*, p. 21.
[139] M. Jones and M. Underwood, *The King's Mother: Lady Margaret Beaufort, Countess of Richmond and Derby*, Cambridge: CUP, 1992, pp. 163-4.
[140] Ibid., p. 163; Prob11/ 20/19 (1514).
[141] Jones and Underwood, *The King's Mother*, p. 162.
[142] W.E.Hampton, 'The Ladies of the Minories', in J. Petre (ed.), *Richard III: Crown and People*, Gloucester: Alan Sutton, 1985, pp. 195-202 (pp. 197-8); Carlin, 'Holy Trinity Minories', p. 16.
[143] Prob11/14/38, Talbot (1505); Prob11/15/25, Norfolk (1506).

[144] GEC, 11, pp. 254, 257; Sir Henry Ellis, *The History and Antiquities of the Parish of St Leonard Shoreditch and the Liberty of Norton Folgate in the Suburbs of London*, London: n.p., 1798.

[145] GEC, 11, p. 257.

[146] Ellis, *St Leonard Shoreditch*, pp. 57-8; Lady Catherine Constable and Lady Adeline Nevill were also granddaughters of Catherine, countess of Westmorland: their father was her eldest son, the fifth earl, and their mother Anne, the countess of Rutland's daughter. GEC, 12 (2), p. 557.

[147] For statistics on widows buried with their husbands, see Harris, *English Aristocratic Women*, p. 75.

Chapter 3

A Rhetoric of Requests: Genre and Linguistic Scripts in Elizabethan Women's Suitors' Letters

Lynne Magnusson

Despite a concerted effort over the last decades to include more women writers in the literary canon, the corpus of sixteenth-century writings by English women that receives serious attention still seems extremely limited. In a seventh edition, the two-volume *Norton Anthology* has recently added short selections by Anne Askew and Isabella Whitney to the snippets by Queen Elizabeth I and Mary Sidney as writing deserving of canonisation. Feminist scholars have explored less well understood or less prestigious forms, including religious verses and closet drama, the material often doubly estranged through its presentation as translations rather than as works of original authorship.[1] Exemplary as this scholarship has been, it is hard not to see the recovered forms as esoteric and peculiar, still relegating women writers to the margins of public life and confirming the successful workings of an all-pervasive ideology keeping women within their modest, obedient and silent places. It is a large task to undermine John Guillory's confident assertion that the 'reason for the absence of great works by women' is 'very easy to determine': there simply were few women who wrote anything at all.[2] Furthermore, Margaret Ezell has analysed ways in which even advocates of a feminist canon have closed out significant early modern voices by upholding assumptions about an evolutionary female tradition. Her suggestions for bringing fresh questions to work on women writers include proposals to 'redirect the current emphasis on the individual as an isolated figure', to pay attention to manuscript writings, and to question the projection of nineteenth- and twentieth-century experience back onto the early modern period – such as the idea that the letter is a form of private expression.[3]

In this essay it is not my intention to promote any single woman writer for her singular accomplishment and potential inclusion in the canon. Instead, I consider a particular genre of Elizabethan women's letters – a genre in which women's written production was prolific, various, at times linguistically sophisticated, political and often consequential. Within the complex arena of request-making constituted by Elizabethan suitors' letters, many noblewomen and gentlewomen managed the skilful performance in writing of social actions that affected the surrounding persons and circumstances. This essay will explore the genre of the suitors' letter – its characteristic purposes and motivations, its recurring linguistic strategies and the subject positions it constructs for participants – and it will assess the nature of Elizabethan women writers' accomplishment in it.

We should not discount the obstacles to arguing for the place of women's suitors' letters in English literary history. The first difficulty is access to texts: not that they are few, but that they are so many. Hundreds are scattered through manuscript collections, but printed examples are still to be found mainly in nineteenth-century biographies and memoirs, although well-edited modern texts of single letter-writers such as Arbella Stuart, edited by Sara Jayne Steen, and Elizabeth Cary, edited by Heather Wolfe, are slowly becoming available.[4] A second obstacle is a bias against the repeated forms that are in the foreground of public discourse; 'convention' tends to get opposed to 'creativity' and is not easily recognised as significant. Third, the women's letters do not exist in a separate economy from men's, and to study female epistolary scripts must also be to take a serious look at the male tradition. Furthermore, our conceptions of authorship may not easily accommodate verbal practices that are social not only in that they repeat set forms but also in that secretaries or family members were often collaborators in the composing process.[5] Nonetheless, recent criticism has interrogated the category of the author, even as it relates to key canonical playtexts, and attention to the social composition of women's letters is of significant use in this revision process. Finally, our ability to assess the verbal accomplishments of women writers in genres like the suitors' letter is seriously limited by the poverty of the methods and tools available in literary studies for the close analysis of language as social action and interaction. Encouraged to turn to the life writings of women, literary critics often lack the vocabulary to describe the texture and interest of the language. Despite the renewed historicism of literary scholars, what Frank Whigham wrote concerning this disjunction in his ground-breaking 1981 article about men's performances in the Elizabethan suitors' letter (to which I am greatly indebted) remains close to the truth today: 'those who study stylistic manipulations do not read historical documents and those who read historical materials do not study style'.[6]

Modern-day discourse pragmatics can work together with traditional rhetorical theory to help us towards the definition we need of a rhetorical or speech-act genre that suggests how the language of letters functions not simply as aesthetic forms in words but as forms of life. It would be misleading to measure the verbal accomplishment of women's suitors' letters in isolation from the field of action in which they participate – to admire the women's letters merely as specimens of verbal virtuosity or as expressions of individual personality. We need to consider the relation between text and context, to ask, with Bakhtin, to what extent the 'internal politics of style (how the elements are put together) is determined by its external politics'.[7] As a first step, both rhetoric and pragmatics encourage us to attend to context. They offer concepts of decorum or appropriateness, the fit of the words to the audience and the occasion, as a critical measure for the value of the verbal performance as social activity. How strongly aware Elizabethan writers were of the adequacy of that fit is suggested when a copy of Lady Catherine Grey's petition for the Queen's forgiveness regarding her illicit marriage to the earl of Hertford is sent by her uncle in advance for advice to Sir William Cecil to guard against there being 'onni faute found w*ith* onni word theerin wrytten'.[8] Politeness analysis, as developed within pragmatics, can help to show that how a gentlewoman frames a request depends to a very large extent on the power relations obtaining in the situation.[9] For example, consider the verbal complexity of Elizabeth Cavendish's request to her mother, the countess of Shrewsbury, that her mother should neither believe nor spread lies about her – 'I myght be so bould as to crave at your Ladyships hands that it wold pleas you to exteme [esteem] shuch falce bruts [rumors] ... as lightly as you have don when others were in the like cas'.[10] The complicated redundancy in the framing of the request reflects the power difference between them and the daughter's corresponding estimation of the repair work required to counter the risk implicit in making the difficult request. Pragmatics is not wholly responsive to the discourse conditions of the Elizabethan political scene, in which a noblewoman's social rank, marital status, property holdings, relationship to a patron or favoured faction, accompanying gratuity, previous expense laid out for a New Year's gift for the Queen, all may affect the reception and efficacy of a supplicatory letter as much as the virtuosity or decorum of its style. In this essay I will eventually draw upon Pierre Bourdieu's economic model for linguistic exchange, which regards linguistic skill as only one among other forms of symbolic capital affecting how an utterance is received in any field or market, to supplement our understanding from rhetoric and pragmatics of the interaction between text and context in women's letter-writing.[11]

The Genre

Social discourse is repetitive: it is in large measure through the repetition with variation of typical scripts that particular social formations with determinate roles or subject positions for participants are produced, reproduced and also slowly transformed. Hence a working concept of discourse type or rhetorical genre is important. Rhetorician Carolyn R. Miller defines rhetorical genres as 'typified rhetorical actions based in recurrent situations', or recurrent social actions situated by exigence and audience.[12] If the suitor's letter is regarded as a social action situated by exigence and audience, how then should we characterise the field of action for the Elizabethan suit – what are its exigencies, or its governing social motives? For male suitors, the situation was effectively described by Sir John Neale, Wallace T. MacCaffrey, Lawrence Stone and Frank Whigham.[13] As a whole, the patronage system of the Elizabethan court was motivated by the crown's need to sustain the loyalty and dependence of the aristocracy without the large-scale use of force and to maintain a competent civil service without the provision of adequate salaries. Distribution of the patronage in the gift of the crown was accomplished through a web of personal interactions, with important members of the court interposed between the monarch and the suitors, the powerful intermediaries either managing access to and influence over the Queen or themselves delegated the gift of certain offices and rewards. Principal among the material advantages sought by male suitors were the offices and posts in the gift of the crown; titles and other honours; royal or confiscated lands up for lease, sale, or available in reward for service; letters patent for monopolies and charters; and wardships.[14] Elizabeth and the officers of her court husbanded the treasure-hoard of these advantages with such extremity as to create what Whigham characterises as a 'context of dissatisfaction': 'letters of supplication', he explains, 'bring us to the center of court life, to the pursuit of opportunity in the face of scarcity'.[15]

This economy of scarcity, the unlimited demand and scant supply of wants, has some fairly obvious (but at the same time remarkable) effects on what Bakhtin calls the 'internal politics' – or the form and style – of Elizabethan request-making. The suit, imagined here as an historically specific variant of the speech-act of request-making, is remarkable for its apparently limitless reiteration of the same request and for the length and extreme elaboration of the rhetoric of each request. In most modern-day situations of request, competent speakers are well aware of the need to limit their repetitions. Beyond asking a few times without a successful result, one crosses the boundary between what is potentially productive and repetitions that are tedious, self-defeating, child-like and humiliating. Elizabethan request-making seems to have known no such limits. Sir Toby Mathew's suit for the deanery of Durham, the suit analysed in detail by Whigham, involved at least seventeen letters of request. The entries in the *Calendar of State Papers, Domestic* for the year 1571 alone show that Sir Thomas Gresham reminded Lord Burghley in writing more than ten times of his request to have the Lady Mary Grey removed from his custody, where she remained at least from 1569 to 1573 after a period of imprisonment for her unauthorised marriage to Henry Keys, the Queen's Serjeant Porter. As remarkable as his unceasing requests 'that it maye pleasse yow ... to have my sewte in remembrans for my ladye Mary Graye'[16] is that Gresham's continuing relation and other business with Burghley do not appear to be significantly disrupted or soured by the persistent reiterations. The court economy of high demand and scarce supply seems to have contributed to an inordinately high tolerance for repetition that itself helps to sustain and multiply what Lawrence Stone judges to be the 'astonishing proportion of contemporary correspondence ... devoted to the fortunes of the chase'.[17] The persistent suit was a regular part of the everyday performance of court life, and as such it carried overall a lower level of speech-act risk than we might otherwise expect. The large demand and scant supply can also be understood as a motive for the stylistic amplification and elaboration of the letters. Two key tropes of the suitor's letter – what I call its 'trouble-making' and its 'trouble-taking' – involve metacommentary: they comment on the dilation of the letter at the same time as they contribute with careful artifice to its copiousness, so that the characteristic but almost infinitely varied apologies for being tedious and troublesome are also among the mainstays of the suitor's deliberate eloquence.[18]

If we can begin to see how exigency shapes generic form in relation to the male tradition, what of the exigencies shaping women's activity in the genre of the suit? The range of activity by women in relation to the Elizabethan suit is less well documented or understood.[19] For the most part, women were not direct suitors for themselves for the courtly offices, the foreign postings, the titles and honours, or the lucrative monopolies sought by male suitors. Nonetheless, they could be very actively engaged in the pursuit of these advantages on behalf of others – especially on behalf of husbands, children, servants, and kinsfolk. Catherine Bertie, dowager duchess of Suffolk, pursued a suit in the early 1570s to regain for her prospective son-in-law, Reginald Grey, titles that had lapsed due to his family's financial hardships and to invest her husband, her former gentleman usher Richard Bertie, with a title out of use in her own family.[20] Mary Sidney (née Dudley), in an unusual reversal of the characteristic pursuit of honours, wrote to Lord Burghley, suing for his influence with the Queen to ensure that her husband,

Sir Henry Sidney, *not* be made a baron, since their shrinking fortunes could not sustain a baron's compulsory outlay.[21] Lady Elizabeth Russell, in the greedier and pushier time late in the reign, demanded that her nephew Robert Cecil 'make my neighbor Mr Rogers a knyght'.[22] Lady Russell was an exception to the general rule that women were not directly awarded the offices or posts in the gift of the crown, for in 1589 the Queen appointed her Keeper of the Queen's Castle of Donnington and Bailiff of the Honor, Lordship, and Manor of Donnington. In relation to this office, Lady Russell engaged in disputes and in suits not to obtain it but to secure her rights in the post, for the Lord Admiral, Charles Howard, obstructed her duties by claiming his own right of residence in the castle.[23] More characteristic, perhaps, is Lady Mary Rogers' effort to have her husband's commission as Justice of the Peace restored when it was withdrawn due to his enforced absence in the Queen's service.[24] Elizabethan noblewomen are well known to have been active in affairs relating to marriage arrangements, but also they pursued suits in relation to the granting or purchase of wardships, perhaps less often for profit out of others' children than to maintain connection with their own, as when Anne Winchcombe sued for her son's wardship to William Cecil as Master of the Court of Wards in 1570.[25] Furthermore, religious patrons like Lady Anne Bacon regularly pursued suits on behalf of ministers for employment or assistance.[26]

Women's suitors' letters represent a surprisingly wide range of public actions. Very often, these actions are prompted not by the thirsty pursuit of opportunity driving male suitors but by the withdrawal of various forms of sustenance. They write in response to their own imprisonment or their husbands'; in efforts to recover incomes, titles, properties, or leases lost to a family through confiscations arising out of accusations of treason or through failures of the male line; they write to recover rooms withdrawn from their use at court; they write to recover access denied them to their children; they write to recover access denied to the Queen's presence or the signs of her favour; they write out of necessity in reaction to deprivations – whether of chamber hangings[27] or of life – of all kinds imaginable.

Linguistic Scripts

Let us turn now to the verbal performances of the letters. Despite some standard shared tropes, we find major stylistic variations among the letters. A more productive way to proceed than to look, on the one hand, for conventions governing all examples or, on the other hand, for individual voices delivering personal expression is to identify the available scripts for this genre and examine how individual women improvised and varied these social scripts. The model scripts for request-making in Angel Day's epistolary rhetoric, *The English Secretorie*, aimed to reproduce actual courtly practices – although always imagined as men's practices – and one can adapt his terms for three principal petitioning styles. His division makes it clear that the different scripts were read not as individualised expression but as an exhibition of the power relations between writer and addressee: an inferior petitions a superior in a style of 'humilitie and entreatie', equals make requests in the style of 'pleasures or curteu[si]e', and a social superior petitions or makes a recommendation to an inferior in a style of 'supposall and assurance'.[28] Given the stereotypical expectation that women's suitors' letters will be pitiful begging letters, it is fascinating to discover that, in fact, they traverse the full power spectrum, including letters loosely resembling Day's supposal and assurance script as well as letters of humility and entreaty.

I will examine women's performances at these two opposite poles, beginning with the humility script.[29] Some features of this script are well known due in part to their similarity to printed letters of dedication. Nonetheless, it is important to be able to recognise the expected moves in this script so that women's copious and competent performances as suitors are not imagined to be uncontrolled products of desperation or of extreme mental states but instead rhetorical performances of power relations, with their own legitimate forms of decorum. Angel Day's treatment makes it clear that decorous subordination involves complex strategies requiring instruction and that powerlessness can be as much a performance in language as domination. Lady Mary Grey's letter to Sir William Cecil, pleading for intercession with Queen Elizabeth for release from confinement and restored favour, exhibits many of the essential features.

Letter 1: Humility and Entreaty

> Good master Secrytary, I must craue pardonn at your handes for trublynge you so oftenn withe my rude letters, but I trust you conceue what a greffe the quenes maiestes desplessur is to me, whiche makes me to wyshe deathe rather thenn to be in thes greatte messery witheout her maiestes fauor, and therfor I am forst to craue your help and goodnes to be a conteneweall meane for me to her maieste, to gett me her maiestes fauor agayen; trustynge if I myghte ons obtayne it neuer to forgoo it, whill I lyue, so nedtlygently [negligently] as I haue donn, god geueinge me his grace, whiche I truste hee will withe my conteneweall prayer for it. and therfor as you haue begonn to forther me to her maiesty for her maiestes fauor, so I truste you will contenewe untell you haue gotten it me, and

> thys I leue to trubell you for thys tyme, prayenge god to send you good spede. from chekers the xxiiij daye of Jenuary 1566.
>
> Yours to com*m*ande duringe my lyfe Mary Graye[30]

As an overall strategy, the suitor directly portrays the letter's advances as 'trouble-making' to the addressee. She makes a direct apology for 'trublynge' Cecil. A related strategy of women's letters of entreaty characterises the request-making explicitly as boldness or presumption. Lady Elizabeth Ralegh, requesting of Sir Robert Cecil a favourable decision for her kinsman Mr Brett in a dispute in which he is entangled, begins her letter: 'Presuming of your honnorabell fafor ever to me, I am bould to trobell you', mentions in the midst of its business why 'I am the mor bouldar to wryt for him', and ends 'desiaring your pardon for my so oft trobelling you'.[31] As part of this trouble-making trope, the writers refer apologetically not only, as Mary Grey does, to the frequency of their letters but also to their length: 'I wold not tyer you with many lines', writes Mary Wriothesley, countess of Southampton, requesting Leicester's assistance over difficulties with her estranged husband's will.[32] Self-deprecation plays a key role in the rhetoric of deference, not only the lowering of the self but also the low estimation of one's own written productions: Mary Grey refers to 'my rude letters', whereas Lady Mary Sidney writing to Burghley refers to her 'rude and tedius letters', to falling 'into a new error with tediusnes' and to 'her rude scryblinge'.[33] These are also features of suitors' letters by well-educated men; they are not transparent confessions of female inadequacy. One feature of the self-humbling shows itself in the choice of the verb for request-making, with 'crave' and 'beseech' the favoured choices. Mary's sister Catherine Grey, in a similar state of deprivation due to her marriage to the earl of Hertford, also writes to Secretary Cecil 'besecheng your farther frendshyp' for obtaining the Queen's favour which 'most humbly I craue'.[34] Deference involves the strategic elevation or praise of the addressee as well as the lowering of the self. In addition to very direct forms of flattery, suitors' letters like Mary Grey's often construct a narrative of past favours leading to the hope of continued help. More elaborate is Elizabeth, countess of Lennox's reminder to Burghley that she

> ...can but yeld your Lo*rdship* most harty thankes for your contenuall goodnes towardes me and my lytell one, and specyally for your Lo*rdships* late good dealynge wth the scotts imbasedor for my poore childs ryght for wch as allso sundry otherwys we ar for euer bounde to your Lo*rdship* whom I besech styll to further that caus as to your Lo*rdship* may seeme best...;[35]

and the countess of Southampton's grateful acknowledgement to the earl of Leicester, 'as ever I helde myself greatly beholding unto you, for your favour and well wyshing of me, so that yt pleased yor Lordship, now in the tyme of my greatest dyscomfort and neede of assestance to offer so honourably of yor owen mocion your helpe'.[36] These rhetorical building blocks of subordination are basically the same ones that Frank Whigham anatomises in male suitors' letters and that Day models in his sample letters of humility and entreaty.

While Whigham's foundational study of men's letters suggested that a witty self-distancing from the deprecation of the begging letters could manifest 'class',[37] he described only a single set of conventions for Elizabethan suitors' letters and did not recognise the strongly contrasted scripts encoding variations in power among the letters – Day's lesson that the letter of petition can also encode the superior's style of supposal or assurance. This omission may have resulted from his focus on a suit in which the client-patron roles invariably coincide with a social inferior writing to his social superior. But among the women's letters, it is sometimes a duchess and often a countess addressing Secretary Cecil, who in the early years of Elizabeth's reign held only the rank of knight and, only in 1571, when raised to the peerage as baron of Burghley, wryly registered the linguistic consequence in a letter to Nicholas White: 'my stile is, Lord of Burghley, if you meane to know it, for your wrytyng, and if yow list to wryte truly, the poorest lord in England'.[38]

By no means are all women's suitors' letters of humble entreaty. Bridget Russell, countess of Bedford, seeking Sir Christopher Hatton's support to recover the 'honour and credit' of the current Lord Deputy of Ireland, her son-in-law, the Lord Grey, offers a good illustration of a noblewoman's petition in Day's aptly named style of 'supposal and assurance'.

Letter 2: Supposal and Assurance

> Good Cosen, I haue by many experiences approuued, that suche is the nature of envy, as it ceaseth not by all indeavours to darken the worthie actions and services of those, that haue dewtifully and faithfully wth their greate p*er*ylls and exceding toyle p*er*formed all good offices in their callings, and in those affayers wherin they were imployed for their Prince and Country. And therefore, though my conscience p*er*swadeth me, that my L*ord* Graye, hath by his travayles in Irelande, done as well, and gouuerned those partes as paynefully, carefully, and iustlie, as any man that ever exercised that place before hym, yet, I feare me, there hath not wanted some suche as haue extenuated his L*ordship*s good services. For this cause, I could nott, but earnestly recommend vnto you, the

> preseruatione of his L*ordships* well deserued honor and creditt wth her Ma*jes*tie against suche as haue, or maye seke to impayre the same. I am loth, often to trouble any of my best frendes (in wch number I recken yor self.); But when I haue cause, I make full accompte, they will not be slack, to further suche reasonable requests as I make vnto them: And boothe the partie, (who p*ar*ticulerly is very dere vnto me,) and the matter assureth me of your best favour herin towards the one and the other. And though I bee not ignorant of yor spetiall affectione to his L*ordshi*p, many wayes witnessed by yor frendshipp, nevertheles, I might not be satisfied vnlesse I had said some what for hym: neither could I bethincke, or make choyse of any, to whome to write that for boeth o^{r} soakes, would be more willinge to yeeld furtherance to all his L*ordships* actions, then yor self. And so I pray God to increase in you, all trewe honor and happynes.
> 1° October 1582.
>
> yor assured frend.[39]

Modern-day discourse pragmatics can help us to expand Day's descriptive terms and relate them to key linguistic features of this style. 'Assurance' matches to the linguistic concept of high modality, that is, the expression of truth claims with a high level of assertion of their likelihood.[40] 'Supposal' matches to the analysis in politeness theory of two contrasting ways of mitigating the speech-act risks that inhere in all verbal interaction: negative politeness, or deference, strategically retains social distance by avoiding assumptions about the wishes or actions of the other; positive politeness, or solidarity, makes explicit assumptions, or 'supposals', about the actions of the other.[41] The countess of Bedford opens her letter asserting as certainty her rule about 'the nature of envy'. Her assurance is warranted not by the authority of others but by her own 'many experiences'. The countess does not 'crave' or 'beseech' Hatton's help. She 'earnestly recommend*s*' to him 'the preseruatione of his L*ordships* well deserued honor and creditt'. She gives an unqualified account of her expectations and supposals regarding Hatton's attitudes and future actions: 'when I haue cause, I make full accompte, they [my best friends] will not be slack, to further suche reasonable requests as I make vnto them: And boothe the partie, (who p*ar*ticulerly is very dere vnto me,) and the matter assureth me of your best favour herin ...'. The countess's acts of cognition are highlighted as important processes by syntactic forms representing them as dramas of deliberation, in which she is gifted not only with assurance but also with agency. Consider, for example, such dilated I-centred phrasings as 'I haue by many experiences approuued', 'my conscience p*er*swadeth me', 'I could nott but earnestly recommend', 'I make full account', and 'though I bee not ignorant of yor spetiall affectione ... nevertheles, I might not be satisfied'. Power is figured in the primacy within the letter of the countess's own mental actions. How marked the contrast can be in levels of assurance and supposal among women's suitors' letters can be emphasised by setting Bedford's power-claiming script against Mary Wriothesley, countess of Southampton's script for humility in her plea to the earl of Sussex to help obtain her sickly husband's release from imprisonment.

Letter 3: Humility and Entreaty

> My Lord, I am now enforced to troble your Lordship with thes fewe lines to crave your helpe for the saiffgard of my Lord his lyffe, who hath ben since your Lordship's departure, being sicke I feare of a burning fever, as also trobled with a swelling in his stomake which he was never tyll this time trobled withall. He fears a dropsy yf presently he syke not remedy. Therefore I beseeche your Lordship for God's sake, be a mean for some more liberty for him, and that I may have recourse to him to ataynd him in his sickness, if his full inlargement will not be obtayned. Truly my Lord, if he be no better atended now in his syckness then comonly he is I much fear his lyffe will not be longe. The necesity of the present cause compelleth me to be thus earnest for lybertye to goe to him, which I hope shall not be denyed him being syck, and have been granted to others in helthe. Thus expecting your Lordship's answer of some good comfort upon the which my Lorde his well-doing restyth, I comytt yor Lordship to God, who send you increase of honor and your hart's desyres. From London the 16 of July.
>
> Your Lordships poure cossen,
> M. Southampton
>
> If yor Lordship or any of my Lords of the Counsell thinke this untrewe, if yt be examyndd yt will be found too trewe.[42]

A conditional 'if' clause and the representation of her claim that her husband is dying as 'her fear' signal the low level of modality: 'Truly my Lord', she writes, 'if he be no better atended now in his syckness then comonly he is I much fear his lyffe will not be longe'. This low register of 'assurance' for her truth claims is further reinforced by the letter's postscript: 'If yor Lordship or any of my Lords of the Counsell thinke this untrewe, if yt be examyndd yt will be found too trewe'. Furthermore, the countess of Southampton's letter illustrates the low level of 'supposal' about the other's willingness or ability – repeatedly giving him 'an out' by imagining only the partial grant of her wishes: she qualifies her expectations as she beseeches Sussex to promote '*some more*' rather than full 'liberty' for her husband that she '*may have* recourse to him to ataynd him in his sickness, *if* his full inlargement *will not be* obtayned'. Mary Grey's letter also looks to the future with this 'if' of non-supposal, 'trustynge *if* I *myghte* ons obtayne it [the Queen's favour], neuer to foregoo it'. Moreover, a downplaying of personal agency marks both the language of Southampton ('I am now enforced') and of Grey ('I am forst to craue').

These examples should make it clear that levels of supposal and assurance do not reflect any objective view of the speaker's knowledgeableness, ability with argumentation, or intelligence, even though they may give the appearance of doing so; instead, they project power relations – the self-assurance of the dominant position versus the self-qualification of the subordinate position. As such, they are forms of social expression, differentially available to the female letter-writers, depending partly upon social rank but also upon other contextual factors affecting relative power. If, however, we are to begin to understand noblewomen's *self*-expression, we are better off looking to the available repertoire of social forms of expression than to an imagined wellhead of personal creativity. Linguists have only recently begun the serious study of how natural languages provide for self-expression. A recent collection of essays titled *Subjectivity and Subjectivisation: Linguistic Perspectives* makes a start, working with John Lyons's characterisation of subjectivity as 'the way in which natural languages provide for the locutionary agent's expression of himself and of his attitudes and beliefs'.[43] In looking at women's language, we can ask an analogous question: how do the available and historically specific social scripts provide for the locutionary agent's expression of herself, or, more simply, for self-expression? In the variations of supposal and assurance among the women's suitors' letters, we have some of the seeds of self-expression – the linguistic materials of boldness or timidity, self-importance or self-diminishment, ownership of one's thoughts and actions or their invisibility.

We still need to ask what kind of power is on display in the choice of scripts – why do noblewomen choose one script over the other (or, alternatively, find them chosen as their voices by their secretaries or advisers)? Is it simply a matter of rank, of duchesses and countesses addressing knights and esquires? Rank or relative status certainly enters into consideration. Anne, dowager duchess of Somerset solicits Sir William Cecil for the release of her son Lord Hertford, imprisoned for his marriage to Lady Catherine Grey, in the assured style, beginning her letter in a way that almost reverses apologies for often troubling, 'good mr secretary, yf I haue let you alone all thys whyle I pray you thynke yt was to tary for my l*ord* of leycesters assystans'.[44] And Elizabeth Talbot, countess of Shrewsbury, though mixing her styles, writes to Cecil as Lord Burghley with assurance, making assumptions about how her Majesty 'can not dyslyke of this my sute in her [Arbella Stuart's] behaulfe' and how she 'dout*s* not her ma*jes*ty wyll well conseue the syxe hondryth poundes yerely' she is asking for 'to be lettell ynough'.[45] But why should the countesses of Shrewsbury and Bedford write with 'supposal and assurance' and the countess of Southampton with 'humility and entreaty'? The countess of Southampton writes to an earl, we might answer, but such an answer does not provide an adequate principle for predicting the stylistic level of the general corpus of suitors' letters. Pierre Bourdieu argues that a key factor bearing on linguistic production is the 'anticipation of profit', the automatic estimation one is always making of one's chances of success in any particular field of action – or linguistic market. In his conception, this estimate is not grounded merely in the immediate situation; linguistic utterances are the product of the relation between a linguistic habitus and a linguistic market. The linguistic habitus of a person is the set of dispositions acquired in learning to speak or write in particular contexts, by a person's history of practice. In Bourdieu's view, the estimate of profit will depend on the history of reception inscribed in the habitus. Linguistic habitus usually coheres with class habitus, but it can vary considerably with an individual's lifetime trajectory of production and reception.[46]

For some Elizabethan noblewomen, the history of their discourse reception was either extremely irregular in its pattern or entirely incongruent with any simple assumptions about how a duchess's or a countess's speech might be received. We might think of Arbella Stuart or Catherine Grey. Despite their high birth, the slight results from their desperate efforts to be listened to at certain crisis points of their lives, could not have shaped confidence about reception. Even though her grandmother, the countess of Shrewsbury, typically wrote suitors' letters, as biographer Maud Stepney Rawson puts it, '*en grande dame*', Sara Jayne Steen observes that the persona Arbella Stuart creates in her court letters is 'humble and lowly' as, of course, are Catherine Grey's (and her sister Mary's) petitions for the renewal of the Queen's lost favour.[47] To understand what shapes the projected estimate of speech profit, or the implicit power relation as it is inscribed in a letter, we must look not only to rank but also to the other forms of symbolic capital a writer has to draw upon – or lacks – in a particular market: Steen emphasises, in addition to Stuart's rank, the dependency of her position, her status as 'a single woman, ... whose political future was uncertain and who had little income beyond a diet from the king's table and her pension'.[48] Other interesting instances include some of the later letters of Catherine Bertie, duchess of Suffolk, and of Lady Mary Sidney, the daughter of a duke, both of whom explicitly register their painful frustration at the accumulating pattern of denied suits, despite the enormous power that these women exerted in public actions in their younger years. Their persuasion styles include clear elements of entreaty and humility, but also with a wandering and at times torturous copiousness that may reflect their bewilderment at the changing conditions of the market they encounter.[49]

The copious performances by Elizabethan women in this genre make the point, in answer to Guillory, that many women *did* write in the sixteenth century. Although these suitors' letters – inaccessible to serious analysis if construed as the works of individual authors – are unlikely to find a place in *The Norton Anthology*, their close study can tell us more than an uninteresting story about formulaic language and stiff verbal conventions. It can begin to tell us something not only of the available scripts for women's social expression but also for their self-expression. The scripts chosen do not merely reflect rank or even an objective power relation. Instead, the script selected and corresponding power stance make a speculative projection of what is likely to be acceptable to its audience, what is likely to be recognised and acted upon. Thus, we find a link between a woman's language and an estimate of her power – just who it is she thinks she is.

Notes

1 For bibliographies of recent work, see Georgianna M. Ziegler, 'Recent Studies in Women Writers of Tudor England, 1485-1603', *ELR*, 24 (1994), 229-42 and its update by Micheline White, *ELR*, 30 (2000), 457-93.

2 John Guillory, 'Canon' in Frank Lentricchia and Thomas McLaughlin (ed.), *Critical Terms for Literary Study*, 2nd ed., Chicago and London: University of Chicago Press, 1995, pp. 233-49 (p. 238).

3 Margaret J. M. Ezell, *Writing Women's Literary History*, Baltimore and London: The Johns Hopkins UP, 1993, pp. 65, 34. For recent work, mainly by historians, on women's letters, see James Daybell (ed.), *Early Modern Women's Letter Writing, 1450-1700*, Basingstoke and New York: Palgrave, 2001.

4 Sara Jayne Steen (ed.), *The Letters of Lady Arbella Stuart*, New York and Oxford: OUP, 1994; Heather Wolfe (ed.), *Elizabeth Cary, Lady Falkland: Life and Letters*, Tempe, AZ and Cambridge: Arizona Center for Medieval and Renaissance Studies, and Renaissance Texts from Manuscripts, 2001.

5 See James Daybell, '"Ples acsep thes my skrybled lynes": the Construction and Conventions of Women's Letters in England, 1540-1603', *Quidditas*, 20 (1999), 207-23; *idem*, 'Women's Letters and Letter Writing in England, 1540-1603: an Introduction to the Issues of Authorship and Construction', *Shakespeare Studies*, 27 (1999), 161-86.

6 Frank Whigham, 'The Rhetoric of Elizabethan Suitors' Letters', *PMLA*, 96 (1981), 864-80 (p. 864).

7 M. M. Bakhtin, *The Dialogic Imagination: Four Essays*, ed. Michael Holquist, trans. Caryl Emerson and Michael Holquist, Austin: University of Texas Press, 1981, p. 284.

8 BL, Lansd. MS 6, fol. 102: John Grey to Cecil, 7 Nov. 1563; quoted from Henry Ellis (ed.), *Original Letters, Illustrative of English History*, 2nd series, 4 vols, London: Harding and Lepard, 1827, 2, p. 281.

[9] For the politeness model, see Penelope Brown and Stephen C. Levinson, *Politeness: Some Universals in Language Usage*, Cambridge: CUP, 1987. For historical applications to Elizabethan letters and dramatic dialogue, see Lynne Magnusson, *Shakespeare and Social Dialogue: Dramatic Dialogue and Elizabethan Letters*, Cambridge: CUP, 1999.

[10] Folger, MS X.d.428 (51): 25 July [1577?]; quoted from Steen, *Letters of Lady Arbella Stuart*, p. 15.

[11] 'The Economics of Linguistic Exchanges', trans. Richard Nice, *Social Science Information*, 16 (1977), 645-68.

[12] 'Genre as Social Action', *Quarterly Journal of Speech*, 70 (1984), 151-67 (p. 159).

[13] See John Neale, *The Elizabethan Political Scene*, London: Geoffrey Cumberlege Amen House, 1948; Wallace T. MacCaffrey, 'Place and Patronage in Elizabethan Politics', in S. T. Bindoff, J. Hurstfield, and C. H. Williams (eds), *Elizabethan Government and Society*, London: Athlone Press, 1961, pp. 95-126; Lawrence Stone, *The Crisis of the Aristocracy, 1558-1641*, Oxford: Clarendon Press, 1965, especially pp. 403-504; Whigham, 'Rhetoric'.

[14] Neale, *Elizabethan Political Scene*, pp. 4-5.

[15] Whigham, 'Rhetoric', p. 866.

[16] BL, Lansd. MS 12, fol. 22^{v}: 15 Sept. 1569; also printed in John William Burgon, *The Life and Times of Sir Thomas Gresham, Knt.*, 2 vols, London: Robert Jennings, 1839, 2, p. 405. On Gresham's custody of Mary Grey, see pp. 383-416.

[17] Stone, *The Crisis of the Aristocracy*, p. 403.

[18] See Magnusson, *Shakespeare and Social Dialogue*, pp. 100-8.

[19] Some excellent work on this subject is, however, emerging, including Caroline Bowden, 'Women as Intermediaries: an Example of the Use of Literacy in the Late Sixteenth and Early Seventeenth Centuries', *History of Education*, 22, 3 (1993), 215-23; Barbara J. Harris, 'Women and Politics in Early Tudor England', *HJ*, 33, 2 (1990), 259-81; Karen Newman, 'Sundry Letters, Worldly Goods: the Lisle Letters and Renaissance Studies', *Journal of Medieval and Early Modern Studies*, 26, 1 (1996), 139-52; Charlotte Isabelle Merton, 'The Women Who Served Queen Mary and Queen Elizabeth', unpublished PhD thesis, University of Cambridge, 1992, esp. pp. 154-202.

[20] Evelyn Read, *Catherine, Duchess of Suffolk, A Portrait*, London: Jonathan Cape, 1962, pp. 171-78.

[21] PRO, SP 12/86/33: 2 May 1572.

[22] Hatfield House, Herts, Cecil Papers 59, fol. 93: 22 Feb. [1599].

[23] See Kathy Lynn Emerson, *Wives and Daughters: the Women of Sixteenth Century England*, Troy, NY: Whitston Publishing, 1984, p. 57; Violet A. Wilson, *Society Women of Shakespeare's Time*, Port Washington, NY and London: Kennikat Press, 1924, p. 225.

[24] BL, Lansd. MS 53, fols 112^{r}-113^{v}: Mary Rogers to Burghley, 9 July 1587.

[25] PRO, SP 12/74/27: [?] Oct. 1570.

[26] On Lady Anne Bacon's correspondence see Magnusson, 'Widowhood and Linguistic Capital: the Rhetoric and Reception of Anne Bacon's Epistolary Advice', *ELR*, 31 (2001), 3-33.

[27] For example, BL, Cott. MS Vespasian, F.XII, fols 179-180^{v}: Mary Sidney to Sussex, 7 Feb. 1574.

[28] Angel Day, *The English Secretorie, or Methods of Writing Epistles and Letters* (1599), intro. Robert O. Evans, Gainesville, Florida: Scholars' Facsimiles and Reprints, 1967, pp. 101-2; for a discussion of these interaction scripts in Day, see Magnusson, *Shakespeare and Social Dialogue*, pp. 80-88.

[29] The 'pleasures' script, though not discussed in this brief essay, is also represented among women's letters, especially when women are themselves serving as patrons or intermediaries.

[30] BL, Lansd. MS 8, fol. 179: 24 Jan. 1567.

[31] Cecil Papers 33, fol. 53: [28] July 1595; quoted from Edward Edwards, *The Life of Sir Walter Ralegh*, 2 vols, London: Macmillan, 1868, 2, pp. 400-1.
[32] Charlotte Carmichael Stopes, *The Life of Henry, Third Earl of Southampton, Shakespeare's Patron*, Cambridge: CUP, 1922, p. 10.
[33] PRO, SP 12/91/19: Apr. 1573; PRO SP 12/108/74: 7 Aug. 1576.
[34] BL, Lansd. MS 6, art. 32: 3 Sept. [n.y]; Ellis, *Original Letters*, 2nd series, 2, p. 278.
[35] BL, Lansd. MS 27, fol. 9, 15 Aug. 1578.
[36] Stopes, *Southampton*, p. 9.
[37] Whigham, 'Rhetoric', p. 874.
[38] BL, Lansd. MS 102, fol. 152: 14 Mar. 1571; quoted in Thomas Wright (ed.), *Queen Elizabeth and Her Times, A Series of Original Letters*, 2 vols., London: Henry Colburn, 1838, 1, p. 391.
[39] BL, Add. MS 15891, fol. 97; also printed in Sir Harris Nicolas (ed.), *Memoirs of the Life and Times of Sir Christopher Hatton, K.G.*, London: Richard Bentley, 1847, p. 272.
[40] As discussed, less technically than in linguistics, in Norman Fairclough, *Language and Power*, London and New York: Longman, 1989, pp. 126-9. In a more technical sense, Susan Fitzmaurice discusses English modal verbs in 'Tentativeness and insistence in the expression of politeness in Margaret Cavendish's *Sociable Letters*', *Language and Literature*, 9 (2000), 7-24.
[41] Brown and Levinson, *Politeness*, p. 70.
[42] BL, Cott. MS Titus, B.II.143, fol. 308: 16 July 1572; quoted from Stopes, *Southampton*, p. 514.
[43] Dieter Stein and Susan Wright (eds), Cambridge: CUP, 1995, pp. 2-3.
[44] BL, Lansd. MS 9, fol. 147: 18 Apr. 1566.
[45] BL, Lansd. MS 34, fol. 143: 6 May 1582.
[46] Bourdieu, 'The Economics of Linguistic Exchanges'.
[47] *Bess of Hardwick and Her Circle*, London: Hutchinson, 1910, p. 84; *Letters of Lady Arbella Stuart*, p. 51.
[48] Steen, *Letters of Lady Arbella Stuart*, p. 52.
[49] Consider Suffolk's suits in the 1570s in pursuit of titles for her son-in-law and husband (Read, *Catherine Duchess of Suffolk*, pp. 171-78) and Mary Sidney's disappointment at denial in PRO SP 12/108/74.

Chapter 4

Politics in the Elizabethan Privy Chamber: Lady Mary Sidney and Kat Ashley

Natalie Mears

Pam Wright's work has been crucial to our understanding of the Elizabethan Privy Chamber and the roles of its female members. She argued that the accession of a female monarch led to the Privy Chamber's eclipse as a political forum because it was numerically dominated by women. Contemporary attitudes towards gender prevented them from assuming key administrative roles such as Keeper of the Privy Purse or the Dry Stamp that had been used so effectively by Sir Anthony Denny and Sir Thomas Heneage (the elder) under Henry VIII. They also prevented women from acting as envoys and ambassadors, increasing the importance of Privy Chamber men and unfeed supernumeraries, though never to the heights achieved by their Henrician predecessors. Most importantly, the Privy Chamber ceased to be a forum for independent initiatives in counselling the monarch over key political issues. Attitudes towards gender were reinforced by Elizabeth's desire that the Privy Chamber should act as a 'barrier or cocoon' rather than a political cockpit. She stamped on independent political initiatives and filled the Privy Chamber with her own relatives whose first loyalties, Wright argued, were to her. As a result, women were restricted to domestic roles, such as Mistress of the Robes, and acting as 'barometers of the queen's mood'. The Privy Chamber's political role was, Wright concluded, 'often accidental, rarely sustained, and never pursued to the uttermost' and its women, unimportant. Their significance was only as patronage brokers, acting on non-partisan lines: 'a free-market economy of favours'.[1]

Wright's arguments have been reappraised by Charlotte Merton and, indirectly, by Joan Greenbaum Goldsmith but neither have seriously challenged her on the fundamental issues of the political role and significance of Privy Chamber women. Both agreed that women played an important role in patronage, as 'points of contact' with Elizabeth and in the circulation of news and information; they also suggested that Wright underestimated women's significance. Significantly, however, neither factored women's activity into the wider workings of court politics to assess their position and importance in the process of policy-making, debate and diplomacy. Goldsmith made an unconvincing case that, in aping men's exercise of influence, women actively worked against the status quo, exacerbating existing hostility to their involvement in politics. Merton's arguments were more sophisticated but, in identifying the driving force for women's activity in personal, familial and friends' interests, she seemed to suggest that women did not interact with the central issues of Elizabeth's reign – marriage, succession and catholic conspiracy – and operated in a sphere partly or wholly disconnected from some of the core concerns of court politics: policy-making and governance.[2]

The insignificance of the Elizabethan Privy Chamber as a political forum has been further reinforced by the direction of the historiography of Elizabethan politics.[3] Despite the work of Simon Adams and Wallace MacCaffrey in particular, who have sought to re-emphasise the importance of individuals, social networks and the relationship between the Privy Council and the royal household, our conceptualisation of Elizabethan court politics remains strongly institutional.[4] Elizabeth's reign is still regarded as the apogee of the Privy Council, a perception reinforced both by Eltonian works like Michael Barraclough Pulman's *The Elizabethan Privy Council in the Fifteen-Seventies* as well as more recent works, like Stephen Alford's impressive *The Early Elizabethan Polity*, which explores high politics with a sensitivity to social and educative backgrounds and political culture. Both present the Privy Council as the main, corporate advisory and policy-making body and suggest extra-conciliar counsel was antipathetical to the 'normal' process of policy-making; little or no attention is paid either to the Privy Chamber or to the role of women.[5] Indeed, even Simon Adams and Wallace MacCaffrey ultimately saw individuals working primarily through the collective body of the Privy Council or an inner ring of its members.[6] The recent emphasis on political culture and gender has not reversed this trend. In emphasising the dominance of ideas of the 'mixed polity' and of classical concepts of citizenship, derived from Cicero and Quintilian, in the first thirty years of Elizabeth's reign, reconstructions of Tudor political culture have continued to privilege the role of the Privy Council as the supreme policy-making body.[7] The council's centrality has been accepted by historians of female monarchy, who have located the impact of gender in conflicts between it and Elizabeth. It has been further underlined by the emphasis placed by John Aylmer on counsel and council to excuse female monarchy in *An Harborowe For Trewe and Faithfull Subiectes* (Strasbourg, 1559) which has defined both the contemporary and modern queenship debate.[8]

This essay reappraises these arguments. First, it re-examines the two cases Wright used to demonstrate that Privy Chamber women played an insignificant political role and places them in the wider context of political activity by Privy Chamber and non-Privy Chamber women throughout the reign. Second, it briefly examines the removal of control of the Sign Manual from the Privy Chamber. Third, it offers a new reading of the nature of Elizabethan court politics that suggests the Privy Chamber, and its female members in particular, could and did have a more significant role in court politics than Wright has suggested. The principal focus of the essay remains on Privy Chamber women, but the role of male servants will also be highlighted.

I

In exploring the political role of Privy Chamber women, Wright focused on two key episodes: Lady Mary Sidney's involvement in Elizabeth's marriage negotiations with the Spanish ambassador, Alvaro de Quadra, bishop of Aquila, for Archduke Charles between September and November 1559, and Katherine Ashley's and Dorothy Broadbelte's support of Eric XIV of Sweden's suit in 1562. Together they demonstrated that Privy Chamber women were prevented from taking independent initiatives on key political issues. Elizabeth used Mary Sidney as a go-between between her and de Quadra until, on 13 November, de Quadra sought a public statement from Elizabeth that she favoured Charles's visit and the marriage, at which point she denied Lady Sidney had acted with her permission. Conversely, Elizabeth commanded Kat Ashley 'to kepe to her chamber' and committed Dorothy Broadbelte to William Cecil's custody in August and September 1562 for independently encouraging Eric to come to England to press his suit directly.[9] As relatively isolated examples, Wright argued, they demonstrated further that Privy Chamber women played an insignificant role in political debate, policy-making and diplomacy either independently or in collusion with Elizabeth. However, when placed in the wider context of the political activity of other Privy Chamber and non-Privy Chamber women, a reappraisal of these two cases reveals that the

Privy Chamber, and its women, was more politically significant than Wright suggests.

Though de Quadra's correspondence is our only source for the events of 1559, Wright's reading can be sustained. Explaining the denouement of 13 November to Philip II the same day, de Quadra was at pains to excuse himself and blame others, but internal and external evidence suggests he had not misread the earlier situation.[10] He and Mary Sidney were able to communicate directly in Italian and had the additional services of an interpreter.[11] Mary Sidney's information was regularly repeated and corroborated by other sources, notably Sir Thomas Parry (Treasurer of the Household), one of Elizabeth's intimates who had served her as Cofferer from 1548 and had been one of her first appointees to the Privy Council in 1558. Moreover, de Quadra tested Mary's information on Elizabeth tactfully and diplomatically, notably on 11 November when Elizabeth effectually confirmed reports that she wanted Charles to visit but could not appear to summon him herself.[12] It was only when, two days later, de Quadra tried to force Elizabeth's hand both on this issue and the marriage proposal itself – even though he had been aware since at least 2 October that Elizabeth feared he might acknowledge publicly her wish that Charles would visit – that she went into denial; she did not even question de Quadra who the 'principal persons of her court' were who had misled him.[13] Her reaction seems to have had little to do with her views on the political role of the women of the Privy Chamber. Her disavowal of Mary Sidney's actions, when they forced her to commit herself to the Habsburg match further than she wished, were comparable to her denial that she had discussed the Anjou match with the French ambassador, Mauvissière, in August 1581.[14]

Wright's reconstruction of the more complex case of Kat Ashley and Dorothy Broadbelte, however, is less easy to sustain. As Susan Doran has briefly indicated, the letter the women wrote to Guilderstern, Eric's Chancellor and ambassador, on 22 July 1562, which suggested Eric's suit would be successful if he pressed it in person, can be linked to the examinations taken of John Dymock – as well as James Goldborne (or Colborne) and John (or Thomas) Keyle – at the beginning of August.[15] Ashley, if not Broadbelte, can be linked to Dymock and Goldborne. Dymock testified that he had visited her, whom he knew from 'mastars watsons', in her chamber at Whitehall in December 1561 to ask her if Elizabeth would marry Robert Dudley. Ashley replied that she did not think Elizabeth would but advised Dymock to come again the following day to speak to her husband. Goldborne, committed to the Tower with

Keyle in August for writing to Eric's servants to encourage the King to come to England, was a former servant of Kat Ashley's.[16] There was a further connection too: Dymock claimed that Ashley knew one Walwicke, possibly a servant of Eric's, with whom he had earlier discussed Elizabeth's marriage and who had encouraged him to investigate the likelihood of its success with a view to selling Eric a number of jewels for the coronation.[17]

These connections are significant. Rivalry between Eric and Dudley over Elizabeth's hand was crucial in uncovering events, with Dudley taking the initiative in trying to secure Dymock's, Goldborne's and Keyle's arrest as early as the end of July, before Ashley's and Broadbelte's detention.[18] But it does not explain why the women were detained. The August examinations and related correspondence, however, suggests it was not because they took independent initiatives. Rather, they were implicated in attempts to manoeuvre Elizabeth into the Swedish match by men who had no authority or responsibility to involve themselves in the *arcana imperii* of Elizabeth's marriage and that these attempts were connected to increasing English aid to the French Huguenots.

According to a contemporary at the Court, who wrote a narrative of events between September 1559 and December 1562, Kat Ashley was detained because Goldborne was revealed as her servant, rather than vice versa.[19] The narrative also stated that Dymock had earlier been arrested in May 1561 either 'for speaking and taking upon him, whilest he was with the king of Swedon, more than he had in commyssion' or for writing to Elizabeth about foreign reports of her behaviour with Dudley.[20] Dymock's card was already marked, either as a dabbler in key, sensitive, political and diplomatic issues for which he had no authority or as a purveyor of slanderous gossip. In December of the same year – and prior to his departure to Sweden – he had consulted with Kat's husband, John, over the sale of jewels to Elizabeth. As Master of the Jewels, John Ashley was the obvious person with whom to consult, but the meeting also acted as an entrée to test and further Eric's suit.[21] Dymock, Goldborne and Keyle were all questioned on whether they were Eric's sworn servants and on the regularity and substance of their correspondence with the Swedish court: Keyle stated that he had 'kept promis' with Eric 'ether [to] ventewr the tower or some other person (or ells) do his majestie som good service' to bring the suit to a successful conclusion.[22] Elizabeth was highly sensitive to interference in what she termed *arcana imperii*, and this may have been heightened by the support Eric appeared to garner.[23] The earl of Arundel and the marchioness of Northampton had both supported the match in

September 1561, while Dymock's examination revealed Lord Strange and Henry Sackford (Groom of the Privy Chamber and Master of Requests) had also been drawn into events: Dymock had shown both of them a letter he had written to Elizabeth.[24]

Furthermore, Goldborne stated that rumours were circulating in London that a number of Frenchmen sought to persuade Elizabeth to 'recover the losses in France'. Keyle made the connection between the Swedish match and English aid of the Huguenots explicit in a letter to Geoffrey Preston (a member of Eric's Privy Chamber) on 27 July. Having told Preston how strong the Guise were against the princes of Condé and Navarre, Keyle said that if Eric came immediately, with his fleet, 'he shall neuer haue the lyke for it wilbe taken that he comes to ayd the Quene as well as for his sute and he shall come to be husband [vnto] a noble Quene and protector of godes quarrel wher bye he shall wyn fame thoroght owt all the world'.[25] If Elizabeth was inimical to interference in the *arcana imperii* by ordinary subjects, then apparent manoeuvrings by them to commit her further to aiding the Huguenots were equally unpalatable, especially for a Queen already burning her fingers over Newhaven.[26]

Though the cases of Lady Mary Sidney, Kat Ashley and Dorothy Broadbelte are the clearest examples of the involvement of Privy Chamber women in diplomatic relations and policy-making, they are not unique. Evidence is fragmentary and scattered but we know Lady Mary Sidney, Lady Frances Cobham (Gentlewoman of the Bedchamber and Mistress of the Robes) and Lady Elizabeth Clinton (unfeed Gentlewoman of the Privy Chamber) were all in contact with the duchess of Feria.[27] Lady Cobham was also Mary Stewart's main contact and ally in the Privy Chamber until her husband was arrested for alleged involvement in the Ridolphi Plot in 1571.[28] Women outside the Privy Chamber were also politically active. One of Elizabeth's intimates, Elizabeth Brooke, first marchioness of Northampton, was the key contact between the court and Spain and was cultivated by both de Quadra and his successor, Guzman de Silva.[29] Lady Mildred Cecil talked with both the Spanish and French ambassadors about the Archduke Charles match in 1566.[30] The visit of Cecilia, marchioness of Baden-Baden and sister of Eric XIV, to the court in 1565 was widely thought to be a means for the marchioness to continue negotiations for the Swedish match.[31] The countess of Westmorland appears initially to have played an important role in persuading her husband to support the Northern Rising in 1569.[32] Eleanor, countess of Desmond, was instrumental in persuading the earl to concede to English reform of Irish government (while also defending his authority over inferiors), resisting the rebellion of

Fitzmaurice Fitzgerald in 1567, obtaining the earl's restoration in 1573, persuading him to accept composition and, during the rebellion of 1579, in conducting negotiations with the English.[33] As Merton noted, and as the countess of Desmond's actions demonstrated, women's activity was partly stimulated by family and friends' interests: the family was, as Barbara Harris has argued, the main political unit in late medieval and early modern England. But, they also reflected a genuine interest in state and European affairs and, at times, an ideological commitment to key issues. In 1596, the countess of Warwick received confidential reports on the Landgrave of Hesse from Edward Monings, a member of the English ambassador's train, and had supplied troops for Leicester's Netherlands expedition in 1585.[34]

If this suggests that the political role of Privy Chamber women, and those outside it, was more significant than Wright argued, then conversely, the administrative changes in the Privy Chamber brought about by Elizabeth's accession seem less important. Wright saw the restoration of control over the Sign Manual (and Privy Purse) to the Principal Secretary as diminishing the Privy Chamber's administrative importance: unable to control the Dry Stamp directly, Privy Chamber women were mere 'barometers of the queen's moods, to be tapped by the secretary to make sure whether the weather were foul or fair'.[35] However, contemporary statements and the actual activity of women indicate this was a crucial function. Robert's Beale's 'Instructions for a Principall Secretarie ... for Sir Edwarde Wotton' (1592) explicitly acknowledged the importance of using Privy Chamber attendants in facilitating the secretary's duties: 'Learne before your accesse her majesties disposicion by some in the Privie Chamber, with whom you must keepe credit: for that will stande yow in much steede'.[36] Beale's advice followed Elizabethan practice by secretaries and other counsellors. Both during and after his tenure as secretary, Burghley maintained contacts with Ladies Cobham and Carew, Sir Thomas Heneage (Treasurer of the Chamber) and the grooms, Thomas Gorges and Thomas Knyvet; Lady Cobham tried to smooth his return to Court in the aftermath of Mary Stewart's execution.[37] Leicester's main contacts from at least 1566 were Dorothy Broadbelte and Blanche Parry.[38] Such practice was established not because Elizabeth was female – importantly, though Beale drew on his own and others' experience in writing the 'Instructions', he did not suggest that the secretary's need to use Privy Chamber attendants was peculiar to female monarchs – but because of Elizabeth's own working methods and the way her servants could tap important information. For instance, in August 1571, Elizabeth used Elizabeth Stafford (later a Chamberer) to recall the earl of Rutland from France because she knew Stafford was in correspondence with him.[39] A letter appointing Sir Edward York to a command of infantry in Ireland was delivered by the countess of Warwick's messenger.[40] Conversely, Lord Chancellor Bromley consulted Lady Mary Scudamore (Chamberer) over whether Sir John Zouche had been appointed to the disputed office of *Custos Rotulorum* of Derby in 1580 by Elizabeth.[41] Thus, Privy Chamber women were important 'information brokers' for those outside the Privy Chamber because of the information to which they had access and their ability to communicate directly with Elizabeth; equally, Elizabeth was able to exploit their social and correspondence networks to convey her wishes easily and informally.

II

The significance of these examples becomes apparent when the nature of Elizabethan policy-making is re-evaluated. A sensitive reappraisal of memoranda prepared for, or reporting on, meetings of Privy Councillors in the 1560s, 1570s and 1580s questions the supremacy of the Privy Council as a policy-making body, thus challenging Eltonian perceptions of Elizabethan policy-making as institutional.[42] The meetings addressed a range of key issues on the Elizabethan political agenda: marriage (December 1567,[43] May-August 1571,[44] 27 March-c. 3 April, 3-4 May and 4-8 October 1579[45] and in 1581[46]); Mary Stewart (20 June 1562,[47] 1 May, 4 June and 24 and 26 September 1565,[48] 29 April 1570[49]); Anglo-Scottish relations (18 July 1571,[50] 18 September 1580,[51] March 1581,[52] March 1583[53]); Dutch aid (on or before 15 January 1576,[54] 22 March 1578,[55] 10 July 1580[56]) and Leicester's Netherlands expedition (9 July 1586).[57]

When mapped onto meetings of the Privy Council, as recorded in the extant Privy Council registers, it is clear that these meetings operated separately from those of the Privy Council. They did not always meet on the same day as the Privy Council (8 July 1571, 22 March 1578 and 26-30 March 1579) and, when they did, attendance was different.[58] For example, on 10 July 1580, Sir Christopher Hatton did not attend the Privy Council meeting while Sir James Croft and Thomas Wilson (excluded from debate on the Netherlands) did.[59] The location of the meeting could also be different: according to the registers, the Privy Council met at Greenwich on 4 October 1579 but the memoranda recording the debate on the Anjou match the same day suggests this meeting took place at Westminster.[60] While ambiguity in the sources, reinforced by gaps in the Privy Council registers between 3 May 1567 to 24 May 1570 and June 1582 and February 1586, make the remaining meetings less easy to define, there are some suggestive hints. Memoranda by Burghley for the meetings on 29 April 1570 and 15 January 1576 report the discussions took place in Elizabeth's presence and with her active involvement, an unprecedented situation for a formal Privy Council meeting, as far as the registers attest, suggesting the meetings functioned separately from the Council.[61] Elizabeth made a clear distinction between the conferences between 29 March and *circa* 3 April (to assess the Anjou proposals) and that of the Privy Council on 3 May 1579 (to discuss the articles for the marriage treaty only).[62] Walsingham's correspondence makes it clear that the conferences in March 1581, March 1583 and July 1596 were not meetings of the Privy Council: attendees were specifically chosen by Elizabeth who also ordered the meetings.[63] The exclusion of the Council's clerks and assumption of secretarial duties by Burghley (or, in 1578, by one of Walsingham's secretaries, Laurence Tomson) during conferences is also suggestive. While clerks were asked to leave the council chamber during sensitive discussions and, as Stephen Alford has shown, the line between conciliar business and councillors' own could be blurred by close working relationships developed between councillors and clerks, the clerks' absence may suggest that conferences on key political issues operated separately from those of the Privy Council.[64]

This suggests that the Privy Council was not the main policy-making body: Elizabeth selected particular individuals to debate key issues separately from Privy Council meetings and left the Council to deal with administrative issues arising from these issues, as well as the wider administration of governance. This probouleutic (primary discussion) format worked alongside Elizabeth's informal and ad hoc consultations with individuals. For instance, in November 1572, she talked 'to and fro' with Leicester about the need to support the Anglophile Scots on receiving news of the death of Regent Mar and, convinced by his arguments that a speedy response was imperative, immediately sought Burghley's opinion on what support would be most effective.[65] Importantly, ad hoc counselling was not restricted to members of the probouleutic group, or to Privy Councillors. Hatton was a key figure – he was, in the earl of Morton's words, a recognised source to tap for 'the better knallege of heir hienes mynd'[66] – but so too were Heneage, Sir Nicholas Throckmorton, Thomas Randolph (a regular agent to Scotland) as well as Henry Killigrew (agent and ambassador), John Somers (Clerk of the Signet, tertiary ambassador to France) and Edward Stafford (Gentleman Pensioner). Heneage was a recognised point of access to Elizabeth by 1565, four years prior to his appointment to the Treasurership of the Chamber; by 1570 he had assumed ad hoc roles as a secretary and counsellor, giving advice when 'yt pleased her [Elizabeth] to aske myne opinyon'.[67] He was a go-between for Elizabeth and Sir Thomas Smith, Principal Secretary, and one of Walsingham's and Lord Buckhurst's main correspondents during the Anjou marriage negotiations in 1571.[68] Throckmorton advised Elizabeth on the proposed interview with Mary in 1562; on appointing a resident agent with Admiral Coligny in 1563 and on the marriage negotiations with the Archduke Charles in 1564.[69] De Silva actually mistook him for a Privy Councillor.[70] Randolph's importance was most clearly demonstrated during his embassy to Scotland to secure Morton's release and impeach Lennox's hegemony in 1581. His advice, to seek Morton's release by negotiations rather than force, overrode contrary counsel from Walsingham and others in London, Hunsdon at Berwick and Huntingdon (President of the Council of the North) at York.[71]

This affects our understanding of the role and significance of the Privy Chamber, and its female members, in key ways. First, it suggests that the Privy Chamber was neither antithetical nor peripheral to the nature of court politics and policy-making. The latter were structured around an informal network of individuals Elizabeth favoured and trusted, rather than institutional bodies: councillors like Burghley, Leicester, Walsingham and Sussex, agents and ambassadors (Randolph, Somers, Buckhurst, Thomas Leighton and Robert Bowes) and household officers, like Heneage, Stafford and others. Those most regularly selected for probouleutic debates were all Privy Councillors – Burghley, Leicester, Sussex, Walsingham and Wilson – but they were chosen because of their personal relationship with Elizabeth rather than their conciliar office. Hunsdon's inclusion in the conference in March 1579 demonstrates this clearly: never politically prominent, he was Elizabeth's cousin and had been able to assume unofficially an ad hoc role as counsellor prior to his formal appointment to the Council.[72]

Most members of Elizabeth's network held Chamber posts: Burghley (Principal Secretary until 1572, and subsequently fulfilling similar responsibilities on an informal basis), Sussex (Lord Chamberlain), Heneage (Treasurer), Randolph (Master of the Posts), Somers (Clerk of the Signet) and Stafford (gentleman pensioner). But key figures also held Privy Chamber posts – Hatton (Gentleman of the Privy Chamber, Captain of the Guard and Vice-chamberlain) – as did lesser individuals: the ambassadors Thomas Leighton and Fulke Greville (Gentlemen Extraordinary, 1568 and 1581 respectively) and Edward Darcy, special ambassador to Anjou in 1583 (Extraordinary Groom, 1583; feed groom, 1595).[73] If not a 'political cockpit', neither was the Privy Chamber a 'cocoon': some of its male members were involved in political debate and diplomacy, suggesting that the actions of Lady Mary Sidney, Kat Ashley and Dorothy Broadbelte were less unusual and controversial than Wright argues.

Second, the practices of receiving information, discussing policy and dispatching commands were not regularised and institutionalised: for example, Elizabeth read only one of Sussex's letters from the Imperial Court about the negotiations for the Archduke Charles match in 1568 because she was about to go hunting and did not want 'to lose the day's pleasure'.[74] Thus, the role of Privy Chamber women as points of access to Elizabeth and 'barometers' of her moods was crucial: counsellors needed to know when to approach Elizabeth. Leicester's discussion with Elizabeth on the death of Mar in November 1572 had to wait because he went to her at six o'clock when she 'was at her wonted repose'.[75] Privy Chamber women were used to communicate royal commands because they were on hand, much as Darcy, Gorges and William Killigrew (grooms of the Privy Chamber) acted as occasional messengers in the late 1570s and early 1580s and ambassadors utilised their own servants as messengers.[76] Bromley consulted Lady Scudamore over the disputed post of *Custos Rotulorum* of Derby *because* she had good access to Elizabeth and would be able to discover easily whether the Queen had granted it to Zouche as alleged. Indeed, the importance of the Privy Chamber, and its women, to policy-making and governance must have been precisely why Beale recommended Wotton maintain contacts with it in his 'Instructions for a Principall Secretary'.[77]

III

The Privy Chamber, and its women, were not as politically and administratively insignificant as Wright suggested. Neither as a body nor as individuals did they achieve the central importance of men like Burghley, Leicester, Walsingham and Sussex: they were not involved in counselling or the regular administration of governance. But neither were they confined to the domestic roles of delivering cloth and clothing, checking fabric receipts and keeping account of Elizabeth's personal jewels.[78] They were involved occasionally in diplomacy on important, sensitive issues both at Elizabeth's request and by independent initiative;

and if the regime was more concerned at the actions of Dymock and Goldborne than Kat Ashley and Broadbelte, then it is less clear that Elizabeth resented independent initiatives by Privy Chamber servants *per se*. They facilitated access to Elizabeth for the secretaries, counsellors and petitioners and delivered royal commands; they were also sources of information on the Queen and court, utilised not only by foreign ambassadors but by fellow members of the political elite. To this extent, they were aided by the close familial relations between Privy Chamber attendants and others in Elizabeth's network: as Simon Adams noted, 'they were practically all each others' cousins in the most literal sense'. For instance, Lincoln's wife, Elizabeth, Edward Stafford's mother (Lady Dorothy Stafford) and sister (Lady Drury) were all royal intimates.[79] Knollys's wife, Catherine, was one of Elizabeth's intimates until her death in 1569; Leighton's wife, Elizabeth, was regularly in attendance from 1583.[80]

If the informal nature of Elizabethan court politics put Privy Chamber women closer to the centre of its workings, then it also had an impact on the Privy Chamber as a whole. First, it retained its significance as representative of the monarch, through its members being intimate body servants of the monarch that Starkey noted operated under Henry VIII. In 1585, knowing how sceptical Mary Stewart was of her custodians' authority, John Somers recommended that William Agarde should be appointed a Gentleman Usher Extraordinary if made Superintendent of her household: Agarde's standing and authority over Mary would be enhanced by being, at least in name, one of Elizabeth's body servants.[81] Second, the role of male attendants in the Privy Chamber was also significant: a number of figures in the outer circles of Elizabeth's political network, often acting as envoys, agents and ambassadors, held posts there on a feed or unfeed basis: Leighton, Greville and Darcy. The latter were not just prestige posts, as Wright argued, but springboards to positions as envoys, mediators and local representatives. As well as an established dimension of Elizabeth's political network, the Privy Chamber was a recruiting ground for its members.

Notes

1 Pam Wright, 'A Change in Direction: the Ramifications of a Female Household, 1558-1603', in David Starkey (ed.), *The English Court From the Wars of the Roses to the Civil War*, London and New York: Longman, 1987, pp. 147-72 (pp. 172, 161-62).

[2] Charlotte Merton, 'The Women Who Served Queen Mary and Queen Elizabeth: Ladies, Gentlewomen and Maids to the Privy Chamber, 1553-1603', unpublished PhD thesis, University of Cambridge, 1993, ch. 6; J.B. Greenbaum Goldsmith, 'All the Queen's Women: the Changing Place and Perception of Aristocratic Women in Elizabethan England, 1558-1620', unpublished PhD thesis, Northwestern University, 1987, ch. 5, pp. 209-12.

[3] See G.R. Elton, *The Tudor Revolution in Government*, Cambridge: CUP, 1953; David Starkey, 'Which Age of Reform?' and 'Court and Government', in C. Coleman and David Starkey (eds), *Revolution Reassessed: Revisions in the History of Tudor Government and Administration*, Oxford: Clarendon Press, 1986, pp. 13-27, 29-58; *idem*, 'Intimacy and Innovation: the Rise of the Privy Chamber, 1485-1547', in *idem* (ed.), *The English Court*, pp. 71-118.

[4] Simon Adams, 'Eliza Enthroned? The Court and Its Politics', in C. Haigh (ed.), *The Reign of Elizabeth I*, London: Macmillan, 1984, pp. 55-77; Wallace T. MacCaffrey, *The Shaping of the Elizabethan Regime: Elizabethan Politics, 1558-1572*, Princeton: Princeton UP, 1968; *idem*, *Queen Elizabeth and the Making of Policy, 1572-1588*, Princeton: Princeton UP, 1981; *idem*, *Elizabeth I: War and Politics, 1588-1603*, Princeton: Princeton UP, 1992; *idem*, 'Place and Patronage in Elizabethan Politics', in S.T. Bindoff, J. Hurstfield and C.H. Williams (eds), *Elizabethan Government and Society: Essays Presented to Sir John Neale*, London: Athlone Press, 1961, pp. 95-126.

[5] Michael B. Pulman, *The Elizabethan Privy Council in the Fifteen-Seventies*, Berkeley, CA. and London: University of California Press, 1971, pp. 52-53 and *passim*; Stephen Alford, *The Early Elizabethan Polity: William Cecil and the British Succession Crisis, 1558-1569*, Cambridge: CUP, 1998, pp. 69-70, 208 and *passim*.

[6] Adams, 'Eliza Enthroned', pp. 62-63; MacCaffrey, *Making of Policy*, pp. 425-26.

[7] John Guy, 'The Rhetoric of Counsel in Early Modern England', in Dale Hoak (ed.), *Tudor Political Culture*, Cambridge: CUP, 1995, pp. 292-310; *idem*, 'The 1590s: The Second Reign of Elizabeth I?', in *idem* (ed.), *The Reign of Elizabeth I: Court and Culture in the Last Decade*, Cambridge: CUP, 1995, pp. 1-19; Quentin Skinner, *Reason and Rhetoric in the Philosophy of Hobbes*, Cambridge: CUP, 1996, pp. 19-110; Alford, *Early Elizabethan Polity*, *passim*.

[8] John Aylmer, *An Harborowe for Faithfull and Trewe Subiectes*, Strasbourg, 1559 [*STC* 1004]; Constance Jordan, 'Women's Rule in Sixteenth-Century British Political Thought', *RQ*, 40 (Autumn 1987), 421-51; Mary Thomas Crane, 'Video and Taceo: Elizabeth I and the Rhetoric of Counsel', *Studies in English Literature 1500-1900*, 28 (Winter 1988), 1-15; A.N. McLaren, *Political Culture in the Reign of Elizabeth I: Queen and Commonwealth, 1558-1585*, Cambridge: CUP, 1999.

[9] Elizabeth St Loe (sister to William St Loe) was sacked as a gentlewoman of the Privy Chamber for supporting Lady Catherine Grey's marriage. Wright, 'Change in Direction', pp. 167-69, n. 86; BL, Add. MS 48023, fol. 366^{r}.

[10] *CSPSpanish, 1558-67*, p. 113.

[11] Though I have been unable to locate corroborating evidence of Mary Sidney's knowledge of Latin, her brother, Robert, did know Italian raising the possibility that Mary was also taught it, especially as her own mother was well-educated. Mary's daughter, Mary, countess of Pembroke, also knew Italian. I would like to thank Simon Adams, Alan Bryson, James Daybell and Alan Stewart for their help on this point. Alan Stewart argues that, as part of her education, Mary Sidney 'learned Latin and French (as witnessed by her annotations on her copy of Hall's *Chronicles*)', was fluent in Italian and corresponded with John Dee: Stewart, *Philip Sidney: A Double Life*, New York: St Martin's Press, 2000, p. 40.

12 *CSPSpanish, 1558-67*, pp. 95-96, 99, 107, de Quadra to the Emperor, 2 and 16 Oct. 1559.

13 *CSPSpanish, 1558-67*, pp. 98-99, 112.

14 PRO, SP78/6/13, fols 34^{r}-34^{v}; PRO, SP78/6/15, fol. 38^{r}, Walsingham to Burghley, 17 Aug. 1581; BL, Harl. MS 6265, fol. 65^{r}, Walsingham, Cobham and Somers to Burghley, 27 Aug. 1581; BL, Cott. MS Galba E. 6, fols 109^{r}-09^{v}, Burghley to Walsingham, Cobham and Somers, 2 Sept. 1581; PRO, SP78/6/19, fol. 46^{r}, Substance of a letter from Burghley to Walsingham, 20 Aug. 1581.

15 PRO, SP70/39, fol. 119^{r}; PRO, SP70/40, fols 60^{r}-62^{r}; PRO, SP70/39, fols 175^{r}-76^{r}, Thomas Keyle to Geoffrey Preston, 27 July 1562; PRO SP70/40, fols 64^{r}-68^{v}, 70^{r}-75^{v}, 77^{r}-80^{r}, 124^{r}-25^{v}; Susan Doran, *Monarchy and Matrimony: the Courtships of Elizabeth I*, London and New York: Routledge, 1996, pp. 35-36.

16 BL, Add. MS 48023, fol. 366^{r}; PRO, SP70/40, fol. 60^{r}; PRO, SP70/39, fol. 118^{r}, Goldborne to Mr Harvey, 22 July 1562.

17 PRO, SP70/40, fols 64^{r}-65^{r}.

18 PRO, SP70/39, fols 175^{r}-75^{v}.

19 BL, Add. MS 48023, fol. 366^{r}.

20 BL, Add. MS 48023, fol. 355^{r}.

21 PRO, SP70/40, fols 66^{r}-67^{v}.

22 PRO, SP70/39, fol. 175^{r}; PRO, SP70/40, fols 60^{r}, 74^{r}.

23 See for example: Leah S. Marcus, Janel Mueller and Mary Beth Rose (eds), *Elizabeth I: Collected Works*, Chicago and London: University of Chicago Press, 2000, pp. 93-98; Peter E. McCullough, *Sermons at Court: Politics and Religion in Elizabethan and Jacobean Preaching*, Cambridge: CUP, 1998, p. 47; Natalie Mears, 'Counsel, Public Debate, and Queenship: John Stubbs's *The Discoverie of a Gaping Gulf*, 1579', *HJ*, 44 (Sept. 2001), 629-50.

24 *CSPSpanish, 1558-67*, p. 214, de Quadra to Philip II, 13 Sept. 1561; PRO, SP70/39, fols 175^{r}-75^{v}.

25 PRO, SP70/39, fol. 175^{v}.

26 MacCaffrey, 'The Newhaven Expedition, 1562-1563', *HJ*, 40 (Mar. 1997), 1-21.

27 *CSPSpanish, 1558-67*, p. 214, de Quadra to Philip II, 13 September 1561; *CSPSpanish, 1558-67*, p. 96; *CSPSpanish, 1558-67*, p. 454, de Silva to Philip II, 23 July 1565.

28 Merton, 'Women who Served', pp. 168-69.

29 *CSPSpanish, 1558-67*, pp. 214, 36, 381: de Silva to the duchess of Parma; 23 Sept. 1564.

30 *CSPSpanish, 1558-67*, p. 544, de Silva to Philip II, 2 July 1565.

31 Letters from Guzman de Silva to Philip II: *CSPSpanish, 1558-67*, p. 445 (2 July 1565), p. 446 (9 July 1565), p. 470 (27 Aug. 1565), p. 505 (5 Nov. 1565), p. 506 (10 Nov. 1565) and p. 492, Philip II to de Silva, 20 Oct. 1565.

32 PRO, SP15/15/49, fols 87^{r}-87^{v}, Hunsdon to Cecil, 26 Nov. 1569.

33 Ciaran Brady, 'Political Women and Reform in Tudor Ireland', in Margaret MacCurtain and Mary O'Dowd (eds.), *Women in Early Modern Ireland*, Edinburgh: Wolfhound Press, 1991, pp. 79-81; *idem*, 'Faction and the Origins of the Desmond Rebellion of 1579', *Irish Historical Studies*, 22, 88 (Sept 1981), 289-312.

34 Merton, 'Women who Served', pp. 165-66; BL, Cott. MS Galba C. 9, fol. 139^{v}, Sir Thomas Sherley to Leicester, 20 Mar. 1585; Barbara J. Harris, 'Women and Politics in Early Tudor England', *HJ*, 33, 2 (1990), 259-81 (pp. 260, 281).

35 Wright, 'Change in Direction', pp. 152-53.

36 BL, Add. MS 48149, fol. 8^{r}. Beale was Clerk to the Privy Council.

[37] PRO, SP12/200/20, fol. 38^{r}, Lady Cobham to Burghley, 10 Apr.1587; PRO, SP12/171/25 fol. 43^{r}, same to same, 15 June 1584; *HMC, Calendar of Manuscripts of Mr A.G. Finch, Formerly at Burley on the Hill, Rutland*, 4 vols, London: HMSO, 1913-65, 1, p. 10, Cecil to Heneage, 30 July 1570.

[38] PRO, SP15/13, fols 11^{r}-11^{v}, John Dudley to Leicester, 29 Mar. 1566.

[39] *HMC, The Manuscripts of His grace the Duke of Rutland, GCB, Preserved at Belvoir Castle*, 4 vols, London: HMSO, 1888, 1, pp. 95-96, Elizabeth Stafford to earl of Rutland, 16 Aug. 1571.

[40] Merton, 'Women who Served', pp. 183-84.

[41] *HMC, Rutland*, 1, p. 121: Sir Thomas Bromley to [Sussex?], 23 Aug. 1580.

[42] The nature of Elizabeth's queenship and Elizabethan policy-making is discussed in more detail in my Counselling Elizabeth I: queenship, politics and public discourse, Cambridge: CUP, forthcoming, 2004/2005.

[43] PRO, SP70/95, fols 133^{r}-33^{v}, Elizabeth to Sussex [draft], 12 Dec. 1567.

[44] DWL, Morrice D, pp. 288-89, Elizabeth to Walsingham, 8 June 1571; DWL, Morrice D, p. 339, Leicester to Walsingham, [15 Aug. 1571].

[45] Hatfield House, Herts, Cecil Papers 148, fols 23^{r}-24^{v}, 25^{r}-26^{v}; PRO, SP78/3/17, fols 34^{r}-35^{r}; Cecil Papers 148, fols 29^{r}-30^{r}, 32^{r}-38^{v}, 39^{r}-41^{r}, 42^{r}-43^{v}, 44^{r}; BL, Add. MS 4149, fols 104^{r}-05^{r}, 105^{v}-08^{r}; Cecil Papers 140, fols 6^{r}-7^{v}, 60^{r}-61^{r}, 59^{r}, 64^{r}-65^{r}.

[46] PRO, PRO31/3/28, fols 285^{r}-87^{r}.

[47] BL, Cott. MS Caligula B. 10, fols 211^{r}-12^{v}, 209^{r}-10^{v}; BL, Lansd. MS 103, fols 6^{r}-6^{v}.

[48] PRO, SP52/10/40, fol. 91^{r}; BL, Cott. MS Caligula B. 10, fols 301^{r}-8^{r}, 358^{r}-59^{v}.

[49] BL, Cott. MS Caligula C.2, fols 63^{r}-65^{v}.

[50] BL, Cott. MS Caligula C. 3, fols 188^{r}-88^{v}.

[51] PRO, SP52/28/85, fol. 238^{r}, Walsingham to Bowes, 18 Sept. 1580; BL, Cott. MS Caligula C. 6, fols 82^{r}-82^{v}.

[52] PRO, SP52/29/46, Walsingham to Randolph, 18 Mar. 1581.

[53] PRO, SP52/31/48, Walsingham to Bowes, 2 Mar. 1583.

[54] *CSPSpanish, 1558-67*, pp. 518-19, De Guaras to [Zayas?], 9 Jan. 1576; PRO, SP70/137, fols 25^{r}-26^{v}.

[55] PRO, SP83/5/93; 'Journal of Sir Francis Walsingham from December 1570 to April 1583', *Camden Miscellany VI*, Camden Society, original series, 106 (1871), p. 35.

[56] PRO, SP83/13/37; PRO, SP94/1/52, fols 146^{r}-48^{r}.

[57] BL, Cott. MS Galba C. 9, fols, 193^{r}-94^{r}, 195^{r}-95^{v}, 290^{v}-91^{r}, Walsingham to Leicester, 25 Apr., 26 Apr. and 9 July 1586.

[58] *APC*, 8, pp. 36-37; 11, pp. 78-79, 86-87.

[59] *APC*, 12, pp. 91-92.

[60] *APC*, 9, p. 276; BL, Add. MS 4149, fols 104^{r}-5^{r}.

[61] BL, Cott. MS Caligula C. 2, fols 63^{r}-65^{v}; PRO, SP70/137, fols 25^{r}-26^{v}.

[62] Cecil Papers 148, fols 42^{r}-43^{v}.

[63] PRO, SP52/29/46, Walsingham to Randolph, 18 Mar. 1581; PRO, SP52/31/48; BL, Cott. MS Galba C. 9, fol. 193^{v}.

[64] *LP*, 16, p. 450, William Paget to Sir Thomas Wriothesley, 27 June 1541; Pulman, *Elizabethan Privy Council*, p. 52; Alford, *Early Elizabethan Polity*, pp. 11, 32, 57, 66, 125-26, 168, 173, 178, 207, 213-14.

[65] Cecil Papers 7, fol. 57^{r}: Leicester to Burghley, 4 Nov. 1572. See also: BL, Harl. MS 6991, fol. 21^{r}, Smith to Burghley, 8 Jan. 1573; Cecil Papers 9, fol. 49^{r}, Sussex to Burghley, [1576?]; PRO, SP83/9/23, Wilson to Burghley, 15 Sept. 1578; PRO, SP12/126/9, fol. 19^{r},

Walsingham to Burghley, 14 Oct. 1578. Examples of Sussex's and Walsingham's role can be seen in PRO, SP83/8/59, Sussex to Walsingham, 29 August 1578, and Cecil Papers 11, fol. 76^{r}, Walsingham to the Lord Deputy of Ireland, 1 Jan. 1582.

66 PRO, SP52/27/47, fol. 98^{r}, Morton to Walsingham, 9 July 1578.

67 Cecil Papers 157, fol. 55^{r}.

68 *HMC, Finch*, 1, p. 10, Cecil to Heneage, 29 July and 30 July 1570; PRO, SP70/119, fols 34^{r}-34^{v}, Heneage to Burghley, 16 July 1571; BL, RP36, pp. 5-26, Buckhurst to Heneage, 8, 11, 15, 21, 24 Feb. and 8 Mar. 1571.

69 PRO, SP70/36, fols 58^{r}-67^{r}, Throckmorton to Elizabeth [draft], 17 Apr. 1562; BL, Lansd. MS 102, fol. 102^{r}, Cecil to Smith, 4 Oct. 1564; PRO, SP70/48/31, fols 75^{r}-75^{v}; PRO, SP70/48/77, fol. 193^{r}, Throckmorton to Elizabeth, 6 and 13 Jan. 1563.

70 *CSPSpanish, 1558-67*, p. 447: de Silva to Philip II, 2 July 1565.

71 Elizabeth was also unnerved by the French ambassador's repeated warnings that Henry III would not tolerate any infringement of Franco-Scottish relations and worried about the financial cost and political aims of military intervention. BL, Harl. MS 6999, fols 39^{r}-40^{v}, Randolph to Walsingham, 8 Feb. 1581; PRO, SP52/29/44, SP52/29/46, Walsingham to Randolph, 7 and [18] Mar. 1581; BL, Harl. MS 6999, fols 84^{r}-84^{v}, [Walsingham] to [Huntingdon], 15 Mar. 1581; Bibliothèque Nationale, Paris, Fonds Français 15973, fols 400^{v}-2^{r}, Mauvissière to Henry III, 10 Feb. 1581.

72 BL, Cott. MS Caligula C. 5, fols 42^{r}-42^{v}, Hunsdon to Burghley, 24 Aug. 1577.

73 Wright, 'Change in Direction', p. 156. Wright argues Darcy's initial appointment was in 1581, *HC 1558-1603*, 1, p. 16 states 1583. BL, Lansd. MS 34/30, fols 76^{r}-76^{v} (1582) lists only feed members of the chamber.

74 *CSPSpanish, 1568-79*, p. 6, de Silva to Philip II, 7 Feb. 1568.

75 Cecil Papers 7, fol. 57.

76 PRO, E351/542, fol. 33^{r}; PRO, E351/541, fols 213^{v}, 224^{r}.

77 BL, Add. MS 48149, fol. 8^{r}. *HMC, Rutland*, 1, p. 121: Sir Thomas Bromley to [Sussex?], 23 Aug. 1580

78 Wright, 'Change of Direction', p. 150.

79 BL, Lansd. MS 59/22, fol. 43.

80 Wright, 'Change in Direction', p. 170.

81 Arthur Clifford (ed.), *The State Papers and Letters of Sir Ralph Sadler*, 2 vols, Edinburgh, 1809, 2, pp. 497-99.

Chapter 5

Portingale Women and Politics in Late Elizabethan London

Alan Stewart

In the summer of 1594, a London woman named Sara Lopez presented a petition to Queen Elizabeth. In it she beseeched the Queen 'for gods sake to have pitifiull consideracion of her aflicted & miserable estate' as 'the contemned & poore widdowe of Docter Lopez'.[1] The case of Sara Lopez's husband is still notorious. On 28 February 1594, Dr Roderigo Lopez, a Portuguese-born denizen who rose to become physician to Queen Elizabeth, was tried by a special commission at London's Guildhall on charges of conspiring to poison his royal patron on behalf of King Philip of Spain, in return for a payment of fifty thousand crowns. Found guilty, Lopez was hanged, drawn and quartered alongside two fellow conspirators, also Portuguese, the following June; despite allegedly confessing at one point, the doctor died protesting his innocence, claiming that his dealings with Spain had been known to, and encouraged by, English government officials.[2] The Lopez case was a *cause célèbre* for several years: not only was it made the subject of an official government publication and several discourses (including one by Francis Bacon)[3], but Lopez was also mentioned, alluded to and even portrayed in a multitude of literary works – by Christopher Marlowe, Thomas Nashe, Thomas Robinson, John Gee, Thomas Middleton, John Taylor, and William Rowley, [4] and even, it has been suggested, by William Shakespeare as Shylock in *The Merchant of Venice*.[5]

Following the execution of her husband, Lopez's widow was now in dire straits: 'vtterlie confounded & dismaied w*i*th the heavie ruin of her late husbande', lying 'in woefull agonye & extremitie of sicknes vtterlye disparinge the recoue*ri*e of her former healthe & strengthe, and rather expectinge the speedie shorteninge of her perplexed lief thoroughe the inwarde conceipte of her p*re*sente desolacion', as 'the sorrowfull mother of ffyve comforteles and distressed children.' In her petition, she made several requests to the Queen: that her 'husbands offence & the rigor of the punishem*en*te thereof may ceasse & be determyned w*i*th the infamous losse of his life'; that she and her children 'maye have the lease of [her] howse for there habitation w*i*th her howsholde stuff', including the 'goods & other thinges' that had been purloined from her during her husband's initial imprisonment; and that Elizabeth would reinstate 'the guife [gift] of a p*ar*sonage to the valew of 30^{li} p*er* annu*m*' to her son Anthony Lopez, 'for his maynetena*u*nce at schoole & learninge' at Winchester.[6]

Sara Lopez usually warrants little more than a footnote in writings on her unfortunate husband. But I shall contend in this essay that to understand the particular status of Dr Roderigo Lopez and his 'Portingale' compatriots in late Elizabethan London, an analysis of the role of his 'poore & contemned' and now largely forgotten widow is essential. In so doing, I hope not merely to correct the erasure from the archive of Sara Lopez and other 'Portingale' women, but also to suggest ways in which that erasure may not be a wholly negative phenomenon: how these Portingale women exploited their invisibility to important commercial and political ends.

I

Dr Roderigo Lopez is now most frequently identified as a Jew, one of what David Katz has dubbed the 'Jewish Conspirators of Elizabethan England'. Yet in the majority of contemporary documents relating to Lopez's interrogation, trial and execution the doctor is significantly *not* identified explicitly as Jewish, but as a 'Portingale', a variant of 'Portugal', the word that in the late sixteenth century denoted both the country Portugal, and a Portuguese man or woman. Lopez was indeed born in Portugal and trained in medicine at the University of Coimbra, before immigrating into England in 1559.[7] By 1567 he was a member of the College of Physicians, and physician to St Bartholomew's Hospital; in time, his personal clients included the earl of Leicester, Lord Burghley and, from 1586, Elizabeth herself, who granted him a lucrative monopoly on the import of aniseed and sumach, two valuable foreign crops, three years later. By the time of the scandal, Lopez was also technically not a 'stranger', as the English referred to people from overseas, but an English denizen by royal patent.[8]

Despite his denizen status, Lopez's Englishness was never fully secure. A denizen's Englishness was always in doubt. Archival traces of Lopez in parish registers and subsidy rolls bear testimony to the confusion. In 1567, living in the ward of Farringdon Without, 'Doctor Lopus and his brother' were described as 'Portingale' *and* 'denizens'.[9] In the following year, in Little St Bartholomew's, the list of strangers was headed by 'Roger

Lopus, doctor in phisick, a Portingale borne, and a denyson'; a note records that the doctor 'goeth to the parishe church', affirming his Anglican credentials.[10] According to a 1571 survey, by which time he was resident in St Andrew's Parish, Holborn, 'Doctour Lopus' is a 'Portingale, howsholder, denizen';[11] in 1583, 'Doctor Lopus', a 'Portingaler' and 'Physicion' was in Aldgate Ward.[12] Lopez's name is usually marked 'denizen', to be sure, but his presence on these lists invariably designates him as first a Portingale, and therefore *de facto* a 'stranger', born overseas, and only second a 'denizen'.

Attacking this vulnerable double status, the official publication on the Lopez case presents the doctor as a traitor to his queen, thus tacitly granting him the status of her (English) subject, but it constantly refers to him as a 'Portingale'. Further, it identifies him as a Portingale in the pay of Spain.[13] As that tri-layered description (English subject-Portingale-in the pay of Spain) might suggest, the status of a Portingale in England in the early 1590s was complex for very specific reasons. While there had long been a Portuguese presence in England (and especially in London and Bristol),[14] in the final two decades of the sixteenth century the political and commercial position of the English Portingale shifted dramatically. In 1580 the elderly Cardinal-King Henry of Portugal died, leaving no obvious heir, and after a brief struggle for power, Philip of Spain annexed Portugal. Local and international opposition to Philip's regime was focussed on the Portuguese Pretender, Dom Antonio, Prior of Crato, who sought refuge and support from England twice during the 1580s. From his first entry into England in 1581, Dr Lopez and other English Portingales played a major role in facilitating Dom Antonio's contacts with the English court. But in the mid 1580s, a new use of the Portingale became evident, when Philip prohibited trade with the English, effectively aborting the lucrative trade between England and Portugal.

The slippery status – and commercial possibilities – of Portuguese-born, English-denizened Portingales can be seen in the depositions produced for a fascinating case in the Court of Chancery, concerning a venture dating from late 1586. A widow named Mary May, acting as executrix of her late husband, the London merchant tailor Richard May, brought a case against Ferdinando Alvares and Alvaro de Lyma.[15] May, it was claimed, had been 'p*er*swaded and assured' by Alvares, de Lyma, and one Barnard Lewis [*alias* Leavis], and by letters from Peter Freire, that Lewis and Freire, 'Portugall m*er*chant*es*', had

> obtained free liberty and licence of the Marques of Sancta Cruce [the Spanish Viceroy in Portugal] or other the kinge of Spaine his deputies and gover*noures* at Lishborne [Lisbon] to bringe thither anie Englishe good*es*

> and Englishe shippes in theire owne names, and as theire owne good*es* w*i*thout anie lett trouble or int*er*rupc*i*on.[16]

May was 'solicited and requested earnestly' by Lewis to consign his goods to Lewis and Freire at Lisbon, on the understanding that they were to be 'by them or either of them bartered, sold, and exchanged in theire owne names, and as theire owne good*es*', or, in the mercantile phrase, 'vnder the culler of the good*es* of the said Barnerd'. Lewis and Freire would take their cut as factors, but the profits were 'to be retorned for the vse benefitt and advantage of the said Richard May'.[17]

The first mission was laded in December/January 1586-7 with two British ships, the Red Lion and the Christopher, carrying 'diu*er*s good*es* and m*er*chandizes of sundry sort*es* to be transported into Portingall belonginge and app*er*teyninge aswell to diu*er*s Englishe m*er*chant*es* as to the saide Barn*ar*d Lewis and to doctor Hector and others',[18] referring to Dr Hector Nuñez, like Lopez a Portuguese-born physician turned English denizen, and leading member of the Portingale community.[19] This was no small venture: the first voyage alone had £25 000 invested in it, with May the principal venturer, consigning merchandise worth £4675, 2s. and 4d. The ships reached Lisbon in March or April 1587, but on their arrival the goods were 'arrested and immediately sequestered for the K*ing* of Spaines vse onely vppon suspic*i*on that the same were Englishe good*es*'.[20] They were held there for some forty days while Lewis travelled the three hundred miles to the King's court, to bribe his way out. It was the additional costs of this mission that were at the centre of the Chancery case brought by Mrs May, who claimed they had diminished her late husband's share in the venture.

This Portingale business venture was, however, more complex than even Mrs May understood. The operation was in fact known to Spanish intelligence agents, thanks to denunciations provided by Francisco de Valverde and Pedro de Santa Cruz to the Spanish ambassador in Paris, Bernardino de Mendoza, on 27 February 1588. They testified that, although a ship would land at Lisbon and claim to be Portuguese, in fact 'The ship and cargo are entirely English property, nothing belongs to the Portuguese who ostensibly own her, but to Mr Cob, Mr Richard Mayo [*sic*], his son-in-law, and other Englishmen'.[21] But the main point of their denunciation was to explain how this international mercantile sleight-of-hand was in reality a cover for an intelligence operation. They described in great detail how two men, Geronimo Pardo in Lisbon, and Bernaldo Luis [Bernard Lewis] in Madrid, were using the ships to supply information to Dr Hector Nuñez – as we have seen, himself a venturer in the plan – in London:

> Last year Bernaldo Luis took a ship from here loaded with cloth worth 70,000 ducats. When the ship arrived in Lisbon it was embargoed, on suspicion that the cargo belonged to Englishmen, as in fact it did. But they arranged so cleverly as to get permission to deal with the merchandize, on condition that neither it nor they were to return to England.[22]

This they accomplished by a clever ruse:

> Geronimo Pardo arrived in London in June last in a ship with a little salt as an excuse, but the rest of the cargo consisting of spices, cochineal, and a large sum of money. He brought on that occasion two packets of letters in cipher, giving a full account of the warlike preparations which were being made in Spain. After translating them, he carried them to Secretary Walsingham, and within two months Pardo was on his way back to Lisbon. Since then he has sent three more ships; the first with raisins and wine, from Ayamonte, the second with wine and cochineal, and the third from Algarves, with wax and figs in barrels, many of the barrels also containing bags of money. By this latter ship full accounts were sent of the ships, men, and stores for the Armada in Lisbon. The despatches were delivered to Dr Hector Nuñez whilst he was at a dinner to which he had been invited. He rose in great haste, and went direct to Secretary Walsingham's house ...[23]

So here illicit trading links between England and Spain, facilitated by the Portingales, are exploited by the English intelligence operation, headed by Principal Secretary Sir Francis Walsingham – indeed, Walsingham's biographer Conyers Read suggests that 'there is some reason to believe that a certain amount of trade with Spain was licensed by the Queen for the express purpose of keeping open a direct channel of communication'.[24] The Chancery case and the denunciations of Valverde and Santa Cruz thus illustrate very precisely the multifarious positions occupied by the Portuguese of England: potentially subjects simultaneously of Portugal (and therefore of Spain) and of England, rendering them commercially and diplomatically valuable. Commercially valuable because under colour of being a Portingale, English subjects could trade in Spain; diplomatically valuable because under colour of these commercial ventures, intelligence against Spain and even secret negotiations with Spain could be facilitated.

II

Thus far, this complex play of politicking, trading and intelligencing has been very much a boys' game, where understandings between men cement alliances, commercial and political. The only women's voices we have heard are plaintive: two widows, Mary May and Sara, the self-styled 'poore & contemned widow of Dr. Lopez', both of whose pleas – one to the Court of Chancery, the other to the Queen – rest on their ostensible exclusion from the negotiations in which their late husbands took part. What I shall argue in the remainder of this essay is that the apparent exclusion of women here is a sleight of hand. This is what we are able to glimpse, I shall suggest, if we uncover the contexts of the complaints of widow May and widow Lopez.

To do this means putting to one side many of our natural assumptions about the social roles of early modern women. Over the past quarter-century, many analyses of the role of women in politics have drawn explicitly or implicitly on what we might call the 'traffic in women' model. Following Gayle Rubin's critique of the anthropological researches of Claude Lévi-Strauss, this model sees women as facilitating and cementing relationships, hostile and friendly, between men. Eve Kosofsky Sedgwick influentially developed this in the field of gay literary studies by re-reading male rivalry over women as the prime feature of male homosociality.[25] For early modern scholars, the pattern persuasively resonates with what we know about the lives of women in the period. In her study of quattrocento and cinquecento Florence, for example, Christiane Klapisch-Zuber has shown how these abstract structures were literalised in practice. 'In Florence,' she writes, 'men *were* and *made* the "houses". The word *casa* designates ... the material house, the lodging of a domestic unit ... But it also stands for an entire agnatic kinship group'. These houses, and kinship in general were 'determined by men, and the male branching of genealogies drawn up by contemporaries shows how little importance was given, after one or two generations, to kinship through women'. She illustrates graphically how, as they married, women moved between houses – both lineage groups and the physical buildings. This demonstrated not only the enduring stability of the houses, but also the radical discontinuity of the lives of the women exchanged between them:

> In these *case*, in the sense of both the physical and the symbolic house, women were passing guests. To contemporary eyes, their movements in relation to the *case* determined their social personality more truly than the lineage group from which they came. It was by means of their physical 'entrances' and 'exits' into and out of the 'house' that their families of origin or of alliance evaluated the contribution of women to the greatness of the *casa*.[26]

One only has to think of Shakespeare's plays to appreciate the power – then and now – of this notion of women's discontinuous lives, defined by movement. When Desdemona rejects her father in favour of Othello; when Helena rejects her father in favour of her lover Lysander in *A Midsummer Night's Dream*; when Juliet rejects her father in favour of Romeo; when Cordelia refuses to divide her allegiance between her father and her hypothetical husband – this structural opposition is the springboard for a thousand romantic fictions. But while this is a powerful fiction, I would argue that it is at heart just that – a fiction; and that in surrendering to its rhetorical persuasiveness, we run the risk first of turning early modern women into a series of discontinuous roles as daughter and wife; and second, of eliding the possibility of women's agency in their exploitation of their dual position between two houses.

I want to suggest that a Portingale woman like Sara Lopez might be more than a 'passing guest'. To pursue this, I turn again to a fiction: to a figurative expression of the lot of the Portingale in England in William Haughton's play *Englishmen For My Money Or A Woman Will Have Her Will* (c. 1598).[27] The play's main plot concerns a '*Pisaro*, a Portingale',[28] an usurer living in London's 'Croched-Fryers' (l. 233) who attempts to deflect his daughters Laurentia, Marina and Mathea from marrying their English gentlemen trueloves, Harvie, Heigham and Walgrave. His opening speech sets the terms for the play, but also says much about the lot of the 'Portingale':

> How smugge this gray-eyde Morning seemes to bee,
> A pleasant sight; but yet more pleasure haue I
> To thinke vpon this moystning Southwest Winde,
> That driues my laden Shippes from fertile *Spaine*:
> But come what will, no Winde can come amisse,
> For two and thirty Windes that rules the Seas,
> And blowes about this ayerie Region;
> Thirtie two Shippes haue I to equall them:
> Whose wealthy fraughts doe make *Pisaro* rich:
> Thus euery Soyle to mee is naturall:
> Indeed by birth, I am a *Portingale*,
> Who driuen by Westerne winds on *English* shore,
> Heere liking of the soyle, I maried,
> And haue Three Daughters: But impartiall Death
> Long since, depriude mee of her dearest life:
> Since whose discease, in *London* I haue dwelt:
> And by the sweete loude trade of *Vsurie*
> Letting for Interest, and on Mortgages,

Doe I waxe rich, though many Gentlemen
By my extortion comes to miserie:
(11-20)

Not only his mind, but also Pisaro's very life is figured as a storm-blown ship. The passage is driven by winds – the thirty-two winds corresponding to the thirty-two points of the compass, and matched (merchandise equalling nature) by his thirty-two ships. But as those winds blow the 'laden Shippes', the 'wealthy fraughts', they also blow Pisaro, 'driuen by Westerne winds on *English* shore'. And rather than being by birth a Portingale *but* by marriage an Englishman, his Portingale status *leads* to his overseas travel ('Indeed by birth, I am a Portingale, *Who* driuen ...'). For Pisaro is 'a *Portingale*',[29] that variant of 'Portugal' that according to the *OED* may be constructed analogous to 'nightingale', a bird carried by the wind, and is also a 'port-in-gale', any port in a storm, a man whose landings are made necessarily through the inclemency of the winds. Pisaro is wind and water, England is 'soyle'. 'On *English* shore' he marries an anonymous woman who is only uttered ('her') as she dies ('Death ... depriude me of her dearest life'). His marriage is to England *land* and his daughters are daughters of the English land: 'Here liking of the soyle, I maried, And haue Three Daughters'. The play's comedy of course relies on the daughters being English rather than Portuguese – while G.K. Hunter sniffed that the 'three daughters are (illogically enough) totally English in outlook',[30] this is precisely an effect of the nature of the windblown Portingale, who has no claims on land. Daughter Mathea makes this very clear, as she berates what she thinks is her French suitor:

Heare you *Frenchman*, packe to your Whores in *Fraunce*;
Though I am *Portingale* by the Fathers side,
And therefore should be lustfull, wanton, light;
Yet goodman Goosecap, I will let you know,
That I haue so much *English* by the Mother,
That no bace slauering *French* shall make me stoope:
(ll. 1782-7)

The Portingale is 'lustfull, wanton, light', and Pisaro's failure to claim Englishness supports this. '[E]uery Soyle to mee is naturall' (l. 10), he proclaims, casting himself as the embodiment of diaspora, as a 'lustfull, wanton, light' (1784) seed that can land on and take root in any soil. What I want to stress here is the way in which the male Portingale is oddly positioned. We hear a lot about Pisaro and almost nothing about his wife, as she is – typically – elided from the play. But his daughters are, like their mother, emphatically English, and insist on the importance of their maternal legacy, which is purposefully opposed to any inherited features of the father.

This dramatic representation of the very different nature of male and female English Portingales points us in a new direction. What if the strong link behind these complex Anglo-Portuguese trade relations is not between men, but in some way between women? And sure enough, there is a hidden level behind the arrangement between May, Lewis, Alvares, de Lyma and Freire, which we can fill in from the pioneering work of the great scholar of English Jewry, Lucien Wolf.[31] Ferdinando Alvares was married to a woman named Philippa Freire. Alvaro de Lyma was married in 1582 to Elizabeth Freire, Philippa's sister. Dr Hector Nuñez had been married since 1566 to a third sister, Eleanor Freire. Philippa, Elizabeth and Eleanor were all sisters of Peter [Pedro] Freire – and of Bernard Lewis, who was known in Madrid as Bernaldo Luis Freyle.[32] In other words, behind the already obfuscatory Portingale connection facilitating Anglo-Spanish trade in the 1580s and 1590s was a sisterhood, which provided the basis for a tangled family web. Moving beyond the Freire sorority, their mother was a sister of Jeronimo Pardo, who was the chief intelligence agent of his niece Eleanor's husband Hector Nuñez, and who captained the second mission of the venture; another relative was Alvaro de Lyma, who was said scandalously to have married his own niece Elizabeth.[33] De Lyma and Alvares encouraged May to consign his goods to Lewis and Freire, who were in truth their brothers-in-law.

Seen through the model proposed by Klapisch-Zuber, these Freire women would become 'passing guests' in the Alvares, de Lyma, Pardo and Nuñez households; but their apparent disappearance into these houses also explains the way in which the Freire women were able to build an ingenious and highly lucrative international trading concern without drawing attention to the intensely personal and familial investment of that concern's main venturers. We might push this further. In Klapisch-Zuber's model, the Freire women would move into separate houses, both symbolically and physically, but once again the archival evidence suggests something importantly different. Examined in Lisbon on 4 July 1588, Pedro de Santa Cruz testified to the presence of Portuguese and Castilian émigrés in London engaged in mercantile enterprises. He named Dr Hector Nuñez, Alvaro de Lyma, Geronimo Pardo, 'Hernan dalbarez' (Ferdinand D'Alvares), Francisco de Tapia, and one Antonio, all of whom, he claimed, resided in the same 'posada' or inn.[34] This detail is significant. These are not merely half a dozen Portuguese male immigrants sharing a lodging; they include five married men, whose wives are all presumably living with them, in the same house. And these wives are all, of course, members of the same *casa*, which is at the same time an extended merchant business.

When Mrs May brought her case against Alvares and de Lyma, she argued that the excessive costs of the venture, which had diminished her husband's share in the profits, were not due to the fact that the goods were English but solely attributable to the venturers' Jewishness. In Lisbon, she claimed, Lewis and Freire were charged that they, their sisters and family were guilty of 'judaism and other haynous crymes', and that they 'did live in Jewish and infedilish ceremonies and superstitions which were punishable by the Laws of Spaine and Portugall with Confiscacon of goods and losse of life'.[35] Much of the venture's profits had been squandered in bribes to ensure that they did not face the Inquisition. Could it be that what we are seeing in the Freire sisters' trade empire was a peculiarly Jewish form?

In recent work, Natalie Zemon Davis has started to develop what she terms an 'ethnographic/comparative approach' to the study of commercial cultures, and specifically seventeenth-century Jewish culture. Striving to avoid 'ahistorical reification' in which a single 'Jewish merchant' figure emerges as representative, Davis aims instead to 'study the culture of a group', European Jews, in all its multifarious forms.[36] She identifies as a salient feature of Jewish culture in the seventeenth century 'the proximity of, the porousness between, family matters and commercial matters':[37] Davis paints a vivid picture of 'crossed-over strands of action and communication networks buzzing with diamond prices, bills of divorces, bans, bankruptcies, and rabbinical admonition'.[38] Such a porousness flies in the face of the influential model of early modern economic evolution familiar from the work of Max Weber and Raymond de Roover, in which 'the separation of business strategy and accounting from domestic strategy and accounting as a necessary and inevitable step toward rational advanced enterprise', but, as Davis asks, is this simultaneous domestic and business arrangement 'perhaps a distinctive Jewish style?'.[39] While admitting that there may well be an intersection of family matters and business matters in the Christian world, she suggests that in the Jewish case the particular 'character of the population and of partnership' is important: 'the German-Jewish commercial families spread across Europe knew each other and the web of in-laws was extensive. Their partnerships were usually among circles of kin or at least familiars'.[40] This arrangement was not merely a necessary reaction to the waves of anti-Jewish expulsions, but also a resourceful exploitation of the possibilities of diaspora. Davis observes 'the Jewish strategy of marrying some of her children close to home and some of them in distant cities' and suggests that 'the wide dispersal of one's kin was an economic advantage and a safety measure'.[41] We can see this at work in the fictional Pisaro's desire to marry his daughters to a wide-ranging set of European merchants; but more powerfully in the Freire family, which had members living not only in London and Lisbon, but also in Madrid (Bernard Lewis) and as far away as Vayaha in India (Alvaro de Lyma); Freire and Lewis also travelled regularly to Antwerp; and the extended family had factors – possibly also relatives – in Morocco.[42]

Roderigo Lopez too had international connections, including familial links in Antwerp, and in Constantinople via his brother-in-law Don Solomon Abenaes, originally known as Alvaro Mendes, whose sister had married Roderigo's brother Diego.[43] But to return to his 'poor & contemned widdowe', Sara Lopez. Accompanying her petition to the Queen was a complex inventory of goods and goods lost that also contains information about her late husband's financial dealings. Dr Lopez, it appears, stood bound for large sums owed by the Portuguese pretender Dom Antonio to various London merchants, a role he undertook alongside one William Añes – who was also a venturer in the May-Freire-Lewis enterprise.[44] Both William Añes and Roderigo Lopez took over the thankless task of English financial agent to Dom Antonio from Benjamin George. As with the Freire business, the focus on male names obscures the true nature of this financial arrangement. Benjamin George was also known as Dunstan Añes, and William was his son. His eldest daughter Sara in 1564 married an up-and-coming physician named Roderigo Lopez. So once again we have a marriage not merely cementing alliances between men, but actively producing trade agreements, with the woman providing the continuity. In this case, although Dr Lopez had been convicted of, and executed for, treason, necessitating the automatic forfeiting of his estate, Elizabeth acquiesced to all of Sara Lopez's requests. She allowed the widow to keep her husband's house, and provided the parsonage that allowed her son Anthony to return to his studies at Winchester the following year.[45]

Davis more tentatively offers a second feature of Jewish culture: its use of secrecy, in the senses outlined in Stephanie Jed's work.[46] At the most fundamental level, Jewish economic practice could be obscured to Christian eyes by the use of account books written in Yiddish in Hebrew characters; in this way, Davis concludes, 'the sense of inside space created by account books and other records in Hebrew characters was more than a family space, it was a larger Jewish space'.[47] But here I want to build on Davis's argument and suggest that women might play a very particular role in this secretive model of Jewish commercial culture. Amy Louise Erickson has noted how the historical records on which feminist historians have to draw are themselves 'obstructive':

> mothers' names are not always recorded in parish baptismal registers; the most common social phenomena, such as women exchanging their family name upon marriage – *every* marriage – create enormous obstacles for the historian. Even for historians not specifically tracing women, kin by marriage are difficult to identify, which has implications for the study of debt and credit networks, as well as kinship ties.[48]

This problem is exacerbated when attempting to trace Jews: as Davis notes, 'Jewish names slipped and slid about in the seventeenth and early eighteenth centuries much more than Christian names, rather to the enjoyment of their referents'; moreover, 'a woman's signature in the Jewish mode associated her not with her husband but with her father'.[49] In short, the nature of the English legal system, the laws governing English marriage and the structures of English family life ensure that we hear precious little of married women, at least until they are widowed, and even less of married Jewish women.

In conclusion, this relative lack of archival trace, this invisibility may seem to be an infuriating stumbling block to any scholar trying to piece together the contribution of early modern women, whether it be in politics, commerce, or whatever. As so often, the laws, courts and scribes that produce, authorise and preserve the archive with which we necessarily work, render up to us a story that is, almost exclusively, about men. But this state of affairs is not merely an archival distortion of a past that obscures for us the multifarious roles of historical women. It was also an early modern reality and, as I have argued, a reality that *enabled* women deliberately to obscure their roles. In the case of these Portingale women it provided a cover for a resourceful, commercially successful and politically influential Jewish family business whose true nature eluded investors and intelligencers in its own day, and historians for centuries to come.

Notes

1 Hatfield House, Herts, Cecil Papers 28, fol. 11: Sara Lopez to Elizabeth, [Aug. 1594]. This letter has recently been printed in Betty S. Travitsky and Anne Lake Prescott (eds), *Female and Male Voices in Early Modern England: an Anthology of Renaissance Writing*, New York: Columbia UP, 2000, pp. 189-93.

2 On Lopez see Frederick George Lee, *The Church Under Queen Elizabeth: an Historical Sketch*, 2 vols, London: W.H. Allen and Co., 1880, 2, pp. 289-91; Arthur Dimock, 'The Conspiracy of Dr. Lopez', *EHR*, 9 (1894), 440-72; Martin A. S. Hume, *Treason and Plot:*

Struggles for Catholic Supremacy in the Last Years of Elizabeth, London: James Nisbet & Co., 1901, ch. 5; John Gwyer, 'The Case of Dr Lopez', *TJHSE*, 16 (1952), 163-84; F.D. Zeman, 'The Amazing Career of Doctor Roderigo Lopez', *Bulletin of the History of Medicine*, 39 (1965), 295-308; David S. Katz, 'The Jewish Conspirators of Elizabethan England', in Katz, *The Jews in the History of England 1485-1850*, Oxford: Clarendon Press, 1994, pp. 49-106.

3 The official publication was *A Trve Report of Svndry Horrible Conspiracies*, London: Charles Yetsweirt, 1594. See also Francis Bacon, 'A True Report of the Detestable Treason, Intended by Dr. Roderigo Lopez', in Bacon, *Resuscitatio*, (ed.) William Rawley, London: William Lee, 1657, pp. 151-61; it will appear in Bacon, *Works*, vol. 1, Julian Martin and Alan Stewart (eds), Oxford: OUP, forthcoming. For the fullest accounts, by Clerk of the Privy Council William Waad, see Folger, MS X.d.348; BL, Add. MS 48029, fols 147^{r}-184^{v}; BL Harl. MS 871, fols 7-64; PRO SP 12/248/7.1. For another account in the Cecil papers see *A Collection of State Papers Relating to Affairs In the Reign of Queen Elizabeth, from The Year 1571 to 1596*, William Murdin (ed.), London: William Bowyer, 1759, pp. 669-75; the manuscript is calendared in *Calendar of the Manuscripts of the Most Hon. the Marquis of Salisbury*, 24 vols, London: Historical Manuscripts Commission, 1883-1976, 4, p. 485.

4 Ch[ristopher] Marl[owe], *The Tragicall History of D. Faustus*, London: Thomas Bushell, 1604, sig. $E2^{r}$; Thomas Nashe, *Have with you to Saffron walden. Or, Gabriell Harueys Hunt is vp*, London: Iohn Danter, 1596, sig. $C4^{r}$; Thomas Nashe, *Nashes Lenten Stuffe*, London: N.L. and C.B., 1599, sig. $I4^{v}$; Thomas Robinson, *The Anatomy of the English Nvnnery at Lisbon in Portvgall*, London: Robert Mylbourne and Philemon Stephens, 1622, sig. C^{r}-C^{v}; John Gee, *The Foot out of the Snare: with a Detection of Svndry Late practices and Impostures of the Priests and Iesuits in England*, London: Robert Milbourne, 1624, sigs $G2^{v}$-$G3^{r}$; Thomas Middleton, *A Game at Chesse*, Ghedruckt in Lydden: Ian Masse, 1624, sig. H^{r}; John Taylor, 'Gods Maniford Mercies in these miracvlovs deliverances of our Church of *England*, from the yeare 1565 vntill this present, 1630. particularly and briefly Described', in *All the Workes of Iohn Taylor The Water-Poet ... With sundry new Additions, corrected, reuised, and newly Imprinted, 1630*, London: James Boler, 1630, 3rd sequence, pp. 142-6 ($Mmm6^{v}$-8^{v}). The poem's running title is 'The Churches Deliuerances'. See stanza 13 (p. 145, $Mmm8^{r}$).

5 William Shakespeare, *The Most Excellent Historie of the Merchant of Venice*, London: T. Heyes, 1600. This is the argument of S.L. Lee, 'The Original of Shylock', *The Gentleman's Magazine*, 246 (Feb. 1880), 185-200.

6 Cecil Papers 28, fol. 11: Sara Lopez to Elizabeth, [Aug. 1594].

7 A 1571 survey claims that Lopez 'came into this realme xij yeares past to get his lyvinge by physycke': *Returns of Aliens Dwelling in the City and Suburbs of London from the Reign of Henry VIII. to that of James I*, R.E.G. Kirk and Ernest F. Kirk (eds), 4 parts, Aberdeen, The Huguenot Society of London, 1900-08, 2, p. 10.

8 See Sidney Lee's standard biographical entry in *DNB* (Dr Roderigo Lopez).

9 Kirk and Kirk (eds), *Returns of Aliens*, 1, p. 365.

10 Ibid., 3, p. 342.

11 Ibid., 2, p. 10.

12 Ibid., 2, p. 319.

13 Lopez is 'a Portingale, fauourably retained in the Queenes Maiesties house of long time, as one of her Phisitians', while his collaborators are 'Portingals, lately reconciled to the seruice of the king of Spaine, and yet colourably residing and resorting into this Realm' (*Trve Report*, $A.iiij.^{r}$). Lopez was 'of late yeeres allured to doe seruice secretly to the King

of Spaine, which hee did by the meanes of one Manuel Andrada a Portingale' and also 'by Roderoquo Marques a Portingale that was employed by the King of Spaine in such purposes' (A.iiij.^{v}). The letter that critically implicated Lopez was carried 'by one Gomez Dauila a Portingale, by order of Doctor Lopez' (B.ij.^{r}).

[14] See Cecil Roth, '5. The case of Thomas Fernandes before the Libson Inquisition, 1556. From the papers of the late Lucien Wolf' in *The Jewish Historical Society of England: Miscellanies part II*, Paulton, Somerset and London: Jewish Historical Society of England, 1935, 32-56.

[15] For the case see file in PRO, Chancery [C] 24/250 [documents relating to Mary May vs Ferninando Alvares and Alvaro de Lyma, 1593]; and entries in PRO, C33/87, fol. 389^{v} [15 Oct. 1594]; PRO, C.33/94, fols 129^{r}-130^{r} [13 June 1598]; PRO, C33/94, fol. 822^{r} [14 June 1599]. This case is discussed in C.J. Sisson, 'A Colony of Jews in Shakespeare's London', *Essays and Studies*, 23 (1938), 38-51, and referred to in Charles Meyers, 'Dr Hector Nuñez: Elizabethan Merchant', *TJHSE*, 28 (1984), 129-31 (p.131, n. 3). For related documents see C3/246/33 [Nuñez vs May, 1591-1596]. In the interests of (admittedly false) consistency I have standardised the spelling of names in my account, although not in quotations from archival documents.

[16] PRO, C24/250.

[17] Ibid.

[18] Ibid.

[19] On Nuñez, see Meyers, 'Dr Hector Nuñez'.

[20] PRO, C24/250.

[21] *Calendar of Letters and State Papers relating to English affairs preserved in, or originally belonging to, the Archives of Simancas*, vol. 4, *Elizabeth 1587-1603*, Martin A.S. Hume (ed.), London: HMSO, 1899, pp. 219-22: Francisco de Valverde and Pedro de Santa Cruz to Bernadino de Mendoza, 27 Feb. 1588, London.

[22] Ibid.

[23] Ibid. This presumably refers to the second voyage of the May-Lewis-Freire syndicate, in the Gift of God, captained by Jeronimo Pardo. In the Chancery case, Pardo is described as 'one of the consort*es* of [the] saide Barnard and Peter and of their complain*antes* [Alvares and de Lyma]': PRO, C24/250.

[24] Conyers Read, *Mr Secretary Walsingham and the Policy of Queen Elizabeth*, 3 vols, Cambridge MA: Harvard UP and Oxford: Clarendon Press, 1925, 3, p. 292.

[25] Rubin, 'The Traffic in Women: Notes on the "Political Economy" of Sex', in *Towards an Anthropology of Women*, Rayna R. Reiter (ed.), New York: Monthly Review Press, 1975, 157-210; Eve Kosofsky Sedgwick, *Between Men: English Literature and Male Homosocial Desire*, New York: Columbia UP, 1985.

[26] Christiane Klapisch-Zuber, *Women, Family, and Ritual in Renaissance Italy*, trans. Lydia Cochrane, Chicago: University of Chicago Press, 1985, pp. 117-18.

[27] William Haughton, *English-men for my money: or, a pleasant comedy, called, A woman will haue her will*, London: W. White, 1616; further editions were printed in 1626 (London: John Norton for H. Perry) and 1631 (London: A. M[athewes] for R. Thrale). References in the main text are to through-line references in *William Haughton's Englishmen For My Money Or A Woman Will Have Her Will*, Albert Croll Baugh (ed.), PhD dissertation, University of Pennsylvania, 1917. For recent discussions of this play, see Jean E. Howard, 'Women, Foreigners, and the Regulation of Urban Spaces in *Westward Ho*', in *Material London ca. 1600*, Lena Cowen Orlin (ed.), Philadelphia: University of Pennsylvania Press, 2000, pp. 150-67 (p. 152); Phyllis Rackin, 'The Impact of Global Trade in *The Merchant of Venice*', *Shakespeare Jahrbuch*, 138 (2002), 73-88 (p. 85 n. 22); and especially Edmund

Campos, 'Jews, Spaniards and Portingales: Ambiguous Identities of Portuguese Marranos', *ELH*, 69 (2002), 599-616.

[28] Haugton, *Englishmen For My Money*, p. 96 ('The Actors names').

[29] At least in the 1616 quarto; thereafter the term reverts, sadly, to 'Portugal'.

[30] G.K. Hunter, 'Elizabethans and Foreigners', in *Shakespeare In His Own Age*, Allardyce Nicoll (ed.), *Shakespeare Survey*, 17 (1964), 37-52 (p. 43).

[31] See especially Lucien Wolf, 'Jews in Elizabethan England', *TJHSE*, 11 (1928), 1-91.

[32] See the genealogical table of the Freire family in Ibid., p.13.

[33] 'el dicho aluaro de lima es fama publica que esta casado con vna sobrina suya'. Archivo General de Simancas, Secretaria de Estado, Legajo 839, fol. 183: 'Deposition of Santa Cruz'; printed in Wolf, 'Jews in Elizabethan England', p. 46. Wolf argues that in fact he was 'only a first cousin of his wife's father'. Ibid., p. 10.

[34] 'Preguntado Diga y declare que gente portuguessa y castellana conosçio este testigo en este tiempo en londres Dixo que conosçio este testigo al doctor Hetor nuñez medico de la rreina de ynglaterra a lo que entendio y a Aluaro de Lima y a geronimo pardo y a Hernan dalbarez y francisco de tapia y a antonio criado e pariente de los suso dichos que todos son portugueses y bibian juntos en va posada y tanbien tubo notiçia y supo que hera pariente de los suso dichos y bibia y estaua con ellos vn bernaldo luis al qual este testigo no conoçio por auer venido a españa en el tiempo queste testigo estubo y llego a londres con vn nauio cargado de mercadurias las quales supo este testigo por ser muy notorio que heran todas de yngleses por que el rretorno que boluio dellas fue sal, passa, y Higo, y vino, y grana cochinilla, especeria, y dinero en talegones metido en los barriles en que yva el higo y en las sacas de la grana cochinilla, y fue anssi mismo notorio que se rrepartio el rretorno que tiene rreferido entre mestre Ricardo mayo y vn su yerno que no le sabe el nonbre y mestre benablo y mestre Vliermames hijo de benjamin gorge y mastre brun y mestre brut y otros que eran dueños de las dichas mercadurias quel dicho bernaldo luis auia traido a españa que valia lo que se cargo en el dicho navio setenta mill ducados largos segun lo que le dixo a este testigo el dicho Hernan dalbarez y asi mismo conoçio a otra camarada de portugueses que se llamaua benjamin gorge y otros nombres desta suerte'. Archivo General de Simancas, Secretaria de Estado, Legajo 839, fol. 183: 'Desposition of Pedro de Santa Cruz', 4 July 1588, Lisbon; printed in Wolf, 'Jews in Elizabethan England', 45-49 (pp. 45-46).

[35] PRO C24/250.

[36] Natalie Zemon Davis, 'Religion and Capitalism Once Again? Jewish Merchant Culture in the Seventeenth Century', *Representations*, 59 (1997), 56-84 (p. 78). See also Davis, 'Arguing with God: Glikl bas Judah Leib, Jewish merchant woman of Hamburg', in *Women on the Margins: Three Seventeenth-Century Lives*, Cambridge, MA: Harvard UP, 1995, pp. 5-62.

[37] Davis, 'Religion and Capitalism', p. 72.

[38] Ibid., p. 73.

[39] Ibid., p. 73.

[40] Ibid., p. 73.

[41] *Eadem*, 'Arguing with God', pp. 12, 13.

[42] See Meyers, 'Dr Hector Nuñez', p.131, ns. 3, 7, 8.

[43] Wolf, 'Jews in Elizabethan England', p. 16.

[44] According to Santa Cruz in his 1588 deposition: 'mestre Vliermames hijo de benjamin gorge'. Ibid., p. 46.

[45] Anthony had been elected to Winchester in 1592, at the age of ten; he was readmitted in 1595, aged 14. See Thomas Frederick Kirby, *Winchester Scholars. A List of the Wardens, Fellows, and Scholars of Saint Mary College of Winchester, near Winchester, commonly*

called Winchester College, London: Henry Frowde and Winchester: P. and G. Wells, 1888, pp. 155, 157; Kirby misreads 'Lopez' as 'Leper'.

[46] Stephanie H. Jed, *Chaste Thinking: the Rape of Lucretia and the Birth of Humanism*, Bloomington, IN: Indiana UP, 1989.

[47] Davis, 'Religion and Capitalism', p. 74.

[48] Amy Louise Erickson, *Women and Property in Early Modern England*, London and New York: Routledge, 1993, p. 18.

[49] Davis, 'Arguing with God', pp. 9, 8.

Chapter 6

Negotiating Favour: the Letters of Lady Ralegh

Karen Robertson

Recent feminist scholarship has begun to analyse the delicate negotiations of Elizabeth I as she constructed for herself a singular position as an unmarried female monarch.[1] One effect of the Queen's own fraught relationship to power led her to insist on the apolitical nature of her Privy Chamber, for her power as a female ruler would be at risk were she to be seen as the leader of a troop of Amazons. For some historians, the Queen's insistence on her singularity has masked the political activities of her court ladies, despite the circulation of stories about conflict in the Privy Chamber during the 1590s, as the Queen's ability to enforce her restrictive code of apolitical femininity on her court ladies began to fracture.[2] These stories of conflict parallel the growing factions at court at large that mark the final decade of the reign. During this period, factions consolidated, one around Essex and the other around a Ralegh-Cecil axis, though the alignments were by no means fixed. In 1597 Henry Howard, in his function as go-between for King James VI of Scotland and Robert Cecil, devoted some lines in his letters to describing the political participation of Elizabeth Ralegh (née Throckmorton), Sir Walter Ralegh's wife: 'The League is very strong between Sir Walter Raleigh and my Lady Shrewsbury and Sir Walter Raleigh's wife'.[3] Howard also assessed Lady Ralegh's capacity: 'Much hath been offered on all sides to bring her into the privy chamber to her old place, because she is a most dangerous woman, and full of her father's inventions; *sed canunt surde* [but they sing to a deaf woman]'.[4] He wrote with satisfaction of the Queen's indifference to the persuasions of Lady Ralegh's supporters. For Henry Howard, so concerned with the antiquity of his lineage and resentful of Elizabeth I's failure to advance him, 'invention' was the mark of dangerous novelty.[5] Yet at the same time, his comments make clear the significance and desirability of a place in the Privy Chamber for, in an era of personal monarchy, proximity to the Queen's body is a crucial conduit to power.

Elizabeth Ralegh, the only daughter of Sir Nicholas Throckmorton and Anne Carew, began her career at court in November 1584, when she was sworn to the Privy Chamber.[6] Her mother's family, the Carews, were long-established gentry in Surrey,[7] while the Throckmortons, like the Tudors themselves, were relative newcomers. The Throckmortons claimed their high status through a tenuous familial link to Queen Katherine Parr, who had acknowledged Nicholas Throckmorton as a first cousin and had taken him into her household as a page.[8] Queen Elizabeth later employed her stepmother's cousin as ambassador to France and his wife as a Lady of the Household.[9] Sir Nicholas was sufficiently prominent that when he was taken ill and died suddenly after a dinner at the house of Robert Dudley, earl of Leicester, he was rumoured to have been poisoned. The death of Elizabeth Throckmorton's father in 1571 when she was six, potentially a disaster for his children, provided the opportunity for a second familial connection to Tudor royalty through the provident remarriage of her mother to Adrian Stokes. He was the widower of Frances Brandon, granddaughter of Henry VII; his royal step-daughter Mary Grey briefly joined his household, though she expected little from him after his remarriage.[10] Thus, for a brief time in childhood after her mother's remarriage, Elizabeth Throckmorton lived as stepsister to the heiress presumptive to the throne of England.[11]

In 1584 at the instigation of her brother Arthur, Elizabeth Throckmorton was taken into the Queen's Privy Chamber.[12] There, she joined a cohort of younger courtiers that included Robert Cecil, born in 1563, Elizabeth Brooke, daughter of Lord Cobham, born in 1565, and Robert Devereux, born in 1567. For this younger generation, the Queen's ageing and approaching death were self-evident. Robert Cecil's steady rise and marriage to Elizabeth Brooke in 1589 and Robert Devereux's jump into the Queen's favour eclipse any mention of Elizabeth Throckmorton's activities as a Maid-of-Honour until the scandal of her secret marriage and the birth of a child to Sir Walter Ralegh precipitated her imprisonment in the Tower in 1592. She was exiled from court to Ralegh's estate, Sherborne in Dorset, where her second child Walter, called Wat, was born in 1593. Not content with this withdrawal to the country after Ralegh's reinstatement to his position in 1597, she began, as Howard's letter attests, to press for her own return to the Privy Chamber.[13] Her refusal at this stage to submit to the decision of the ruler reveals a stubborn determination to maintain a position of influence, a persistence evident throughout her life.

Entrance into the Privy Chamber put women of prominent families in closest proximity to the Queen, a position of access to her ear and favour. Attendance upon the Queen also had the advantage of favourably placing young single women in circulation in the marriage market at court, though the Queen's notorious reluctance to see her ladies marry caused some difficulties. Marriage in the final decade of her reign seemed particularly fraught, in part because the fertility of the maids made only too apparent the discrepancy between the mask of the ever youthful virgin Queen and the ageing body beneath, however much representational efforts denied that fact.

The young women who entered the Privy Chamber as Maids of Honour performed minor domestic tasks, entertained the Queen and, being young and marriageable, amplified the Queen's display of virginity.[14] She used her ladies as elements in her own decorative self-presentation, rather as a *corps de ballet* surrounds and presents the prima ballerina. For example, for one reception of the Dutch ambassador, the ladies and the Queen appeared all in white.[15] In the 1590s, as the Queen aged, the discrepancy between her putative nubility and the actual fertility of her ladies became a gap difficult to disguise. During this time stories circulated about conflict in the Privy Chamber.[16] Bridget Manners secretly married Robert Tyrwhit in the summer of 1594; Elizabeth Vernon secretly married the earl of Southampton in 1598; and Mary Fitton was seduced by the earl of Pembroke, who refused to marry her.[17]

Elizabeth Throckmorton's liaison with Sir Walter Ralegh and the secret birth of a child was the first of these court scandals of the 1590s. Not only did she marry secretly, but also she gave birth to a child at her brother's house and then returned to her position as a Maid-of-Honour. Sir Walter had attempted to disguise the connection by lying about it to Sir Robert Cecil. After the child was shown to Ralegh at Durham House in May, rumour became so extensive that finally in July Elizabeth Throckmorton and her husband were sent to the Tower, where they were imprisoned in separate quarters.[18] Her betrayal of the Queen was never forgiven.

Biographers of Queen Elizabeth have tended to attribute such reactions to feminine jealousy. Edward Thompson's psychological comment gives the twentieth-century gloss: 'Her hatred of everything sexual was pathological'.[19] Instead of presuming that Elizabeth's reactions can simply be explained by resorting to a set of misogynist presumptions about jealousy and competition between women over men, one must consider the particular injury embedded in Elizabeth Throckmorton's deception of her mistress. With the Queen's increasing age and loss of fertility, the marriage of any of her ladies made pointed the loss of one of her major diplomatic strategies: the dynastic marriage. While the Queen's reaction to the secret marriages of Essex to Frances Walsingham and of

Southampton to Elizabeth Vernon registers indignation, her punishment of these ladies was not as long lasting as that of Elizabeth Throckmorton. In the former cases, the marriages violated the Queen's position as protector and paternal substitute – the final arbiter of marriage. Charlotte Merton explains the Queen's anger about the flouting of her authority when the daughters of prominent households married in secret:

> Personal preference, expressed in the form of secret marriages and illegitimate children, created financial chaos for the families of both parties anywhere in the social scale, but it took on even greater significance when the huge estates and reputation of a leading aristocratic family were in question, and the queen herself had been made to look foolish.[20]

In short, aristocratic marriages during the early modern period formed and cemented political alliances; Elizabeth was, therefore, careful to control the marriages of those closest to her.[21]

In the case of Elizabeth Throckmorton, the Queen's namesake, though she was not a major heiress her marriage to Ralegh engendered an even greater animus. Orphaned in 1592 by the deaths of her mother and of her stepfather, she had no protectors other than her brother and uncle. At twenty-five, with little property to her name, she had served in the Privy Chamber for seven years and may have seemed dedicated to a life of virginity like the Queen, perhaps ready to emulate a constant servitor like Mary Radcliffe who had died in service, unmarried. Elizabeth Throckmorton's choice of reproduction and marriage was a direct challenge to the Queen's assertion of the virtues of single blessedness. A further violation lay in the duplicity of her return to her position after the birth of a child. The action violated the intimacy of the Privy Chamber and her bond to the Queen. She insulted her monarch by living a lie for months. Finally, by her return after parturition, she exposed the Elizabethan's court display of virginity as simply a performance, thus casting a shadow on the Queen's own claims of virginity.[22]

Elizabeth Throckmorton's first extant letter, written from the Tower during her imprisonment in the autumn of 1592, is remarkably unrepentant over her violation of the Queen's trust. She wrote to Sir Moyle Finch and his wife, thanking them for both medicine and advice. At the core of her letter is her assertion of devotion to Sir Walter Ralegh:

> I asur you treuly I never desiared nor never wolde desiar my lebbarti with out the good likeking [sic] ne advising of Sur WR; hit tis not this in

> prisonment if I bought hit with my life that shuld make me thinke hit long if hit shuld doo him harme to speke of my delivery.[23]

That devotion was to structure the rest of her life. Supplementary to that devotion, she set out her plans for the management of her return to court.

In this letter she displays her intimate knowledge of court hierarchy and the meaning of access to the monarch. She chose her correspondents carefully. Lady Finch was the daughter of Sir Thomas Heneage who, as Vice Chamberlain of the court, would have administrative responsibility for the conduct of the Privy Chamber.[24] The Finches' assurance of the sympathy of their father gave Lady Ralegh the confidence to write a letter of exculpation to Heneage in the full expectation that he would show it to the Queen, a delicate writing exercise with a double audience: 'I thank for your advis to wryt to Mr. vis-Chambarlin: I will parform hit to moro in such sort as hee may shoo hit the q*ueen*: I can most willingly wryt to him wher I assur my selfe of helpe'.[25] She confessed that her previous epistolary task, a letter to the Lord Chamberlain Hunsdon, the Queen's cousin, had been more inhibited: 'Sinc I have wrytten to me L*ord* Chambarlin wher I much hope for non: but so must I be reuled [ruled]'.[26] She noted briefly that Sir Robert Cecil's predictions in the matter of the length of her imprisonment were inaccurate: 'but Sur R.S. [Cecil] was somwhat deseved in his Judgment in that and hit may be hee findeth his error'.[27] This letter makes clear that Elizabeth Throckmorton considered herself responsible for the management and protection of her own position. Separated from Sir Walter in the Tower, ill, alone, and disgraced, she assessed her friends, wrote letters, and formulated strategies for her release. At this crisis point in her life she drew support by mobilising allies and utilising kinship networks.

Her brief mention of Sir Robert Cecil in the letter registers her major court connection, a personal friendship with Cecil, evidently formed during her seven years at court prior to her marriage and registered by a decade-long correspondence with him.[28] The correspondence is unusual in its informality, intimacy and playfulness, and contrasts with the more formal letters of petition by other women to Robert Cecil and his father, Lord Burghley, which are preserved in the archives at Hatfield House. Lady Ralegh's work in maintaining the Cecil connection was a crucial element in the political manoeuvres that led to Sir Walter Ralegh's return to his old position as Captain of the Queen's Guard in 1597.

The importance of Lady Ralegh's correspondence with Cecil, which forms one strand of the political pressures and tactics that led to Ralegh's re-instalment to royal favour, becomes all the more apparent when read in the context of the shifting political configurations of the last decade of Elizabeth's reign. The deaths of Leicester in 1587 and Walsingham in 1590, and the disgrace of Ralegh, removed from the court the dominant figures who had balanced the caution of William Cecil with a more belligerent Protestantism. Their absence made space for the remarkable rise of the earl of Essex, a figure whose meteoric tragedy tends to obscure the steady consolidation of power by the less dazzling Sir Robert Cecil, who was elevated to the Privy Council in 1591, and took on his father's tasks as Secretary of State, an office to which he was formally appointed in 1596.[29] Anticipating the Queen's death, Cecil dangerously opened a secret correspondence with the man he expected and intended to succeed to the throne, James VI of Scotland.[30] Meanwhile, Ralegh was forced to manoeuvre for a return to court. To return to his old position Ralegh needed both a coup of some sort and the support of Essex and Robert Cecil. At this time, when Ralegh was engaged in exploits abroad, notably the voyage to Guiana in 1595 and the attack on Cadiz in 1596, Elizabeth Ralegh maintained her connection with Robert Cecil through her correspondence.

Her first extant letter to Cecil displays a remarkable trust in him, for it alludes covertly to the death of the Queen. In the letter written from Sherborne in February 1594, she thanks Cecil for a gift, a set of tables, engravings or paintings with both words and an image. Skilled in the verbal games of the court, Lady Ralegh found comfort in the riddle enclosed with the gift: 'I reseved our tabells of no less rare device then the sentans within was cumforttabell'.[31] The gift itself, from a recently elevated Privy Councillor to a disgraced former Maid-of-Honour, was a signal of Cecil's favour, which she matched with her veiled anticipation of the death of the Queen:

> If faith wear broken with mee I was yet farr a way, but I feare that my mistris, if all hartes weare opene and all desiars knowne, might without so gret curiosetye of desciphering reed her owne desteni in a playne alphebett, but wee ar both great belevars, and therin we flatter our seuleus and nurishe our owne mindes with what wee would.[32]

The line is so obscure that A.L. Rowse attributes the letter to Sir Walter Ralegh.[33] That the letter is her own is suggested by the characteristic difficulty that she had with spelling. 'Curiosetye' is begun with the three letters 'cau', then crossed out and begun again.[34]

Further evidence of her composition is the allusion in the phrase 'if all hartes weare opene and all desiars knowne'. This echo of a familiar text, the opening collect of the Holy Communion service in the *Book of Common Prayer*: 'Almighty God, unto whom all hearts be open, all desires known and from whom not secrets are hid', which is not an abstruse reference. While Lady Ralegh had an educated italic hand, her letters demonstrate no evidence of wide reading and contain no other literary allusions. The overt meaning, invoking the opening lines of the collect for purity, prays for an end to rancour, a perfectly appropriate wish on the part of an estranged subject and amplifies her insistence that if faith were broken, she was far away from such an act: true, 'I was yet farr a way'. Yet the line shifts from that decorous wish to a more disturbing suggestion. The allusion momentarily situates the Queen in the god-like vantage of the creator, a necessity for omnipotence that she then tartly dismisses by pointing out that the Queen might read her own destiny in a 'playne alphebett'. While the plain alphabet that the Queen might read is overtly the loyalty of her former servant, a second alphabet that she must learn to decipher is the inevitable approach of her own death. This riddling hint at the Queen's mortality, a natural fact only too apparent to the Maids of Honour, signals Lady Ralegh's trust in her correspondent. The generalisation of the final clauses, 'but wee ar both great belevars, and therin wee flatter our seulevs and nurishe our owne mindes with what wee would' is an unusual formulation in her letters, and again offers a riddle, in the obscurity of the pronoun reference. With 'we' she seems to be describing the optimism the Raleghs felt about a return to favour, but she may also be aligning herself with the Queen, in identifying shared tendencies toward wishful interpretations.

The second half of her letter encases a request for Cecil's help in dissuading Ralegh from his plans to sail to Orinoco. 'Now sir, for the rest, I hope you will rather draw Sir Walter towards the East than help him forward toward the sunset, if any respect to men or love to him be not forgotten'. In imagining an alliance between Ralegh and Cecil, she deftly subordinates her own heterosexual bond with her husband to the homosocial bond between the former favourite and the rising Privy Councillor. Cecil is to be the lodestone to draw Sir Walter back to the court and away from his projects to sail westwards. She punches the compliment home with a reminder about the gratitude owed to her husband. She confirms her intimacy with Cecil with a joke about councellors, a sly glance at his recent appointment. 'But eueri monthe hath his flouer and eueri seusan his contentment, and you greate counselares ar so full of new councels as you are steddi in nothing'. Her playful mockery of great men manages to conjoin both her husband and Cecil in a comic deflation and masks gently the wound of Ralegh's continued exclusion from the Council. Only at the end of the letter does she temporarily fall into the conventional rhetorical posture of the disgraced lady: 'We poor souls that hath bought sorrow at a high price desiar and can be plesed with the same'.

Her request that Cecil dissuade her husband from his adventures to the West failed and Ralegh sailed to Guiana. During the six months of that voyage, Elizabeth Ralegh wrote three times to Cecil.[35] In her first letter after Ralegh's departure, dated March 1595, she made an unusually formal tribute to Cecil's friendship: 'Amoungest many vertues hit is not your least to be a cumfort to the greeued, and so ar you to me with your honnorabell and kind lettar'. She further promised 'I shall fly to you in all my cumbars as to the shurest staf I trust to in Sur Wattar's absens'; and greeted Cecil's wife, Elizabeth Brooke, with an acknowledgement of her vulnerability over her separation from Ralegh that signals the intimacy of their friendship:

> I thank my honnorabell mistris for wishing me neer heer, to doo heer sarvis, and to injoy both you companies, I oft wish hit with heer, els, is an hermit's sell most fit for me and my mind at this time, beeing for a tim thus desevered from him that I am.[36]

At the end of the letter, she tucked in the information that she meant to pursue a suit for the money owed her by the earl of Huntington, her inheritance of £500 loaned by her mother years before her marriage.[37]

Ralegh's grand gesture of seeking the gold of Eldorado reverberated through the court. Rowland Whyte reported to his master, Sir Robert Sidney, far from court in Flushing, the reactions to Ralegh's return later in the summer:

> Sir Wal*ter* Ralweys friends doe tell her ma*jes*ty what grate service he hath done [indecipherable] her by the late voiage in discovering the way to bring home the wealth of India and in making known to that nation her worthe, her justice. he hath brought hither a supposed prince and lefte hostages in his place; the q*ueen* giving good eare unto them.[38]

These reverberations of court gossip signal the excitement and expectation surrounding Ralegh's voyage, even though the promises of gold came to nothing. In July 1596, while Ralegh was on the voyage to Cadiz, Lady Ralegh defended him to Cecil. Reporting to Cecil the return of Ralegh's lieutenant from a second voyage to Guiana, she promised 'I will sende then on*e* to them: that you may knoo what thay have broute: witch cannot bee ani thing as I thinke much worthe, for that the spanniardes ar allredi possessid in gueano'.[39] She closed the letter with a bitter defence: 'Thus, sur, you heer your poour absente frindes fortune: who, if hee had bin as will credited in his reportes and knooleges as hit simmethe the spanniardes wear, thay had not now bin poscisars [possessors] of that plas'.[40] The success of the Cadiz expedition, despite the failure to secure the treasure fleet, reconciled Ralegh and Essex and, during the spring of 1597, Essex and Ralegh were reported to be in secret counsel with Sir Robert Cecil.[41] In June 1597, Ralegh was restored as Captain of the Guard. The first element in restoring favour at court had succeeded, and Lady Ralegh now began to press for her own return to court.

In the period before and after Ralegh's reinstatement as Captain of the Guard, power relations between Ralegh, Cecil, and Essex shifted and realigned.[42] Essex remarkably had served as godfather to the first, secret child of Ralegh and Elizabeth Throckmorton. During the years of Ralegh's disgrace, Essex was the Queen's prime favourite. In 1596, quarrels broke out during the expedition of Cadiz over command and strategy, but these were soon patched up.[43] The honour earned at Cadiz opened the way for Cecil to piece together a wary triumvirate in the spring of 1597, with dinners and a performance of *Richard II*, and Cecil brokered Ralegh's restoration to his old position as Captain of the Guard.[44] Yet, conflicts soon arose among the three, in part because after 1597, the Queen used Ralegh to check the ambitions of Essex. Ralegh's suit for Cobham to succeed to the Wardenship of the Cinque Ports was successful and Essex's support of Robert Sidney failed.[45] Yet Ralegh's ambitions too were thwarted. He was never elevated to the Privy Council and, despite his desire for the Vice-Chancellorship of the duchy of Lancaster, was granted only the Governorship of Jersey, far from court. Paradoxically, the fall of Essex damaged Ralegh irreparably. Not only was he depicted by Cecil to James VI as an enemy to Essex, but also the earl's death set him in direct competition with Cecil for control over the succession.[46]

Throughout these years of fluctuating political alliances, Elizabeth Ralegh's correspondence with Sir Robert Cecil did much to nourish the Cecil-Ralegh connection. The teasing intimate friendship of her first letter marks the rest of her correspondence with Cecil. Her greetings to Cecil are also contained in her husband's letters.[47] She was also sufficiently confident to announce in a postscript to one of Ralegh's letters that she forgave all quarrels: 'Bess returns yow her best wishes notwithstanding al quarrels'.[48] Without a hint of self pity, in 1600, she gaily reported the damage to Durham House caused by a fire.[49] In a letter of 25 November 1601, she announced she would serve as godparent to Sir John Throckmorton's child, if Cecil would do so as well.[50] Most significantly, Cecil sent his son Will to her household in 1600, a sure sign of his bond of friendship.[51]

The cheer and ease of Lady Ralegh's letters are very unlike the formal petitionary letters that Cecil received in his position as Secretary of State. Only one letter hints at difficulty in her relationship with Cecil, the stiff formal apology that Lady Ralegh wrote concerning her conflict with Lady Cobham.[52] Other than this, there is no evidence of the rage that Henry Howard attributes to her in his letters. Presumably Howard assumed that Robert Cecil shared his dislike of Elizabeth Ralegh's energy and forcefulness. In an insulting metaphor that elevates Ralegh's wife to the presidency of the Durham chapter of atheists. Howard urged Cecil to inform the Queen 'what cannons are concluded in the chapter of Durham where Rawley's wife is president'.[53] He continued:

> His wife, as furious as PROSERPINA with failinge of that restitution in Court which flatterie had moved her to expecte bendes her whole witts and industrie to the disturbance of all motions, by councell and encouragement that may disturbe the possibilitie of others' hopes, since her owne cannot be secrid.[54]

Howard's epithet, Proserpina, glances sideways at rumours of Ralegh's atheistic leanings and names his wife as consort of the ruler of the underworld. For a misogynist reactionary like Howard, Lady Ralegh's gender made her an easy and useful target; Cecil, however, seems to have made no defence of the woman who was supervising his son.

Elizabeth Ralegh's apology to Cecil and her dislike of Lady Cobham raise as yet unanswerable questions about the political activities of women in the factional struggles over the succession.[55] The matter of the quarrel between Lady Ralegh and Lady Cobham is overshadowed by the far greater matter of their husbands' trial for treason and the death sentences imposed upon them in the early months of James I's reign. Just before Ralegh's scheduled execution in November 1603, Elizabeth Ralegh wrote again to her friend, Sir Robert Cecil. The letter is unusual. The language, which petitions Cecil to intercede for Ralegh's life, is more formal than her earlier letters, but the presentation is even more intimate. Written on a half sheet of paper, the letter is folded repeatedly to create a tiny packet, one that could fit into the palm of the hand. After the seals are broken, the letter requires multiple unfolding, rather like a miniature, acting as an epitome or a material embodiment of her emotions sent to him. The presentation of the letter in this manner emphasises the depth of grief she reveals to him in the formal rhetoric of her invocation: 'If the greved teares of a unfortunat woman may resevef [receive] ani fafor, or the unspekeabell sorros of my ded hart may resevef ani cumfort, then let my sorros cum before you'.[56]

When the crisis of immediate execution was averted, Elizabeth Ralegh energetically engaged in the defence of her property. Thrust into a legal limbo, as the wife of a legally dead man who yet breathed, she chose to share Ralegh's imprisonment in the Tower, though she was free to come and go. She remained steadfastly loyal to her husband and bore Ralegh a third son in 1604.[57] Despite the legal ambiguity of her status as wife of a breathing dead man, in defending her property, she drew on the conventional stereotype of the petitioning widow with orphaned children, in one last letter to Robert Cecil. While the opening is formal and formulaic,

> As it hath plesed your Lordshept hetherto to be our only cumfort in our lamentabell misfortuns, so I most humbly beseich your Lordhsept, both in cumpassion and Justes, to speke one word to me Lord Admerall not to take from us by strong hand that which his magisti hath geven us for our relife[58]

the formality is not sustained as the letter turns to criticise the earl of Nottingham. In assessing Nottingham's profit from the fall of Ralegh – he had been granted Ralegh's patent for wine-licenses and threatened to claim the arrears[59] – she is tart. 'I might have hoped that me L*ord* Admerall (if wee might hope for ani thing from any leving man) would rather have geueng us sumthing Back agayne of his great porcion'. This letter unusually is endorsed with the names of eighteen other women and may signal her mobilisation of her female kin links for defence of a widow's property.[60] Some of her tartness was also directed at her husband. Sir Walter voiced a private complaint to Robert Cecil, now viscount Cranborne. From the Tower, Ralegh bewailed his physical condition and his emotional distress.

> The other [is] that I shalbe made more then weary of my life by her criing and bewayling, who will return in post when shee heares of your lordships departure and nothing don. She hath alreddy brought her eldest sonn in one hand and her sutting [sucking] child in another, criing out of her and their destruction, charging me with unnaturall negligence and that, having provided for myne own life, I am without sense and compassion of theirs.[61]

In this private complaint, Ralegh attempted to align Cecil with him in a masculine alliance against the tears and complaints of railing women. Lady Ralegh also managed a meeting with Cecil, which seems to have been disappointing, for the long correspondence ceases.

Although her connection to Cecil was insufficient to protect Sherborne from the demand of Robert Carr for the property, Lady Ralegh did receive a £8000 grant and an annuity of £400.[62] She and her son Carew never ceased in their persistent claims on the property. She can be seen challenging regal authority in her son Carew's description of her in his *Brief Relation* in 1659. 'The Lady Ralegh with her children humbly and earnestly petitioning the King for compassion on her and hers, could obtain no other answer from him but that he mun have the land, he mun have it for Car'. The King's rejection precipitates a dramatic and theatrical gesture.

> She being a woman of very high spirit and noble birth and breeding, fell down upon her knees, and in the bitterness of spirit beseeched God Almighty to look upon the justness of her cause and punish those who had so wrongfully exposed her and her poor children to ruin and beggary.

Carew drives home the point that the plea was more than satisfactorily answered: 'What hath happened since to that royal Family is too sad and disastrous for me to repeat, and yet too visible not to be discerned'.[63] The sober satisfactions of a long-term vengeance reverberate in the son's description.

The catastrophe of Ralegh's sentence for treason forced his wife into political gestures more public than her letters to Robert Cecil. On the stage of the court she enacted her pleas for pity and property. Yet these gestures were an intensification, not an alteration, of the strategic alignments she nurtured in her letters in the first decade of her marriage. In 1605 after the exposure the Gunpowder Plot, the government set a watch on her at Sherborne when she ordered the armour scoured.[64] That official anxiety over her potential as a threat to security registers the gravity with which the political energy of a highly placed woman was viewed.

Notes

My thanks to James Daybell, Susan Frye, Michael Hobbs, Benjamin Kohl, Elizabeth Robertson and Paul Russell for their insightful readings of drafts of this essay.

1 The major work is Susan Frye, *The Competition for Representation*, New York: OUP, 1993. See also Carole Levin, *The Heart and Stomach of a King: Elizabeth I and the Politics of Sex and Power*, Philadelphia: University of Pennsylvania Press, 1994; Constance Jordan, 'Woman's Rule in Sixteenth-Century British Political Thought', *RQ*, 40, 3 (Autumn, 1987), 421-51.

2 See Pam Wright 'A Change in Direction: the Ramifications of a Female Household, 1558-1603', in David Starkey (ed.), *The English Court from the Wars of the Roses to the Civil War*, Harlow: Longman, 1987, pp. 147-72. Charlotte Merton, in her unpublished thesis 'The Women Who Served Queen Mary and Queen Elizabeth: Ladies, Gentlewomen and

Maids of the Privy Chamber, 1553-1603', unpublished PhD thesis, University of Cambridge, 1993, recognises the political potential of the Privy Chamber women. See especially chapter 6, 'Influence and Politics', pp. 154-202.

[3] Henry Howard served as a surrogate for Robert Cecil and wrote to James VI's courtiers, in this case Edward Bruce: *The Secret Correspondence of Sir Robert Cecil with James VI, King of Scotland*, (ed.) Lord Hailes, Edinburgh: A. Millar, 1766, p. 68.

[4] Ibid., p. 68.

[5] Linda Levy Peck, *Northampton: Patronage and Policy at the Court of James I*, London: George Allen & Unwin, 1982, p. 21.

[6] The major biographical source has been A.L. Rowse, *Ralegh and the Throckmortons*, London: Macmillan, 1962, p. 106. Rowse discovered her brother Arthur's diary which records details of her first pregnancy, the birth of a son Damerei, and her marriage to Ralegh. See Anna Beer's recent work, *My Just Desire* (London: Macmillan, 2003).

[7] The Carew family tombs can be seen in the parish church beside the family estate at Beddington: Bridget Cherry Smith and Nikolaus Pevsner, *The Buildings of England: London 2: South*, Harmondsworth, Middlesex: Penguin, 1983, p. 640. The Throckmortons were linked to the Tudors via the placement of a maternal grandfather, Sir Nicholas Vaux, in the household of Henry VII's mother, Margaret Beaufort. See Susan E. James, *Kateryn Parr: the Making of a Queen*, Aldershot: Ashgate, 1999, p. 24.

[8] The connection was through a shared grandmother. The Queen's grandmother Elizabeth Parr married Sir Nicholas Vaux, after the death of her first husband, Sir William Parr; her daughter Catherine Vaux was viewed by the Queen as an aunt, and Catherine's seventeen children by Sir George Throckmorton were acknowledged as first cousins: James, *Kateryn Parr*, pp. 23, 24, 44.

[9] Merton, 'Women who Served', p. 173. For a description of the hierarchy of positions within the Privy Chamber, see p. 6. The titles given to the ladies can be confusing. 'Maid' meaning servant could be a term applied to a married Gentlewoman of the Bedchamber or of the Household (p. 10). The portrait of a Lady Throgmorton in court dress may be of Elizabeth Throckmorton's mother, since her husband was given the court appointment as Butler of the Household before he was sent as ambassador to France. See Janet Arnold, *Queen Elizabeth's Wardrobe Unlock'd*, Leeds: W. S. Maney, 1988, p. 134, fig. 285.

[10] Frances Brandon survived the executions of her husband and their daughter, Lady Jane Grey, married her Master of Horse, Adrian Stokes, sixteen years her junior, and lived for a further five years, dying in 1559. Thirteen years later in 1572, Adrian Stokes married Anne Carew, widow of Sir Nicholas Throckmorton. Mary Grey, Frances Brandon's daughter, wrote of her financial situation to William Cecil, 'Of my own I have but twenty pounds and as your lordship knoweth, there is nobody will board me for so little. As for my father-in-law [Stokes], I know he will give me nothing now; for before his marriage I had little; and now I look for less'. Cited in Alison Plowden, *Lady Jane Grey and the House of Suffolk*, London: Sidgwick & Jackson, 1985, pp. 183-84.

[11] Her stepsister established her own household in 1572-3 and died in 1578: Plowden, *Lady Jane Grey*, p. 184.

[12] Her brother's diary records her swearing in as a member of the Privy Chamber in Nov. 1584: Rowse, *Ralegh and the Throckmortons*, 1962, p. 104.

[13] *Secret Correspondence*, p. 68: Howard to Lord Mar.

[14] Merton, 'Women who Served', p. 48.

[15] Rowland Whyte reports the audience of Vereken, the Audientary of Archduke Albert, in 1600: *HMC, Report on the Manuscripts of Lord De L'Isle & Dudley, Preserved at Penshurst Place*, 6 vols, London: HMSO, 1935-66, 2, p. 441.

[16] See, for example, Lady Newdigate-Newdegate, *Gossip From the Muniment Room Being Passages in the Lives of Anne and Mary Fytton, 1574 to 1618*, London: David Nutt, 1897.
[17] Merton, 'Women who Served', p. 139. See also Paul Hammer, 'Sex and the Virgin Queen: Aristocratic "Concupiscence" and the Court of Elizabeth I', *Sixteenth Century Journal*, 30, 1 (2000), 77-97.
[18] The date of the couple's wedding remains obscure. On 10 March 1592, Sir Walter had denied the rumours of marriage, lying to Sir Robert Cecil that he of all men would be the first to know of any marriage (Agnes Latham and Joyce Youings (eds), *The Letters of Sir Walter Ralegh*, Exeter: Exeter UP, 1999, p. 63). Her brother records the birth in his diary on 29 March 1592. The baby was baptised Damerei on 10 April, with Essex and Arthur Throckmorton and his wife as godparents. Elizabeth Throckmorton returned to court on 27 April. Contracts over the marriage settlement are recorded in the diary on 19 May. Just over a week later, on 28 May, the child was shown to Sir Walter. In July the Queen imprisoned the couple (Rowse, *Ralegh and the Throckmortons*, pp. 161-62). When Elizabeth Throckmorton wrote her letter from the Tower to the Finches, she signed it with the initials E. R., indicating her belief in a valid marriage (*HMC*, *Report on the Manuscripts of George Finch, Esq., of Burley-on-the-Hill, Rutland*, 4 vols, London: HMSO, 1913-65, 1, p. 34). Her brother recorded learning of their marriage in November, 1592 (Rowse, *Ralegh and the Throckmortons*, p. 162).
[19] Edward Thompson, *Sir Walter Ralegh*, London: Macmillan, 1935, p. 80.
[20] Merton, 'Women who Served', p. 138.
[21] On arrangement of marriage in aristocratic families see Barbara J. Harris, *English Aristocratic Women, 1450-1550: Marriage and Family, Property and Careers*, New York and Oxford: OUP, 2002, ch. 3.
[22] Rumours about the Queen's giving birth to illegitimate children by Robert Dudley, earl of Leicester, had circulated (Levin, *Heart and Stomach of a King*, p. 76).
[23] *HMC, Finch*, 1, p. 34.
[24] Wright, 'A Change in Direction', p.154.
[25] *HMC, Finch*, 1, p. 34.
[26] Ibid., p. 34.
[27] Ibid., p. 34.
[28] The majority of Lady Ralegh's extant correspondence is at Hatfield House, which I consulted. Unless otherwise indicated, the transcriptions are mine. Her letters have been transcribed and printed by Edward Edwards in his biography of Ralegh, *Sir Walter Ralegh*, 2 vols, London: Macmillan, 1868, 2, pp. 397-414. She and Cecil were of the same generation and began their entry into court service in the same year, 1584. During this year Cecil also travelled abroad in the Netherlands and sent reports back to his father (*DNB*).
[29] For a recent reappraisal of the 1590s see John Guy (ed.), *The Reign of Elizabeth I: Court and Culture in the Last Decade*, Cambridge: CUP, 1995.
[30] *Secret Correspondence*, p. 68.
[31] Hatfield House, Herts, Cecil Papers 2, fol. 50: 8 Feb. 1594.
[32] Ibid.
[33] Rowse, *Ralegh and the Throckmortons*, p. 181.
[34] Cecil Papers 2, fol. 50. Her holograph letter is written with great care and seems copied from a first draft because of the neatness of the hand, far neater than her later bolder hand. Despite copying, she makes mistakes. In addition to the double attempt at 'curiosetye' she crosses out a florid valediction, though the testimony, 'to love and serve you for ever' is still legible. The signature is set very neatly below and close to the body of the letter, unlike her

later signatures that became bolder and larger on the page, though always indented far to the right.

[35] Cecil Papers 31, fols 29, 77, 53.

[36] Ibid., 31, fol. 29.

[37] The letter discussed here is followed in the next month by a recommendation for Arthur Radford (Cecil Papers 31, fol. 77) and in July by a letter supporting the suit of Alexander Brett (Cecil Papers 31, fol. 53).

[38] CKS, De L'Isle MS U1475 C12/4: Rowland White to Sir Robert Sidney, 27 Sept. 1595.

[39] Cecil Papers 43, fol. 20: July 1596.

[40] Ibid., 43, fol. 29: July 1596.

[41] *HMC, De L'Isle & Dudley*, 2, p. 308: Rowland Whyte to Sir Robert Sidney, 3 Jan. 1598.

[42] The sequence can be followed in the letters of Rowland Whyte to Sir Robert Sidney which formed the basis for Thomas Birch's biography of Sir Walter Ralegh, which prefixes *The Works of Sir Walter Ralegh*, London, Dodsley, 1751.

[43] CKS, U1475/C12/116: Rowland Whyte to Sir Robert Sidney, 20 Dec. 1597.

[44] *HMC, De L'Isle & Dudley*, 2, pp. 243, 285-86: Rowland Whyte to Sir Robert Sidney, 5 Nov. 1597, 2 June 1597.

[45] Ibid., 2, p. 258: Rowland Whyte to Sir Robert Sidney, 3 Apr. 1597.

[46] Ibid., 2, pp. 478-79: Rowland Whyte to Sir Robert Sidney, 23 Aug. 1600.

[47] Latham and Youings (eds), *Letters of Sir Walter Ralegh*, p. 221: Oct. 1601.

[48] Comment in the lefthand margin, 13 Aug. 1601. Ibid., p. 206.

[49] Cecil Papers 250, fol. 36: Oct. 1600.

[50] *HMC, Calendar of the Manuscripts of the Most Honourable The Marquess of Salisbury, Preserved at Hatfield House Hertfordshire*, 24 vols, London: HMSO, 1883-1973, 11, p 503: Capt. John Throckmorton to Cecil, 25 Nov. 1601.

[51] Ralegh reports on his health on 27 March 1600, Latham and Youings (eds), *Letters of Sir Walter Ralegh*, p. 188.

[52] Cecil Papers 85, fol. 134.

[53] *BL*, Ms Cotton Titus C. VI, fols 386-92; also in Edwards, *Sir Walter Ralegh*, 2, p. 438. Durham House, Ralegh's London residence, had formerly belonged to the Bishop of Durham.

[54] *Ibid.*

[55] Lady Dorothy Devereux, for example, reported her husband's oaths against the succession of James: *Secret Correspondence*, pp. 31-32. Northumberland was imprisoned in the Tower soon after Ralegh.

[56] Cecil Papers 102, fol. 29: 18[?] Nov. 1603.

[57] Carew Ralegh was baptised on 15 Feb. 1605 at the Chapel Royal of St Peter Ad Vinculam: personal communication, Terry Radley, Sexton of the Chapel Royal.

[58] Cecil Papers 190, fol. 6 [1604].

[59] Rowse, *Ralegh and the Throckmortons*, p. 245.

[60] See Robertson, 'Tracing Women's Connections from a Letter by Elizabeth Ralegh', in Susan Frye and Karen Robertson (eds), *Maids and Mistresses, Cousins and Queens: Women's Alliances in Early Modern England*, New York: OUP, 1999, pp. 149-64.

[61] Latham and Youings (eds), *Letters of Sir Walter Ralegh*, p. 189: July 1605.

[62] Steven W. May, *Sir Walter Ralegh*, Boston: Twayne Publishers, 1989, p. 22.

[63] Carew Ralegh, *A Brief Relation*, London, 1659, p. 7.

[64] Rowse, *Ralegh and the Throckmortons*, p. 251.

Chapter 7

'Suche newes as on the Quenes hye wayes we have mett': the News and Intelligence Networks of Elizabeth Talbot, countess of Shrewsbury (c.1527-1608)

James Daybell

Recent work, by both historians and literary scholars, has recognised the manuscript newsletter as an important means by which news and political information or 'intelligence' was spread throughout the early modern period.[1] Richard Cust and F.J. Levy, in seeking to understand the formation of political attitudes in the period prior to the Civil War, have emphasised the role of newsletters, which circulated with relative freedom from censorship, in the dissemination of political ideas and information from the capital to the provinces. During this period, letters from family and friends, servants and London agents, government and court officials, as well as semi-professional and professional letter-writers, worked in close relation with other non-printed and printed news forms, such as 'separates', libels, corantos, pamphlets, newsbooks, newspapers and oral exchanges.[2] News pamphlets or quartos from the late Elizabethan period, as Paul Voss has shown, often in their titles announced letters as their primary source of information.[3] Harold Love in his work on 'scribal publication' has further detailed how manuscript newsletters were produced, copied and circulated within 'local reading networks'.[4] Other scholars have shown the ways in which reports of the latest political and religious developments abroad were fed back to England through continental correspondence networks. Alan Stewart's work on Francis Bacon and Philip Sidney, for example, details how both men were at the centre of webs of foreign intelligence networks.[5] Scholars, therefore, have a good idea of how different kinds of information were gathered and disseminated, and the kinds of channels and mechanisms through which written news travelled, locally, nationally and internationally.

What is little understood, however, is the nature and extent of women's involvement in these correspondence and news networks.[6] Ian Atherton in an important recent article on 'Manuscript Transmission of News in the Seventeenth Century' offers a very male world of news transmission and readership, one that largely excludes women. According to Atherton, whose own work on news stems from his expertly detailed study of viscount Scudamore, men could draw on a wider range of news sources than women, and the environments in which news flourished and circulated – St Paul's, the Inns of Court, and the royal court – were frequented by men: lawyers, courtiers and merchants. Men were, therefore, the source of news. He further argues that female correspondents 'rarely included even a line of news in their letters', unlike their male counterparts, that newsletters were generally procured by men, and that women may in fact have been 'less interested in news'. To Atherton, 'the private world of the family, not the public world of politics, was seen as the sphere of women'[7] – a dichotomy that this essay seeks to explode.

This depiction of manuscript news and information networks as exclusively male, and confinement of women to an apolitical 'private world', rests rather uneasily with current scholarship on women's political and patronage roles within the family, locality and on a wider national stage. In fact, women at court were at the very centre of where news was exchanged: Anne Talbot (née Herbert) thought the court a place to 'learn' news 'worthey the wrytynge'.[8] Female courtiers were also themselves a forum for news: conduits to the monarch, courtiers and officials, and purveyors of intelligence more generally, intelligence that found its way into the counties through correspondence and by word-of-mouth, and abroad through ambassadors' despatches.[9] Olwen Hufton has argued that 'a court without women is like a body without a nervous system. Women are part of a vital system of communications through which messages are transmitted, channels opened up'.[10]

The study of sixteenth-century women's letter-writing further shows that women participated in a broad range of news-related activities.[11] Women were indeed the recipients of newsletters, and the letters they wrote themselves frequently contained news of family, household and locality, and items of 'national' interest. For example, Margaret Hill wrote regularly from London to her cousin Richard Carnsew in the West Country, keeping him informed of events in the capital, and in one of her letters she enclosed a newsbook and a copy of the earl of Essex's funeral sermon.[12] Likewise, the letters of Frances Seymour and Margaret Clifford to their husbands brim with news from the court and, as Elizabeth McCutcheon has recently shown, Lady Elizabeth Wolley acted as a court commentator for her father and brother when they were based in Surrey.[13] Female correspondents were also central to the maintaining of patronage and kinship relations, and passing on news in letters was one of the chief ways in which these networks were strengthened. During the seventeenth century women were also involved in sending newsletters: during the 1640s women often addressed letters containing important news because their letters were less likely to be confiscated, opened and read;[14] Claire Walker has highlighted the ways in which Ghent Benedictines in the 1650s put their postal services at the disposal of Charles II for delivering royalist mail; and during the early seventeenth century the staunchly Puritan widow, Lady Joan Barrington, regularly received copies of corantos or newsbooks with letters from family and friends.[15]

By way of a detailed case study of the correspondence of Elizabeth Talbot, countess of Shrewsbury (c.1527-1608), herself the recipient of substantial numbers of letters containing news, this essay explores more fully the roles of women within news networks, as gatherers, readers, purveyors and writers of news. In particular, it looks at the types of people who wrote to aristocratic women with news, the nature of the information they supplied, the role of news within a hierarchical society, and the purposes for which it was collected. More broadly, the essay examines the extent to which news was gendered during this period. Did men and women consume different types of news? Was news written differently and made more palatable for women than for men? Whereas women are traditionally seen as 'gossips', peddlers of ephemeral and trifling tittle-tattle, men are described as 'intelligencers', suppliers of information of serious import.[16] I argue in this essay for a rethinking of how we employ the terms 'gossip' and 'intelligence'. This fits in with the work of other feminist scholars who have sought to re-conceptualise a range of seemingly 'female' or 'domestic' and 'household' activities as political. Barbara Harris has argued for the importance of gift-giving, hospitality, marriage arrangement, and placing children as secondary patronage activities; Georgianna Ziegler has read as diplomatic the calligraphy of Esther Inglis; and Susan Frye has highlighted the political significance of needlework and embroidery – one of the tasks most clearly associated as 'feminine' and 'domestic'.[17] This essay's contribution to this re-conceptualising of women's history is the *politicisation* of gossip.

The letter-writing activities of Elizabeth Talbot, countess of Shrewsbury (c.1527-1608), who is probably better known to modern readers as 'Bess of Hardwick', are the best documented of any sixteenth-century aristocratic English woman. Well over 200 of her letters, to and from over 60 correspondents, are extant, many preserved among her own papers, which are held mainly at the Folger Shakespeare Library (X.d.428), and which are distinct from the Shrewsbury/Talbot manuscripts relating to the family of her last husband, George Talbot, seventh earl of Shrewsbury, now kept at Lambeth Palace Library and Longleat.[18] From these surviving letters, Bess of Hardwick, well known to the 'romance, sex and violence' school of history as the indiscrete gossiper to Mary, Queen of Scots about Elizabeth I, and the ambitious dynast who made a career out of marriage, emerges as a serious political operator.[19] Just as Paul Hammer's study of the earl of Essex's secretariat repackages the Elizabethan playboy as a serious contender for the office of Secretary of State, so too this essay repackages the cantankerous Elizabethan matriarch as a woman at the centre of an extensive correspondence, news and intelligence network.[20]

When absent from London, Bess received a stream of letters from family, servants, friends, wider social contacts and semi-professional writers of newsletters, which kept her current with court and national events, and news from the capital: the monarch's health and moods, court progresses, fluctuations in royal favour, appointments to office, parliamentary sessions and aristocratic marriages. Conversely, when at court or absent from one of her residences, she received regular reports from her servants, estate stewards and legal advisors on a range of matters: household and estate management, children and other family members, the numerous legal cases in which she was involved, the progress of her building works, and events within the locality. The countess was also regularly kept up-to-date with the latest religious and political developments in Europe by correspondents who recycled for her the contents of continental newsletters. Hugh Fitzwilliam reporting on the Revolt of the Moriscos informed her: 'may it please [you] ... tunderstand that by l*ett*res of the xxiiiith of the last out of Spayne from a towne bordering upon the mores, sayth that the king hath driven them in to the mountaynes agayne'.[21]

The newsletters received by the countess of Shrewsbury vary greatly both in nature and content. At one extreme, there are letters similar to what Richard Cust has defined as 'pure' newsletters – long detailed letters the sole concern of which was to impart news.[22] A letter from an unknown correspondent, for example, dated January 1569 provided a detailed overview of developments in Europe. It reported that 'the Duke of Alva hathe for the lacke of mony disarmed the moost p*ar*te of his army'; 'the new king of Sweden and the king of denmarke being frendes; they haue set out the duke of Holste*in* w*ith* a good power of suche soldiers bothe horsesmen and footemen as they may well spare'; and 'In France there is a great sturre to let the prince of conde to ioiyne w*ith* the prince of Orange'.[23] The structure of these letters, as with Fitzwilliam's letter of 28 July 1570 (see Figure 7.1), written in 12 or so short paragraphs, each dealing with a different topic, may reflect the way in which news was compiled from different sources – from printed documents, letters and conversations. But also, the formality of the letters, the lack of personal details, the absence of comment or opinion, suggests an intended wider readership. The letters, however, were personal in the sense of being personally addressed to the countess, different from more general newsletters that were directed to her households at Hardwick or Chatsworth.[24] Most letters were addressed to the countess using her name and title, some were addressed merely 'to my lady', and others also specified the place of delivery: Hardwick, Chatsworth and London. While the countess received most of her letters when she was away from her husband, the earl of Shrewsbury, or when he himself was absent, she also received news independently of him when they were together. In like manner, correspondents writing to Lord Lisle in 1530s Calais often sent accompanying letters to Lady Lisle.[25]

At the other extreme, are letters that merely mention news in passing, almost as an afterthought. James Hardwick, in a postscript, reported to his sister, the Lady St Loe: 'My cosyn wylloghbe ys maryed to mr Lytelltons daughter of worcestshyre'; William Cavendish informed his mother in July 1604, 'the erle of Penbrocks mariage is deferred for iii moneths stayed by great p*er*sons as I credibly here'.[26] The majority of letters, however, lie somewhere between these two ends of the spectrum, a mixture of 'public' and 'private' matters, as defined by Erasmus, where news of parliamentary bills sits next to complaints of suffering from attacks of gout.[27] In a letter from her step-son Gilbert Talbot, written from 'the cowrte at Grenewidg' in 1574, news of London and the court is interwoven with more personal concerns:

> ...her ma*jes*tie styrreth litell abrode and since the stay of the navy to sea, here hathe bene all thinges very quieat, and almoste no other taulke but of this late proclamation for apparell w*hi*ch is thought shallbe very severely executed, both here at the cowrte & at London / I haue wrytten to my Lorde of the brute th*at* is here of his beyng sick agayne w*hi*ch I nothing doubte but yt is utterly untrew ... I can not chuse but be sumwhat trobled & yet I consyder the like hathe bene often reported moste falcely and withoute cause, as I beseche god this be / My Lady Cobham asketh daly how yo*u*r La*dyship* dothe, and yesterday prayed me the next tyme I wryt to doe her very hartie comendacons vnto y*our* La*dyship* saying openly she remayneth unto yor la*dyship* as she was wonte as unto her deereste frend:

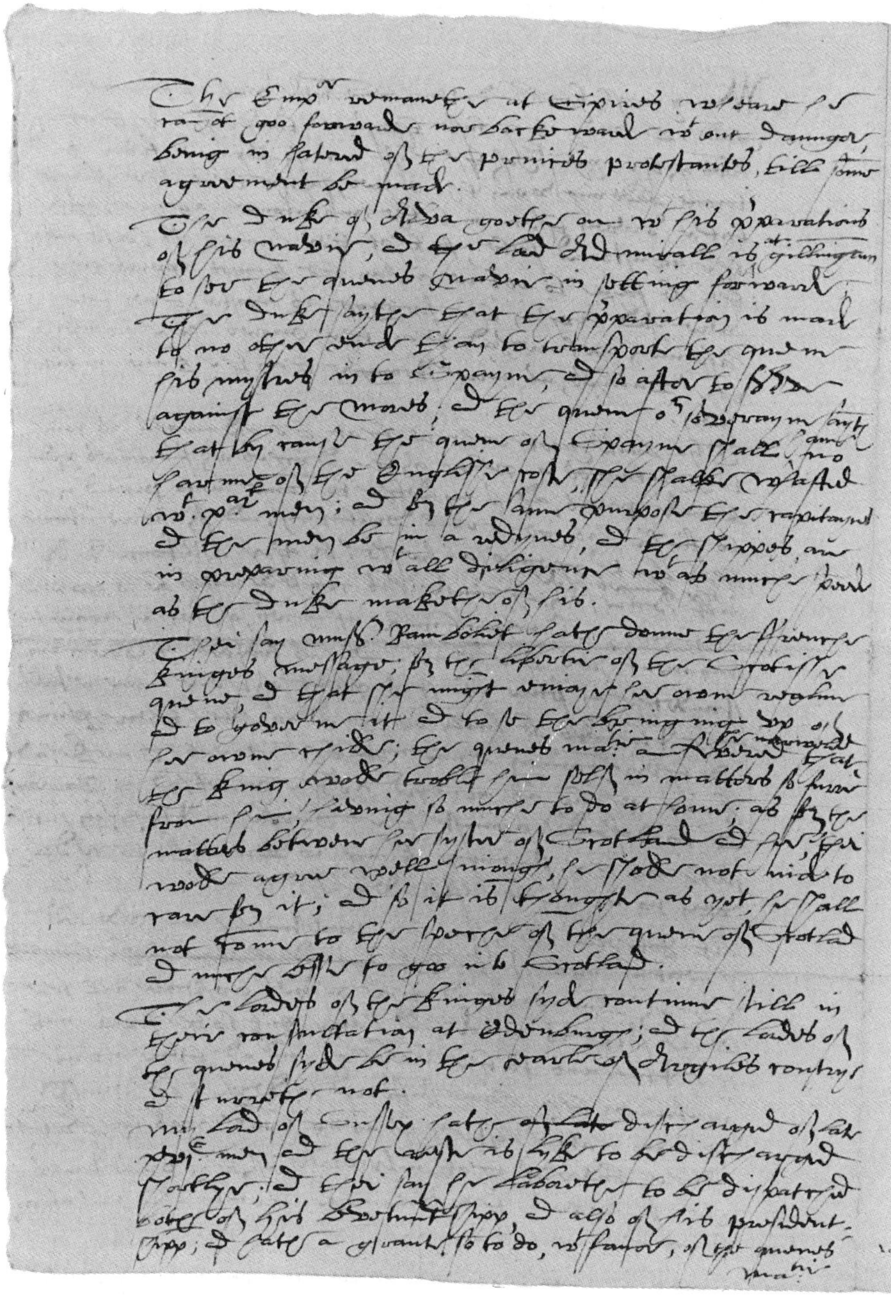

Figure 7.1 Letter from Hugh Fitzwilliam to Elizabeth, countess of Shrewsbury, 28 July 1570

> my La*dy* Lenox hathe not bene at the cowrte since I came / On Wednesday next I truste (god willing) to goe hence towarde Goderidge, and shortely after to be at sheffeld.[28]

This form of mixed or 'informal' manuscript newsletter was the predominant written mode by which news circulated throughout the early modern period, even when printed news forms become more established.[29] Printed materials such as proclamations, bills and sermons were also often enclosed in correspondence to further supplement reports. A letter to the countess written on the 31 August 1570 included, 'the articles of peace concluded and proclaimed through all Fraunce', which the correspondent added were 'in Frenche bycause thei be not at this hower to be had in Englishe, w*hi*ch be translated and in printing'.[30] This in itself suggests not just a superficial acquaintance with current affairs, but rather a well-informed, detailed understanding of political events.

The letters that Bess of Hardwick received represent a distinct stage in the development of the genre, before the increasing professionalisation of newsletters during the seventeenth century, when John Pory was paid £20 a year in the early 1630s for his weekly letters to Lord Scudamore.[31] As far I can establish, Bess appears not to have paid for newsletters, although one of her later correspondents, James Montague, Dean of the Royal Chapel, was bequeathed £20 in her will.[32] For the most part, those who wrote to her about news were family and servants, people who by ties of blood, kinship or service were duty-bound or obligated to write. In reporting news to his mother-in-law, Gilbert Talbot was 'fulfilling' her 'commandement' and 'discharging' his 'duty by wryting';[33] after their return to Dunstable, he and his wife Mary felt called upon to deliver 'Suche newes as on the Quenes hye wayes we have mett'.[34] Duty, however, is only half the explanation: Bess also solicited news. Anne Talbot wrote to her:

> I humbly craue your la*dyships* good openyon of me not to decreasse rememberynge your la*dyships* comandement here to for to wryt to you as often as I coulde, whych nowe In thys plase [Baynard's Castle, London], I shall haue better meanes then I haue had In the country, and ther vpon pressuming to lenghten my letter vpon any occasion.[35]

The transmission of news in these letters flows from social inferior to superior: from son or daughter to mother, from kinsman or kinswoman to aristocratic relative, from servant or agent to mistress, and from client to patroness. Rarely did news travel down the social hierarchy, although occasionally it was passed between equals. As is customary, news in letters from social subordinates is presented couched in a language of deference, familial obedience and service, which allowed the writer and addressee to uphold social decorum. While 'humbly craving' her mother's 'moste honorab*le* and continuall bo*u*nty', Frances Pierrepont conveyed news of an insurrection heard from 'on*e* of the kinges chamber'.[36] William Kniveton, the son of Bess's half sister, Jane, closed a detailed report on enclosure riots in Lincolnshire, the current parliamentary session, and King James's progress to the Isle of White with the phrase, 'Thus being bould to troble yor ho*nour* w*i*th these small matters w*hi*ch are the certaynest newes that I can att this tyme write to yo*u*r ho*nour*'.[37] This concern about the 'certainty' or credibility of news is a recurrent theme of newsletters. An unnamed correspondent prefaced a three-sided letter to Bess on national and international news with the disclaimer:

> Yf it were not for my bounden duetie sake, I wolde be lothe to write, bycause there is so smale certaynetie in occurrences but seing I am bounde to write it is but smale that I see w*ith* my owne eyes, that is worthe writing; and therefore I am forced to supplye by that I do heare; w*hi*ch I write as I do heare by credeble reporte; other wyse I sholde not write at all; and therefore, if I do erre, it is p*ar*donable.[38]

This manner of self-deprecating downplaying of the importance of news, indicative of an awareness of the unreliability of information received second- or even third-hand, is again symptomatic of the deferential nature of the relationship between the newsletter writer and the recipient of his or her letter. Because of the unequal balance of power within the relationship, the letter-writer distances himself from the news in case it is inaccurate, absolving himself from blame in advance so as not to lose favour for supplying incorrect information.

In many ways, news acted as a kind of gift (solicited or otherwise), which helped to cement the relationship between sender and addressee.[39] The supplying of news was a tangible service demonstrating a writer's usefulness as a source of intelligence or information, a service that the female patron was obligated to reciprocate. George Chaworth, a kinsman and legal adviser to Bess, whom he addressed as his 'best patron', reminded her of his last 'intelligence' by way of apology: 'I could not in so short tyme make them fytt for your honours readeinge or heareinge'.[40] He then introduced his suit, which was that she speak to his uncle about his inheritance, beseeching her to stand by him as his 'p*ro*tectress and defender'.[41] Thus, news fitted into the patronage and clientage system as a form of exchange: the trade was information in return for favour.

For much of her news-gathering Bess relied on letters from immediate family, kin, household members and other dependents. Indeed, her female correspondents at court – Mary Scudamore, Frances Cobham, Susan, countess of Kent, Elizabeth Wingfield, and Katherine, countess of Pembroke – were mostly relatives either by blood or marriage. This is not to say, however, that she did not cultivate contacts from wider social groups; these include the aforementioned James Montague, John Lenton who predicted a 'violent death' for Elizabeth I, and Dorothy Lady Stafford, a close friend from early in Bess's court career.[42] Epistolary relationships were developed with these well-placed correspondents precisely because they were at the heart of court and political events; these were people cultivated in the main for their power, influence, and the types of news they could offer.

All too often, the purpose of news appears somewhat nebulous. Interest in news is often vaguely attributed to the 'inquisitiveness' of the country gentry or a desire among the aristocracy to be kept well-informed when absent from London. Newsletters in this sense are treated merely as precursors of newspapers, news a staple to be consumed.[43] More tangible is Jason Scott-Warren's detailed reading of Sir Thomas Cornwallis's 'oulde' man's 'fancye' for 'newes', which he argues stemmed from a 'bookish' interest in his own particular political and religious agenda.[44] With the countess of Shrewsbury, however, one detects a very utilitarian attitude towards news. While news reached her in a continuous stream, it was gathered with particular assiduity at key periods, to serve very specific and practical ends. In this way, her activities in acquiring information and in cultivating useful correspondents more closely resemble those of a government official at the heart of an intelligence network than those of a country gentleman distracted by affairs in the capital. To illustrate this more fully, the remainder of this essay concentrates on three distinct groups of letters, each of which were solicited or written for different ends: first, the letters she received in the 1570s, second, those from the last years of her life, and third, those from court women. From these three case studies, one gets a sense of the kind of news the countess required, the different ways that news worked, and the roles it played in her life.

The largest cluster and most detailed of newsletters survive from the period 1569 to 1574, during which time Bess's then husband, the earl of Shrewsbury, acted as the keeper of Mary, Queen of Scots.[45] At this point, despite her fall from power, the Scottish queen was still very much at the centre of European politics and court intrigue: Mary was implicated in the Rising of the Northern Earls and the Ridolphi Plot, Walsingham intercepted her correspondence, and she was forced to send letters secretly in cipher, letters later found under stones, and even in the staff of a visitor.[46] Given their royal prisoner, there was a real need for the Shrewsburys to keep in touch with mainstream political events both at home and on the continent. During these years, largely spent away from London in Derbyshire, the countess received regular letters from a range of correspondents. Chief among these was Hugh Fitzwilliam, a distant relative. Typical of Fitzwilliam's letters is one dated 28 July 1570, which provides an overview of continental and court news. It reported (without comment or opinion) that the Italians were fully occupied 'with their comon enemye the great Turke'; the Huguenots at La Rochelle had 'p*re*valed greatly against the king'; and the duke of Alva 'goethe on w*ith* his p*re*parations of his navie'.[47] Related to these foreign developments were detailed reports on Mary, Queen of Scots.[48] The second and third sides of the letter reported the French envoy's message from the French King that Mary, Queen of Scots 'might enioye her owne realm and govern it', and that the duke of Norfolk 'hathe set out a submission in writing ... and hath utterly renunced the mariage w*ith* the Scottish quene'.[49] Likewise, a letter of 21 September 1571 is concerned almost exclusively with Mary and Thomas Howard, duke of Norfolk. Fitzwilliam described at great length Norfolk's committal to the tower, and the discovery of secret letters between the earl and Mary, including 'a l*ett*re of her owne hand' in which the Scottish queen urged him to 'send ayde to her frendes in Scotland'. The letter continues with a description of the arrest of the duke's secretary Hicford, his forced confession, the subsequent search for the 'sifer' for the clandestine correspondence, and ends with the arrest and questioning of another of Norfolk's servants Bannister: 'I canot lerne Banisters confession upon the racke as yet, but he was put to the racke for the denying of moost manifest trothes at the first'.[50]

John Kniveton, another servant, provided a similar service to Fitzwilliam during this period for the earl of Shrewsbury, writing detailed letters on European politics. These letters the earl then passed on to his wife for her to read.[51] 'I have sent you John Knyftons lettar' he wrote on one occasion 'that you may p*er*seve what is bruited of the yonge king [James VI of Scotland]'.[52] While Bess gathered intelligence independently, she also had access to reports produced for her husband. This in itself presents conceptual and methodological problems. First, in terms of defining what constitutes a woman's correspondence, should one include as well as letters written by and addressed to her, general letters to which she had access? In the case of the Shrewsburys, the customarily strong notion of personal correspondence that emerges during the sixteenth century is replaced by something altogether more fluid: Gilbert Talbot, for example, informed his step-mother, 'wher I wryte to one it is to bothe'.[53] This inter-changeability of letters also makes it difficult to analyse how news was reported differently according to the gender of recipient. The second problem is a recurrent theme of women's history, that social transactions of this nature all too often go undocumented: where women's names are absent on address leaves they are 'hidden from history'! How many wives read their husbands' correspondences that now remain silent to historical record?

Although much of the information concerning Mary, Queen of Scots, was for personal use (the Shrewsburys were largely kept in the dark about their captive), the countess also fed details to Burghley and Walsingham.[54] One of the earl's servants, Hersey Lassels, having gained the confidence of the Scottish queen, acted as spy for Bess, reporting on Mary's 'doings and devices'. He was dismissed in 1570 for taking gifts from Mary and for suspected subversive activities, and was later cross-examined by the council.[55] At this time Bess passed on to Burghley Lassels' intelligence, partly for her own preservation: Lassels had implicated her in his 'dealings' with Mary, and furthermore Bess was herself accused of enjoying too great an intimacy with the Queen of Scots. Among other matters, she told the Secretary of State what she knew of Mary's relationship with Norfolk. Under less pressure to divulge information in 1578, the countess conveyed news of her captive to Walsingham, informing him that Mary had 'misliked' the 'contents of the articles' he had sent her, adding 'she is grown lean and sickly and saith want of exercise rings her into a weak state'.[56] These snippets of information probably also helped to lubricate the passage of suits which the countess pushed in other letters to officials – where her role is more that of suitor than patron – in much the same way that news received by her obligated her to act 'favourably'.

The other period in which newsletters played an important role in keeping Bess in touch with events is the last years of her life, when she more or less retreated to Hardwick. One suspects here, perhaps not unfairly, that letters conveying news were a handy way of keeping in favour with a woman almost in her eighties, who had made her will in 1601. Here again news assumes the role of gift. A disproportionate number of letters from her son William Cavendish, who was a major beneficiary of her will, date from 1604 and 1605.[57] In an extravagant letter dated 22 April 1605, he informed his mother that 'my la*dy* Arbell & my lady marquesse shall christen the Q*ueen* ma*jes*tis daughter, but w*hi*ch of ye lady marquesses I know not / for yo*ur* la*dyshi*ps matters I shall plie them ernestly'. He also reported that 'the quene of Spayne is lately brought a bed of a sonn', and that the 'Spanish Imbassador here for ioy made many fireworks in the street before his howse & cast gold & siluer amongst the peple to ye value of CC li'. He continued to report that the 'Cardinall of Medices unckell to the duke of Florence is chosen Pope' and that 'yt is thought he will fauour the french more then the Spanyard'.[58] The news offered here is exactly the sort of news found in the letters of John Chamberlain, a man described by modern-day scholars as an 'insatiable gossip', a commentator on the 'abnormal and unusual', 'the sordid and repellent'.[59] Here, the term 'gossip' is applied regardless of gender in order to trivialise news and suggest its untrustworthiness. And yet, the sorts of newsworthy items traditionally referred to by scholars as 'gossip' and which might be seen as a 'female' domain – rumours about suitors vying for the hand in marriage of a rich heiress, tales of how much money the Spanish ambassador spent on fireworks, talk of what colour gloves the Queen most liked – in actual fact assume *political* importance in a society preoccupied with rank, status, reputation, power and influence, a society in which such details as what gifts would best please the monarch was important political capital. Equally, rumours such as insulting remarks about Elizabeth I's temper and vanity, which the countess herself perpetuated, whether grounded in truth or not, take on a particular importance when circulated.[60]

Another key correspondent in the latter stages of the countess's life was Dr James Montague, Dean of the Royal Chapel, and later Bishop of Bath and Wells.[61] At almost eighty, and with matters of her own mortality on her mind, Bess's relationship with a clergyman is perhaps understandable. However, this was an epistolary relationship based on the transaction of news, different from the kind of spiritual, in many ways confessional, relationships evidenced by Protestant women's correspondence with preachers that Patrick Collinson has so fully described.[62] Montague, in his position as Dean, was a man at the centre of the court and well placed to comment on events there; in his own words he was in 'continuall followinge of his Ma*jes*tie in his iourneys', a polite excuse he used on at least two occasions for not writing 'so often to your honour as I would'.[63] His letters, though, do not divulge the intimate secrets of the royal chapel, but offer a staple diet of parliamentary affairs, conspiracies and religious persecutions of 'preests and recusants'. In his letter of 20 February 1606, he wrote 'I think my lo*rd* Ca*ev*ndish acquynteth you with all the parlament newes. It is a very joyfull matter to see how well the Kinge his lordes and commons doe agree together in one this parlament: and all agaynst the papistes'. He continued by describing the execution of the Gun Powder Plot conspirators, and the capture and trial of the Jesuit Henry Garnet.[64] A second letter of 7 March followed similar lines: 'the newes heer is all parlament business. The matter of religion to compell every man to comunion within the space of 2 years or else they shalbe the nature of recusants'. It continued with further reports on the examinations of Garnet, that 'notorious traitor'.[65]

Importantly, news in the countess's relationship with Montague ran both ways: he was a source of news, as well as a conduit to King James. In 1605, when Bess thought that Arbella Stuart was after money from her (with the tacit support of the King), she wrote to Montague explaining that her granddaughter had been provided with land worth £700 and gifts totalling £100, with the hope that it would reach James's ears.[66] The obvious confessional bias of Montague's letters hints at an ideological or religious agenda in the countess's choice of correspondents, despite her supposed 'conservative' religious inclinations.[67] In addition to Montague, himself a leading Protestant, she received letters from Richard Topcliffe, the renowned recusant hunter, and regularly corresponded with her kinsfolk the Wingfields, who were Protestants under Elizabeth.[68]

In contrast to these former two groups of letters, the news supplied by the countess of Shrewsbury's female contacts at court was privy and personalised. Their letters largely concerned the status of Bess's general standing at court, her favour with the Queen, the monarch's reactions to her gifts, and the progress of suits. Several letters from the period 1568 to 1585 survive from her half-sister Elizabeth Wingfield, the wife of Anthony Wingfield, one of the Queen's Gentleman Ushers, and herself Mother of the Maids.[69] In one letter, Lady Wingfield wrote that the Queen in conversation had stated, 'I assure you there ys no lady yn this land that I beter loue'; another letter told of how the Queen 'toulde my lo*rd* of Lester and my lo*rd* chamberlen that you had geven her such garments thys yere as she neuer had any so well lyked her and sayd that good nobell copell the*y* show in all things what loue the*y* bere me'; and during Bess's turbulent separation from the earl of Shrewsbury, Elizabeth Wingfield kept her informed of efforts to move the Queen on her behalf, 'your good frende my la*dy* cheke had longe talke w*ith* her ma*jes*ty latly of my lo*rdships* harde dealinge and the quene gaue many good wordes what she woulde do for your la*dyship*'.[70] Royal favour and intimacy of this sort, as David Starkey has shown, had important symbolic resonance.[71] The kind of news that court women wrote about was highly specialised; these were intimate firsthand accounts from the Privy Chamber, rather than the generalised rumour that reverberated around the corridors and halls of court, and that characterises the letters of her male correspondents. Whereas other letters and other forms of news may have circulated more widely, the news conveyed by court women was highly privileged and in some cases confidential. Dorothy Lady Stafford was concerned that the details of her discussion with the Queen regarding potential husbands for Arbella Stuart, an account of which she imparted in a letter to Bess, should go no further:

> I beseeche you good Maddam seing it pleased her Ma*jes*tie to saie so muche unto mee touching her care of my La*dy* Arbella that yor La*dyshi*p will vouchesafe mee so muche favo*u*r as to kepe it to yor selfe not making anie other acquainted wth it but rather repose the truste in mee for to take my opportunitie for the puttinge her Ma*jes*tie in mynde thereof w*hi*ch I will doe as carefullie as I can.[72]

While Montague did not divulge secrets of this nature in his letters, the close familial and social bonds that Bess had with her female court contacts perhaps explains their willingness to commit intimate and privy news to paper.

The correspondence of the countess of Shrewsbury illustrates women's interest in areas of news traditionally viewed as 'male': parliamentary business, war, armed rebellions and naval preparations. Hers was an interest fuelled by necessity and grounded in the need to be informed. The inimitable Bess of Hardwick, popularised by historical romances, emerges at the centre of a network of correspondents and intelligence gatherers, both male and female. Viewed from the perspective of women's reading, it suggests a broader, less restricted range than might hitherto have been assumed. The assassination of the French King, Henri III, by Jacques Clément in 1589, for example, is reported to her in all its macabre details: the letter describes the 'cruel varlet' priest who when delivering a letter to the monarch drew a 'sharpe poynted knyfe' from his sleeve and stabbed the King several times in the side.[73] Her example also highlights the *political* significance of news traditionally dismissed as trivial gossip. When she informed Burghley of the marriage of her granddaughter Grace Pierrepont to George Manners, the countess presented her new grandson-in-law to the Lord Treasurer as a 'friend', a political ally.[74] Although tempting to read news as gendered according to environment, women writing about household, family, and locality, men about affairs in London, the court or abroad, this public/private split is too schematic and oversimplified. Through conversation, social interaction and correspondence aristocratic women had access to a range of news from beyond their immediate locale.

Notes

The research for this essay was supported by the generosity of the Folger Shakespeare Library, Washington, D.C., in the form of a short-term Research Fellowship, and by a Postdoctoral Fellowship at the University of Reading. I would also like to thank the audiences at the 'Rethinking Women and Politics' conference at the University of Reading, and at the Center of Renaissance and Baroque Studies at the University of Maryland, College Park, who heard this essay in its incarnation as a paper. I thank especially Alan Stewart, Ralph Houlbrooke, David Norbrook and David Como for their helpful comments.

[1] On the importance and development of newsletters in early modern England see Richard Cust, 'News and Politics in Early Seventeenth-Century England', *P&P*, 112 (Aug. 1986), 60-90 (pp. 62-63); F. J. Levy, 'How Information Spread Among the Gentry, 1550-1640', *The Journal of British Studies*, XXI, 2 (Spring 1982), 11-34 (pp. 20-23); *idem*, 'The Decorum of News', in Joad Raymond (ed.), *News, Newspapers, and Society in Early Modern Britain*, London: Frank Cass, 1999, pp. 12-38; Harold Love, *Scribal Publication in Seventeenth-Century England*, Oxford: Clarendon Press, 1993, pp. 9-22; Gary Schneider, 'The Culture of Epistolarity: Letters and Letter-Writing in Early Modern England, 1500-1700', unpublished PhD thesis, Wayne State University, 2001, ch. 4.

[2] Cust, 'News and Politics', 60-90; Levy, 'How Information Spread', 11-34. See also, Joad Raymond, *The Invention of the Newspaper: English Newsbooks, 1641-1649*, Oxford: Clarendon Press, 1996; Adam Fox, 'Rumour, News and Popular Political Opinion in Elizabethan and Early Stuart England', *HJ*, 40, 3 (1997), 597-620.

[3] Paul J. Voss, *Elizabethan News Pamphlets: Shakespeare, Spenser, Marlow and the Birth of Journalism*, Pittsburg: Duquesne UP, 2001.

[4] Love, *Scribal Publication*, pp. 9-22, 190-91.

[5] Lisa Jardine and Alan Stewart, *Hostage to Fortune: the Troubled Life of Francis Bacon*, London: Victor Gallancz, 1998; Alan Stewart, *Philip Sidney, A Double Life*, London: Chatto and Windus, 2000.

[6] By contrast, scholars have recognised women's involvement with newspapers during the seventeenth century as readers, printers and publishers: Marcus Nevitt, 'Women in the Business of Revolutionary News: Elizabeth Alkin, "Parliament Joan", and the Commonwealth Newsbook', in Raymond (ed.), *News, Newspapers, and Society*, pp. 84-108. For women's political involvement in the popular press see Lois G. Schwoerer, 'Women's Public Political Voice in England: 1640-1740', in Hilda L. Smith (ed.), *Women Writers and the Early Modern British Political Tradition* (Cambridge: CUP, 1998), pp. 56-74.

[7] Ian Atherton, 'The Itch Grown a Disease: Manuscript Transmission of News in the Seventeenth Century', in Raymond (ed.), *News, Newspapers, and Society*, pp. 39-65 (pp. 49-50); *idem*, *Ambition and Failure in Stuart England: the Career of John, first Viscount Scudamore*, Manchester: Manchester UP, 1999. Scudamore received letters from over 43 correspondents, including letters from professional newsletter-writers, such as John Pory, government and court officials, and family and friends.

[8] Folger X.d.428 (122): Anne Talbot to countess of Shrewsbury, 29 May 1575.

[9] Pam Wright, 'A Change in Direction: the Ramifications of a Female Household, 1558-1603', in David Starkey (ed.), *The English Court From the Wars of the Roses to the Civil War*, Harlow: Longman, 1987, pp. 147-72 (p. 153).

[10] Olwen Hufton, 'Reflections on the Role of Women in the Early Modern Court', *The Court Historian*, 5, 1 (May 2000), 1-13 (p. 1).

[11] James Daybell, 'Women's Letters and Letter-Writing in England, 1540-1603', unpublished PhD thesis, University of Reading, 1999, esp. chs 6, 7.
[12] PRO, SP 46/71/223, 224, 226, 228: Margaret Hill to Richard Carnsew, 10 May 1601, 29 Mar. 1602, 23 Oct. 1602, n.d..
[13] Longleat House, Seymour Papers 5, fols 144-45: Frances Seymour, countess of Hertford to Edward Seymour, earl of Hertford, 9 June [1584-85]; Kendal RO, WD/Hoth Box 44: Margaret Clifford, countess of Cumberland to George Clifford, earl of Cumberland, n.d.; Elizabeth McCutcheon, 'Playing the Waiting Game: the Life and Letters of Elizabeth Wolley', *Quidditas*, 20 (1999), 31-53 (pp. 43-46).
[14] I am grateful to Germaine Greer for discussion on this point.
[15] Claire Walker, '"Doe not supose me a well mortifyed Nun dead to the world": Letter-Writing in Early Modern English Convents', in James Daybell (ed.), *Early Modern Women's Letter Writing, 1450-1700*, Basingstoke: Palgrave, 2001, pp. 159-76; *eadem*, 'Prayer, Patronage, and Political Conspiracy: English Nuns and the Restoration', *HJ*, 43, 1 (2000), 1-23; Arthur Searle (ed.), *Barrington Family Letters, 1628-1632*, Camden Society, 4th Series, 28, London: Royal Historical Society, 1983, pp. 201, 215, 223, 206-7.
[16] Sara Mendelson and Patricia Crawford, *Women in Early Modern England, 1550-1720*, Oxford: Clarendon Press, 1998, p. 215.
[17] Barbara J. Harris, 'Women and Politics in Early Tudor England', *HJ*, 33 (1990), 259-81; Georgianna Ziegler, '"More Than Feminine Boldness": The Gift Books of Esther Inglis', Mary E. Burke *et al.* (eds), *Women, Writing, and the Reproduction of Culture in Tudor and Stuart Britain*, Syracuse, NY: Syracuse UP, 2000, pp. 19-37; Susan Frye, 'Sewing Connections: Elizabeth Tudor, Mary Stuart, Elizabeth Talbot, and Seventeenth-Century Anonymous Needleworkers', in Susan Frye and Karen Robertson (eds), *Maids and Mistresses, Cousins and Queens: Women's Alliances in Early Modern England*, New York and Oxford: OUP, 1999, pp. 165-82.
[18] Bess of Hardwick's outgoing correspondence is scattered throughout numerous collections.
[19] The best biographical study of Bess of Hardwick is David N. Durant, *Bess of Hardwick: Portrait of an Elizabethan Dynast*, London: Weidenfeld and Nicolson, 1977; rev. ed. 1999. Also see E. Carleton Williams, *Bess of Hardwick*, London: Longman, Green & Co., 1959; Maud Stepney Rawson, *Bess of Hardwick and Her Circle*, London: Hutchinson, 1910; Alison Plowden, *Mistress of Hardwick*, London: BBC Publications, 1972; Kate Hubbard, *A Material Girl: Bess of Hardwick, 1527-1608*, London: Short Books, 2001.
[20] Paul E.J. Hammer, 'The Uses of Scholarship: the Secretariat of Robert Devereux, Second Earl of Essex, c. 1581-1601', *EHR*, 109, 430 (1994), 26-51.
[21] Folger, X.d.428 (28): 28 July 1570.
[22] Cust, 'News and Politics', p. 62. Although the distinction between 'unformalised' and 'pure' newsletters has been challenged by Ian Atherton as too simplistic (Atherton, 'The Itch Grown a Disease', p. 41), Cust's definition of 'pure newsletters' most closely describes Fitzwilliam's letters, and those of several other correspondents.
[23] LPL, MS 3196, fol. 221: 24 Jan. 1569.
[24] I am grateful to Alan Stewart for discussion on this point.
[25] Muriel St Clare Byrne (ed.), *The Lisle Letters*, 6 vols, Chicago: The University of Chicago Press, 1981.
[26] Folger, X.d.428 (34, 23): 1 Dec. 1565, 4 July 1604.
[27] D. Erasmus, *De Conscribendis Epistolis*, (1522), in *Collected Works of Erasmus*, 25, (ed.), J.K. Sowards, Toronto: University of Toronto Press, 1985, p. 225: 'private matters would include informing an absent person of our state of health, or our progress in our

studies, of how our affairs are progressing in the country, at court, in building concerns, and in the lawcourts, or of any new undertakings of ours in other spheres right down to trivial details of parties and conversations; public news concerning peace, war, kingly exploits, treaties, plagues, floods, earthquakes, storms and other such things'.

[28] Folger, X.d.428 (107): 28 June 1574.

[29] Levy, 'The Decorum of News', p. 18.

[30] LPL, MS 3206, fol. 565: unknown to countess of Shrewsbury, 24 Jan. 1569.

[31] William S. Powell, *John Pory 1572-1636. The Life and Letters of a Man of Parts*, Chapel Hill, NC: The University of North Carolina Press, 1977, p. 55.

[32] For Bess's will, see A. Collins, *Historical Collections of Noble Families of Cavendish*, London, 1752, pp. 15-19.

[33] Folger, X.d.428 (107): 28 June 1574.

[34] Folger, X.d.428 (114): [1589].

[35] Folger, X.d.428 (121): 8 May [1575].

[36] Folger, X.d.428 (68): [1603].

[37] Folger, X.d.428 (41): 22 June 1607.

[38] LPL, MS 3195, fol. 221: unknown to countess of Shrewsbury, Jan. 1569.

[39] On the importance of sixteenth-century gifts see Natalie Zemon Davis, *The Gift in Sixteenth-Century France*, Oxford: OUP, 2000.

[40] The reference here to 'heareinge' letters may well indicate the practice of letters being read out aloud.

[41] Folger, X.d.428 (15): 13 Feb. 1607.

[42] Taken as a whole, Bess's letters show that her correspondence networks were more widely spread. She numbered among her correspondents the earls of Essex, Leicester, Cumberland, Arundel and Rutland, Lord Burghley and Sir Robert Cecil.

[43] Lawrence Stone, *The Crisis of the Aristocracy, 1558-1641*, Oxford: Clarendon Press, 1965, p. 388.

[44] Jason Scott-Warren, 'News, Sociability, and Bookbuying in Early Modern England: the Letters of Sir Thomas Cornwallis', *The Library*. 7th Series, 4 (Dec. 2000), 382-402 (p. 388, also see 386, 394).

[45] Durant wrongly describes the writers of these letters as 'professional newswriters' (p. 74), when in fact the letters appear to have been written by her servants. On Mary, Queen of Scots' captivity in England with the Shrewsburys see: Patrick Collinson, *The English Captivity of Mary Queen of Scots*, Sheffield History Pamphlets, 1987. During this period Mary was shuttled between Tutbury, Chatsworth, Wingfield Manor and Sheffield Castle.

[46] Durant, p. 75.

[47] Folger, X.d.428 (28): 28 July 1570. Two other detailed letters of national and international news written by unnamed correspondents also survive from this period: LPL, MS 3196, fol. 221, Jan. 1569; LPL, MS 3206, fol. 565: 31 Aug. 1570.

[48] Other writers also wrote about Mary, Queen of Scots during this period. An unknown correspondent writing in January 1569 reported, 'the newes is heere that my lord yo[u]r husband is sworne of the privie Counsel; and that the Scotishe quene is on her iourney to Tutbury, something against her will, and shal be under my lordes custody there': LPL, MS 3196, fol. 221: to countess of Shrewsbury, 24 Jan. 1569.

[49] Folger, X.d.428 (28): 28 July 1570.

[50] Folger, X.d.428 (29): 21 Sept. 1571.

[51] John Kniveton was the younger brother of Thomas Kniveton (d.1591), MP for Derbyshire in 1559, and wife of Bess of Hardwick's half sister Jane Kniveton (née Leche): *HC 1558-1603*, 2, p. 407. For John Kniveton's correspondence to Shrewsbury see LPL, MS 697,

fol. 131, MS 700, fol. 77, MS 708, fol. 29, MS 3206, fols. 305, 575, 669, 729, 747, 15 June 1570, 22 Nov. 1570, 11 May [1573], 24 June 1571, 30 Jan. 1571, 19 Jan. 1574, 16 Apr. 1575, 23 Nov. 1573.

[52] Folger, X.d.428 (93): [1574].

[53] Folger, X.d.428 (108): 14 May 1575.

[54] Collinson, *The English Captivity of Mary Queen of Scots*, p. 25.

[55] Williams, *Bess of Hardwick*, pp. 99-100; Edmund Lodge, *Illustrations of British History, Biography and Manners in the Reigns of Henry VIII, Edward VI, Elizabeth, and James I*, 3 vols, London: John Chidley, 1838, 1, pp. 528-29: Burghley to countess of Shrewsbury, 13 Oct. 1571.

[56] Hatfield House, Herts, Cecil Papers 10, fol. 27: 29 Dec. 1578.

[57] Folger, X.d.428 (22, 23, 24, 25), 12 Nov. 1600, 4 July 1604, 1604, 23 Apr. 1605.

[58] Folger, X.d.428 (25).

[59] Levy, 'The Decorum of News', p.12; N.E. McClure (ed.), *The Letters of John Chamberlain*, 2 vols, Philadelphia: The American Philosophical Society, 1939, 1, p. 21.

[60] Alexandre Labanoff (ed.), *Lettres, Instructions et Mémoires de Marie Stuart, Reine d'Ecosse*, 7 vols, London: Charles Dolman, 1844, 6, pp. 50-57.

[61] Folger, X.d.428 (59, 60); LPL, MS 3202, fol. 7: 'I haue writt to my ladye the news of her maiesties safe deliverye'.

[62] Patrick Collinson, 'The Role of Women in the English Reformation Illustrated by the Life and Friendships of Anne Locke', G.J. Cuming (ed.), *Studies in Church History*, 2, London: Nelson and Sons, 1965, pp. 258-72.

[63] Folger, X.d.428 (59): 20 Feb. 1606.

[64] Ibid.

[65] Folger, X.d.428 (60).

[66] Durant, p. 219.

[67] Collinson, *The English Captivity of Mary Queen of Scots*, p. 13.

[68] Folger, X.d.428 (125): Richard Topcliffe to countess of Shrewsbury, 9 July 1577; *DNB* (Topcliffe, Richard, 1532-1604); Folger, X.d. 428 (129, 130, 131); *HC 1558-1603*, 3, p. 634 (Winfield, Anthony II, c.1550-c.1615).

[69] Durant, pp. 7, 55, 82, 91-92, 118, 167; Charlotte Merton, 'The Women Who Served Queen Mary and Queen Elizabeth: Ladies, Gentlewomen and Maids of the Privy Chamber 1553-1603', unpublished PhD thesis, University of Cambridge, 1992, p. 269.

[70] Folger, X.d.428 (129, 130, 131), 21 Oct. 1568, 2 Jan, 1576, 8 Dec. 1585.

[71] David Starkey, 'Representation Through Intimacy: a Study in the Symbolism of Monarchy and Court Office in Early-Modern England', in I. Lewis (ed.), *Symbols and Sentiments: Cross Cultural Studies in Symbolism*, London, New York and San Francisco, 1977, pp. 187-224.

[72] Folger, X.d.428 (120): 13 Jan. 1601.

[73] Folger, X.d.428 (115): Gilbert and Mary Talbot, to countess of Shrewsbury, 1 July 1589.

[74] *HMC, The Manuscripts of His grace the Duke of Rutland, GCB, Preserved at Belvoir Castle*, 4 vols, London: HMSO, 1888, 1, p. 317: 9 Aug. 1593.

Chapter 8

Esther Inglis and the English Succession Crisis of 1599

Tricia Bracher

To the majority of modern critics the work of the writing master Esther Inglis (1571-1624) is an inspiring example of what could be achieved by a woman writer. Indeed Inglis' calligraphic skill in manuscripts copied from the work of other writers and from the Bible between 1586 and the year of her death has attracted the interest of a range of scholars including Susan Frye, Lisa M. Klein, Anneke Tjan-Bakker, Kim Walker, Georgianna Ziegler, and Ann Rosalind Jones and Peter Stallybrass.[1] In different ways each critic stresses the unique aura of the hand-wrought present and the possibilities for a female gift-exchange community headed by Elizabeth I. While Jonathan Goldberg has emphasised Inglis' 'limited empowerment' within a culture that attempted to regulate the act of writing and to control the extent of women's education, modern scholarship continues, whatever its ideological slant, to treat Inglis' work as a corpus, rendering the author herself just one more *woman writer* whom we can discuss in general.[2] In turning away from analyses focussing on the question of gender, I do not pretend that the political can be separated from the personal. Instead I want to suggest that at least in the case of Inglis, the lack of a fully historicised account of her 1599 manuscripts has deprived Inglis scholarship of the key to her literary success and to her textual audacity in the face of massive cultural prohibitions against the early modern women writer. Building on Georgianna Ziegler's proposition that Inglis' husband Bartholomew Kello might have worked as a 'kind of double agent' between James VI of Scotland and both the Cecil and Essex factions at the Elizabethan court, I will focus for the first time on the political context to the manuscripts written in 1599 and will propose that year as a historical moment that made the services of a husband and wife uniquely valuable.[3]

Bartholomew Kello

In 1599 Kello journeyed from Scotland to the court of Elizabeth I carrying a letter of introduction to the Queen's Principal Secretary Sir Robert Cecil from James Hudson, a representative of James VI of Scotland. In it Hudson commended Kello, the bearer of a letter from the King to the Queen, and proclaimed:

> The present which he has is esteemed to be of singular rarity. I know the king has very favourably commended the party to her Majesty's good liking and holds her to be a most excellent and skilful judge in all virtues.[4]

From other contemporary letters we know this present to be *Le Livre des Pseaumes escrites en diverses sortes de lettres par Esther Anglois francoise*, a manuscript book of psalms written by Kello's wife and dedicated to Elizabeth on 27 March 1599.[5] After the courtesy of Kello's introduction to the Queen, more quotidian issues soon arise. On 14 July Kello wrote to an unnamed recipient regarding the dilatory behaviour of Henry Sackford, the Keeper of the Queen's Privy Purse, in providing him with money. Kello explained:

> ...efter I resaved your l*ett*re on Wedinisday last at morne; I went praesentilie to Grenewhiche and delyverit the samyn to Mr Sackforde, who tooke and red the same, and thane delyverit it agane to me, and said he haid no money, nathair culd he know when to get money, and so gaif me ane infinit answer. I went agane to hym yisterday, and was so instant with him as I could, that he would be no hinderer of me, for alreadie I haid lost one ship, and if he maid me to losse ane uthair, that wes to saill one of thir tuo dayis, I sould be constrayned to stay heir perchance till I spendit all hir Ma*jes*ties rewaird, and so be this doing, it sould ceas to be my rewaird at all, for yea know sir, qui cito dat, bis dat [who gives quickly, gives twice].[6]

Kello went on to recount how Sackford explained to him that the Queen was very willing to give him the money but that there was no money in her Privy Purse and suggested that he return on Monday. Earnestly requesting that the recipient of the letter speak to Sackford, Kello expressed his fear that no payment would be made, raising the possibility that something should 'be done as the present maybe returnit bak agane to me, and so he sall get money to hir Ma*jes*teis purs befoir I truble him moir thairwith, for I am indead almost wereit in my sute'.[7]

Despairing of his situation, Kello took up his own pen and importuned Elizabeth on 18 July 1599:

> It may pleas your [blank] Ma*jes*tie the booke of psalmes wreaten be my wyfe in french and in divers soirtis of Carectaris adornit everie way so far as wes possible to ane simple woman, being presentit to Your Ma*jes*tie togidder with ane l*ett*re of my Souverane lords the kings Ma*jes*tie of Scotland in my recommendatioun: I did understand be repoirt of certane your Ma*jes*ties serviteurs, the work wes verie acceptable to your Ma*jes*tie wherof indead I could noght bot greatlie rejose, and so will the wreater therof when shoe sall heir your Ma*jes*tie to have taiken ony small pleasour or delyt in hir handywork: lykwayis your Ma*jes*ties most princelie will thereanent a long tyme since wes declarit to me, bot I am sorie that ther is no Mecoenas in regia Augusti [Maecenas (or patron) at the court of Augustus], bot I constraynit to my great hurt heir to stay (whilk I am sure is unknowen to your Ma*jes*tie) inrespect of your Ma*jes*ties deliberation past therin. It may therfore be your Ma*jes*ties princelie pleasour to give ordour for my spedie dispatch.[8]

Whether or not Kello ever received any remuneration for Inglis' book, he had returned to Edinburgh by 15 August from where he again wrote to an anonymous associate. Having recounted at great length the causes of delays in his sea journey from London to Scotland, Kello made an impassioned plea for understanding:

> ...during this storme no thing trublit me so mekle (I assure you sir, noght my oune lyfe, my wyf, nor children) as the things yea knowe I haid to do and to discharge; for tuiching my lyfe it wes never deir to me, knowing perfytlie my tyme to be in the lordis counsell and where ever it pleasit his divine Ma*jes*tie I wes sure it should be in him; concerning my wyfe and children I assured my selfe the lord hes hethairto and sall to there lyves end have ane speciall cair of theme. Bot my intolerable greif (during thay 12 hours of exceading storme) wes that I should be so unhappie that such thingis as wer to be redelyverit be me et verbo et facto [in both word and deed] fra such ane rair, singular and most worthie persoun, to such ane great persoun &ct [etc] and uthair verteous personis besyd, should all with me be overwhelmed in the deip of the seas, so that noght onlie had I finishit my terme; bot my proceedingis, my treuth, my honestie, (be my misgouvernement or small cair in my adois [duties], as lesullie [leisurely] it would have bene thoght) might have bene randerit suspitious to you, of whome I resaved bothe the credeit and courtasie above mereit, and lykwayis I haid bene evill thoght of be thais to whome I wes committed.[9]

Speaking of his dealings on his return to Edinburgh with the mysterious 'male and female' and with people identified in the letter only as 'B.' and 'E.', Kello wrote:

> ...all things wer done so gravelie and circumspectlie, bothe thay things that wer manu trandendis et ore communicandis [passed by hand and communicated by mouth] and so greatlie to the males lyking and contentment, as I am assurit na thing hethairto better done, for diligence, treuth, secresie, and wisdome wes usit in the haill action, as yea ar to be (I houp) informed of hearefter; alwayis my sweit and deir sir I will noght pen doun herr particularis for mony respectis, and chieflie becaus of great dainger in noght sure delyverie of letters in thir perilous dayis.[10]

What then was the danger of which Kello spoke? Moreover, why were James VI and a mystery correspondent interested in the fate of a manuscript book of psalms by a Scottish woman? Reading Inglis within the context of textual diplomacy, I propose that Kello's fretting over his wife's *Livre des Pseaumes* can only be understood if we consider it alongside the books dedicated just weeks later to Robert Devereux, second earl of Essex, the Queen's one-time favourite and now political rival, and to Anthony Bacon, his unpaid secretary and friend. In foregrounding Kello's previously undiscovered involvement with Bacon (whom I will argue to be the anonymous recipient of Kello's letter written in London), I want to suggest that, in 1599 at least, Inglis and Kello must be considered as a couple working together to promote a secret or not-so-secret alliance between James VI of Scotland and his Essexian allies in England.

James' Exquisite Writers and the Bacon Connection

In December 1595, just prior to his marriage to Inglis in or around 1596, Kello first appears in the extant records as the writer of a newsletter, now found among the Bacon Manuscripts in Lambeth Palace Library. The letter reported on the covert support offered by various governors and officials of Brittany to the Spanish forces who had landed there at the beginning of the decade.[11] Such newsletters were the staple of Anthony Bacon's co-ordination of the intelligence activities that underpinned Essex's continuing campaign to assert himself militarily on the continent and his attempts to support the French Protestant cause. Indeed as Paul E.J. Hammer has recently shown, while Cecil was Elizabeth's official intelligencer, his supremacy was increasingly rivalled by Essex's news network as operated by Bacon.[12] Thus

Kello's first visible role within politics was as one of Essex's many intelligence agents, his associations on the continent perhaps strengthened by his relationship with the French-born Inglis.

In 1596, Kello worked as an intermediary between Bacon and John Bothwell, Abbot of Holyroodhouse (and thus attached to James VI's palace in Edinburgh), and a trusted envoy and negotiator of the King who became a non-official member of the Scottish Privy Council.[13] Writing on 4 October 1596 in response to a letter from Bothwell, Bacon noted that as he was persuaded that Kello, whom he named as a relation ('parent') to the abbot, had already informed Bothwell of the reasons for his silence, he would not insist on that point.[14] Having assured the abbot of his friendship, Bacon enclosed some papers for him to read, asking him to keep them to himself lest 'l'eccho de mon nom rebonde aus oreilles de n*ost*re Ambassadour' [the echo of my name rebound in the ears of our Ambassador].[15] Regarding other particulars concerning himself, Bacon referred his correspondent to the 'present Porteur mon trecher et intime amy' [present bearer, my most dear and intimate friend].[16] Whether or not the bearer of this letter was Kello, he is clearly implicated in a secret relationship between Bacon and Bothwell which side-steps the official ambassadorial communications between England and Scotland. Thus, while scholars such as Ziegler and A.H. Scott-Elliot and Elspeth Yeo continue to assert Kello's connections with Cecil, the evidence here suggests that Bacon was Kello's primary contact at the English court.[17] Indeed, Kello's London letter of 14 July 1599 to an anonymous recipient is as least as likely to have been written to Bacon as Cecil given the composition of British Library, Additional Manuscript 4125. A note on the first folio of this volume describes the contents as 'Letters of Secretary Cecill, Robert, Earl of Essex and others and also many Letters to them'. The book, however, was compiled by the eighteenth-century historian Thomas Birch and corresponds to a large extent with Lambeth Palace Library, Bacon MS 662 from which Birch worked and which comprises letters relating to Anthony Bacon from the period 1596-1603.

While Kello had secured employment with Bacon and in the secret networks of Scottish intelligence, he and his wife were aiming higher. In 1865 the Scottish antiquarian David Laing noted the existence of a warrant, dated by Laing to 1598, appointing Kello 'Clerk of all Passports'.[18] In this warrant, the poor quality of letters being produced in the King's name is bemoaned and Kello is requested to ensure that all letters in the future be written by himself or by 'the maist exquisit & perfyte wreater within this Realme', a clear reference to Inglis.[19] At the centre of the document's claims is the notion that the King's textual honour abroad has been under threat:

> ...quhairin [wherein] fault sumtyme may be found in the forme of the lettir throu imperfection of the wreater, and sumtymes for that the autentick copies ar not referuit [sic] in register, quhairthrow [through which] his Hienes is oftymes circumuenit [thwarted] it being ane mater tending to the aduancement of his honour.[20]

Conflating legibility with penmanship, the document threatens those who would seek to circumvent Kello's authority. The text submits that such individuals should 'do nor attempt na thing to the breaking & violation of the said lettir in ony point vnder al hiest payn, charge, & offence' and proposes a scenario in which Kello would act as a kind of permanent de facto Principal Secretary, controlling the production and dispatch of court letters 'during al the dayes of his lyftyme'.[21] The warrant declares:

> With power to the said Barthilmo Kello, to wreat or cause al the sadis lettiris be his direction be wreatin BE THE MEST EXQUISIT WREATER WITHIN THIS REALME, iniunand [enjoining] also to the said Barthilmo Kello to put and commit to register all sik wreatis as salbe wreatin be him or be his direction, and subscryuit be his Ma*jes*tie to the effect that accompt and tryal may be taken thereof as necessitie sal requyre, & the saming lettir to be extendit in the best forme, with al clausis nedful, with command therein to the keiparis of his Hienes seilis, and signetis that nane of thame ressaue or passe ony siklyk forrayne wreatingis to be subscryuit be his Hienes in tyme cuming except the saming be wreatin be the said Barthilmo Kello or be his direction and marked at vnder with his name, dischairging thame thereof & of there offices in that pairt, dischairging also al his hienes Leiges and vtheris quhom it effeiris of all wreating of ony sik lettiris without the said Barthilmo Kellois gude wil and command.[22]

Twice calling Inglis 'the most exquisite and perfect writer within this realm', the text appears to betray something of an authorial ego. Indeed this warrant is not an unbound single document, but a page (fol. 31) now missing from the middle of a composite volume of specimens of writing attributed to Inglis that includes various Latin translations and verses by different authors.[23] Given that this document is also unsigned and incomplete (the blanks left for the date at the end of the text remain unfilled), this text must surely be seen as a somewhat optimistic draft for a warrant that Inglis and Kello hoped might be authorised. While Inglis' calligraphic virtues alone never garnered her the official role advertised in the 'warrant', the combination of Kello's intelligence connections and the aesthetic flexibility and potential secrecy of the manuscript gift did, however, culminate in a moment of textual and political efficacy: the production and transmission of the 1599 books.

Inglis' 1599 Manuscripts

To return to the letters written by a troubled and weary Bartholomew Kello in 1599, we recall the source of his trepidation, the question of whether he would be paid by Elizabeth for his wife's *Livre des Pseaumes*. In this manuscript we encounter two statements designed to suggest the goodwill of the Scottish monarch toward his English counterpart. Speaking of the excellence of her subject matter 'digne d'une Roine, laquelle entre tous les Princes approche de plus pres a ce Royal Prophete' [worthy of a Queen who, among all Princes most closely resembles this Royal Prophet], the Scottish-based Inglis first silently places Elizabeth above James as the prince who most closely resembles David, the royal prophet and author of the psalms.[24] Completing this gesture of submission, Inglis prays for Elizabeth's longevity: 'ie supplie le Roy des rois honorer vostre Ma^{te} en toutes vos actions de sa presence par son Esprit, vous donnant en toute foelicite tres heureuse et longue vie' [I pray the King of kings will honour your Majesty in all your actions with his presence through his Spirit, blessing you with a happy and long life].[25] While a general expression of goodwill is traditional in dedicatory letters, Inglis' reference to Elizabeth's life is nonetheless pointed. As one of the most powerful potential heirs to the English throne, James was daily waiting for news of the ageing Queen's death, and the image of respectful patience conveyed by Inglis is surely double-edged. Indeed, it is precisely this strategic Scottish threat to Elizabeth that becomes apparent when we read the *Livre des Pseaumes* alongside Inglis' other 1599 manuscripts. In these texts there is conveyed a broader and more subtle message of the King's fidelity to the earl of Essex who (through the services of Anthony Bacon) was both a rival to Elizabeth's official intelligencer Cecil, with access to a large number of Cecil's correspondents, and a potential threat to the English throne.

In her dedication to Essex of *Les Proverbes de Salomon* on 13 April 1599, Inglis described her reasons for addressing the work to him:

> ...ce mien petit labeur, duquel je n'ay que l'exterieur, et l'interieur a vous proprement s'addresse, paterne de toute sagesse, oracle de prudente, et vray Salomon de cest aage [sic]. Il plaira doncques a vostre Seig*neu*rie si gratieuse et debonnaire de ne reietter le pauvre artifice de celle qui ne manque que le moyen pour vous donner preuve de son affection, et n'ayant autre sujet plus digne de vous que la source de toute sagesse manant l'Esprit de Dieu par ce bon Roy Salomon.[26]
>
> [this my little work, of which I have only the exterior, and the interior addresses itself properly to you, pattern of all wisdom, oracle of prudence and true Solomon of this age. It will therefore please your most gracious and good-natured Lord not to reject the poor artifice of she who only lacks the means to give you proof of her affection, and having no other subject more worthy of you than the source of all wisdom, leading the Spirit of God through this good King Solomon]

Although Inglis appears to have made an entirely uncontroversial explanation for her choice of texts, her use of the image of Solomon is in fact highly charged. As Frank Livingstone Huntley has pointed out, the three books of the Bible ascribed to Solomon, the Canticles, the Proverbs and Ecclesiastes, were among James' favourite books.[27] Huntley makes the crucial connection with James' *Basilikon Doron* (1599) in which the King as Scotland's Solomon addresses his son (as in the book of Proverbs) thus:

> Reade the Prophets, and likewise the bookes of the *Prouerbs & Ecclesiastes*, written by that great paterne of wisdome *Salomon*; whiche will not onlie serue you for instruction, howe to walke in the obedience of the Lawe of God, but is also full of golden sentences, & morall precepts, in all things that can concerne your conuersation in the worlde, as amonge all the prophane Philosophers and Poets, ye shall not find so riche a storehouse of precepts of naturall wisedome, agreing with the will & diuine wisedome of God.[28]

Although this passage is found only in Robert Waldegrave's London 1603 printed edition, the Solomonic tone and structure is equally visible in Waldegrave's Edinburgh 1599 first edition and in the manuscript original in James' hand,[29] and forms the precedent for Inglis' description of Solomon as the 'paterne de toute sagesse'. In fashioning his son as Solomonic heir, James effectively produced a manual on the Stuart succession to the English throne, a project which was naturally shrouded in secrecy, with the first printed edition of 1599 running to only seven copies. It is my argument here that Inglis would have been aware of the new symbolism of the books of Solomon and precisely reflected this in her choice of texts to copy in 1599: Essex's *Proverbes de Salomon* and Bacon's *Livre de l'Ecclesiaste, ensemble le Cantique de Salomon* (dedicated on 14 April 1599) were exactly those advocated by the King.[30]

Having named Essex the true Solomon of the age, the Scottish divine Andrew Melville's laudatory verse in Inglis' text focuses upon Essex's martial glory as the symbol of his true leadership of England. Such focus was highly appropriate since the field of battle had always been the arena in which he endeavoured to shine, Ireland being the latest place to which he was expected to go as the Queen's commander. Between October 1598 and March 1599 the court anxiously awaited news of the Queen's command and of Essex's attitude toward his commission. Since his frequent quarrels with the Queen (the latest dispute leading to his storming out of court in April 1598), it was becoming clear that she and the earl stood in a perilously rivalrous relationship to each other. As Fynes Moryson recorded in 1617, during this period the earl gave his enemies at court 'power to make his imbracing of militarie courses, and his popular estimation so much suspected of his Soueraigne, as his greatnesse was now iudged to depend as much on her Maiesties feare of him, as her loue to him'.[31]

By 27 March 1599 the opportunity for the earl to promote his martial skills had arisen. On this day Essex left London through reverential crowds of onlookers to subdue the earl of Tyrone and other Irish nobles rebelling against English rule, the public expectation of this glorious military exercise being as high as the earl's profile at this time.[32] Melville's verse (taken from *Les Proverbes de Salomon*) runs:

> Angle Heros, quibus Angla polo te laudibus aequem?
> Seu pax, seu bellum munia ad alta vocet.
> Fortis auita novis auges decora alta triumphis:
> Teq$_e$ patrem patriae mater ELISA vocat.
> Te pietas virtutum alis caelestibus ambit.
> Qui divina pius prae SOLOMONTE sapis
> Accipe quae sapiens SOLOMON dedit enthea dicta: (xiii)
>
> [English Hero, how should I sing your praises to an English sky?
> Whether peace, or war calls you from your duties to the heights.
> You enrich noble ancestral graces with new triumphs:
> And mother ELISA designates you father of the fatherland.
> Courage from other heavenly bodies surrounds you.
> You, the dutiful one, who discern divine things ahead of SOLOMON
> Accept the inspired words that wise SOLOMON offered:][33]

Although the capitalisation of the names superficially links Solomon to Elizabeth, the actual text overwhelmingly allies him to Essex. While remaining officially true to Elizabeth as the mother ('mater ELISA') of her country, Inglis' ventriloquisation of the Queen's commendation of Essex as England's father ('patrem patriae') threatens to subordinate her as the woman in a standard patriarchal marriage, a figure who merely speaks in the domestic sphere while others (Essex) truly advance the cause of the country abroad.[34] Dedicated just weeks after Essex's departure, Inglis' manuscript (having been authorised by James' discourse on kingship) inescapably conflates the respective causes of James and Essex within the metaphor of Solomonic self-fashioning.

If the integrity of purpose behind Inglis' 1599 manuscripts was not clear enough, Melville's verse, found in each of the manuscripts dedicated to Essex and Bacon and usually taken to be a testament to the wonders of Inglis' hand,[35] gives a huge clue:

Aemula Naturae manus exprimit una figuras
Mille, animans pictis signa pusilla notis.
Signa creans animata, polum spirantia signa:
Quae picturato margine limbus obit.
Mirum opus: at mage mira manus, mira o*mn*ia uincit
Mens manuj moderans dum manus urget opus.[36]

[One hand, Nature's rival, portrays a thousand forms
Lifelike, tiny signs from embellished letters.
Creating lively images, inspired signs of the sky:
Which the border, with its painted/embroidered edge, encompasses.
A wonderful work: and, more wonderful, the hand, surpasses every wonderful thing
The mind controlling the hand while the hand presses on with the work.]

Although the specific content of the texts dedicated respectively to the Queen, Essex and Bacon differs, each book contains identical rectangular borders showing on a stippled ground a chain of oval beads divided from each other by three small round balls.[37] In addition, each bears virtually identical self-portraits of Inglis within pages of an almost identical size.[38] While these 1599 books are an aesthetic triumph, it is their border or 'margine' (as Melville terms it) which signifies their ultimate meaning as texts which serve to ally James with Elizabeth as well as with Essex and Bacon.

In dedicating *Le Livre des Pseaumes* to Elizabeth on 27 March, the day of Essex's departure for Ireland, Inglis marked a national event with a text which voices the Queen's role as Protestant leader and which subordinates James to her in a hierarchy of European monarchs.[39] Yet within the context of the other 1599 manuscripts, this gesture of praise and humility appears to be perfunctory and to a certain extent even compensatory. For whatever the importance of Bartholomew Kello's introduction to the Queen (as witnessed by James Hudson's letter of commendation), the dedications a fortnight later (on 13 and 14 April respectively) of similarly highly detailed and technically complex manuscripts to Essex and Bacon must indicate that Inglis (and through her the King) fully intended to use Kello's visit to communicate with the earl and his secretary.

Given Essex's absence in Ireland during April, it is probable that on 13 April Kello delivered the book dedicated to the earl to Essex's house in the Strand in London, also the home of Anthony Bacon to whom the second book was presented the following day. At the helm of Essex's secret dealings with James over the succession to the English throne, Bacon was a pivotal figure and was perhaps the most functionally important (if the least grand) of all the recipients of Inglis' books in that year. Indeed, in her dedication of *Le Livre de l'Ecclesiaste* to Bacon, Inglis hinted at the secretary's activities: 'n'avant autre chose que vous donner que un sujet, auquel pour vostre prudences estes assez verse' [having no other thing to give you than a subject in which your cares make you well versed].[40] Further verses by the Scottish divine John Johnston strongly allude to Bacon's intelligence work, casting him as a panoptic figure able to see both the rising and the setting of the sun:

> Adde quod Eoo simul et spectaveris orbe
> Occiduo ipse oculis plurima rara tuis.[41]
>
> [Take into consideration that which you yourself (will) have seen
> At the same time in the East and in the West most extraordinary sights for your eyes.]

Crucially here Inglis echoes the references to the heavenly signs produced by her hand in the dedication of her book to Essex, securing the unity of theme and purpose of the Bacon and Essex books and casting her writing as a kind of astrological chart through which the Scottish future of England might be divined.

Referring (in the third person) to 'les bons offices faits a son mary en particulier' [the good offices done toward her husband in particular][42] as one of the motivating factors behind her book, Inglis' parting shot is one which implies that the text is the product of an ongoing relationship between Bacon and his Scottish associates.[43] She implores that the Creator 'vous donner ce que desirez pour l'accroissement de son honneur et vostre felicite' [gives you what you desire for the increase of his honour and your happiness].[44] This is a wish that permits Bacon as reader to infer that behind the dedication there lurks the presence of a creator, a *deus ex machina* who will reward his efforts to increase his honour. In other words, we have a Scottish king looking to double his status as the monarch of two nations.

Thus Kello, writing to the Queen and to Bacon in 1599, had as his joint concern the transport of manuscript books which sought to establish the earl of Essex and his secretary as symbolic sons to the Scottish king, and the acceptance by Elizabeth of a book of psalms. The latter served not only as a pretext for his visit to London, but also as a kind of textual contract advertising James' patience in the matter of the succession. That the Queen delayed Kello's financial reward is a testament not only to her famed parsimony, but also to the troubling and edgy nature of such a contract. For in its obliquity, its touching upon questions which could not but remind Elizabeth of the danger of her position, Inglis' *Livre des Pseaumes* was both a gift and a profound political threat that mocks the concept of a purely feminine alliance.

In its textual and social chiasmus in which the male sovereign authorises a book produced by a woman, entrusted to a man and offered to the female sovereign, Inglis' *Livre des Pseaumes* models an idealised courtly intimacy between James VI and Elizabeth I. Yet at this time of profoundly divided loyalties, Inglis' books and Kello's letters also represented a kind of cynical marital rupture. Inglis' margins and Kello's background communications with Bacon both destabilised the unity and beauty of the *Livre des Pseaumes*, and intimated the divisions that lay at the heart of Elizabeth and James' political partnership.

Notes

I would like to thank Prof. Alan Stewart for commenting on an earlier draft of this essay.

1 Susan Frye, 'Esther Inglis and Early Seventeenth-Century Print Conventions of Authorship', *The Journal of Medieval and Early Modern Studies* (forthcoming); Lisa M. Klein, 'Your Humble Handmaid: Elizabethan Gifts of Needlework', *RQ*, 50 (1997), 459-93; Anneke Tjan-Bakker, 'Dame Flora's Blossoms: Esther Inglis's Flower-Illustrated Manuscripts', in Peter Beal and Margaret J.M. Ezell (eds), *English Manuscript Studies, 1100-1700, vol. 9: Writings by Early Modern Women*, London: British Library, 2000, pp. 49-72; Kim Walker, *Women Writers of the English Renaissance*, New York: Twayne

Publishers, 1996, pp. 147-51; Georgianna Ziegler, 'Hand-Ma[i]de Books: the Manuscripts of Esther Inglis, Early-Modern Precursors of the Artists' Book', in Beal and Ezell (eds), *Writings by Early Modern Women*, pp. 73-87; Ann Rosalind Jones and Peter Stallybrass, 'The Needle and the Pen: Needlework and the Appropriation of Printed Texts', in *Renaissance Clothing and the Materials of Memory*, Cambridge: CUP, 2000, pp. 134-71 (pp. 146-48).

[2] Jonathan Goldberg, *Writing Matter: From the Hands of the English Renaissance*, Stanford: Stanford UP, 1990, p. 153.

[3] Georgianna Ziegler, '"More Than Feminine Boldness": the Gift Books of Esther Inglis', in Mary E. Burke *et al.* (eds), *Women, Writing, and the Reproduction of Culture in Tudor and Stuart Britain*, Syracuse, NY: Syracuse UP, 2000, pp. 19-37 (p. 24).

[4] *Calendar of State Papers Relating to Scotland and Mary Queen of Scots, 1547-1603 Preserved in the Public Record Office, the British Museum and Elsewhere in England*, 13 vols in 14, Edinburgh: HMSO, 1898-1969, vol. 13 part 1 (1597-1603), p. 589. The letter is undated but is signed by James Hudson and endorsed by Cecil's clerk, '1599. Mr. James Hudson to my master'.

[5] Esther Inglis, *Le Livre des Pseaumes escrites en diverses sortes de lettres par Esther Anglois francoise. A Lislebourg en Escosse 1599* (Christ Church, Oxford, MS 180).

[6] BL, Add. MS 4125, fol. 354: Bartholomew Kello to unknown, 14 July 1599.

[7] Ibid.

[8] BL, Add. MS 4125, fol. 355: Bartholomew Kello to Queen Elizabeth, 18 July 1599. The letter is signed 'your Ma*jes*ties Most humbill most obedient and fayt*h*full serviteur Bartholomew Kello'.

[9] BL, Add. MS 4125, fol. 357: Bartholomew Kello to unknown, 15 Aug. 1599.

[10] Ibid.

[11] LPL, MS 660, fols 231^{r}-32^{r}: Relation of 'm*onsieu*r kello' on the commanders in Brittany, Dec. 1595.

[12] See Paul E.J. Hammer, 'The Uses of Scholarship: The Secretariat of Robert Devereux, Second Earl of Essex, c. 1585-1601', *EHR*, 109 (1994), 26-51; *idem*, *The Polarisation of Elizabethan Politics. The Political Career of Robert Devereux, 2nd Earl of Essex, 1585-1597*, Cambridge: CUP, 1999, pp. 152-98.

[13] David Masson (ed.), *Register of the Privy Council of Scotland, 1545-1625*, 14 vols, Edinburgh: HM General Register House, 1877-1970, vol. 5 (1592-99), pp. xlvi, lix; for Bothwell's political career, see *DNB*, revised ed.; London: OUP, 1973, vol. 2, pp. 906-9.

[14] Bacon wrote: 'Monsieur D'autant que ie m'asseure que mons^{r} kello vostre parent a presente et vous auez desia accepte mes tresiustes excuses de mon sylence pour lors, Je n'y insisteray point d'aduantage': LPL, MS 659, fol. 216^{r}. My translations of Bacon's letter are based on Thomas Birch, *Memoirs of the Reign of Queen Elizabeth From the Year 1581 till her Death*, 2 vols, London: A. Millar, 1754, vol. 2, p. 158.

[15] Bacon wrote: 'que ie presume vous ne trouverez pas indignes de vostre cognoissance et Lecture vous payant de les reseruer a vous mesmes ne desirant point que l'eccho de mon nom rebonde aus oreilles de n*ost*re Ambassadour': LPL, MS 659, fol. 216^{r}.

[16] Ibid.

[17] Ziegler, 'More Than Feminine Boldness', p. 24; A.H. Scott-Elliot and Elspeth Yeo, 'Calligraphic Manuscripts of Esther Inglis (1571-1624): a Catalogue', *The Papers of the Bibliographical Society of America*, 84 (1990), 11-63 (p. 12). Scott-Elliot and Yeo cite Cecil as Kello's correspondent: p. 12.

[18] David Laing, 'Notes Relating to Mrs Esther (Langlois or) Inglis, the Celebrated Calligraphist, with an Enumeration of the Manuscript Volumes Written by her Between the

Years 1586 and 1624', *The Proceedings of the Society of Antiquaries of Scotland*, 2 (1865), 284-309 (p. 288).
[19] Ibid., p. 288.
[20] Ibid., p. 288.
[21] Ibid., pp. 289, 288.
[22] Ibid., pp. 288-89.
[23] Esther Inglis (attrib.), University of Edinburgh Library, MS La.III.522; see Scott-Elliot and Yeo, 'Calligraphic Manuscripts', p. 33.
[24] The manuscript of the 1599 *Livre des Pseaumes* is in a severely decayed condition. Hereafter, quotations from this manuscript will be taken from Laing, 'Notes', pp. 292-93, which cites Rev. W.D. Macray's transcription.
[25] Ibid., p. 293.
[26] Esther Inglis, *Les Proverbes de Salomon escrites en diverses sortes de lettres par Esther Anglois Françoise. A Lislebourg en Escosse, 1599.* (Bodl., MS 990), xi-xii.
[27] Frank Livingstone Huntley, *Essays in Persuasion: On Seventeenth-Century English Literature*, Chicago and London: The University of Chicago Press, 1981, p. 49.
[28] King James VI of Scotland, *Basilicon Doron. Or His Maiesties Instructions to his Dearest Sonne, Henry the Prince*, Edinburgh: Robert Walde-graue, [1603], sigs. C4^{v}-C5^{r}, quoted in Huntley, *Essays*, pp. 49-50.
[29] For this manuscript see BL, MS Royal 18 XV.
[30] Inglis' practice here might also be viewed within the context of early modern women's use of images of Solomon in their embroidery; see Jones and Stallybrass, *Renaissance Clothing*, p. 162.
[31] Fynes Moryson, *An Itinerary Written by Fynes Moryson, Gent. First in the Latine Tongue, and then Translated by Him into English*, London: John Beale, 1617, part 2, p. 26.
[32] For an account of Essex's departure, see Lisa Jardine and Alan Stewart, *Hostage to Fortune: the Troubled Life of Francis Bacon*, London: Victor Gollancz, 1998, pp. 214-15.
[33] I am grateful to Eleanor Merchant of Queen Mary, University of London, for this and other Latin translations.
[34] *Pater Patriae* was also the title awarded in 1464 to Cosimo de' Medici by the Council of Ten on Liberty in respect of his enormous services to the city of Florence, a title first given to Cicero after he foiled the Catiline Conspiracy against the Roman Senate; see Vincent Cronin, *The Florentine Renaissance*, Bungay, Suffolk: Collins/Fontana, 1972, p. 74.
[35] Ziegler, 'More Than Feminine Boldness', p. 34.
[36] This commendatory verse is taken from Esther Inglis, *Le Livre de l'Ecclesiaste, ensemble le Cantique de Salomon. Escrites en diverses sortes de Lettres par Esther Anglois Françoise a Lislebourg en Escosse, 1599* (Bodl., MS 990, p. xviii).
[37] See Scott-Elliot and Yeo, 'Calligraphic Manuscripts', p. 33. While the text dedicated to Elizabeth is now in too fragile a state to examine, J.J.G. Alexander and E. Temple, *Illuminated Manuscripts in Oxford College Libraries, The University Archives and the Taylor Institution*, Oxford: Clarendon Press, 1985, Plate 51, shows a photograph of one of the pages of this book, which clearly demonstrates its visual similarity to the works dedicated to Essex and Bacon.
[38] See Scott-Elliot and Yeo, 'Calligraphic Manuscripts', p. 38. The books dedicated to Elizabeth and to Bacon measure 185mm x 130mm and that dedicated to Essex measures 184mm x 128mm.
[39] In 1599 Inglis also dedicated a collection of psalms to Maurice of Nassau, in which she likened him to Alexander the Great. Her varied dedicatory strategies will be the subject of my forthcoming book on the life and works of Esther Inglis.

[40] fol. 3^r.
[41] fol. 4^r.
[42] fol. 3^r.
[43] In Inglis' dedication of *Les Proverbes de Salomon* to the earl of Essex she again refers to 'la faveur particuliere departie de vostre grace a mon mary' [the particular favour shown by your grace to my husband].
[44] fol. 3^v. The translations from French are mine.

Chapter 9

The Cavendish-Talbot Women: Playing a High-Stakes Game

Sara Jayne Steen

When scholars began rewriting the Renaissance[1] with more attention to women, the royal women of Tudor and Stuart England were, by the sheer quantity of material, the easiest women to rediscover. There were many more extant documents or texts related to Anne Boleyn or Elizabeth I than there were to Isabella Whitney, the gentlewoman in service whose 'Last Will and Testament' so wonderfully evokes Tudor London's shops and prisons. For England's monarchs and consorts, and for those close to them, the archives supplied numerous diplomatic and legal records, portraits, histories, biographies, and fictional representations. As a result, many early modern scholars focussed on recovering what was less accessible. Sustained and dedicated interdisciplinary research has led to the publication of more texts written by women than scholars once imagined could be possible – diaries, memoirs, letters, poetry, plays, fiction, translations and treatises. Scholars have begun to re-imagine a manuscript culture that included writers of both sexes. And material goods that could be 'read' – embroidery, handkerchiefs, jewellery, and household objects – have facilitated recovery of women's everyday experiences. This recent scholarship raises significant methodological questions for the interpretation of aristocratic women's letters. For example, how might these women's letters be read with an understanding of the manuscript culture in which they were formulated? What linguistic subtleties might be lost to modern readers?[2] How did these women operate within an elaborate system of court politics, of patronage and material gift-giving? In this essay I would like to discuss the lives and letters of three Cavendish-Talbot women and begin to explore their writing within the context of the questions above.

The first letter-writer is Elizabeth Talbot (née Hardwick), by her fourth marriage countess of Shrewsbury, and popularly known as 'Bess of Hardwick' (a familiar name she did not use). The second is her daughter by her husband William Cavendish, Mary Talbot (née Cavendish), also later countess of Shrewsbury when her husband Gilbert became the seventh earl upon the death of George, Mary's father-in-law and step-father. The third is Lady Arbella Stuart, not a Cavendish or Talbot in the sense of naming but in the early modern sense of kinship. As the daughter of Elizabeth Cavendish and Charles Stuart, countess and earl of Lennox, she was the niece of Mary Talbot, and the granddaughter of Elizabeth Talbot. These individuals represent three generations of aristocratic women in a single family, one of them – Lady Arbella Stuart – a potential heir to the throne. Their portraits suggest a family resemblance; the women even may have worn the same pearls for their sittings (see Figures 9.1-9.3).

Although all three women were at court on occasion and sometimes for sustained periods, their lives were spent largely in Derbyshire, away from court and the advancement that regular attendance on the monarch could bring. They understood that information was critical and powerful and relied on letters to and from intermediaries and friends, and sometimes even paid informants. In another essay in this collection, James Daybell discusses in more depth Elizabeth Talbot's elaborate news network.[3] All three women worked, sometimes more and sometimes less successfully, within a political system that required intellectual ability and social adroitness. They were of a rank and level of influence to compel consideration. Their lives and letters suggest that, rather than viewing themselves as definitively removed from the sphere of politics because of their gender or geographic isolation, they played politics as a high-stakes game and both actively and reactively shaped themselves as players.

Elizabeth Talbot, countess of Shrewsbury, had extended experience with the seriousness of court politics. In 1561, as Lady St Loe and a lady of the Privy Chamber to Queen Elizabeth, she had been an observer of, and perhaps associated with, the Catherine Grey scandal.[4] Catherine Grey – friend, godmother to Lady St Loe's daughter Elizabeth, and co-Lady-in-Waiting to the Queen – had clandestinely married Edward Seymour, earl of Hertford and another claimant to the throne, and had become pregnant. That marriage was declared invalid and any children thus illegitimate; Catherine Grey died in prison. Recent scholars argue that the Lady St Loe who was imprisoned in connection with the case was another Lady St Loe, Elizabeth's sister-in-law (also Elizabeth),[5] but regardless of who was imprisoned, Elizabeth Talbot was clearly made aware of the potential consequences of defying the Queen. It, however, seems unlikely that she personally incurred the Queen's displeasure. After her marriage to George Talbot in 1568, a friend at court, Elizabeth Wingfield, reported the Queen's reaction:

> I haue bene glade to se my lady Sayntloa but now more dyssirous to se my lady Shrewsbury I hope sayd she my lady hath knowne my good opennon of her and thus muche I assure you there ys no lady ys [in] thys land that I beter loue and lyke.[6]

In 1569, Elizabeth Talbot received Mary, Queen of Scots, now in the custody of the earl of Shrewsbury, as a prisoner and certainly understood that even an anointed queen was not invulnerable to royal disfavour.

Nonetheless, Elizabeth Talbot took the risk of supporting and probably arranging the clandestine marriage of her daughter Elizabeth Cavendish to Charles Stuart, earl of Lennox, last surviving son of the countess of Lennox, younger brother of Henry Lord Darnley and thus brother-in-law to the queen of Scots, and, most importantly, an heir to the throne. It was a bold gamble. Although Queen Elizabeth was angry, investigated the marriage, and even imprisoned the countess of Lennox, Elizabeth Talbot survived with her fortune and reputation intact. The Queen of Scots remained in George Talbot's custody, surely an indication of Queen Elizabeth's on-going confidence in the couple; and even after the countess's granddaughter and royal claimant Arbella Stuart was born, the Queen wrote to the earl and countess acknowledging her debt, 'as great as a Sou*er*aigne can owe to a subiect', and noting that England's peace was maintained by their safekeeping of Mary of Scots.[7]

Not surprisingly, given the countess of Shrewsbury's well-known passion for building, many of the letters she wrote over decades have to do with the construction of Chatsworth and Hardwick Hall. She sent lists of work to be done to stewards, gave directions to her builder, forwarded seeds for a garden, detailed instructions for erecting a battlement, wrote to her husband George for timber, iron, and money for oxen, lamented when she could not provide beer for her workmen, debated hangings and carpets, and called for a plumber.[8] She maintained family bonds with letters about health and wellbeing.[9] She also received information at a significant rate; she knew the articles of peace concluded with France before English translations were available, was given details of treason trials, and was updated on the foreign news circulating at court.[10] After her daughter Elizabeth, Arbella's mother, had died and the countess's relationship with her husband George had soured, he wrote that he had been 'moved' to take Elizabeth of Lennox's men into his household; however, he was aware that numerous people regularly reported to his estranged wife and said he did not need more of them: 'I have too many spyes in my howse alredy'.[11]

Elizabeth Talbot's letters also reflect the delicate negotiations involved in promoting and maintaining relationships with Queen Elizabeth and those around her. In a gift-giving culture in which the personal and the

Figure 9.1 Elizabeth Talbot, countess of Shrewsbury

Figure 9.2 Mary Talbot, countess of Shrewsbury (misidentified as Queen Elizabeth)

Figure 9.3 Lady Arbella Stuart

political were intertwined, gifts and responses to them held special significance. Not long after granddaughter Arbella's birth, an event that could have led to further disfavour, Lady-in-Waiting Elizabeth Wingfield wrote that the countess's New Year's gift to the Queen had been well received. The Queen had told the earl of Leicester and the Lord Chamberlain that 'she neuer had any [garments] so well lyked her'[12] – words that likely relieved the countess, since in saying so the Queen was making a political statement that clearly would be passed to the countess by her friends, in letters that would themselves be gifts. Within the aristocratic community, words like 'friend' and 'friendship' were politically weighted; access, influence, and networking were features of the political game and required regular reaffirmation of one's friendships.[13]

The Queen's pleasure with a New Year's gift did not mean, however, that the Queen would automatically accede to one's requests, especially if they involved money. After Arbella's parents died, her grandmother wrote to both Francis Walsingham and William Cecil asking them to urge the Queen to transfer Lady Lennox's portion to her daughter. Consistently Elizabeth Talbot's language emphasises her service and Arbella's future service to the Queen. The portion was necessary, the countess argued, because preparing the child so that she 'may the sooner be ready to attend on her Majesty'[14] would be expensive: 'her better education her servauntes that are to loke to her, her masters that are to trayne her upp in all good Learninge and vertue will require no small charges'.[15] The countess describes Arbella in phrases that called attention to the child's royal rank and blood relationship to the Queen but that also highlighted the countess's own loyalty, which well might have been called in question:

> ...neare well towards vij yeares ould she ys of very greate towardnes to learne anytheng, and I very careful of her good educatyon as yf she were my owne and only chyld, and a great deale more for the consanguynitye she ys of <to> her majesty whos happye raigne over us I dayly with most zealous mynd pray the allmeghty governor of allthenges long to contenew.[16]

Well educating her grandchild, as the countess cast it, was another form of loving and serving her Queen. The suit, however, was not successful, and the Queen was said to have been exceedingly annoyed when she learned not long afterwards that the countess was negotiating the child's marriage to Robert Dudley, earl of Leicester's son, Robert. Because of the Queen's affection for Leicester, the countess might have thought the Queen would be likely to declare Arbella her successor; instead, the Queen blocked the marriage. It is not surprising that at court words of affection and loyalty were scrutinised for motive and nuance.

Having once shared the custody of Mary, Queen of Scots, who had been executed for plotting against Queen Elizabeth, Elizabeth Talbot now was the guardian of another claimant, her granddaughter, about whom plots were swirling. In 1592, Lord Burghley wrote to warn the now dowager countess of Shrewsbury of a conspiracy, a 'wycked practyse' against her and Arbella, as the countess phrased it. Her reply emphasises her vigilance, and again she carefully constructs herself in her letter as a reliable supporter of the crown who, much as she loves this grandchild, honours and loves equally her queen:

> I wyll not have any unknowen or suspected person to come to my howse, uppon the least suspicion that may happen here, any wey, I shall give advertisement to your Lordship/ I have litle resort to me, my house is furnished with sufficient company, Arbell walks not late, at such tyme as she shall take the ayre, yt shalbe nere the howse, and well attended on; she goeth not to any bodyes howse atall, I se hyr almost every howre in the day, she lyeth in my bed chamber, yf I can be more precise then I have bene I wylbe. I am bound in nature to be careful for Arbell; I find her loving and dutyfull to me; yet hyr owne good and safety is not dearer to me, nor more by me regarded then to accomplish her Majesties pleasure and that which I think may be for her service.[17]

The countess detailed her past care in taking precautions against a seminarian in the area and her dismissal of one Morley, a tutor to Arbella whom she distrusted (a tutor thought by some current writers to have been Christopher Marlowe, sent by Burghley as a spy).[18] Because Burghley, who had corresponded regularly with the dowager countess, would recognise that this letter was not in her handwriting and thus might suspect her friendship or her discretion if she had allowed a secretary to read his letter or record her response on such a sensitive issue,[19] she added an explanatory note:

> I am inforced to use the hand of my sonn William Cavendysshe / not beinge able to wryte so much my self for feare of bringing greate payne to my hed / he only is pryvy to your Lordships letter / and neyther Arbell nor any other lyuinge / nor shalbe.[20]

As the Queen grew older and had not named her successor nor matched Arbella, now in her mid-twenties, in marriage, Elizabeth Talbot continued to press for a suitable match for her granddaughter, attempting to influence the Queen through letters and an extended network of friends. In

January of 1601, Dorothy Stafford, a Lady-in-Waiting to the Queen, wrote to the dowager countess with good news and bad news. The good news was that the Queen had especially liked Lady Arbella's New Year's gift, a scarf of lawn cutwork, with silver and silk of many colours. Lady Stafford had presented it on her behalf. The bad news was the subsequent discussion. The countess had requested that Arbella be bestowed in marriage. Although the Queen responded that she would be careful of Arbella and sent a token in return, her response was polite but dismissive, and the token was not as good as that Arbella had provided or as Stafford would have wished. Stafford urged the countess to continue to trust her to move the Queen, likely from personal and political interests that are hard to separate: Stafford seems to have cared about the countess's interests, but she also would have been significantly rewarded had her intervention produced the desired outcome.[21] The letter well illustrates the complex role of a Lady-in-Waiting and the potential importance to those removed from court of having supportive friends with personal access to the monarch.[22]

In the early months of 1603, two of the Cavendish-Talbot women were in direct opposition over a royal marriage, and they contested for control of letters and information. Lady Arbella Stuart was a bright, well-educated woman now in her later twenties who had become increasingly frustrated by her grandmother's restrictions and the Queen's refusal to allow her to come to court. As a result, she attempted to contract a marriage with Edward Seymour, the grandson of the earl of Hertford, also an heir to the throne. The marriage of two claimants doubtless would have been forbidden and, had it occurred, considered treasonable, as had Hertford's marriage to Catherine Grey. But Queen Elizabeth was ill and failing, as both women at Hardwick Hall knew from their correspondents, even though the court was trying to maintain a façade of normality; the question of the succession was unresolved; and no one could estimate how many northerners might rally to Arbella Stuart if the Queen died. After Sir Henry Brounker, the Queen's representative, investigated, he became convinced that the dowager countess had been entirely unaware of the proposed marriage. She also may have been surprised that her sophisticated intelligence network had failed her and that some of her servants had chosen to obey the young claimant; the countess described them as having been 'corrupted' by her granddaughter.[23] Her response was to tighten security; Stuart would have no visitors, no walking, no riding, no music, and no unmonitored letters or conversations.

In the correspondence that follows, we see feints within feints from both women, with strategies that are both political, in the sense of court politics at the highest level, and intensely personal, with an antagonism that suggests mutual feelings of betrayal. Lady Arbella Stuart received the Queen's pardon, but was not removed from her grandmother's custody or summoned to court as she had requested. Her response was to turn Hardwick Hall's security system to advantage. She knew her letters were being intercepted by her grandmother and forwarded to Robert Cecil, and perhaps also to the Queen. She risked toying with the royal power and used her words to create a fictional second conspiracy with a lover whose seeming existence she must have hoped would cause as much concern as had the first. In a letter supposedly written to her grandmother to explain fully the Hertford conspiracy, she enlarged the plot to include her lover, a wonderful man, high in the Queen and court's esteem, for whom she would abandon everyone except the Queen.[24] Her revisions to the letter indicate that she imagined the Queen as audience, since she occasionally had to modify a phrase like 'your Majesties knowledge' to 'your Ladyships knowledge' as she recalled the ostensible addressee. She pretended in a letter to Sir Robert Cecil and Sir John Stanhope to be abashed by the discovery of her lover and continued to provide hints, but no identifying information, about 'my dearest', whose name 'I dare not trust paper with all'.[25] She requested the opportunity to speak with the Queen or, failing that, to have Sir Henry Brounker again sent to Hardwick Hall so that she could speak to the Queen through a trusted representative. Initially, her bluff was successful. Her grandmother credited the fictional lover or, having been once discovered unaware, feared to dismiss the idea; the dowager countess wrote to the Queen that another match appeared to be in the works, adding the weight of her opinion to the evidence the crown would assess.[26]

In the meantime, because the dowager countess was having Stuart's letters intercepted, Stuart had her attendant Mrs Bridget Sherland write to friends and supporters on her behalf. For example, Sherland wrote to John Hacker, who worked for Mary Talbot (née Cavendish), saying that Stuart wanted him to ask her aunt to come to Hardwick Hall because Stuart was now fully a prisoner. (Presumably it would have seemed reasonable for Mrs Sherland to be writing to Mr Hacker.) At least some of these letters, too, were intercepted, and the dowager countess then wrote feigned replies to them, indicating that the recipients could not come right away or would send on the letter to the appropriate person or wanted more information. The countess then forwarded her secretary's copies of the letters and her feigned replies to court, adding 'They growe nowe so warie [wary] that I doubt I [shall] hardly meet with any more'.[27] Her language – 'They growe nowe so warie' – indicates the degree to which the dowager countess established herself as allied with Cecil and Stanhope, separate from and in opposition to her granddaughter's supporters.

In early March, the contest escalated in intensity. According to Elizabeth Talbot, Arbella Stuart attempted to escape from Hardwick Hall with her uncle Henry Cavendish, who had forty horsemen hidden beyond the gates. This time, the dowager countess's servants obeyed her, and the attempt failed. The countess in a letter to Sir Henry Brounker urged that her granddaughter be moved south where she would have fewer friends,[28] and Brounker, again the crown investigator, wrote to Cecil that he too thought Stuart should be removed. Stuart received, he said, 'dayly advertisements' about 'the Queenes daunger', one of which he had intercepted and enclosed; and, if the Queen died, Stuart could not be 'kept in this place ij dayes' because the dowager countess was weary and her son William Cavendish 'but a weake man for such a pourpos [purpose]'.[29] Brounker, who was unsure of his own role during this transition and would not have wanted to underestimate the danger, presented both women as significant players in a potentially explosive situation. Queen Elizabeth died before Stuart was relocated, and once the succession was settled in King James's favour, Stuart went to Wrest Park in the custody of Henry Grey, earl of Kent, whose nephew, Henry Grey, later the seventh earl of Kent, was married to Arbella's cousin Elizabeth. Eventually Arbella joined James's new court.

Arbella Stuart's interactions with her grandmother afterwards were few. One set of letters, however, is of particular interest in discussing women and politics. When the dowager countess became ill in 1605, Stuart returned to Hardwick, perhaps to nurse her grandmother (or, if one takes a more cynical view, to increase her inheritance). With her, she brought a letter from the king asking that the dowager countess receive her granddaughter with her former kindness, a request politically difficult to refuse. The dowager countess was offended, but she could not directly chastise the king. Instead, she wrote a letter ostensibly to the Dean of the Royal Chapel, one of her informants at court. In it she described her surprise that her granddaughter brought James's letter, 'as either doubting of her entertainment or desiring to come to her from whom she had desired so earnestly to get away'. The dowager countess said she already had expressed her kindness by providing for a small inheritance and had bestowed much considering her 'poor ability' – the latter a comment that doubtless provoked incredulity. In an accompanying letter, the dowager countess instructed the dean to make sure the king read her letter. Although she could not openly criticise the monarch, Elizabeth Talbot did not choose silence. She employed an indirect and thus more politically acceptable means of communicating her response through letters.[30]

The Cavendish-Talbot woman who thus far has been discussed little is Mary Talbot, of the generation between Elizabeth Talbot, her mother, and Arbella Stuart, the niece whom Mary treated as a daughter. Mary Talbot was considered one of England's intellectual women; she was a patron of and regularly contributed financially to St John's College, Cambridge. Often she and her husband Gilbert wrote to and received letters from family, friends, and servants as the partners they were. Letters from the couple may be written in Gilbert's hand and signed by both, written in a secretary's hand and signed by both, or written in both hands, less often with the majority in Mary's handwriting.[31] Mary probably collaborated in their joint responses or at least read and discussed what Gilbert had written before adding notes of her own. Other people also felt comfortable, however, writing to the countess separately about her or the couple's concerns, on topics such as debts, cattle, land leases, mortgages, and lawsuits, anything from her foundry to potential water mills on the River Trent.[32]

Lady Arbella Stuart in her extant letters wrote to her aunt and uncle separately. Her early letters to Gilbert Talbot are the more amusing now, because they are filled with affectionate teasing and court news. In the early court letters, she writes from the perspective of an outsider recently come inside, offering us as readers a privileged glimpse of what we otherwise might not see because those in regular attendance at court would not mention what could be assumed. Her early letters to Mary, however, are the more direct and political in terms of patronage and the exercise of influence. She wrote to Mary, for example, about what she needed from Gilbert, a member of the Privy Council: 'I beseech you gett him [my uncle] to write to my Lord Cecill in my behalfe' about her allowance of diet.[33]

What is most intriguing in the correspondence between aunt and niece and indicative of their closeness is what is absent. Mary had been a surrogate mother during Arbella's childhood, and Arbella apparently had been open in conversations with her aunt. Their correspondence contains repeated indications of the countess's care that Stuart not be equally direct in letters, which could not be trusted to remain private. For example, in September 1603, while the government was investigating a conspiracy to depose James and crown Arbella, her aunt must have sent a veiled postscript. Stuart commented in reply:

> Madame./ if you receive the letters I write I am sure you see I faile not to write often how the world goeth heere both in particuler with me and otherwise as farre as my intelligence stretcheth wherfore I rather interpret

> your postscript to be a Caveat to me to write no more then How I do, and my desire to understand of your health[,] that is no more then is necessary, then a new commaundemente to do that which I already do.[34]

In another letter, Stuart informed her that she awaited a messenger who could be trusted: 'I will bethinck my selfe against your long expected trusty messenger comme whatsoever he be, and that expectation shall keepe me from troubling you with so plaine and tedious a discourse as I could finde in my hart to disburden my minde withall to you'.[35] Once she apologised because a servant sent a packet of her letters by official post, rather than conveying them personally or through an approved messenger: 'I beseech you let us know if you received them safe if I had thought they would have binn sent by post I would have written more reservedly'.[36] During that tense first year, Thomas Cooke, a servant to the earl and countess of Shrewsbury, wrote to the countess about the directions that she and her husband had sent with him and assured her that Stuart had watched him burn them.[37] Letters or instructions could be dangerous and subject to varied interpretations by readers other than the intended audience.

By 1610, and despite repeated promises to match her in marriage, King James still had made no provision for his cousin Arbella. In June, Stuart took matters into her own hands and clandestinely married William Seymour, a grandson of Edward, second earl of Hertford. Both were imprisoned. Stuart's letters of appeal for freedom were considered well written and reasoned by those who read them, but they had little effect on the king, who said she had 'etne of the forbidne trie'.[38] He planned to send her north in the custody of William James, Bishop of Durham, to live much as her aunt Mary, Queen of Scots had lived. Lady Arbella employed her considerable linguistic tools to stay near the court. In one petition, she thanked James for his generosity in allowing her a respite from the journey because of her recent illness; assured him that she would no longer resist the journey and now understood her duty to him; and requested just a little more time.[39] James granted the additional weeks, although he might not have done so had he seen the draft with the angry marginal notes in which she responded to her own text: 'as thoughe I had made resistans ... whereuppon I must confess I bely myselfe extreemely in this'.[40] Her marginal notes argue that she saw her submissive prose here as political strategy. During the weeks of reprieve James granted, the disgraced couple coordinated escapes to France.

The prison escapes were successful; however, for Stuart, the freedom was short-lived. Seymour had been delayed and forced to take a different ship than they had planned, and because Stuart waited for him before landing on the continent, she was re-taken, and he went on safely, of significantly less importance once Stuart, the primary claimant, was again in custody.

Mary Talbot was imprisoned in the Tower after her niece's escape and recapture. The countess probably had participated in planning the attempt or at least was aware of it; she was said to have queried Stuart's Gentleman Usher Hugh Crompton in advance about the plans,[41] and to have bought from Stuart some of Mary, Queen of Scots' needlework to finance the escape.[42] A Roman Catholic, she was suspected of wanting Stuart to join Catholics on the continent. But I have found not a single letter to or from her during these years that offers unequivocal evidence of her awareness or participation; perhaps she had maintained her wonted care in correspondence. Of her few extant letters from this time, those most directly related treat her imprisonment – for example, she wrote to her servant Henry Butler from the Tower that she needed money and knew not which way to turn – and her grief over Stuart's death in 1615.[43]

Ironically, given her discretion in letters, the countess was usually described as lacking diplomacy in speech. She was criticised for answering boldly when questioned about her niece's escape. Over a year after being imprisoned in the Tower, Mary Talbot repeatedly was questioned about Stuart's flight. According to a transcript now in the British Library, when the countess was questioned by Solicitor General Francis Bacon and the Privy Council and assembled justices, she 'refused and persisted in refusall to answer as by her duty & allegeance and by Law and the Custom of the Kingdom she was bound'. Thrice she refused. After the first round, she was described as 'impertinent but ending in an absolute refusall to answer to particulars'; in the second and third rounds she said she was forced to honour a 'rash vowe that she had made not to answer otherwise then in course of ordinary Justice' – and this was not ordinary justice, that is, not a trial. She was reported to have said 'she had rather obey God than Man' and asserted 'priviledge for the Nobility that should exempt them from answer upon Examynation'. The countess then allegedly added that 'if she could have devised to have carried herselfe in a more humble and submissive manner she would have done it'. Her response was termed a 'very high and great Contempt'. Had they been in Star Chamber, the examiners said, they would have imposed a £20 000 fine. As they had no authority to fine her, they returned her to the Tower with a recommendation that her imprisonment be perpetual 'unless she should desist from her Contumacy, & dutifully conforme her selfe to answer as a Subject should'.[44]

In 1618, three years after Stuart's death, Mary Talbot was re-condemned, this time because she refused to answer questions about the rumour that Stuart had given birth to a child 'Kepte privatelye bee yonde the Seas'. Stuart's trusted attendant Anne Bradshaw testified that her mistress was ill, but never pregnant. From everything I have discovered about Stuart's health, there was no pregnancy, and the now dowager countess of Shrewsbury would have had nothing to hide, no one to protect. In any case, she easily could have reassured the king had she wanted to do so. But she did not. Instead, according to extant accounts, the countess 'contemptuouslye refused to make Answere thereunto or to give his Majestie satisfaction'; she again claimed a 'vowe to the Contrarye' and said she 'would respect her soule before a world of Lives'. Her position was derided as a failure of allegiance and 'obstinacye without example'.[45]

When I suggest that the Cavendish-Talbot women played politics as a high-stakes game, it should be clear that my use of 'game' does not mean their actions were without real-life consequences. Quite the contrary was true. But all three employed the system of personal politics to take positions and exert influence; all three took what we would consider bold measures in spite of their awareness of the potential consequences and sometimes were successful; all three were willing in various ways to challenge the crown. Perhaps we should not be surprised that they acquired negative and sexualised reputations, Elizabeth as the builder of halls and dynasties, often described as 'ambitious' or 'redoubtable', with the implication that her authority was unwomanly; Mary as a female intellectual who was domineering and manipulative; and Arbella as a female scholar who was romantic and politically naive. If we begin to remove the layers of repeated opinion accumulated over centuries and review their letters, more detailed and complex portraits emerge of them and of their society. Many questions remain, but we can say that despite their gender and their distance from court the Cavendish-Talbot women were acutely aware of, and active participants in, the game of Tudor and Jacobean politics.

Notes

[1] An allusion to the influential *Rewriting the Renaissance: the Discourses of Sexual Difference in Early Modern Europe*, Margaret W. Ferguson, Maureen Quilligan and Nancy J. Vickers (eds), Chicago and London: The University of Chicago Press, 1986.

[2] See, for example, Lynne Magnusson's *Shakespeare and Social Dialogue: Dramatic Language and Elizabethan Letters*, Cambridge: CUP, 1999; her work-in-progress on women's letters is tentatively entitled 'The Language of Letters: Scripting Social Relations in Englishwomen's Letter-Writing, 1535-1635'.

[3] Ch. 7.

[4] For biographical information on Elizabeth Talbot, see David N. Durant, *Bess of Hardwick: Portrait of an Elizabethan Dynast*, London: Weidenfeld & Nicolson, 1977; rev. paperback ed., London: Peter Owen, 1999.
[5] See Durant, *Bess of Hardwick*, rev. ed., addendum.
[6] Folger, MS X.d.428 (129): to Elizabeth Talbot, 21 Oct. [1568].
[7] LPL, MS 3206, fol. 819: 25 June 1577. Partial transcripts of the Talbot papers now held at Lambeth Palace Library are printed in G. R. Batho, *A Calendar of the Shrewsbury and Talbot Papers in Lambeth Palace Library and the College of Arms*, London: HMSO, 1971.
[8] Folger, X.d.428 (82): to Francis Whitfield, 14 Nov. [1552]; X.d.428 (83): to James Crompe, 8 Mar. [1560?]; X.d.428 (84): to Francis Whitfield, 20 Oct. [1560?]; LPL, MS 3205, fol. 58: to George Talbot, n.d. [1570s]; LPL, MS 3205, fols 66, 68: both to George Talbot, n.d. [1577].
[9] See, for example, LPL, MS 3205, fols 64, 72: both to Mary Talbot, n.d. [1580s].
[10] LPL, MS 3206, fol. 565: from unknown, 31 Aug. 1570.
[11] LPL, MS 3197, fol. 120: to Thomas Baldwin, 10 Feb. 1582.
[12] Folger, X.d.428 (130): 2 Jan. [1576 or 1577].
[13] Elizabeth McCutcheon, 'Playing the Waiting Game: the Life and Letters of Elizabeth Wolley', *Quidditas*, 20 (1999), 31-53, (pp. 45-47); Linda Levy Peck, *Court Patronage and Corruption in Early Stuart England*, Boston: Unwin Hyman, 1990; paperback, London: Routledge, 1993, pp. 12-29.
[14] Elizabeth Cooper, *The Life and Letters of Lady Arabella Stuart*, 2 vols, London: Hurst and Blackett, 1866, 1, pp. 61-62: to Sir Francis Walsingham, 28 Jan. [1582].
[15] BL, Lansd. MS 34, fols 4-5: to Burghley, 28 Jan. 1582.
[16] PRO, SP12/153/ 84: to Sir Francis Walsingham, 6 May 1582. Words in brackets (< >) represent additions or deletions in the MS.
[17] BL, Lansd. MS 71, fol. 3: 21 Sept. 1592.
[18] See, for example, John Baker and Susan Olsen, 'Marlowe and the Girl Who Would be Queen', *The Marlovian*, 2, 1 (Winter 1995), 1-2. The controversy is discussed by Charles Nicholl, *The Reckoning: the Murder of Christopher Marlowe*, New York: Harcourt Brace, 1992, pp. 340-42; although Nicholl doubts that the tutor was Marlowe, he suggests further investigation is needed.
[19] James Daybell, '"Ples acsep thes my skrybled lynes": the Construction and Conventions of Women's Letters in England, 1540-1603', *Quidditas*, 20 (1999), 207-23 (p. 215); *idem*, 'Women's Letters and Letter Writing in England, 1540-1603: an Introduction to the Issues of Authorship and Construction', *Shakespeare Studies*, 1999, 161-86 (pp. 176-77).
[20] BL, Lansd. MS 71, fol. 3: 21 Sept. 1592.
[21] Folger, MS X.d.428 (120): 13 Jan. 1601.
[22] See, for example, McCutcheon, 'Playing the Waiting Game'.
[23] Hatfield House, Herts, Cecil Papers 135, fol. 129: to Sir John Stanhope and Sir Robert Cecil, 2 Feb. 1603.
[24] Sara Jayne Steen (ed.), *The Letters of Lady Arbella Stuart*, New York and Oxford: OUP, 1994, letter 7: n.d. [29 Jan. - 2 Feb. 1603]. Subsequent references to Stuart's letters will refer to this edition.
[25] Steen (ed.), letter 8.
[26] Cecil Papers 135, fol. 127: 29 Jan. 1603.
[27] Ibid. 135, fol. 127: Elizabeth Talbot to Queen Elizabeth, 29 Jan. 1603.
[28] Ibid. 135, fol. 167: 10 Mar. 1603.
[29] Ibid. 135, fol. 175: 19 Mar. 1603.
[30] As cited in Cooper, *The Life and Letters of Lady Arabella Stuart*, 2, pp. 48-49.

[31] See, for example, LPL, MS 3197, fol. 307: to George Talbot, 4 Apr. 1579; LPL, MS 3206, fol. 903: to George Talbot, 14 Oct. 1578; Folger, X.d.428 (112): to Elizabeth Talbot, 1 Aug. 1577; Folger, X.d.428 (113): to Elizabeth Talbot, [19 Sept. 1583?]; Folger, X.d.428 (114): to Elizabeth Talbot, [Feb. 1589]; Folger, X.d.428 (115), to Elizabeth Talbot, 1 July 1589; LPL, MS 697, fol. 53: to George Talbot, 6 Mar. 157[9]; LPL, MS 702, fol. 21: to Thomas Cooke, 5 Feb. 1604. Partial transcripts of the Shrewsbury papers are printed in Catherine Jamison, *Calendar of the Shrewsbury and Talbot Papers in Lambeth Palace Library and the College of Arms*, London: HMSO, 1966.

[32] LPL, MS 3203, fol. 288: from Sir Francis Leake, 10 Apr. 1605; LPL, MS 3203, fol. 570: from Sir John Bentley, 23 Feb. 1609; LPL, MS 3205, fol. 108: from Lucrece Hatcliffe, 30 June 1606; LPL, MS 698, fol. 137: from William Kirkbye, 10 Jan. 1599; LPL, MS 698, fol. 139: from John Hacker, 19 Jan. 1596; LPL, MS 709, fol. 15: from one Ratclyff, 8 Dec. 1589.

[33] Steen (ed.), letter 24.

[34] Ibid., letter 26.

[35] Ibid., letter 30.

[36] Ibid., letter 37.

[37] LPL, MS 3203, fol. 182: 12 Feb. 1604.

[38] Steen (ed.), letter B15.

[39] For discussion of Arbella's use of illness as a strategy, see Sara Jayne Steen, '"How Subject to Interpretation": Lady Arbella Stuart and the Reading of Illness', in James Daybell (ed.), *Early Modern Women's Letter Writing, 1450-1700*, Basingstoke: Palgrave, 2001, pp. 109-26.

[40] Steen (ed.), letter 101.

[41] BL, Stowe MS 424, fol. 165.

[42] David N. Durant, *Arbella Stuart: A Rival to the Queen*, London: Weidenfield and Nicolson, 1978, p. 191.

[43] LPL, MS 3205, fol. 97: 16 Dec. 1610; *HMC* Eleventh Report (1887), Appendix, Part 7, p. 83, 'Manuscripts of Lord Hothfield': Mary Talbot to countess of Cumberland, 8 Dec. 1615.

[44] BL, Stowe MS 424, fol. 165 (early eighteenth-century copy of the 1612 proceedings).

[45] University of London, Senate House, ULL MS. 20, fols 145-50: 'Examination of Mary of Shrewsbury'; BL, Trumbull Add. MS 36: 'Privy Council Orders'.

Chapter 10

Aristocratic Women, Power, Patronage and Family Networks at the Jacobean Court, 1603-1625

Helen Payne

Around 1617, a rare pictorial representation of a Jacobean family group was painted, possibly by Paul van Somer, a Flemish artist patronised by Anne of Denmark, consort of James VI and I (see Figure 10.1). This portrait – of Sir Robert Carey (later first earl of Monmouth), his wife and three children – is also a unique visual record of a family with a long tradition of royal service which, during Elizabeth I's reign, owed much to their close kinship with the Queen.[1] This tradition continued into the reign of James VI and I, with four of the five members of Sir Robert's family serving various members of the royal family. Sir Robert stands in the centre of the portrait – as *pater familias* – holding his white staff of office as Chamberlain of Prince Charles's household, a post he gained after Charles was created Prince of Wales in November 1616. Elizabeth Lady Carey is placed between and behind her husband and son Thomas, but it was she who played a central role in the establishment of her family at the Jacobean court.

This essay seeks to restore Lady Carey and other aristocratic women to their rightful place as active and significant members of family networks at the Jacobean court – networks upon which power and patronage in that institution were based. Jacobean court women – like early modern elite English women in general – served the political as well as the dynastic and economic ambitions of their families through marriage. They also served the interests of their families through their activities as courtiers and Ladies-in-Waiting.[2]

Aristocratic women were present at the Jacobean court as the kin and friends of prominent male household officials, ministers, councillors, courtiers and favourites, as well as holders of household posts in their own right. Kinship connections also provided a means by which women could secure a place in the Queen consort's Privy Chamber.[3] Once appointed to court posts, membership of family service networks stretching across the various royal households facilitated the court careers of these women enabling them not only to participate in court politics and patronage for their own purposes, but also to promote family interests.[4] Roger Manners' advice to his niece, Lady Bridget Manners, when she was accepted into Queen Elizabeth's service in 1589, indicates how useful her Privy Chamber post could be to family and friends. Manners advised her *inter alia* that she was to be 'dyligent, secret and faythfull' in the Queen's service, and to 'be no medeller in the causes of others [and] that [her] speech and indevors ever tend to the good of all and to the hurt of non'. Not only would Lady Bridget benefit by following these rules, but also her friends would 'rejoyse of [her] well doying': that is, through her they too would benefit.[5]

Some women were central to court family networks; for example, Queen Anne's principal Ladies-in-Waiting: Elizabeth (née Trevannion) Lady Carey, Lucy Russell (née Harington), countess of Bedford, and Jane Drummond (Lady Roxburghe from 1614 and countess of Roxburghe from 1616). All three were long-serving career courtiers and their cases are discussed in more detail below. Other women with close connections to influential men and the King's favourites also played their part. Among the most prominent of these was Katherine Howard (née Knyvett), countess of Suffolk, wife of the King's Lord Chamberlain and later Lord Treasurer, and an intimate friend of Robert Cecil, first earl of Salisbury, Secretary of State and Lord Treasurer. Prominent later in the reign were the countesses of Buckingham and Denbigh, mother and sister respectively of the favourite, George Villiers, duke of Buckingham. Nevertheless, the concomitant opportunities for the exercise of female power and influence offered by kinship and royal service should not be exaggerated and account must be taken of the limitations that the patriarchal structures of family and court placed on the activities of these women.

Family

The court family networks of aristocratic women included not only those of their husbands and children, but also of their parents and siblings; what Charles T. Wood describes as 'a dual kinship relationship'. 'By way of contrast', he observes, 'a man's place tended to be defined primarily by his membership in a single patrilineal family'.[6] An example of this 'dual kinship relationship' is expressed visually in a portrait of the countess of Bedford in the Swedish National Portrait Collection at Gripsholm Castle in Sweden (see Figure 10.2). She is splendidly attired in robes of estate and coronet, which identify her as a countess through marriage to an earl. However, the presence of her parents' coat of arms on the chair cushion rather than that of her and her husband's (the more usual practice) represents her as a daughter as well as a wife, and reflects her significant kinship connection at the Jacobean court – that of her paternal family.

As successful courtiers, aristocratic women could, and did, benefit their families, but they also had to balance the commitments of marriage, children and family with their duties as Ladies-in-Waiting and obligations as members of family service networks. Moreover, 'family' was a double-edged patriarchal sword for court women: on the one hand, it enabled and facilitated their participation in court service, politics and patronage, but, on the other hand, as most were wives and mothers, pregnancy and other family responsibilities could limit their activities in this sphere.

The progresses made by the King and Queen around the countryside in the summer offered an opportunity for courtiers to absent themselves from duty in order to spend time with their husbands and wives, and to visit their extended families and country estates. The Queen's Ladies-in-Waiting sometimes accompanied her for a part of the progress, then slipped away.[7] Courtiers whose country houses were situated on the King's route to his favourite hunting grounds at Newmarket and Royston were best placed to combine royal service with family life. Susan Herbert (née de Vere), countess of Montgomery – a Lady of the Withdrawing Chamber – found this a solution to the problem of balancing family life with a husband who was in constant attendance on the King as a Gentleman of the Bedchamber and one of his regular hunting companions. During her child-bearing years in the 1610s Lady Montgomery was based at Enfield, a royal house in Middlesex, of which her husband was then keeper.[8] Conveniently located near the King's great house of Theobalds, which he used as a regular stop between London and his hunting lodges, Enfield became a kind of unofficial 'court' as Lady Montgomery was visited by the King and courtiers, and entertainments and the baptisms of the Montgomery infants were held there.[9]

Producing an heir and ensuring its survival was a critical part of every aristocratic woman's life. Thus, pregnancy, childbirth and child-rearing could have a marked effect on service and attendance. Elizabeth Stanley (née de Vere), countess of Derby, for instance, withdrew from service as a Lady of the Withdrawing Chamber some time before the birth of her eldest son James, the Derby heir, on 31 January 1606 and did not return.[10] Even the countess of Bedford, at court without her husband (except when he attended on ceremonial occasions), absented herself from

Figure 10.1 1st Earl of Monmouth and his family

Figure 10.2 Lucy Harington, countess of Bedford (misidentified as Queen Elizabeth)

service to have children (although one child died shortly after birth and she miscarried the other).[11] Pregnancy and childbearing though was not necessarily incompatible with court service. The births of two children only briefly interrupted the service of the 'first lady' of the Bedchamber, Jane Drummond. She returned to her duties almost immediately following each childbirth.[12]

The Court, Power and Patronage

The patriarchal norms of the court also imposed restrictions on women. With the exception of the monarchy, women were excluded by virtue of their sex from high office; that is, from those positions in government and in the royal households which gave the degree of authority necessary for the exercise of significant *direct* and *formal* power, major influence and patronage.[13] Of course, most men at court were in the same situation.[14] As men, however, there was a critical difference – they could aspire to such positions and power where women could not.

Moreover, the accession of a male monarch in 1603 displaced court women from the personal access they had enjoyed as Ladies-in-Waiting or favoured companions of the regnant queens, Mary and Elizabeth. Exceptions were the Villiers women whose kinship with the King's favourite, the duke of Buckingham, gained them intimate access to James in the last half of his reign. The Villiers family became the King's surrogate family and James's deep personal attachment to his favourite extended to Buckingham's mother and sister, and to his wife Katherine (née Manners) after their marriage in 1620.[15] A 'Relation of England' written in September 1622 by Girolamo Lando, the Venetian Ambassador, sheds an interesting light on the role of these women. According to Lando, 'the favourites' (presumably Buckingham and James Hay, viscount Doncaster) used the intimacy of their closest female relatives with the King to keep an eye on James and to ensure that he remained firmly attached to them in their absence.[16]

The exercise of power by women at court, as in early modern society generally, is thus difficult to evaluate, as Sharon Kettering demonstrates in her study of early modern French noblewomen.[17] This difficulty, as I have already discussed, arises from the fact that the 'actual power of women was hidden behind institutional powerlessness'. However, French noblewomen in this period were able to exercise 'a considerable amount of patronage power' because 'the patron-client ties and networks dominating noble society were informal, fluid, non-institutional, and well suited to the exercise of indirect power through personal relationships by women [who] exercised political influence through these ties'.[18] The nature of patron-client networks in England mirrored those of the French nobility, and personal relationships were the key to the participation of aristocratic women in Jacobean court politics and patronage. The power, influence and patronage of Jacobean court women, like that of many men, was contingent on their relationships with powerful men, both family members and friends.[19]

With both direct access and the formal channels of power closed to them, most Jacobean court women were obliged to operate through those informal channels which were available: an important place in the Queen's service and favour, significant kin and other personal relationships, patronage networks and judicious hospitality.[20] Aristocratic court women pursued their interests through these different avenues with great skill and enterprise. They often pushed the boundaries of patriarchal constraints and, in certain circumstances, an association with a particular woman could serve the interests of a powerful man. The countess of Suffolk, for instance, acted as a go-between with Salisbury and successive Spanish ambassadors, lining her own pockets in the process. In 1604 at the time of the signing of the Anglo-Spanish peace treaty in London, Taxis, the Spanish ambassador, acceded to Lady Suffolk's requests for money and jewels so that she would keep Salisbury 'well disposed' towards his country. Although Taxis did not consider her services to Spain 'to be so great', he argued that not to keep her satisfied financially 'would be dangerous now and for the future'.[21]

Kettering's qualification of French noblewomen's power as 'indirect power' thus comes closest to defining that exercised by their Jacobean counterparts. Lady Suffolk had the power to demand money and jewels from successive Spanish ambassadors based on her relationship with Salisbury, and the power to extort money from suitors during her husband's term as Lord Treasurer based on his position.[22] She, like other aristocratic court women, also had the power to influence or to mediate, the power to recommend a person or a suit, and occasionally the power to broker, but this power was wholly dependent on relationships with powerful men. On the other hand, Jane Drummond's position was unique among Jacobean court women. A Scottish baron's daughter who had been in the Queen's service in Scotland, she was not only 'first lady of the Bedchamber' but also a fervent Roman Catholic. Jane's confessional allegiance and her position as the Queen's most intimate attendant and closest confidante made her particularly useful to diplomats from Catholic Europe. On the mistaken assumption that Anne had significant influence with her husband, many ambassadors cultivated Jane as a confidential informant and go-between with her royal mistress. Spain even paid her a secret pension for her services.[23] Jane's power was thus contingent on her close relationship with the Queen and dependent on maintaining the fiction of Anne's influence with the King in the sphere of foreign politics. The countess of Bedford, Jane's Puritan Bedchamber colleague, on the other hand, worked principally through powerful ministers, officials and favourites at the King's court to achieve her ends.

Kinship and Family Networks

Female as well as male kinship connections at court could be useful. Husbands could benefit from their wives' positions in the Queen's Privy Chamber and from their favour with the Queen. Sir Thomas Walsingham was appointed joint Keeper of the Queen's Robes with his wife Audrey Lady Walsingham in 1608, a post she had held on her own since 1603, and Sir Geroge Carew reportedly gained the Mastership of the Court of Wards in 1612 'by his wives grace with the Quene as is thought or rather as others say by the Lord of Rochester [later earl of Somerset]'.[24] Conversely, other husbands – notably the earls of Somerset and Suffolk – were ruined by the criminal activities of their wives (murder in the case of the countess of Somerset and extortion in the case of the countess of Suffolk, her mother).[25]

Female kin could assist with suits and disputes. Lady Arbella Stuart was pushed hard by her uncle, Sir William Cavendish, to forward his suit to be created a baron, although Cavendish also sought the help of the countess of Bedford.[26] The countess of Shrewsbury's niece, Elizabeth Stapleton, personally pursued a suit at court for a pension in 1605, the ground having been initially prepared by her aunt who wrote to her friend, Salisbury (then Lord Cranborne), on her behalf. [27] Once Mistress Stapleton had established that Cranborne would look favourably on her suit 'if it came before him', the earl of Northampton (Lord Privy Seal) presented her to the King. Mistress Stapleton was required by the King to modify her suit and then to proceed through Cranborne and Lord Treasurer Dorset, to which end she requested her aunt to write letters to them on her behalf.[28] Ultimately she gained a pension for life of £200 per annum through

Northampton, and through Dorset's daughter, Lady Glemham who, she reported, had 'bean most Honorabli kind and carefull of my well doing'.[29]

The Carey family offers a striking example of the importance of kinship at court and the significant role that women could play. Sir Robert Carey had made a headlong dash on horseback to Scotland to be the first to inform James of his accession to the throne of England. For his efforts, Carey was initially made a Gentleman of the Bedchamber but demoted to the Privy Chamber a short while later.[30] In his *Memoirs*, Carey stated that his wife waited on the Queen when she arrived from Scotland, and that at Windsor in July 1603 she 'was sworn of her Privy Chamber, and Mistress of her Sweet Coffers, and had a lodging allowed her in court'.[31] Around October 1604 Lady Carey was also appointed Keeper of the four-year-old Prince Charles, duke of York.[32] According to Carey, 'the queen (by approbation of the Lord Chancellor [of Scotland]) made choice of [his] wife to have the care and keeping of the Duke'.[33] As a result of his wife's appointment and his 'necessary' residence' with the prince, the King gave Carey, on 25 February 1605, 'the charge and rule' of Charles' household, while Lady Carey had the 'charge and oversight of the person' of the prince.[34]

Lady Carey also maintained her post in the Queen's Privy Chamber and, as well as the Mastership of the prince's household, secured for her husband 'a suit of the King that was worth ... afterwards four or five thousand pounds' while he was 'from court'.[35] The Careys consolidated their family network at court by also securing places for two of their children in royal service. Their daughter, Philadelphia, was 'brought up with [Princess Elizabeth] and served her, and had the happiness to be allowed to wait on her in the privy lodgings', and Thomas, one of their sons, 'by the Queen's means, ... was, before [Prince Charles's creation as Prince of Wales in 1616] sworn a Groom of his Bedchamber'.[36] While Lady Carey's initial appointment to the Queen's Privy Chamber may have been a gesture to soften her husband's demotion in the King's household, she was pivotal in establishing her husband and family securely in royal favour and service.

The countess of Bedford is well known to historians and literary scholars as the leading female Jacobean patron and, as a Lady of the Bedchamber, one of Queen Anne's principal women favourites, from 1603 until the Queen's death in March 1619.[37] Lady Bedford's most significant kinship network at court was that of her paternal family, the Haringtons: her husband rarely came to court after the experience of his involvement in the Essex rebellion in 1601. The Haringtons, unlike the Careys, were not an established court family. It was only the resourcefulness of the countess and her mother, Anne Lady Harington, in travelling to Scotland unofficially to be among the first English women to make the new Queen's acquaintance that secured the Harington family in royal service and favour.[38] It is also probably to the efforts of his wife and daughter that John, first Lord Harington of Exton, owed the Governorship of Princess Elizabeth, and his son, Sir John Harington, owed his favoured place in Prince Henry's entourage. Furthermore, the importance of kinship and the role of women in serving the ambitions of a family newly arrived on the court scene can be seen in Lord Harington's attempt to convince the earl of Salisbury to place his daughter, Lady Frances Cecil, in the princess's entourage. This proposal, although itself a failure, was made by Harington perhaps in the hope that having Lady Frances in his care would prove a successful alternative to his failed proposal to marry her to his son.[39]

The countess of Bedford's other Harington connections at court included her first cousin James Montague, Bishop of Bath and Wells and Dean of the Chapel Royal. His brother, Chief Justice Henry Montagu, enjoyed a brief moment of power as Lord Treasurer in 1620-21. Another first cousin, Theodosia Noel (daughter of Mabel Harington) was the wife of Salisbury's favourite nephew, Sir Edward Cecil. However, in July 1603 Theodosia's father, Sir Andrew Noel, approached Salisbury, not the countess, to take his son under his patronage at court 'and wholly at his disposition'.[40] Noel's approach to Salisbury is an indication that Lady Bedford's patronage power at court was limited despite her high standing with the Queen. Nevertheless, Lady Bedford was successful in preferring the female relatives of her paternal and maternal families to the Queen's service. In the first few years of the reign she 'stacked' the Queen's Bedchamber with her own kin: the two Bulstrode sisters (Dorothy and Cecilia, grand-daughters of her mother's half-sister) and a Harington first cousin, Bridget Lady Markham.[41]

In addition to her place in the Queen's Bedchamber and that of her immediate Harington family in the households of the elder royal children, Lady Bedford (and indeed other Haringtons) were still obliged to cultivate, maintain and, if possible, extend their patronage by Salisbury, to whom they had turned after the fall of the earl of Essex. Until Salisbury's death in May 1612, Lady Bedford repeatedly worked through him on behalf of herself, her Harington family and others, such as the four men who shared her patent, granted in 1611, for the manufacture of gold and silver thread.[42] In 1607, for instance, Lady Bedford wrote to Salisbury on behalf of an uncle. In her letter, which she signed as his 'affectionnat friend, to do you service', she made clear the reliance of both herself and her family upon the patronage of the Secretary of State: 'thus you see my Lord owr holl family have eyther owt of ellection or fortune a dependensy on you [their] affection to serve you'.[43]

Salisbury's death robbed the countess of her powerful patron and the Haringtons' other significant royal connections were dissolved by death within the space of a little over twelve months. Prince Henry died in November 1612 and Lord Harington in August 1613. Six months later Lady Bedford's brother was also dead. Instead of establishing herself again with a single patron she developed a network of male courtiers and household officials. Principal among these was her second cousin, William Herbert, third earl of Pembroke, appointed Lord Chamberlain of the King's household in December 1615, and James, marquess of Hamilton, the King's Scottish favourite from 1617.[44] Lady Bedford continued to be active at court on her own behalf and that of others, including her niece, Anne Chichester, for whom she endeavoured unsuccessfully to secure a politically advantageous match with Hamilton's son.[45]

Even Jane Drummond, the Queen's Roman Catholic Scottish 'first lady', did not lack significant kin connections at the Jacobean court. She was a member of two families prominent at James's court in Scotland: her paternal family, the Drummonds, and her maternal family, the Lindsays. Members of these families had served James in Scotland and some continued to do so after he acceded to the throne of England, including her brother, the first earl of Perth. Jane's Drummond kinship connections through blood and marriage were wide-ranging, extending from the Stuart royal family, across the Scottish aristocracy and the highest officers in the government of Scotland, to members of the King's Bedchamber in Scotland. Several Lindsays were also intimate royal servants.[46] From 1603 until her departure from the Queen's service in 1617, Jane Drummond's political interests and activities at court were shaped not only by her Roman Catholicism, her privileged place as the Queen's closest attendant and confidante, and by her support for Spain, but also by her Scottish kin connections. Indeed, she may have gained her original place in Anne's service in Scotland through these kin connections.[47]

Significantly, but not surprisingly, all the members of Jane Drummond's Scottish 'circle' were (or became) Roman Catholic and nearly all are identifiably pro-Spanish. Prominent among this circle were her brother-in-law, Alexander Seton, earl of Dunfermline, Lord Chancellor of Scotland,[48] her Drummond kinsman, Sir James Elphinstone (first Lord Balmerino), Secretary of State in Scotland, and her maternal Lindsay kin.[49]

Jane's support for Spain (which earned her a secret pension and enabled her to seek Hapsburg patronage for a kinsman of her husband) may thus have been influenced as much by her kinship with these men as by her religion.[50]

The Anglo-Spanish peace in 1604 enabled Jane to profit financially and provided her with the opportunity to participate informally in foreign politics and patronage. In doing so, she maintained the tradition of support for Spanish interests by prominent members of the Lindsay family in the 1580s and 1590s and into the first decade of the seventeenth century.[51] In 1604, for instance, the Spanish Ambassador reported that Sir James Lindsay, one of Jane's kinsmen, had 'been of great use and help to me and by his own hand he readied the necessary means to correspond with the Queen, who trusts him, and with Lady Drummond, her favourite'.[52]

Jane's major achievement on behalf of a kinsman was the role she apparently played in saving the life of Lord Balmerino. In October 1608 Balmerino found himself obliged to 'confess' to allegedly having falsely obtained the King's signature on a letter to the Pope in 1598.[53] James summoned Balmerino to London for the purpose of extracting his 'confession' in order to clear himself from the claim made by Cardinal Bellarmine 'that he misled the papacy in [this] letter ... about his intentions [regarding Roman Catholics] before his accession'.[54] James forbade Balmerino to go to the Queen's court, where he would find support from Anne and his kinswoman Jane Drummond.[55] That James was concerned about what Jane could do is borne out in a letter he wrote to Salisbury. In this letter James reported a visit made by Lord Hay to the Queen at Hampton Court with the purpose of determining her attitude and deflecting her 'first lady' from influencing her mistress on Balmerino's behalf. According to James, Hay informed him that the Queen

> ...would never open her mouth for [Balmerino] if it were not by Mistress Drummond's persuasion, which he says he told to Drummond, who answered him only with a blush; and therefore he advised me to seem angry at the Chancellor [Dunfermline] for another cause for which they already feared my wrath and he said that would move Drummond, who loved the Chancellor much better than the other, to be so careful for appeasing me towards him as she would gladly let the other run his destiny.[56]

If James did take Hay's advice – of feigning anger at Dunfermline in order to deflect Jane from supporting Balmerino – the tactic did not succeed. Nor did James ultimately ignore his wife's intercession on Balmerino's behalf, despite initially claiming that if she tried to mediate in the matter he 'would constantly go on [his] own course without the least alteration'.[57] Balmerino returned to Scotland and was convicted of high treason at St Andrews on 10 March 1609 and sentenced to death.[58] Two days later the earl of Dunbar wrote to Salisbury from Edinburgh that he had recently received a letter 'written from the hands of one near to the Queen's majesty, assuring that if death and wrack befel Balmerinoe the Queene would keep it in her heart upon you and me so long as she lived in this world'.[59] Balmerino's brother, John Elphinstone, was a Gentleman Usher of the Queen's Privy Chamber, but the author of the letter is more likely to have been Jane Drummond.

The Venetian Ambassador reported that the Queen had personally interceded to save Balmerino's life, but that the King had told her that he had already sent to have the sentence carried out.[60] Nevertheless, Balmerino's life was spared and he was later allowed to return to his estates where he died in 1612. Balmerino had claimed that he was the victim of a plot, which may ultimately have swayed James to be merciful.[61] Yet the intercession of the Queen, undoubtedly influenced by his tenacious kinswoman who refused to be intimidated, still appears to have been a significant factor in saving Balmerino's life.[62]

Conclusion

Not all aristocratic women at the Jacobean court, however, played such positive roles in promoting family interests, nor did even the most exalted kin connections guarantee continued success. Families could abandon individual members when they fell from favour, a hard fact which Anne Cranfield (née Brett), countess of Middlesex, discovered when her husband lost the Lord Treasurership in 1624. She was unable to prevail on her husband's behalf either with the King or with his powerful favourite, her first cousin, the duke of Buckingham.[63] Aristocratic women were also at the centre of family disputes which could bring ruin on high-ranking royal servants. One such dispute over land involving the family of Salisbury's elder half-brother, Thomas Cecil, first earl of Exeter, escalated into allegations of incest and poisoning brought against his much younger second countess by her step-grand-daughter-in-law, Lady Roos. The matter, which was finally settled in the countess's favour in Star Chamber in February 1619, resulted in the fall of Lady Roos's father, Sir Thomas Lake, the King's Principal Secretary of State.[64]

Such examples apart, aristocratic women usually made positive contributions to family interests at court and were integral to court family networks. Although their power was contingent and indirect, thus limiting the extent of their patronage and political activities, such women were nonetheless integral to court family networks. As Pauline Croft has recently observed, 'Even in an allegedly patriarchal society, the sustained and successful prosecution of family interests depended heavily on the skills of worldly-wise women'.[65] Lady Carey, the countess of Bedford and Jane Drummond are striking exemplars of such women at the Jacobean court.

Notes

1 Sir Robert's grandfather, William Carey, had been an 'Esquire of the body to Henry VIII' and the husband of Mary Boleyn, Anne Boleyn's sister: F.A. Mares (ed.), *The Memoirs of Robert Carey*. Oxford: Clarendon Press. 1972, p. xiii. [hereafter Carey, *Memoirs*].

2 See Barbara Harris, 'Women and Politics in Early Tudor England', *HJ*, 33, 2 (1990), 259-81. For the roles played by the daughter and grand-daughters of Lord Burghley, Lord Treasurer to Elizabeth I, see Helen Payne, 'The Cecil Women at Court', in Pauline Croft (ed.), *Patronage, Culture and Power: the Early Cecils 1558-1612*, New Haven & London, Yale UP, 2002, pp. 265-81; Linda Levy Peck, *Court Patronage and Corruption in Early Stuart England*, London: Routledge, 1990, 1993, pp. 68-74.

3 See also Harris, 'Women and Politics', p. 274.

4 Barbara Harris's observation about early Tudor court women applies equally to Jacobean court women: 'the select group who held appointments in the royal household or resided at court at the king's expense were particularly well placed to participate in politics': Harris, 'Women and Politics', p. 275.

5 *HMC, The Manuscripts of His Grace the Duke of Rutland, K.G. Preserved at Belvoir Castle*, 4 vols, London, HMSO, 1888, 1, p. 275 (*HMC, Twelfth Report*, Appendix, Part IV). See also Harris, 'Women and Politics', pp. 275-76.

6 Charles T. Wood, 'The First Two Queens Elizabeth, 1464-1503', in Louisa Olga Fradenberg (ed.), *Women and Sovereignty*, Edinburgh: Edinburgh UP, 1992, pp. 121-31 (p. 127).

7 For example, the gathering of the extended Salisbury Cecil family during the 1608 progress (BL, Lansd. MS 90, fol. 157); *HMC, Report on the Manuscripts of Lord De L'Isle & Dudley Preserved at Penshurst Place, Kent*, 6 vols, London: HMSO, 1935-66, 4, pp. 158-59: Lord Lisle to Lady Lisle, 15 Sept. 1609. [hereafter *HMC, De L'Isle*].

8 H.M. Colvin (gen. ed.), *The History of the King's Works*, 6 vols, London: HMSO, 1963-82, vol. 4, 1485-1660, part. 2, pp. 86-89; David Pam, *A History of Enfield*, 3 vols, Enfield Preservation Society, Enfield, 1990-94, *A Parish Near London: Volume One - before 1837*, p. 56.

9 Helen Margaret Payne, 'Aristocratic Women and the Jacobean Court, 1603-1625', unpublished PhD thesis, University of London, 2001, p.189, ns 125, 126.

[10] Payne, 'Aristocratic Women', p. 53, n. 37. Her sister-in-law Alice Stanley (née Spencer), dowager countess of Derby, is the Derby countess at court from 1606.
[11] *HMC, De L'Isle*, 4, p. 229: Lord Lisle to Lady Lisle, 3 Sept. 1610; N.E. McClure (ed.), *The Letters of John Chamberlain*, 2 vols, Philadelphia: American Philosophical Society Memoirs, vol. 12 (parts 1 & 2), 1939, vol. 12, part 1, p. 306: Chamberlain to Carleton, 5 Oct. 1611. [hereafter *Chamberlain Letters*].
[12] PRO E351/544, mem. 43; Lord Braybrooke (ed.), *The Private Correspondence of Jane Lady Cornwallis, 1613-1644*, London: S & J Bentley, Wilson & Fley, 1842, p. 35; *Chamberlain Letters*, part 2, p. 626: John Chamberlain to Sir Dudley Carleton, 30 Apr. 1616.
[13] Robert P. Shepherd, 'Royal Favorites in the Political Discourse of Tudor and Stuart England', unpublished Ph.D dissertation, Claremont University, 1985, p. 12; Sharon Kettering, 'The Patronage Power of Early Modern French Noblewomen', *HJ*, 32, 3 (1989), 817-41 (p. 817).
[14] I am grateful to Professor Barbara Harris for discussion on this point.
[15] David M. Bergeron, *King James & Letters of Homoerotic Desire*. Iowa City: University of Iowa Press, 1999, p. 115.
[16] *CSPVenice*, 17, p. 442.
[17] Kettering, 'Patronage Power', pp. 817-41.
[18] Ibid., p. 818. See also Harris, 'Women and Politics', p. 289.
[19] Payne, 'Aristocratic Women', pp. 198-228.
[20] See also Harris, 'Women and Politics', p. 281.
[21] A.J. Loomie, 'Toleration and Diplomacy: the Religious Issue in Anglo-Spanish Relations, 1603-1605', *Transactions of the American Philosophical Society*, n.s, 53, part 6 (1963), p. 53.
[22] Ibid., Loomie, 'Sir Robert Cecil and the Spanish Embassy', *BIHR*, 42 (1969), 30-57; Pauline Croft, 'The Reputation of Robert Cecil: Libels, Political Opinion and Popular Awareness in the Early Seventeenth Century', *TRHS*, 6th Series, 1 (1991), 43-69 (pp. 58-60); Peck, *Court Patronage and Corruption*, pp. 182-84.
[23] Horatio F. Brown (ed.), *CSPVenice*, London: HMSO, 1900, vol. 10, p. 341; C.H. Carter, *Secret Diplomacy of the Spanish Hapsburgs 1598-1625*, New York and London: Columbia UP, 1964, pp. 127-28; Loomie, 'Toleration and Diplomacy', pp. 54, 55; BL, Add. MS 31111, fols 17, 145.
[24] *Chamberlain Letters*, pp. 357-58: Chamberlain to Carleton, 17 June 1612.
[25] Anne Somerset, *Unnatural Murder: Poison at the Court of James I*, London: Weidenfeld & Nicolson, 1997; Peck, *Court Patronage*, pp. 181-84.
[26] LPL, MS 3202, fol. 13: Edmund Lascelles to the earl of Shrewsbury, 30 Apr. 1605.
[27] LPL, MS 3205, fols 102-102v: Elizabeth Stapleton to the countess of Shrewsbury, 20 Feb. 1605; LPL, MS 3203, fol. 298: same to same, 1 July [n.y.] [1605].
[28] LPL, MS 3205, fols 102-102v.
[29] LPL, MS 3203, fol. 298.
[30] Carey, *Memoirs*, pp. 64-65.
[31] Ibid., p. 66.
[32] PRO, SP 15/37/21.
[33] Carey, *Memoirs*, p. 68. The Lord Chancellor of Scotland had had the young prince in his care since the Queen's departure for England.
[34] PRO, SP 15/37/21.
[35] Carey, *Memoirs*, p. 68.

[36] Ibid., pp. 68, 76.
[37] See, for example, Leeds Barroll, *Anna of Denmark, Queen of England: a Cultural Biography*, Philadelphia: University of Pennsylvania Press, 2001; Barbara Kiefer Lewalski, *Writing Women in Jacobean England*, Harvard: Harvard UP, 1993, pp. 95-123; Peck, *Court Patronage*, pp. 47, 68-74.
[38] John Nichols (ed.), *The Progresses, Processions, and Magnificent Festivities of King James the First, his Royal Consort, Family and Court...*, 4 vols, London: n.p., 1828 [Reprint. New York: Burt Franklin, n.d.], 1, p. 168.
[39] See Payne, 'Cecil Women', p. 276.
[40] *HMC, Calendar of the Manuscripts of the Most Hon. the Marquis of Salisbury, K.G. &c. Preserved at Hatfield House. Hertfordshire*, 21 vols, London: HMSO, 1883-1973. 15, p. 187. [hereafter *HMC, Salisbury*]
[41] Payne, 'Aristocratic Women', p. 77.
[42] Wallace Notestein, Frances Helen Relf and Hartley Simpson (eds), *Commons Debates 1621*, 7 vols, New Haven and London: Yale UP, 1935, 2, p. 164.
[43] Hatfield House, Herts, Cecil Papers 123, fol. 61.
[44] Payne, 'Aristocratic Women', pp. 218-20.
[45] For a detailed discussion of this proposed match and its failure, see Ibid., pp. 174-76.
[46] Ibid., p. 229, n. 133.
[47] Ibid.
[48] The earl's brother whose brother was Master of the Household to Philip II of Spain, and Dunfermline himself was a personal friend of Gondomar, the Spanish Ambassador to England. J.D. Mackie, 'The Secret Diplomacy of King James VI. in Italy prior to his Accession to the English Throne', *Scottish Historical Review*, 21 (1924), 271, n 5; Albert J. Loomie, *Spain and the Jacobean Catholics*, vol. 2, 1613-1624, Catholic Record Society, n.pl., 1978, no. 68, p. xviii.
[49] Payne, 'Aristocratic Women', p. 229, n. 133.
[50] For her secret pension see Loomie, 'Toleration and Diplomacy', pp. 54, 55; BL, Add. MS 31111, fols 17, 45. In 1614, Jane requested Gondomar, the Spanish Ambassador, to prefer a suit to the duke of Lerma on behalf of Sir George Ker, a kinsman of her husband, for a place in the service of Anne of Austria, queen of France and daughter of Philip II of Spain: Antonio Ballesteros Beretta (ed.), *Documentos Ineditos Para la Historia de Espana: Correspondencia Oficiel de Don Diego Sarmiento de Acuna Conde de Gondomar*, 4 vols, Madrid: Tipografía de Archivos, 1936-44, 3, p. 297.
[51] W.B. Patterson, *King James VI and I and the Reunion of Christendom*, Cambridge and New York: CUP, 1997, pp. 13-14.
[52] Loomie, 'Toleration and Diplomacy', p. 53. See also Payne, 'Aristocratic Women', p. 231, n. 141.
[53] For a good summary of the affair, see Patterson, *King James VI and I* , pp. 86-88. For a more detailed account, see Robert Pitcairn, *Ancient Criminal Trials in Scotland; compiled from the Original Records and MSS., with Historical Illustrations*, 4 vols in 10, Edinburgh: Maitland Club, 1831-33, vol. 2, part 2, pp. 568-604.
[54] Patterson, *King James VI and I*, p. 87.
[55] Pitcairn, *Ancient Criminal Trials*, p. 586.
[56] G.P.V. Akrigg (ed.), *Letters of King James VI & I*, Berkeley: University of California Press, 1984, p. 307.
[57] Ibid.

[58] T.B. Howell (comp.), *A Complete Collection of State Trials and Proceedings for High Treason and Other Crimes and Misdemeanours From the Earliest Period to the Year 1783...*, 33 vols, London: Longman, Hurst, Rees, Orme and Brown, 1816-26, 2, p. 723.
[59] *HMC, Salisbury*, 21, p. 30.
[60] *CSPVenice*, 11, p. 249.
[61] Pitcairn, *Ancient Criminal Trials*, p. 584.
[62] John Spottiswoode, *The History of the Church of Scotland*, 3 vols, Edinburgh: Spottiswoode Society, 1847-51, 3, p. 20.
[63] Mary Anne Everett Green (ed.), *Calendar of State Papers, Domestic Series, of the Reign of James I, 1603-[1625]*, 5 vols, London: HMSO, 1857-72, 4 (1623-1625), p. 314; *Chamberlain Letters* 2, p. 571; Menna Prestwich, *Cranfield: Politics and Profits Under the Early Stuarts: The Career of Lionel Cranfield Earl of Middlesex*, Oxford: Clarendon Press, 1966, pp. 472-74.
[64] Samuel R. Gardiner, *History of England from the Accession of James I to the Outbreak of the Civil War 1603-1642*, 10 vols, London: Longmans, Green & Co., 1901, 3 (1616-1621), pp. 189-95.
[65] Croft (ed.), *Patronage, Culture and Power*, pp. xvi-xvii.

Chapter 11

Anne of Denmark and the Historical Contextualisation of Shakespeare and Fletcher's *Henry VIII*

Susan Frye

The characters and events of *Henry VIII* stage connections across eighty-five years between the courts of King Henry and Queen Katherine of Aragon, King James and Queen Anne of Denmark. Yet Anne, who like Katherine had been crowned queen consort, has until recently been ignored in historical discussions of the period. *The Narrative History of King James, for the First Fourteen Years* (1651) fails to mention Anne, recounting instead gossip about James's favourites and the Overbury murder; *The Memorials of Affairs of State* (1725), produced from the papers of Ralph Winwood, gives Anne three cursory entries in its index although the letters themselves mention the Queen dozens of times in relation to foreign and domestic affairs.[1] Anne has been ignored and even denigrated throughout the twentieth century, often by otherwise reliable historians. In 1966, for example, Menna Prestwich described Anne as James's 'vain and vapid queen'; in 1969, Robert Ashton described this queen as one who was 'incurably frivolous, and lacked a sense of adult – let alone regal – responsibilities'.[2] With the publication of Leeds Barroll's *Anna of Denmark, Queen of England: a Cultural Biography*, a book anticipated in articles by Barroll and Marion Wynne-Davies,[3] the reinstatement of Anne's importance to English culture and politics is well underway. While the trajectory of Anne's historical reinstatement began with her involvement in the creation of the Jacobean court masque, for Leeds Barroll the project became one of recovering her widespread cultural and political influence. To study Anne as part of the context of *Henry VIII* requires rethinking court politics during the period 1603-1619 in accordance with the substantial historical record of ambassadorial correspondence and domestic letters that credit Anne with political influence and activity. To understand Anne as a public figure, it is necessary to acknowledge that as queen consort her every action carried political weight, from giving birth to going on progress, from entertaining ambassadors to following the intrigues of dynastic marriage. Reading *Henry VIII* as a play that in part stages the political importance of queens – Katherine of Aragon, Anne Boleyn (in the play, spelled Anne Bullen), and the future Queen Elizabeth as a newborn, but especially Katherine – prompts us to recover both Anne of Denmark's political functions, together with a sense of her contemporaries' acknowledgment of them.

The play titled *All is True* when it was first acted in the spring of 1613, then titled *Henry VIII* in the First Folio ten years later, was produced through the collaboration of William Shakespeare and John Fletcher.[4] Although it may have been begun earlier, it was doubtless completed in the months following the death of Henry, Prince of Wales in November of 1612, which had followed closely on the death in June of the family's most reliable civil servant and confidant of the Queen, Robert Cecil, earl of Salisbury. As Linda Levy Peck summarises the political moment with which this play interacts, in England 'the centre of power shifted in 1612 and 1613'.[5] Into the gap created by the deaths of Henry and Salisbury stepped James's current favourite, Robert Carr, viscount Rochester, soon to be earl of Somerset. Carr's was an ascent initially opposed by Anne and Henry together, and then by Anne alone. With Salisbury dead, James used Carr as his Secretary of State while, as *The Narrative History of King James* summarises his position, 'No suite, no petition, no grant, no letter, but Mr Carr must have a hand in it'.[6] Meanwhile, James had ordered the mourning period for Henry to be shortened considerably in order to begin the several months of ceremonies and celebrations surrounding the wedding of his and Anne of Denmark's daughter, the Princess Elizabeth, to the Elector Palantine on Valentine's Day, 1613. It has long been conjectured that *Henry VIII* was performed as part of those celebrations, and that seems likely, as does the possibility that the play was written in part with such a performance in mind. If *Henry VIII* was not preferred it may well have been because, in spite of its pageant-like qualities and its final blessing on the House of Stuart, the play engages the delicate interactions of discarded queens and male favourites.

Produced in a time of loss, a new favourite, and a dynastic marriage, *Henry VIII* was acted in the spring of 1613, the one Shakespeare play we can date to the time of its first performance because in May the discharge of chambers attending the banquet at which Henry meets Anne Bullen set the Globe theatre on fire. The play recalls the interconnections between Henry VIII and James I at a time when queens, royal offspring, and male favourites shaped both domestic and foreign policy: both kings had produced an heir and daughters; both maintained male favourites who opposed their queens; both were known to act in public as if they valued their queens while not hesitating to humiliate them. The play interweaves the worlds of Henry and Katherine and that of James and Anne by playing on the very names that the Stuarts had chosen to link their family with the Tudors – Henry and Elizabeth were James and Anne's first born, while Henry was the name given to Henry and Katherine's first son who did not survive infancy. In addition, the very places staged and mentioned in the play allow the past to intrude into the present, while reminding the audience of the royal prerogative to seize the properties of fallen favourites, and of the interconnections between royal houses and the playhouse: Whitehall, initially Wolsey's, becomes Henry's and eventually James's great palace, the sight of court-performed plays, masques, and other entertainments; Hampton Court, likewise; and the scene during which Queen Katherine is confronted with Henry's need for a divorce at Blackfriar's was acted at both the Globe and at the Blackfriar's theatre, which was, by the turn of the seventeenth century, the indoor theatre of Shakespeare's company, the King's Men.

These names and places provide points of connection between the court politics of the Tudors and Stuarts, many of which have long been recognised by the play's literary critics, who have elucidated the play's relation to its context in a variety of illuminating essays.[7] Stuart Kurland, for example, notes that 'the characters' interest in politics is focused on the rivalries at court'.[8] But Kurland and other critics failed to consider the conflicts between Queen Katherine and Wolsey because the Queen's participation in the political events outside her divorce did not yet seem worth noting. Even though a number of studies focus on the character of Katherine – as she relates to Hermione or Vittoria Corombona, to the Virgin Mary, or to Frances Howard, whose divorce trial was ongoing – the points of resemblance with Anne of Denmark are only now becoming apparent.[9] But in 1613 and probably until the Civil War, when *Henry VIII* staged the Tudors for the benefit of Stuart audiences, the play's relation to seventeenth-century anxieties must have been apparent.

Within *Henry VIII*, Queen Katherine frequently claims centre stage, even in a play about the man who was prepared to split from Rome in order to be rid of her. In contrast to an earlier, more popular play, Samuel Rowley's *When You See Me, You Know Me*, about the relations among Henry, Jane Seymour, Katherine Parr, and Edward, Prince of Wales, the change of religion in England receives no real attention in

Shakespeare and Fletcher's *Henry VIII.*[10] And yet their play stages the shift in religion embodied in Katherine and her successor, Anne Bullen. Wolsey describes Bullen as 'A spleeny Lutheran' (III.ii.100), and Cranmer replaces Wolsey as the King's favourite, but little is made of the King's role in affecting the important religious changes of this period. The ways in which *Henry VIII* sidesteps the Reformation allow Katherine to present a Catholicism that is low-key, central to her femininity, and unchallenged. She is a reformist whose attitude towards Wolsey suggests distaste for clerical corruption that Henry comes to share. In not making the Catholic Queen's religion a dramatic issue, Shakespeare and Fletcher preserve her virtuous centrality while evoking the living queen widely suspected of being a Catholic, Anne of Denmark. The longstanding question of why the Catholic Queen, Katherine, receives the play's sanction as a chaste and truly royal queen, even though the Protestant Anne Bullen is the baby Elizabeth's mother, may in large part be answered when we acknowledge the extent to which Henry's queen of twenty years resembles James's queen of twenty-four.

If Katherine's Catholicism is toned down in favour of representing a chaste and pious queen resembling Anne, the connection between the two queens is made stronger by the play's repeated staging of Katherine's resistance to her husband's court favourite. Queen Anne's opposition in 1612-13 to Carr, during the period when the play was being written, resembles that of Queen Katherine's opposition to Cardinal Wolsey in *Henry VIII* in that Katherine, like Anne, demonstrates herself to be a worthy politician. Wolsey and Katherine quarrel first over the duke of Buckingham, then over the taxation of the clothiers, over her divorce, and, finally, over whether she ought to appeal to the pope. What is at stake is simultaneously the King's love and who will help him to determine public policy. Thus, Katherine intercedes when King Henry believes Buckingham's surveyor, when he testifies that Buckingham has often contended 'that if the King / Should without issue die, he'll carry it so / To make the sceptre his', even as the duke is said to have mingled this treasonous version of the succession with an 'oath' of 'revenge upon the Cardinal' (I.ii.134-36, 138-39). The play suggests that Wolsey has paid for the surveyor's testimony in order to eliminate Buckingham's opposition, so that the Queen's position in this quarrel is distinctly that of the anti-Wolsey faction. Moreover, Wolsey has placed in the surveyor's mouth the threat of Buckingham's interference with the Tudor succession, the very charge most likely to infuriate Henry. At this point in the play, because he has not produced a living son with Katherine, Henry has pinned his dynastic hopes on what Wolsey can achieve abroad by persuading the pope that his marriage to Katherine is incestuous: Wolsey's power as favourite depends on his ability to achieve a foreign solution. As a result, Katherine, in pleading for Buckingham, is participating in a struggle over the control of both the succession and England's foreign policy. She is not simply taking pity on a doomed man; she is engaged in court politics. Although in the end she sees she cannot win and so resigns herself to her husband's decision with a simple 'God mend all' (I.ii.202), she allows herself one protest in which she shows that she has done her homework, telling the surveyor, 'If I know you well, / You were the Duke's surveyor and lost your office / On the complaint o' the tenants' (I.ii.172-74). Thus, in a stroke she makes it clear that the surveyor's character is as questionable as his motives, that he must be Wolsey's creature and so a conspirator in the Cardinal's corrupt pursuit of power.

Katherine's further confrontation with Wolsey in act one, scene two over taxing the clothiers also has a foreign-policy dimension: the clothiers are being taxed in order to carry on the war in France, which the play describes as entirely Wolsey's doing. As she points out, 'The subjects' grief / Comes through commissions which compels from each / The sixth part of his substance to be levied ... / the pretence for this / Is named your wars in France' (I.ii.57-61). In this quarrel, Katherine wins by arguing that such taxation has brought these good citizens to the brink of rebellion: 'Their curses now / Live where their prayers did ... I would your highness / Would give it quick consideration, for / There is no primer business' (I.ii.66-68). Henry responds, 'By my life, / This is against our pleasure' (I.ii.68-69). After Wolsey backs down, the King phrases the danger of such a policy in words that suggest that childbirth and the succession again are at stake: 'Things done without example [taxing the clothiers], in their issue / Are to be feared' (I.ii.91-92). The 'issue' of this policy, like Buckingham's supposed threat to the succession, promises a monstrous outcome.

These confrontations between Katherine and Wolsey take place toward the beginning of the play in a sequence of scenes splicing together the clothiers' taxation and Buckingham's fate. First we see Buckingham imprisoned; then the dispute about the clothiers; then the surveyor's testimony against Buckingham. The only thematic connection between them is the Queen's fight with a favourite for the King's support in making foreign and domestic policy. Then follows Wolsey's banquet at which Henry meets and kisses Anne Bullen, Anne Bullen's talk with a Lady-in-Waiting about the possibility of Anne's becoming queen, and then the next confrontation between Katherine and Wolsey at her trial for divorce at Blackfriars. Katherine must lose the battle over the divorce – although she never admits as much – in the interests of the succession. And even though she is by far the most sympathetic character in the play, she must lose so that Edward and Elizabeth Tudor and, eventually, James and Anne, may reign.

Conflicts similar to those played out between Katherine and Wolsey prevailed between Anne of Denmark and James's favourites even before their arrival in England. As Archbishop Abbot wrote in 1627 looking back on George Villiers's supplanting of Robert Carr, the Queen had 'been bitten with Favorites both in England and Scotland'.[11] In his letter of May 1603, regarding their ongoing quarrel about Henry's living with John Erskine, earl of Mar as well as allegations of Anne's conversion to Catholicism, James attempted to put his wife in her place outside the power relations he enjoyed with his male favourites. He sets out to 'cure' Anne 'of that rooted error' by which he meant her 'prejudice' against his favourites. These men, whom she believed were 'unfriends', the King found were 'true servants to me'. He asks her to 'leave these womanly apprehensions, for I thank God I carry that love and respect unto you which, by the law of God and nature, I ought to do to my wife and mother of my children'. But in the next sentence, he reminds her that, regardless of her royal birth, her place in the world depends entirely on his honour, which her protests oppose:

> ...not for that ye are a king's daughter, for, whether ye were a king's or a cook's daughter, ye must be all alike to me being one my wife.... The love and respect I now bear you is for that ye are my married wife and so partaker of my honour, as of all my other fortunes.

He threatens that if she continues to question 'an honest servant for his true service to me ... then neither ye or I be ever at rest'.[12]

James's fury attests to Anne's ability to exercise power through the Scottish factions, an ability that adumbrated her political activities in England. Like Katherine, Anne of Denmark was a queen consort and so exercised nothing like the power of Elizabeth I. But that does not mean that such queens were without power whether they won or lost their political battles at court, as the opening scenes of *Henry VIII* make clear for us. And the fact that both were queen consorts for over twenty years meant that they were inevitably compared. Upon her arrival in England in 1603, for example, the precedents cited for determining the new queen's jointure were those of 'Elizabeth of York, Catherine of Aragon, Anne Boleyn, and

Catherine Parr'.[13] Like these Tudor queens, Anne of Denmark was involved in the court politics of her time: the records provide a wealth of detail demonstrating that her life was one of continual political activity. From time to time her contemporaries sought to belittle her authority, but such remarks have frequently been taken out of context. In March 1612, a few months before Henry's death and a year before *Henry VIII* was first acted, Antonio Foscarini, then Venetian Ambassador, noted of Anne that 'the Queen does not mix herself up in affairs', a quote commonly associated with Anne, but which tells only part of the story. For Foscarini's entire sentence reads, 'I have reported all this because though the Queen does not mix herself up in affairs, still she may sometimes know what is going on as the King tells her any thing she chooses to ask, and loves and esteems her'. Even this complete sentence belies the extent of Anne's political interest and knowledge that Foscarini details at the beginning of this same letter:

> She asked me what news I had from Italy, and what they thought at Venice about the Franco-Spanish matches. I said I had nothing worthy of her Majesty's notice ... I added that the matches here were also on a fair way to conclusion. The Queen showed that she understood my allusion to the Palatine, and said that the King and the Council were greatly in its favour but did not express her views one way or another.[14]

Regardless of Foscarini's denigrating the Queen's relation to foreign policy later in this same letter, at the start he pictures not a queen without influence in the affairs of state, but a savvy queen, too discreet to voice her opposition to her daughter's match with the Elector Palatine, imbrued in the politics of dynastic alliance through which so much early modern foreign policy was expressed and conducted.

In spite of James and Anne's domestic disagreements that resulted in what Barbara Lewalski portrays as Anne's 'oppositional stance' to James,[15] reading between the lines of the ambassadorial correspondence for Venice and Italy, it becomes clear that, like Henry and Katherine in the discussion about the clothiers, James and Anne functioned as a kind of foreign policy team. Within this team, Anne's influence on policy was less direct than had she been a member of the Privy Council; on the other hand, as queen consort, as Foscarini acknowledges, she was in a position to influence James and other members of the Council, as well as to help the government implement its policies by participating in the ritualised and highly significant interchanges with foreign ambassadors. In the correspondence of foreign ambassadors James and Anne emerge as reasonably dextrous managers of English foreign policy. In these letters, the ambassadors pass from King to Queen and back again, the royal couple giving lip service to the ambassadors' concerns, while feeding them the bits of inside information so important for their reports. And just as the King and Queen judiciously allowed the ambassadors a few sprinkles of news, so the Queen might be sent to pump the ambassadors, albeit with mixed results. In 1608, for example, when the King 'closed the passage between Dover and Calais in order to intercept the message which the French Ambassador here was sending his master', the Queen gave a breakfast for Zorzi Giustinian at which she broached the subject, but, reports the ambassador, 'I took care to avoid all discussion'.[16] Sentences like Giustinian's in his report back to Venice are common: 'The Queen expressed the great affection of the King and herself for the Republic'.[17] The same letter from John Chamberlain to Sir Ralph Winwood that contains news of 'the burning of the Globe or Playhouse on the Bankside on St. Peter's Day' contains as well a report that the marquess de Villa, Ambassador of Savoi, 'staid at least three Weeks' in England 'to present certaine Toys of Chrystall to the Queen ... He had a Present of Plate at parting of 1000 *l.* and a Jewell from the Queen of 1500 *l*'.[18] Such receiving and giving of gifts expressed mutual regard and understanding in the most personal and personally appropriate of forms, the giving of valuable objects. Other courtly forms of interaction were similarly important in the early seventeenth century. For the ambassadors, invitations to the masques, especially the Queen's, became the occasion for bitter fights over precedence, as when the ambassadors of France and Spain fell out over the King's inviting the Spanish ambassador rather than the French; Anne was forced 'to put off her Masque for a few days' so that a solution could be found.[19] When the wedding of John Ramsay and Elizabeth Ratcliffe was in the offing, Giustinian reported that the Austrian ambassador, 'having failed to obtain an invitation to the Masque, though he made handsome presents for this purpose to the Queen's first Ladies-in-Waiting, has been obliged to accept the invitation to the wedding'.[20] Although the King and Queen experienced many personal and political differences, Anne and James agreed on the need for and use of the foreign ambassadors who waited on them.

While Anne and James worked together on maintaining foreign contacts, Anne also upheld the family's commitment to royal progresses through the English countryside, to attend the baptisms of the children of the elite, and to hear the suits for position and possession that formed so much of government business in this period. Anne's numerous political activities, however, many of them conducted in loose partnership with James, could not erase the King's preference for a group of male courtiers. In particular, Robert Carr's ascendance to the position of Secretary of State formerly held by Robert Cecil, with whom the Queen had been in constant contact, made effective her increased exclusion from much political decision-making. In *Henry VIII*'s versions of the homosocial and suggested homoerotic relations driving the courts of kings, Queens Katherine and Anne Bullen must both share the stage with male favourites, first with Wolsey and then with Cranmer, with whom Henry enjoys greater physical intimacy than with either queen. Henry's initial entrance leaning on Wolsey, as Stuart Kurland notes, replicates James's well-known habit of leaning on his favourite courtiers, particularly on Carr.[21] As Thomas Howard, earl of Suffolk informed John Harington in a letter of 1611 delivered by Howard's son, Carr was quickly ingratiating himself, for the King 'leaneth on his arm, pinches his cheek, smoothes his ruffled garment'.[22] The First Folio's stage directions, '*Enter King Henry, leaning on the Cardinals shoulder*' (entry at I.ii), connect the physical behaviour of James toward Carr, with its homoerotic overtones, with that of the King on the stage.

As the actions of the play work to equate female and male favourites, they deny the reproductive capacity of queens and their ability to influence policy because of their birth and social status, their family's international alliances, and their proximity to the King. In singling out the three Tudor queens, Katherine, Anne Bullen, and Elizabeth, who failed to produce a male heir, the play creates a need to consider the alternative forms of reproduction available to a king – even a king like James, with his spare but young and sickly son positioned as heir. Significantly, Katherine calls Wolsey 'that great child of honour' (IV.ii.6), a phrase that exposes the extent to which such kings, by choosing favourites, seek to reproduce themselves without the help of queens. Moreover, *Henry VIII* demonstrates that the king's ability to choose queens and create favourites is only part of his power. For if he can reproduce himself through these relations, he can also destroy those whose intimacy proves unnecessary or undesirable. Both heterosexual and homosocial/homoerotic forms of reproduction carry risks: a son may not be born; a son may die young; a son may inherit the throne and be beheaded. Or, alternatively, the male favourite may help to poison someone in his way, as Carr was said to have helped his new wife, Frances Howard, to murder Thomas Overbury. Or, as in the later case of George Villiers (the favourite supported by Queen Anne), produce a family toward whom the King shows more affection than to his own but that cannot be substituted for his own when it comes to inheriting the crown in spite of the King's swearing to 'advance' the Villiers family 'above all others'.[23]

But *Henry VIII* is not just about the powerlessness of queens in the face of favourites. Although the King's players were his liveried servants, 'technically members of the royal household',[24] they did not doggedly set out the King's point of view. Shakespeare and Fletcher's play is far more than a celebration of the King's closeness to his male favourites in opposition to the reigning queen. Instead, there is a general sense of the importance of male-female reproduction set forth in the two crowd scenes featuring the energy and importance of female fertility on a civic, even national, scale. Twice in the play, a crowd, including many women, wait at the gates in the hope of seeing, first, the processions of Anne Bullen's coronation and, second, Elizabeth's christening. These scenes describe a kind of rampant heterosexual fertility. The Third Gentleman who recounts the spectators during Anne's procession says that she showed 'the beauty of her person to the people. / Believe me, sire, she is the goodliest woman / That ever lay by man; which when the people / Had the full view of ... Hats, cloaks – / Doublets, I think – flew up' (IV.i.78-79). The consequence of her eroticised appearance is reproduction on a large scale: 'Great-bellied women / That had not a half a week to go' 'shake the press' (IV.i.79-80); among the crowd 'No man living / Could say 'This is my wife' there, all were woven / So strangely in one piece' (IV.i.81-83). In the second such scene, just before the christening of the Princess Elizabeth at the play's close, the porter together with a servant from the larder hold off an unruly crowd, of whom the porter exclaims, 'Bless me, what a fry of fornication is at door! On my Christian conscience, this one christening will beget a thousand' (V.iii.31-35). This time it is the prospect of seeing yet another royal female, Elizabeth, that produces this reaction. In these fertile crowds, as even the men become indistinguishable from one another – 'Here will be father, godfather, and all together' (V.iii.35-36) – it is as if the spectacles of Anne Bullen and her daughter, Elizabeth, both brushed with the favour and fertility of Henry VIII, spread dynastic fertility into the streets, giving rise to a nation of subjects.

The fear and awe that the crowds of fertile women incite in their onlookers function as unruly versions of the emotions evoked by *Henry VIII's* queens. For if the play stages a Jacobean fantasy of a queen who offers nothing more than male favourites and may as easily be removed, the play, by making Katherine dominate the central scenes, also serves as a reminder of the Queen's political importance, an importance that gives rise to the play's acknowledgment of the feminine in both the prologue and epilogue unprecedented in Shakespeare's plays. When the prologue warns that 'those that can pity here / May, if they think it well, let fall a tear' (prologue. 5-6), it foretells Katherine's position as the only character whose downfall occasions strong emotion. Returning to the prologue's implicit emphasis on the feminine, the epilogue asserts that 'this play at this time is only in / The merciful construction of good women, / For such a one we showed 'em' (epilogue. 9-11). 'Such a one' showed the 'good women' of the audience may refer to the infant Elizabeth Tudor, whose christening we have just witnessed.[25] But 'such a one' also presents a wonderfully ambiguous 'good woman' who seems an amalgam of the women 'shewn', of Katherine, Anne Boleyn and Elizabeth in particular. The 'good woman' may also suggest a living woman, perhaps even one present at a performance, like the Princess Elizabeth, who may have seen this play alongside her new husband and representative of English commitments abroad, the Elector Palantine. The fact that the epilogue, like so much of the play, celebrates the power of women as politicians, mothers, and daughters, suggests that the play might have been acted for mother and daughter together, or that this epilogue seeks to recall a vision uniting the infant Elizabeth, Queen Anne, and the Princess Elizabeth in a tableau of resemblance and recognition. If so, this moment would resemble the closeness between mother and daughter displayed in the Queen's masque in celebration of Henry's investment as Prince of Wales, when Anne as Tethys appeared in an elaborate scene featuring 'the queen in the middest' of the show 'and the lady Elizabeth at her feet'.[26] Such a concluding emphasis on queen and princess, mother and daughter – on the centrality of the feminine in a ruling dynasty – counterbalances the play's exploration of Henry's relations with his favourites as well as his regal willingness to set aside queens and daughters in pursuit of a son.

Notes

Quotations are from Jay L. Halio (ed.), *King Henry VIII, or All is True*, Oxford: OUP, 1999.

[1] *The Narrative History of King James, for the First Fourteen Years*, London: printed for Michael Sparke, 1651 [Reprint. Walter Scott, *A Collection of Scarce and Valuable Tracts*, London: T. Cadell and W. Davies, 1809], vol. 2, pp. 262-80 (p. 262); *Memorials of Affairs of State*, 3 vols, London: W.B. for T. Ward, 1725.

[2] Menna Prestwich, *Cranfield: Politics and Profits Under the Early Stuarts*, Oxford: The Clarendon Press, 1966, p. 12; Robert Ashton, *James I By His Contemporaries*, London: Hutchinson & Company, 1969, p. 86. Ashton, a remarkable scholar of the period, here repeats the prevalent assessment of Queen Anne in the context of the denial of James's erotic attraction to men. It may well be that the need to explain James's turning to male favourites produced or contributed to the devaluation of Anne's reputation. As Ashton

continues, while acknowledging that 'not all the blame for the failure of the marriage should be laid at the door of the Queen', she nevertheless 'lacked the qualities and failed to supply the companionship which might have made a crucial difference not only to the king's private but also to his public life' (pp. 86-87).

3 See Leeds Barroll, *Anna of Denmark, Queen of England: a Cultural Biography*, Philadelphia: University of Pennsylvania Press, 2001; *idem*, 'The Court of the First Stuart Queen', in Linda Levy Peck (ed.), *The Mental World of the Jacobean Court*, Cambridge: CUP, 1991, pp. 192-208; *idem*, 'Theatre as Text: the Case of Queen Anna and the Jacobean Court Masque', *Elizabethan Theatre*, 14 (1996), 175-93; Marion Wynne-Davies, 'The Queen's Masque: Renaissance Women and the Seventeenth-Century Court Masque', in Susan Cerasano and Marion Wynne-Davies (eds), *Gloriana's Face: Women, Public and Private, in the English Renaissance*, Detroit: Wayne State UP, 1992, pp. 79-104. See also Barbara Kiefer Lewalski. 'Enacting Opposition: Queen Anne and the Subversions of Masquing', in her *Writing Women in Jacobean England*, Cambridge: Harvard UP, 1993, pp. 15-43.

4 *All is True* was apparently the play's initial title, but the First Folio's editors chose to place it at the end of the histories, titled *The Life of King Henry the Eighth*. See Gary Taylor, 'Textual Note' in Stephen Greenblatt, Walter Cohen, Jean E. Howard, and Katharine Eisaman Maus (eds), *The Norton Shakespeare Based on the Oxford Edition*, New York: W.W. Norton & Company, 1997, p. 3118.

5 Linda Levy Peck, *Northampton: Patronage and Policy at the Court of James I*, London: George Allen & Unwin, 1982, p. 40.

6 *The Narrative History of King James*, p. 268; Linda Levy Peck, *Court Patronage and Corruption in Early Stuart England*, Boston: Unwin Hyman, 1990, p. 43.

7 In this essay, I am relying on a number of works that connect *Henry VIII* and related plays to their historical context. These include Judith Anderson, *Biographical Truth: the Representation of Historical Persons in Tudor-Stuart Writing*, New Haven: Yale UP, 1984; William M. Baillie, '*Henry VIII*: a Jacobean History', *Shakespeare Studies*, XII (1979), 247-66; Edward I. Berry, '*Henry VIII* and the Dynamics of Spectacle', *Shakespeare Studies*, XII (1979), 229-46; Anston Bosman, 'Seeing Tears: Truth and Sense in *All is True*', *SQ*, 50, 4 (1999), 459-76; Howard Felperin, 'Shakespeare's *Henry VIII*: History as Myth', *Studies in English Literature*, 6, 2 (1966), 225-46; Barbara Hodgdon, *The End Crowns All: Closure and Contradiction in Shakespeare's History*, Princeton: Princeton UP, 1991; Jean Howard and Phyllis Rackin, *Engendering a Nation: a Feminist Account of Shakespeare's English Histories,* New York: Routledge, 1997; Ivo Kamps, 'Possible Pasts: Historiography and Legitimation in Henry VIII', *College English*, 58, 2 (Feb. 1966), 192-215; M. Lindsay Kaplan and Katherine Eggert, '"Good queen, my lord, good queen": Sexual Slander in *The Winter's Tale*', *Renaissance Drama*, n.s. 25 (1994), 89-118; Stuart M. Kurland, '*Henry VIII* and James I: Shakespeare and Jacobean Politics', *Shakespeare Studies*, XIX (1987), 203-18; Gordon McMullan, 'Introduction', in Gordon McMullan (ed.), *King Henry VIII (All is True)*, London: Arden Shakespeare, 2000, pp. 1-199; Kim H. Noling, 'Grubbing Up the Stock: Dramatizing Queens in *Henry VIII*', *SQ*, 39, 3 (Fall 1988), 291-306; Annabel Patterson, '"All is True": Negotiating the Past in *Henry VIII*', in R.B. Parker and S.P. Zitner (eds), *Elizabethan Theater: Essays in Honour of S. Schoenbaum*, Newark: University of Delaware Press, 1996, pp. 147-66; Peter L. Rudnytsky, '*Henry VIII* and the Deconstruction of History', *Shakespeare Survey*, 43 (1991), 43-57; Camille Wells Slights, 'The Politics of Conscience in *All Is True* (or *Henry VIII*)', *Shakespeare Survey*, 43 (1991), 59-68; Leonard Tennenhouse, 'Strategies of State and Political Plays: *A Midsummer Night's Dream, Henry IV, Henry V, Henry VIII*', in Jonathan Dollimore and Alan Sinfield (eds), *Political*

Shakespeare: Essays in Cultural Materialism, 2nd edition; Ithaca: Cornell UP, 1994, pp. 109-28.

[8] Stuart Kurland, '*Henry VIII* and James I', p. 204.

[9] On Katherine of Aragon's centrality and range of historical reference, see Jane Lapotaire, 'Queen Katherine in *Henry VIII*', in Robert Smallwood (ed.), *Players of Shakespeare 4: Further Essays in Shakespearian Performance by Players with the Royal Shakespeare Company*, Cambridge: CUP, 1998, pp. 132-51; Linda Micheli,'"Sit By Us": Visual Imagery and the Two Queens in *Henry VIII*', *SQ*, 38, 4 (Winter 1987), 452-66; Jo Eldridge Carney, 'Queenship in Shakespeare's *Henry VIII*', in Carole Levin and Patricia A. Sullivan (eds), *Political Rhetoric, Power, and Renaissance Women*, Albany: State University of New York Press, 1995 , pp. 189-202; Joseph Candido, 'Katherine of Aragon and Female Greatness: Shakespeare's Debt to Dramatic Tradition', *Iowa State Journal of Research*, 54, 4 (1980), 491-98; Ruth Vanita, 'Mariological Memory in *The Winter's Tale* and *Henry VIII*', *Studies in English Literature*, 40, 2 (spring 2000), 311-37.

[10] Samuel Rowley, *When You See Me, You Know Me*, 1605, 1613 [rpt. New York: AMS Press Inc., 1913]. For the relation between Anne of Denmark and the structure of *Henry VIII*, including a comparison of dynastic issues in *When You See Me, You Know Me* and *Henry VIII*, see Susan Frye, 'Queens and the Structure of History in *Henry VIII*', in Jean Howard and Richard Dutton (eds), *A Companion to Shakespeare, Volume IV: The Poems, Problem Comedies and Late Plays,* Oxford: Blackwell's Publishers Limited, forthcoming.

[11] Ashton, *James I By His Contemporaries*, p. 127.

[12] G.P.V. Akrigg (ed.), *Letters of King James VI & I*, Berkeley: University of California Press, 1984, pp. 214-15.

[13] *CSPDom, James I, 1603-1610,* London: HMSO, 1857, p. 35.

[14] Ibid., pp. 312-13.

[15] Lewalski, 'Enacting Opposition', p. 43.

[16] Horatio F. Brown (ed.), *CSPVenice*, London: HMSO, 1904, vol. 11, p. 87.

[17] *CSPVenice*, vol. 11, p. 14: 18 July 1607.

[18] *Memorials of Affairs of State*, 3, pp. 468-69: 8 July 1613.

[19] Ibid., p. 83: 18 Jan. 1608.

[20] *CSPVenice*, 11, p. 97.

[21] Kurland, '*Henry VIII* and James I', p. 205.

[22] John Nichols (ed.), *The Progresses, Processions, and Magnificent Festivities of King James the First, his Royal Consort, Family and Court...*, 4 vols, London: n.p., 1828 [Reprint. New York: Burt Franklin, 1964], 2, pp. 412-14.

[23] Ibid., 4, p. 484; transcription of BL, Harl. MS 6986.

[24] Stephen Orgel, 'Making Greatness Familiar', *Genre*, 15, 1&2 (Spring and Summer 1982), 41-48 (p. 44).

[25] See Barbara Hodgdon, *The End Crowns All*, whose discussion of this final scene in the context of its stage history is crucial to my understanding of it (pp. 229-34).

[26] Samuel Daniel, *Tethys Festival: Or the Queenes Wake. Celebrated at Whitehall, the fifth Day of June, 1610* [Reprint. Walter Scott (ed.), *A Collection of Scarce and Valuable Tracts,* London: T. Cadell and W. Davies, 1809] vol. 2, pp. 191-99 (p. 196).

Chapter 12

Mothers, Lovers and Others: Royalist Women

Jerome de Groot

> Moreover it is as lawfull for women as men to be Bishops (if Bishops were lawfull).[1]

This essay discusses the representation of women by Royalist writers, beginning with caricatures of Parliamentary women transgressing and misbehaving, and then moving to a discussion of the idealisation of Queen Henrietta Maria in the panegyric collection *Musarum Oxoniensum Serenissimæ*. I will be using these representations of Henrietta Maria and Parliamentarian women to consider the discursive field of Royalism and in particular the issue of gender in the complex nexus of loyalty and identity. Royalists reacted to the Parliamentary challenge by asserting a model of identity that was essentially circumscribed and limited. The representation of political identity during the war, as opposed to the physical experience of life on the ground, was far less concerned with the ambivalence of loyalty than with using polemically informed definitions of behaviour to exclude and attack perceived enemies. The texts I analyse in this essay show how Royalism was concerned with the construction of a set of binary roles and behavioural models designed to perpetuate a certain paradigm of social stability. Royalism attempted to impose a structure of social identity that rejected these transgressions and was premised upon obedience and a hierarchy of 'normality'. Violation of these codes led to instability, social inversion, anarchy and dissolution. The Parliamentarian experiment challenged and questioned the structure of society and politics.[2] Royalism desired a social order dependent on pre-ordained and fixed roles for the obedient subject and of the reader. The play of identities and the questioning of role involved in the Parliamentarian dispute threatened this order and structure. However, as I will show, Henrietta Maria was a unique and problematic woman in Royalist discourse. Her status and influence meant that she did not meekly fit into a simple binary categorisation. She was trouble simply through being a powerful woman, and the only way to deal with her was to construct her, to colonise and control her before her deviant but powerful sexuality started to undermine the stability of the nation.

For Royalists national identity was gender-based and centred upon male hierarchies and the King himself. It was predicated upon family structures and particular social models. Royalist tract writers and theorists interpreted the fifth commandment in a general way, arguing that the King was political father to the nation and therefore any challenge to his authority was blasphemous. The use of a traditional familial model predicated upon patriarchal infallibility is a common trope for Royalist theories of society, and, as we will see, particularly important in Royalist constructions of gender roles. Henry Ferne was in no doubt as to the reason for the present troubles: 'Tis the spirituall whoredome of Lay-Preachers, and Shee-Divines that hath procreated these monsters in Religion, that hath engendered this Viporous Brood of Schismaticall Tenets, which like the Ægyptian flyes darken the aire, blind the eyes of the vulgar with sencelesse ignorance'.[3] Ferne's carefully polemic syntax expresses the horror at social and gender experiment found in all Royalist literature of the First Civil War. The language of monstrous feminine creation allied with apocalyptic and serpentine imagery caricatures recognisably Parliamentary egalitarian roles and identities with destructive and abnormal characteristics. The flawed magistracy of 'ignorant and mechanick Divines' (sig. A1^{v}) has allowed the 'vulgar' and ignorant populace to become powerful and begin to intervene in the political life and debate of the nation. Rather than allow humanistic debate which leads to truth and understanding, this new social order threatens to 'darken the aire' and 'blind the eyes'. Ferne sees popular enfranchisement as a physical invasion: 'they must be entring into Kings Chambers, entrenching upon the Prerogative of Princes' (sig. A1^{v}). The material space of monarchy is violated. Challenges to traditional familial paradigms were represented as profound disruptions to the social fabric.

Women, in particular, were castigated if they attempted to interrogate their social and political definition. The Royalist newsbook *Mercurius Aulicus* portrayed the emasculating consequences of the lack of patriarchal structures through accounts of the socially transgressive actions of Parliamentarian women. Sir William Waller's wife, Lady Waller, is portrayed as an interfering dominatrix whose aim is to set up a 'Reformed Nunnery; where none must be admitted, but First, Such as are married: Secondly, Such as can preach: Thirdly, Such whose husbands have beene exceeding well beaten'.[4] She flirts with other soldiers, interprets the bible, preaches, and is generally master of the general.[5] This dominance leads to frequent jokes about Waller's impotence and effeminacy: 'if he offered to speake about Doctrines or Uses, her Ladyship would rebuke him, saying Peace Master Waller, you know your weaknesse in these things; since which time Sir William hath ever gone for the Weaker Vessell'.[6] Lady Waller assumed a public role independent of her husband and took on religious, social and political power. This promotion of women to abnormal roles is part of the egalitarian nature of the Roundhead caricature drawn by the court newsbook and Royalist texts in general. John Taylor dismissed the 'dangerous disease of Feminine Divinity', and Abraham Cowley attacked women preachers in *The Puritan and the Papist*: 'For to outdoe the story of Pope Joane: / Your Women preach too, and are like to bee / The Whores of Babylon, as much as Shee'.[7] Women in public roles are transgressive and socially destructive, spreading vice and disease. They invert social normality, trespassing into spaces not intended for them. They disrupt gender boundaries, questioning the nexus of power that subjects and defines them. Pointedly, they begin to self-construct; where Henrietta Maria would be safely fashioned by Royalist poets and writers, Lady Waller and the Parliamentarian preachers attain a level of self-expression and a voice that is not mediated through the standard channels of male ordering. This model of identity is querying, self-creating, and individual. It is thus troubling for a regime concerned with establishing set boundaries of power relations predicated upon state, religious and patriarchal institutions.

Royalism therefore defined Roundhead women as evil witches, anti-social and disruptive. In particular, Parliamentarian women were constructed as sexually voracious and active. Attacks on dominant women, particularly preachers, combined sexual insults with general social rebukes, in an attempt to construct a monstrous Otherness directly linked to rebellion and transformation. The decentred and fluid identities of women who challenged gender structures were translated into anti-social depravity. In early 1643 *Mercurius Aulicus* reported how the formerly 'zealous young Maids' of Norwich had now become pregnant: 'And let all Virgins looke to it, for people hereafter will scarce thinke them honest, who are so bold and shamelesse as to joyne in a Rebellion against their own Soveraigne'.[8] The same edition of the newsbook satirised the entry of women into politics, attacking the 'Shee Committee of Coventry' for petitioning the 'pretended Houses'. This explicit link between transgressive social roles – political and religious power, involvement in government, dominance in the household – and sexual dissipation is common in Royalist construction of Parliamentary women. Degenerate behaviour is directly aligned with political thinking – rebellion is 'bold' and 'shamelesse'.

Licentiousness and hypocrisy are regularly linked as characteristics of Parliamentarian women. Roundhead women were regularly attacked for their loose morals: 'Professing purity, chaste, undefil'd, / Yet in a Gravell pit was got with childe'.[9] They claimed to be 'chaste', but poets knew this to be false: 'She loues it wel enough, why then doth she spit / Her teeth doe water for to think on it'.[10] The 'Holy-Sister' is one that 'will lie, yet sweares she hates a lyer, / Except it be that man will ly by her'.[11] She is rude, gossipy, drunken, greedy and vain, foolish and ignorant: 'Shee that at Christnings thirsteth for most sack' (l. 13). This charge of drunkenness in women was particularly contrasted with the model of the demure and virtuous domestic wife. Drinking was a male preserve, and female desire for alcohol was one more challenge to the set roles assigned the subject within patriarchal Royalist culture. Sexual identity was tied to models of the family and to anthropocentric notions of the wholeness of the body within society. Royalists accused Parliamentarians of collapsing sexual and gender distinctions completely: homosexuality was seen as a rife plague, and *Mercurius Anti-Britannicus* went so far as to accuse the London newsbook *Mercurius Britannicus* of being 'an Herm Aphrodite Rebell'.[12] They dissolve the either/or binary, challenging compulsory heterosexuality.

The sexual libertinism associated with Roundhead or Parliamentary women was part of a consistent discourse of sexual difference and exclusion. Royalism presented a sexual orthodoxy of compulsory heterosexuality within a fixed family unit. Roundheads were hypocrites because they were promiscuous, were voyeurs, committed buggery, incest, adultery and transmitted sexual diseases. Roundheads are those 'That hate the flesh yet ferke the Dames' ('The Oxford Riddle', l. 7), hypocrites who disdain the orthodox sexual family unit.[13] They 'will not sweare, when's found fast with a sister, / But yet, by Yea and Nay, deny he kist her'.[14] Their sexual profligacy is barbaric and alien: 'The number of their Wives their Lusts decree; / The Turkish Lawe's their Christian Libertie!'.[15] Roundheads reject the normality of compulsory familial heterosexuality, and instead embrace a strange polygamy and sexual dissolution. Parliament was characterised by Royalists as questioning and challenging the order of things, subverting and undermining established patterns of behaviour and modes of identity. Part and parcel of this challenge to hierarchy and normality was a monstrous blurring of gender roles, an unsettling fluidity which allowed women to interrogate the discourses of patriarchy fundamental to the stability and harmony of the family of state. Sexual and gender deviancy was rampant in Royalist versions of the enemy.

In contrast, Royalism presented various models of virtuous femininity. For instance, a variety of Royalist women in non-traditional roles figure in *Mercurius Aulicus'* narratives generally as victims or martyrs, separated from their menfolk by the strictures of war. The countess of Derby was a special favourite of *Aulicus*', representing martial femininity and duty to the Royal cause. The long siege of Latham House was reported at length on several occasions, and the stubborn refusal of the countess to yield her ancestral home became something of a symbol of aristocratic political defiance:

> ...wherein it hath pleased God to grant her such matchlesse courage, that she still holds Lathom House against them (having now beene besiedged full Twelve weekes) and this day seavennight (April 10.) this most noble Countesse made a sally out upon the Rebels which was performed so gallantly; that she killed 45, wounded above 60 more, and tooke two Peeces of Ordinance, with Colonell Moores Colours and Drummes, on who theretofore hath eaten much bread in Lathom House, and therefore this brave Lady caused his Colours to be nayled on the top of the highest Tower of the house, that all the world may see the ingratitude of a Rebell.[16]

The countess is forced to act in a masculine role by the absence of her husband. Her courage is celebrated in patronising fashion ('gallantly' is disingenuous) but the reader is never allowed to forget that she steps out of her traditional gender roles in order to defend them. She is not challenging the structures of society, but defending them; she is not interrogating, but sustaining loyalist identity models. This kind of contained transgression is common in Royalist accounts of social behaviour. It pre-empts shifting identities and roles by configuring them within an overarching structure of allegiance.

After her controversial trip to Europe, Henrietta Maria returned to England in July 1643, and her eventual arrival at Oxford after meeting Charles at Edgehill was attended by wine, strewn flowers, and literary rejoicing. It was a muted return to court; there is little evidence of masquing or official entertainment organised to welcome her. A book of University poetry, however, published as *Musarum Oxoniensum Serenissimæ*, stood as a public testament of loyalty and political engagement. Whilst recalling the halcyon days of the 1630s, the volume answered Henrietta Maria's critics and bore testament to the cultural and poetic changes the country had undergone since her flight abroad in 1642. The collection configured the image of Henrietta Maria in an extensive fashion not attempted by other media during the war. It was produced at a time when the King's army was successful in the field, and confidence was high. It thus presents us with a Royalist version of femininity projected onto a figure that was at the centre of a complex nexus of religious, public and political signification.

The university verse collections of the 1620s and 1630s had evolved a form of panegyric which had roots in the demonstrative oratory taught in the Schools. Poets used various classical forms and epideictic topoi, notably the genethliacon, but rearranged and remoulded the structures in subtle and pointed fashion. In particular the poems emphasise the potent and creative union between Charles and Henrietta Maria, and celebrate a pastoral harmony and cosmic stability which echoes the language and action of court masques. The Queen is feted for her creative role in giving birth to both children and poetry. Poems elide poetic creation with birth, both of royalty and nation. Whilst privileging the Queen in panegyrics of birth, poems highlight the fact that her role was simply to facilitate the creation of a dynasty, whereas the state is focused through the King. *Musarum Oxoniensum* is a volume characterised by many of the same practices and thematic concerns as those previously published by the University. The contributors were a mixture of old and new voices; senior poets who had contributed to many other university volumes, like Mayne, Cartwright and Birkhead, all wrote new verse.[17] Whilst this emphasised a continuity of tradition it also established the differences from that tradition. The presence of a poem by John Berkenhead, for instance, politicised the volume and underlined how different it was from those which had preceded it. Bodleian MS Rawlinson Poet. 26 includes a poem 'The true Puritan w'out disguise' (109^{r}–110^{v}) that begins 'A Puritan is such a monstrous thinge / that loues Democraties, and hates a kinge / for royall issue never making praiers', conflating otherness with egalitarian politics and focussing this through loyalist poetic practice of the 1630s. The writing of such panegyric verse was in itself a political act. The older poets had also changed during the war, choosing more to give sermons and write pamphlets (or contribute to *Mercurius Aulicus*) rather than write verse. *Serenissimæ*, and the companion volume *Bevill Grenville*, are unique poetic texts of the period. Published within a fortnight or so of each other, they represent the end of Oxford Royalist panegyric, and a unique corpus of poetry produced from within the city-court during the war.[18] They demonstrate the fracturing and rupturing of generic rules and poetic expression during the war identified by James Loxley and Nigel Smith.[19]

The Queen has become the entire focus of the work and the renewal of her union with Charles the locus for a regeneration of poetic and social normality:

> Every Look which You reveale,
> Will compose our Commonweale.
> And Your bright Eyes will create
> Once more a well orderd State.

From Your Returne, Lawes will obtaine
Their Force, and be once Lawes againe.
(Jaspar Mayne, 'Whilest *Orpheus* toucht his Harpe', ll. 47–52)

Mayne's poem opens the collection's English poems and establishes the tone of the following verses. The poet compares the Queen to Orpheus, who brought calm and peace to the forest with his song. The absence of her person, and by extension the songs or verses inspired by her presence, has led to chaos and sociological inversion. In particular it is the glory of her outward appearance that reasserts hierarchical normality. Mayne gives her external virtues the power of verbs; her visage will 'Smile' war away, her looks 'compose' the state and her eyes will 'create' an ordered state. He is careful to insert 'Once more' into this sentiment, encouraging a notion that this is a return to normality. The absence of the calming influence of the Queen had broken apart fragile civilisation:

Having lost the Harmonye,
Which combined us in one knot,
Concord, Rule, and Lawes forgot
Every Thing did loose its Name,
A People a wild Rout became
(ll. 31–5)

The exile of the Queen allows the entire space of the nation to be reduced to chaos. The loss of language is foregrounded by the poem as the most destructive consequence, more important than civic peace or legal clarity. Linguistic confusion follows the loss of national harmony, and this leads to civil unrest and the debasing of the country.

There is also a terrible confusion involved in the loss of nomenclature; Adam named the world for God in Eden, and this divinely ordered linguistic system has been undone. Even the poem's form reflects this corruption as the rhyme scheme inverts normality: 'And those parts which lowest lye / Striv'd to chance place with the skye' (ll. 41–2). However, this piece of wit is partially corrected through the stability attained by the full rhyme. Metric and rhyming uniformity is a characteristic of the verse as a whole, contributing a firm exoskeleton to the poem. The piece controls language to illustrate the renewed vigour and harmony brought by the return of the Queen. Mayne traces a political shift which highlights the reconfiguration of panegyric verse:

And where You Your Beames display
'Twill be pleasure to Obey.

And our Bodyes, which before
The Style of Subjects only Wore,
Henceforth will but one halfe be
Of their Princes Soveraignty.
You'l enlarge His Realmes, and find
A greater Empire in each mind.
And His other Titles fill
With his Peoples Hearts, and Will.
When it shall be said in storye
You made these his Territory.
(ll. 47–64)

Subjects are bodily part of the 'Princes Soveraignty'; where before livery had clothed them in the colours of obedience, now they are incorporated into the representative commonwealth themselves, becoming 'one halfe [...] / Of their Princes Soveraignty'. Their minds are colonised individually as the notion of partnership opens up greater empires for Charles than those he already owns. What is striking about this section is the sense that the removal of Henrietta Maria has led to a collapse of order and normality. Her return will revivify the country, give laws their bite, and create the state anew as 'well orderd'. The return of the Queen therefore imbues her with a fundamentally important agency, an ability to focus and heal the wounds of the kingdom that the King seemingly lacks alone. Their union is celebrated and apotheosised, but this ability of Henrietta Maria to knit together the nation is not dependent on the King. Whilst she is his possession, and posited as part of a structured patriarchal system, she is the figure who brings all together. The reassertion of the family of state stabilises the disharmonious nation.

W. Barker figures the newly revived kingdom of *Serenissimæ*:

That State, which 'twixt two Hands does Bleeding ly,
The Hand of Murther and of Chirurgie,
(While this Cuts off Bad limbs, and that the Sound,
Till there be scarce a Body to be found)
Now gathers breath againe, and hopes to Live,
Not by what strength it hath, but what She'l give.
('Go burne some Rebell Towne', ll. 7–12)

The verse extends the Queen's creative potency to enabling a resurrection of sorts. England has been butchered, both geographically and institutionally, and it is only Henrietta Maria's intervention that can recreate the anatomised body politic. Barker's physiological vocabulary is echoed in Henry Birkhead's poem 'Till with Your selfe' which desires that the Queen 'unite us, and distempers cure' (l. 36). The state is revitalised by the Queen's return, highlighting the mutual relationship between commonwealth and monarch that had been established by Charles' speeches. The verse maps a Harveian model of the mutual dependence of the body's limbs and organs onto the state, a trope of circulation used by Charles throughout his public speeches. Henry Birkhead goes further in describing the 'numerous Unitie' which holds together the British state, 'Fowre bodies being so wrapt up together, / That every part at once is all, and neither' (ll. 10, 11–12). Birkhead deplores the strain placed on identity by the strictures of the war: before the combat, 'Traitour, and Subject undistinguisht stood, / Since 'twas all one to seeme, and to be good' (ll. 5–6). The war has fractured normality, and only the reappearance of the Queen can heal the ruptures, or 'stop their wild Career' (John Berkenhead, 'Now let them Vote, Declare, Contrive', l. 5). The Queen can bring closure to the awful fracturing where 'every part at once is all / and neither' (ll. 11–12). She is mother and healer, salvation and conclusion. Where Parliamentary women signify disruption and transgression, Henrietta Maria reconstitutes the state and mediates a return to normality.

Other poets marry the new martial voice of poetry with the idealised neo-platonic character of 1630s modes. John Dale's poem 'The Muses heretofore' sets the new collection in its tradition and highlights the shift in emphasis and content of the war poems:

> The Muses heretofore were wont to wait
> Vpon you at your Childbed, to relate
> The dangers there o're pass'd, no thought was then
> We should have had such matter for the Penne
> Your Travailes then were shorter, in the space
> Of a small month we saw your Princely face,
> (ll. 1–6)

Dale refers to the earlier University volumes celebrating the birth of Henrietta Maria's children, establishing his poem within that panegyric tradition. The verse is conscious of the changes imposed upon loyalist poetics and traces this shift. By emphasising what had previously (or 'heretofore') been the model for praise poetry, the poet highlights the gradual movement toward a different style and stance. Henrietta Maria's maternal agency, which had been so important in earlier volumes, is here reflected upon as something potentially harmful. Dale extends the childbirth metaphor, comparing her 'Enemies' then, which were 'Pangs and Groanes / Which breeding caus'd within Your Royall Bones' (ll. 9–10), with the malicious 'Rout' which threaten her now. Parliamentary opposition is likened to the illnesses attending pregnancy. It is part of the body politic that must be purged or endured; the Queen's innate virtue and divinity will protect her from these labour pains until her arrival gives birth to a new state and she becomes, as Strode later describes her, 'Mother of [the] Country'.[20] Dale's verse reworks the ritualised praise normally associated with the birth of a new member of the royal family to fit this new conception.

Throughout the poem, Dale establishes the ritualisation of conflict. Henrietta Maria's courtly entourage becomes indistinguishable from her conquests. Her return turns war into a ceremonial or ritual, a stately progress across the country toward Oxford:

> Your sweet celestiall Voice doth farre more cheare
> Then any Trumpet, and forbids all feare.
> Your Maids of honour with their glorious fight
> Millions of Preaching Citty dames will fright.
> Each beauty takes a Pris'ner, and what hand
> Can hurt those Starrs which doe the hearts command?
> Newes of your Victories, like Pages, came
> Before your Person, to proclaime your fame.
> To take a Towne by th'way it was your sport,
> Nor was your prosp'rous Iourney hindred for't.
> (ll. 25–34)

War is a 'glorious' undertaking, and the battle itself becomes an idealised 'sport' or pastime; almost a masque to divert the court. Comparable is the closing progress of I. Goad's pastoral dialogue 'Pan Blesse us', in which the Queen appears as if dressed for the *Shepherd's Paradise*:

> You may descry a Crowne and Crooke,
> That Gold, this Silver: then I see
> Our wood and Flockes shall setled be.
> Welcome from Low-country Land
> To once-fairer Englands Strand.
> (ll. 52–6)

Goad's attendant shepherds emphasise that the Queen's return will not transform the country or provoke a return to the golden age when England was 'fairer'; the transcendent power of the court entertainment has been diminished. The outdated pastoral allegory can only comment upon what has once been and will not return.

In Dale's poem, 'Pages' and 'Maids of honour' attend the triumphant and 'prosp'rous' apotheosis toward the King and court. Despite the power attributed them, women can only fight with traditional weapons: grace and beauty. The generic expressions of the wounded lover are redeployed in a different, although still figurative, setting ('Each Beauty takes a Pris'ner'). Puritan women are 'dames', ugly old wenches ignorant of all but preaching. Whilst this line satirises all female discourse emanating from Parliamentarian sources, it specifically picks up on the extensive public criticism of Lady Waller. By contrast, members of the Queen's entourage are young and pretty. They do not want to preach, they are happy being objectified. Dale appropriates military metaphors for his poem which mix pastoral fantasy and panegyric with a new sense of engagement:

> The Birth of Princes the chiefe Theme hath beene
> For Scholars, now, the safety of the Queene.
> We now doe runne to meet You in the Field
> Wherein we see your Fanne turn'd to a Shield
> Vpon Your Cheekes the Royall Colours lye,
> The Rose and Lilly in full Majesty,
> Your lovely Look Commander is in Chiefe
> Of all the Hearts; your Hands powre out releefe
> To needy Souldiers; 'mongst your Femall train
> The Lady Money followes, to sustaine
> Your Army with full store, which was not got
> By th'publike Faith, that hansome sugred plot.
> (ll. 13–24)

The rhetorical model of poetry has shifted from celebrating birth to idealising military engagement. The scholar-poets, rushing to meet the Queen with praise, discover that as a Muse she has become distinctly militarised (although her garb owes something to *Salmacida Spolia*). The work she now inspires is martial and situated on the battlefield. The Queen's complexion exhibits her innate nobility. She becomes a physical site of allegiance, as symbolically important as the Royal colours themselves. The trappings of monarchy and femininity are turned to martial use, protecting her subjects. The two external examples of Henrietta Maria's new power, make-up and fans, are those traditionally associated with disguise, covert asides and subterfuge. These ambiguous and problematised items are reclaimed and represented as indexes of symbolic strength. However, the acceptance of her femininity is still mediated by her construction by male poets who have shaped her to their own purpose. A line in the following poem, Richard Steevenson's 'What? Scholars digge' uses a similar model: 'Each Maid of Honour's Fanne's become a Shield / Indeed no honour like to that o'th field' (ll. 17–18). Whilst Dale fetishises the Queen's idealised role as protector and inspiration, her courtly protection or exterior now changed to armour, Steevenson instead highlights how all servants of the Queen, from courtly maidservants to poets, must engage with the enemy and use their natural tools in that fight. What outwardly seems empty of purpose and simply beautiful must be turned to practical use in the Queen's defence.

Both poets engage with the Parliamentarian criticisms of Henrietta Maria's sojourn on the continent. This is a motif of the majority of the volume. Steevenson celebrates the 'Queene's Army' (l. 16), highlighting Henrietta Maria's agency in the physical running of the conflict and her inspirational role. Rather than try to excuse her fundraising, Dale paints it as a charitable act, giving the Queen a faintly religious aura as the dispenser of peace, grace and 'releefe' (l. 20). Indeed, many of the poems in the volume seem to bring an underlying catholic discourse to their work. Henrietta Maria attains the status and power of her namesake, bringing 'the chast Birth of a Victory' (J. Read, 'Welcome, from Tempests to a Calme', l. 18). They rework platonic catholic virtues that had been commonly attributed to Henrietta Maria during the 1630s: her role as a mother, as an inspiration, as an intercessor or facilitator of reconciliation, as a leader to truth. Various puritan critics had picked up on this representative association in their attacks on the Queen, and their responses range from attacking the creeping papacy of Charles' court to the perceived impotence of the King within such a model. William Prynne complained about the popish cult of the Virgin which claimed 'That all things are subject to the command of Mary, even God himselfe'.[21] The *Serenissimæ* poets take these criticisms and make them virtues, creating a martial Virgin crusading for the cause of justice and divine right, turning her religion into a trope of polemic significance. They defend the honour of the Queen, protecting her from the criticism of the enemy. She is produced as an image of virtue and patience, her example of fortitude and loyalty something to be admired and followed.

The volume is closed by William Strode's 'Speech made to the Queenes most Excellent Majesty' (sig. D2^{v}). Strode is identified as the 'Orator of the University', the public mouthpiece of the institution. His speech is cast as an official declamation welcoming the Queen. Rhetorically the piece relies on a layered repetition which progresses towards the Queen's eventual apotheosis as the beloved of 'every thing that hath Breath or sound' (sig. D3^{v}). Henrietta Maria's absence from 'that Company [...] which you most Lov'd' was 'so barbarously forc'd with danger, persued by Calumnies, so patiently born' (sig. D2^{v}). The repetition of 'so' gives the line a circularity which allows her grace to replace or triumph over the barbarity of her enemies. Her patience is an early indication of her divinely appointed status and another echo of the Virgin in constructions of the Queen. Later in the speech this resolute virtue becomes a political stance, the dialectic opposite of the savage Parliamentary troops: 'for how much greater Your vertue, 'tis with so much the fiercer malignity aimed at, and with so much more prevalent Grace defended' (sig. D3^{v}). The actuality of Henrietta Maria's physical movement from exile is given a religious inflection, as the orator describes her 'second comming' (sig. D3^{v}). Her progress toward Oxford is celebrated as the return of stability and harmony: 'You have left behind you Victory in the North; You find it spreading in the South; and Victory from the West hath been seasonably stayed till this poynt, as ordain'd to salute your approach, and celebrate Your entertainment' (sig. D3^{r}).[22] Tactfully leaving out the Parliamentarian strongholds in the East, Strode conceives of victory attending the Queen's movement south. Decisive conflicts have been specially staged for Henrietta Maria's benefit, and the war itself is reconfigured as an entertainment. The arrival of the Queen heralds the movement from antimasque to peace and revelry, the renewal of harmony and stability defeating the lords of misrule and confusion. At a later point his vision of the returning Queen becomes a description of a masque-like entrance: 'We behold a strong Hoast of Men in Your attendance below, and with other eyes a stronger Hoast of Angells hovering above, under Gods ordering' (sig. D3^{v}). The Royal marriage is 'renew'd' and 'all the Spectators are as joyfull Now, as Then' (sig. D3^{v}). The Queen's body is again the nexus of obedience and national identity, as 'a union of the Rose & Lillies springs a fresh on Your cheeks' (sig. D3^{v}). This echoing of Dale's earlier poem highlights a profound difference in approach, even though both pieces celebrate the joining of the pastoral and the martial. Dale's image of the Queen is revelatory, a new ideal for the new situation. Strode situates himself firmly along a continuum, assuring the reader that Henrietta Maria's exile has been a temporary hiccup. He is careful to emphasise the similarity between 'now, as Then', and highlights the glow returning 'a fresh' to the Queen's cheek.

By reinserting the Queen back into a recognisable trope of masquing, Strode and the poets reassert the generic rules challenged by the Parliamentarian women. Furthermore, where the masque itself would seem to be the ultimate expression of personal power and political influence, the poets' representation of the masque mediates the power of the Queen; she is *represented*, rather than *presented.* She becomes part of a symbolic hierarchy, panoptically constructed through the male gaze as the idealised mother of the nation. Strode emphasises that she has returned to 'the Eyes of Your loving People' (sig. D3^{v}). They construct her, watch her, contain her. Strode emphasises the importance of the image in Royalist identity: 'to greet your most desired Presence; which, in beholding your Picture, we longd for, and in beholding Your Person, we are ready to dye for' (sig. D3^{r}). She is a morale-boosting, desirable poster girl representing virtue and fidelity. There is once again the sense of completion attending Henrietta Maria's return, emphasised by Strode's insistent recounting of the problems caused by her 'absence'. She fulfils a need, concludes, and brings stability and closure. Whilst she is celebrated as the mother of a renewed England, she is also part of the empire, colonised and appropriated, meaning inscribed upon her, a locus of idolisation and an ideal to adore. She is 'By Dangers made more pretious / As Things put on new price and cost/ When most in perill to be lost.' ('Whilest Orpheus toucht his Harpe', ll.70–3). The poet and people value her as a lost possession. They are 'as He, who his Iewell threw / Into the Sea, received it new' (ll. 74–5), welcoming the return of a precious cargo: 'We doe receive you back as Treasure [...] Or as the longing Merchant prizes / By th'Wracks they scape his Merchandizes' (ll. 82, 84–5). John Fell desires 'Neighbour Hollander', that particularly mercantile nation, to give up 'that Prize, / So farre aboue thy richest Merchandize [...] Returne our Lillies, we will ask no more, / Nor envie thee the Indies in thy store' ('When we remember those affronts', ll. 29–34). Henrietta Maria is granted status as commodity, something to be prized for its extraneous rather than innate value; indeed, Fell's verse expresses neatly the underlying gendered imperialist impulse of a male body politic that needs to possess its Queen. She is greatly important in a symbolic or idealised sense, but not a physical. The abstraction of the panegyric mode works to allow this gendered distancing, as the subject of the verse becomes exulted and objectified. However, these poems further suggest that the Queen was constructed as part of the locus of Royalist national identity mediated through the necessities of a masculine war effort. She is a morale boosting pin-up, idealised and unattainable. The Queen is a possession, a passive item necessary for the wholeness of the nation but without innate agency.

Despite her status as key figure in Royalist identification, the Queen was idealised simply as the perfect companion for the King, a platonic symbol of Caroline harmony and purity that the opposition were attempting to tarnish through untruth:

> She regards their many forces no more then their more numerous Lyes and forgeries, which have been let loose from Presse and Pulpit in such shamefull, filthy, abhominable plenty against Her Majestie, that as we all know there are Angels which guard the innocent from that end these

> Libels ayme at; so there are Devils which taught them how to slander, and will see them paid for the great paines they have taken.[23]

Aulicus' construction of the Queen is echoed throughout Royalist verse and prose of the period; she is innocent of all accusations due to her innate virtue, and this is proven by establishing the evil nature of those who arraign her. The poems in *Serenissimæ* idealise her feminine virtues and her martial prowess; the mutually creative union between the 'Sacred Couple' or the 'Great Best Paire' is still strongly emphasised (John Berkenhead, 'Now Let Them Vote, Declare, Contrive', ll. 13, 42). However, Henrietta Maria had no independent voice during the war. Unlike other members of the Royal family, she produced no (official) publications, took a low public profile, and was deployed only to complete the model of familial normality and compulsory heterosexuality key to Royalist configurations of the subject. She was simply as the poem 1641 'Maria Regina' categorised her, 'largely Graced, by th'Almighties Hand / To be a fruitfull Vine'.[24]

In Royalist discourse Henrietta Maria is presented as a fetishised and idealised paradigm for behaviour in contrast to the libertine and lascivious enemy. Parliamentary women preached, stole, drank, had public roles and forsook the domestic sphere. The Queen's example illustrated how they were unnatural and subversive. The opposition was deviant and transgressive, acting outside of the traditional space of the family and of structured gender roles. Roundhead women disrupted the hierarchies of society and ruptured the order of things, violating norms and flaunting sociological rules. They challenged the stability of family, both as a symbol of national unity by undermining the King's role as father of his people, and as a controlling network of localised patriarchy that confirmed and sustained the social order. The primacy of the loyalist Royalist family unit in contrast to this image of debauchery is demonstrated through the panegyrics written in praise and defence of Henrietta Maria. She was important to the Royalist project as a symbol of dutiful and normal femininity. Royalist poets simultaneously lauded the Queen and objectified her, emphasising her regal aspect whilst establishing her status as Charles' possession and subject. Poets celebrated her as the mother of England, her maternal role clearly defined within a standard family unit. She is colonised and appropriated, has meaning inscribed upon her, becomes a locus of idolisation and an ideal to adore. Her female power is at once celebrated and constrained – she is simultaneously lauded as unique and important, and assigned a voiceless symbolic value within a discourse of familial obedience and patriarchal subservience. As Leonard Lichfield wrote, the poets and the press are instruments of mediation, theatrical technologists that 'discover' the Queen in various emblematic poses – inspiring the troops, meeting the King on Edgehill, in the night sky ('The Printers Conclusion to Her Majestie', l. 24). They reveal the Queen to the audience, presenting her image, categorising and controlling her role and status as Royalist fetish, exemplar and pin-up.

Notes

1 *Three Speeches*, Printed at London for S. R. 1642, p. 6.

2 See, for instance Rachel Trubowitz's discussion of female divinity and agency in 'Female Preachers and Male Wives: Gender and Authority in Civil War England', in James Holstun (ed.), *Pamphlet Wars*, London: Frank Cass, 1992, pp. 112-33.

3 *The Soveraignty of Kings*, Printed at London, 1642, sig. A1^{v}.

4 *Mercurius Aulicus*, 30 July 1644.

5 Ibid., 23 Feb. 1644; 17 Aug. 1644.

6 Ibid., 18 Aug. 1644.

7 *The Diseases of the Times*, London: Printed for R. T. [1642], Sig. A3^{r}; *Puritan and the Papist*, in Thomas O. Calhoun, *et al.* (eds), *The Collected Works of Abraham Cowley*, 6 vols, London and Toronto: Associated University Presses, 1989, 1, ll. 196–98.

8 *Mercurius Aulicus*, 8 Jan. 1643.

9 John Taylor, *A Swarme of Sectaries*, [London], 1641, p. 7.

10 'An Epigram on a puritan': Beinecke Library, MS b.62, fol. 7^{r} ll. 3-4.

11 'The Holy-Sisters Character', *A Puritane Set forth in his Lively Colours*, London: Printed for N. B., 1642, p. 6, ll. 11-12.

12 *Mercurius Anti-Britannicus*, [Oxford, 1645], sig. 2^{v}.

13 Bodl., Rawlinson Poet. MS 71, p. 139.

14 'The Round-Heads Character', *A Puritane Set forth in his Lively Colours*, London: Printed for N. B., 1642, p. 5, ll. 29-30.

15 *The Collected Works of Abraham Cowley*, 3, pp. 95-96.

16 *Mercurius Aulicus*, 17 Apr. 1644.

17 Berkley, Strode, Fell, Hakewill, Bathurst, Rudyerd, Underwood, Barker, Mayne, Goad, Dale, Sandys, Cartwright, Stevenson and Howe contributed to both *Serenissimæ* and the most recent collection, *Eucharistica Oxoniensia In Exoptatissimum.*

18 Bevill Grenville died on 5 July 1643, and the Thomason copy of *Bevill Grenville* is annotated 'Aug: 12'. The Queen entered Oxford in late July of the same year, and the Thomason copy of *Serenissimæ* is annotated 'July 31'.

19 James Loxley, *Royalism and Poetry in the English Civil Wars*, Basingstoke: Macmillan, 1997; Nigel Smith, *Literature and Revolution in England 1640-1660*, New Haven and London: Yale UP, 1994.

20 *Musarum Oxoniensum*: 'Speech made to the Queenes most Excellent Majesty', sig. D3^{r}.

21 *The Popish Royall Favourite*, quoted in Erica Veevers, *Images of Love and Religion: Queen Henrietta Maria and Court Entertainments*, Cambridge: CUP, 1989, p. 108.

22 This movement is replicated in E. Gayton's poem 'Fall back you sonnes of Treason': 'Here Eagle-wayes thy Victories doe Fly / The West, and North is talk'd in every Mouth, / We must salute Thee now the Queene o'th South;', ll. 18–20. National identity is mapped onto compass-points which signify particular areas of the country.

23 *Mercurius Aulicus*, 17 Apr. 1644.

[24] *The True Effigies of our most illustrious Soveraigne Lord, King Charles Queene Mary, with the rest of the Royall Progenie*, London, 1641, ll. 12-13.

Chapter 13

Beyond Microhistory: the Use of Women's Manuscripts in a Widening Political Arena

Elizabeth Clarke

I have deliberately set myself a challenge in this essay by promising to go beyond microhistory. In women's history this is a rather rash thing to do, because at the aristocratic level it is the individual woman's rank, family and contacts which dictate her political influence. This is why the letter is the characteristic mode of political intervention by elite women, as demonstrated by so many of the other essays in this volume: it is the dominant writing practice for aristocratic women who wanted to engage in political projects of whatever nature using their own personal tokens of influence, such as rank, family and property. The Perdita Project – which was conceived to catalogue women's manuscript compilations from the sixteenth and seventeenth century – does not consider letters, at least not individual ones. However, I am going to look at the non-aristocratic manuscripts in the Perdita catalogue, which because of rising literacy rates tend to date from the later period, the second half of the seventeenth century, coinciding with the involvement in politics by a much larger proportion of the population. In this essay I am concerned with several questions. How different is political writing when mass audiences are the target? Do rhetoric and trope play a bigger part in political writing than the biography of the author? What role can women have within this kind of politics, when their writing is thought of as 'personal' and 'private'?

Although the women I shall discuss here are of 'the middling sort', the fact that they engaged in any kind of literary activity places them in the upper element of that category. These women may be descended from gentle families, and may marry wealthy merchants: many wealthy merchants gentrified themselves in this period, through a process which involved buying estates in the country. They were often closely connected with ordained ministers, who were usually treated as 'honourary' gentry.

They probably received some kind of education; one of the manuscripts I am going to discuss describes a kind of sub-university for women in the 1630s, made up of women who were sent to be educated by the wife of the Principal of New Inn Hall, Dr Rogers. Another mentions a kind of Nonconformist academy for the daughters of Dissenting families, run by Mr. Hill in Godmersham in Kent in 1671.[1] All of these manuscripts date from a period in the second half of the seventeenth century when historians like Tim Harris and Mark Knights have substantially charted involvement in politics by 'the middling sort'.[2]

This essay will chart the tones of what Bahktin calls a 'double voice' in these manuscripts. I will argue that the voice that many women ventriloquise has the ideal feminine tones of early modern patriarchy, masking any dissent. This rules out for most women publication in print, which tended to mark the female author as beyond the cultural pale; too rich, or too radical, or simply too vain. Attitudes to female publication are shown in Robert Boyle's dedication of his book, *Occasional Reflections,* to Katherine Ranelagh. Although she was 'so great a Mistress of Wit, and Eloquence', and encouraged him to publish his writing, she refused herself to publish anything at all: 'her Modesty did … confine her pen to Excellent Letters'.[3] This in itself is probably at once a statement of gender limitation in early modern culture, and a revelation of how a powerful woman might work effectively within it by avoiding publication: Katherine Ranelagh joins the list of early modern literary figures who thought Margaret Cavendish seriously deranged – 'I am resolved she scapes Bedlam onely by being too rich to [be] sent thereto' she wrote in1657.[4] If you were a Quaker of course you did not worry about your reputation, at least pre-1673. In 1673 the Second Morning Meeting was set up to censor manuscripts, and the minutes of these meetings reveal that the Quaker authorities were anxious about conforming to wider society's attitudes to gender and to politics: in fact none of the works they passed are as radical as the earlier Quaker publications of women like Elizabeth Hincks.[5] Male-authorised female writing like the mother's advice book was carefully constructed to avoid the criticism that attended the publication of women's work.[6] There is only one document in the Perdita catalogue that seems to have been originally intended for publication in print, and there are actually two manuscript copies of this work, one in the Dr Williams's Library, and one incomplete one in the British Library.[7] Both are entitled 'The Life of Christopher Love', by his wife, Mary Love. Christopher Love was the Presbyterian leader of the 1651 Love Plot, otherwise called the Presbyterian Plot, which aimed to put Charles II back on the throne.[8] Many

Presbyterian ministers and merchants were implicated in this conspiracy, but only Christopher Love was executed, for treason, in 1651.

Samples of Mary Love's writing had previously appeared in print, in *Loves Letters, His and Hers, to Each Other, a Little Before his Death* published in 1651, just after Love's execution in August, and in *Loves Name Lives*, apparently intended to give a fuller record of Love's correspondence, and published a few months later. This kind of authorship is well within that allowable to women: the letters are assumed to be private, the solemnity of the occasion and the intimacy of the relationship ruling out the rhetorical self-display that was particularly blameworthy in the female sex. Measures were taken, by the author herself or by editors unknown, to ensure that the manuscript 'Life' conveyed the same impression of feminine submission. The aim of the manuscript is of course to draw attention to her husband rather than herself. Mary even erased her own name, which was now Bradshaw: she remarried in 1654, a fact that would clearly have detracted from the devotion to Christopher expressed in the manuscript. Both manuscripts include a prefatory epistle by a man, 'T. H.', who has yet to be identified, who spends some time justifying and apologising for the fact that the author is female.[9] There is an apologetic letter to the 'Christian Reader' from Mary herself, couched in terms deeply familiar to any student of women's writing: 'Grudge not now to receive this unexpected Birth from a Woman ... it is the only one of its Mother'.[10]

It is obviously important for the impact of the work that Mary Love should be considered inexperienced and indeed reluctant as an author. She does not consider her letters, already published and to be republished in 1663, to be an act of authorship as such, a judgement consistent with cultural expectations of letter-writing as private and unrhetorical. Such letters from women were to become familiar features of Nonconformist martyrology during the Restoration, beginning with the accounts of the deaths of the regicides, and containing until the famous western martyrologies in the final decade of the seventeenth century that commemorated the victims of Judge Jeffries. Because they were considered to be without rhetorical strategy they were offered as proof of the character of the martyr.[11] The 'Life' is also a genre associated with martyrology, of course. The publication of Samuel Clarke's volumes of *Eminent Lives* in 1660 and 1662, which are probably contemporary with Mary Love's work, and which included a number of women's biographies, established a new political potential for the exemplary life: the familiar patterns of Foxean martyrology are wrested from their anti-Catholic context and made to perform in the service of resistance to Tory

Anglicanism, a function which they performed well. These early 1660s publications clearly form part of a Presbyterian drive for recognition, if not full political power, at the Restoration of Charles II. Love's was a name to conjure with at the Restoration for those Presbyterians who had hoped for some recognition for their support for the King in less happy days. Presbyterian poet Robert Wild, the most popular poet in London according to Dryden, had published *The Tragedy of Christopher Love at Tower-Hill* in 1660, clearly intended to prompt the King's memory.[12] There followed a rash of publications and re-publications all exploiting the name of Love: the village scribe of Ashton-in-Makefield, Presbyterian Roger Lowe, purchased a volume of Love's sermons in 1663.[13]

Mary Love's 'Life' probably dates from the same period, in the immediate aftermath of the Restoration in the early 1660s. The political message of this work is clear, and is expressed in her prefatory epistle: 'none know better how to love their King even to the death then they who but know how to love their God'. This represents an unequivocal plea for the Presbyterians to be included in politics. The document must date from before 1663, as Faith Lanum has recently established that she died in this year, and the epistle by T.H. speaks of her as if she is still alive.[14] The composition of the 'Life' itself probably dates from before 1662, as she celebrated the absence from church life of the Book of Common Prayer, and of ceremonies: 'which in those Evening times were more then in use, but for these many years these shadows have dispersed before the Sun'. She added, darkly, 'God grant that our abuse of light may not cause them to appear again'.[15] Of course, by summer 1660, the diarist Thomas Rugge reported the Presbyterian Thomas Manton using the Book of Common Prayer in his services, and one of the first acts of the Cavalier Parliament in May 1661 was to insist that its members received the Sacrament according to the Church of England rite.[16] The manuscript ends with a thinly-veiled plea for vengeance on Christopher Love's killers, a sentiment that certainly was in harmony with the mood of the summer of 1660, for some of those who had condemned Love had also condemned the King, and were on trial for their lives. One of the charges of the State against the regicide Major-General Harrison, executed in October 1660, actually related to the death of Christopher Love. In the letter prefacing Mary Love's account, 'T.H.', confirming a date for composition of the discourse by 1660, is puzzled as to why it was not published immediately at the Restoration.[17] It may be that circumstances changed too quickly. In 1658, prior to the Restoration, Charles II was writing to Thomas Cawton, another Presbyterian Plot conspirator in exile in Holland, looking for his support, stressing his

Protestant credentials, and asking Cawton to make these known among his colleagues in the Reformed Church.[18] This letter, a propaganda coup for the Presbyterians, was published in 1660, along with a Latin translation for the benefit of French and Dutch ministers by Major-General Massey which made clear that he was with the King when he wrote the letter. Major-General Massey was another Presbyterian Plot conspirator and civil war hero: in April 1660 *A Letter From an Eminent Person in Gloucester* described his rapturous return to Gloucester, where he was made a freeman of the city and elected burgess.[19] In March 1660 Alderman Bunce, also a Presbyterian plotter, arrived to great acclaim on the floor of the Royal Exchange. It was assumed in many quarters that Presbyterian fortunes were on the rise. However, the Worcester House Declaration of September 1660, rather favourable to Presbyterians, never passed into law. By October the consecration of new bishops was beginning. As Mary Love wrote in the prefatory letter to her manuscript, 'some constellations seeme to threaten at the instant of its Nativitys'.

It may be that potential publishers of Mary Love's treatise missed the moment: the stars that threatened at the moment of its birth were not deceptive. At the beginning of 1662, in reward for his relentless pursuit of subversive printers, Roger L'Estrange was made Surveyor of the Press. His 1661 publication *The Holy Cheat* had made it clear what he thought of Presbyterian pretensions to Court favour; thereafter, Presbyterian publications had a rough ride. State papers reveal that in the secret service in the 1660s a history of support for Love was considered a minus rather than a plus: to would-be absolutists, resistance to any authority, including that of the usurper Cromwell, was potentially dangerous.[20] Mary Love's 'Life of Christopher Love' did not achieve printed publication in the early 1660s, but it probably circulated in manuscript. Watermarks and handwriting suggest that the Dr Williams's Library manuscript was transcribed much later than the early 1660s, possibly in the early eighteenth century, when once again Presbyterians were striving for influence, and Christopher Love again seemed a name with some political resonance. In *The Dissenter's Answer to the High Church Challenge,* a 1704 pamphlet written to defend the political interests of Nonconformists, Daniel Defoe mentions that he is proud to possess a mourning ring given out at the funeral of Christopher Love.[21]

Thus far in this essay I have in fact indulged in microhistory, in contravention of earlier claims, but the context I have sketched is relevant for a significant cluster of manuscripts for which I am also going to suggest a similar mode of circulation, 'scribal publication'. These manuscripts can loosely be described as 'spiritual journals', documents of religious devotion that are tied to specific dates: the structural similarity of *Robinson Crusoe* to the spiritual journal is no coincidence. It is surprising that so many have survived, lacking the natural repository of the stately home where so many aristocratic manuscripts were preserved, and I suspect that they are representative of a far larger body of writing. They are probably the biggest homogenous group within the Perdita project apart from the receipt books, of which well over one hundred survive. In total, there are 15 'spiritual journals' in our catalogue, more than the number of conventional diaries which tend to come from aristocratic contexts and which, I think, fulfil a completely different function.[22]

The most famous spiritual journal of the period is actually that of an aristocrat, the countess of Warwick, Mary Rich, sister of Katherine Ranelagh. Although her writing clearly helped to establish the rhetorical form – extracts from it were printed in her lifetime by her chaplain – it does not share the features I am going to identify as political in other spiritual journals. This may be because her manner of political operation was that which I have suggested is characteristic of aristocratic women: she was consulted by many influential politicians and churchmen of the period – indeed, she was related to many of them – which meant that she was able to exercise personal influence. The remaining spiritual journals are almost exclusively a product of wealthy women of the merchant classes, on the margins of the gentry, who have close ties to the Nonconformist ministry; women like Mary Love, who was the daughter of wealthy City merchant Matthew Stone, or Mary Roberts, member of an extremely influential Nonconformist family from Sussex, or Ollive Cooper, daughter of a Presbyterian businessman from Nottingham or, of course, Mary Penington, wife of prominent Quaker Isaac Penington.

The writing of the spiritual journal was clearly a widespread literary practice. In funeral sermons, quoting from the spiritual journals of godly women from merchant and gentry classes was common in the pre-Civil War period, to establish the dead women's elect status and holy lives.[23] Samuel Clarke's 1662 volume of *A Collection of the Lives of Ten Eminent Divines* contained two extracts from women's spiritual journals in the women's *Lives* which constitute the second part of the volume. The link between hagiography and spiritual journal is obviously very close – the latter could be the material for the former – but I suggest that the political power of the spiritual journals was in their reader's capacity to read hagiography (a blatantly political form) into the spiritual journal, which was perceived as primarily devotional. The Henry family of

Cheshire, famous Presbyterians, read Clarke's *Eminent Lives* to each other, and at least one of the daughters, Ann Hulton, knew some them off by heart.[24] Her sister, Sarah Savage, describes reading other women's *Lives* which were sent to her: these *Lives* may have been the spiritual journals themselves. Philip Henry seems to have made a practice of using his sisters' spiritual journals to compile memoirs of them after their deaths; his memoir of Eleanor Radford, Matthew Henry's third daughter, did exist in the Henry papers in the nineteenth century, in Sarah Savage's handwriting. A memoir of Ann Hulton, his youngest sister, composed in this way, circulated in manuscript in the early eighteenth century with a preface by the learned and persecuted Presbyterian James Owen, and it contains extracts of her spiritual diary, in true Samuel Clarke fashion.[25] Certainly, Sarah Savage's journal circulated: two of her numerous volumes exist in later copies in the Bodleian Library and the Dr Williams's Library, and demonstrate that she had internalised the characteristic rhetoric of providential intervention and divine deliverance.[26] In the later seventeenth century, in a period of intense persecution of Nonconformists, such circulation was obviously a spiritual encouragement, but spiritual and political are always extremely close in this period, as I hope to show. Sarah Savage's father Philip Henry burnt his journal when he heard there was a warrant out for it.[27]

Although the surviving spiritual journals appear to be texts of private devotion – deliberately so, I believe – their circulation and in some cases their very composition was politically motivated. With one or two exceptions these later seventeenth-century journals are written by Independents or radical Presbyterians. From the late 1660s onwards, the more politically active wing of Presbyterianism, whose leaders were called the Ducklings, because of their readiness to abandon the idea of comprehension into a State Church and 'take to the waters' of Dissent, was linked by the government with Independency and Anabaptism in the pejorative term 'fanaticism'.[28] In the politico-religious crises of the Clarendon Code and the London riots, the Exclusion Crisis and the Monmouth rebellion, Presbyterians and Independents tended to act together.

Unlike aristocratic and Anglican diaries of this period, Nonconformist journals do not give specifics of the author's secular circumstances: the symbolic capital they drew on was not linked to the individual attributes drawn on by aristocratic women. Even names are omitted or referred to in code. The first manuscript I would like discuss is in some ways not a conventional journal, although it is a dated record of spiritual experience. It is in poetry, and its author Julia Palmer acknowledged the transgressive nature of her inspired act by explicitly renouncing what she called the 'sin' of modesty. However, it is in the simple non-rhetorical form which is considered to be the kind of poetry appropriate for women in the seventeenth century. Her poems are in two groups of one hundred, mimicking the most famous Presbyterian collection of hymns in the period, William Barton's 'Centuries'. Many of her poems are in the metres of his hymns, and they conceivably might actually have been sung: according to the introductory poems for each 'Century', she certainly intended them for circulation, and she left the copy of the manuscript that we have to a wealthy apothecary who was linked with the famous centre for Independent and Presbyterian cooperation, Pinner's Hall.[29] *The 'Centuries' of Julia Palmer* cover a crucial period of Nonconformist activity, including the response to the Declaration of Indulgence in the early 1670s, and clearly respond to specific political events, often included in the titles of the poems: but she encrypted those details in her own personal shorthand, a prudent strategy which is deeply frustrating to a modern reader. Several of her poems seem to refer to the Dutch War, such as the poem below, responding to what she calls 'this sad news' in the previous poem.

6 From dark, and cloudy providences, upon the church, & people of god. June 25 72

Shall wee, our father angry see
And shall we, unconcerned bee
Oh shall we not, be sore afraid
When we doe see, the rod is laid
On others, whilst we ar as much,
Or rather more, in fault then such
Who have already smarted by
The hand of him, who dwells, on high
Whilst we doe know our selfs as deep
In giult, shall we not att thy feet
Throw our selfs down, and lye prostrate
Untill thou shalt comiserate
And take away, the guilt of sin
In which we have walowed in
How should we wrastle, with thee now
By faith, and pray'r, least thou shouldst vow
The vialls of thy wrath, to poure
And all thy Judgments, on us showr
What arguments should we now use

That thou mayst not our pray'rs refuse
Wee can out of our selfs draw none
But what we fecth from thee alone.
And from the glory of thy name
Which wicked men doe now profane
Oh wilt thou on, the wicked shine
whilst thou dost seem, to cast of thine
Thou smilst upon their eterprise
And wilt not hear thy peoples crys
Oh wilt thou favour their design
Whilst they against thee, doe combine
And plot how they may doe their best
For to destroy, thine interest
And from the earth cut off the race
Of thosse that love, and seek thy face.[30]

(ll. 1-34)

This poem, in the tradition of the Psalms, manages at the same time to ask forgiveness for guilt and lay blame firmly at the door of 'the wicked'. 'Interest' is a word from the controversies surrounding the Restoration, and refers to God's stake in human politics, which is seen by Palmer as being firmly located in the godly, reformed Protestants of England and of Holland. I think that this poem reflects her response to the news of June 1672, which was of the bloody victories of the English and French fleet, and the flight of the Dutch before a land invasion by the French.[31] The plotters in line 31 are the Royalist government of Charles II who are seen as in league with the French Catholics. At this stage Palmer and her contemporaries knew nothing about Charles' secret promise to the French at the treaty of Dover, to bring the country to Catholicism, but they suspected the worst. An interesting feature of this poem is in its date, soon after the Declaration of Indulgence in March 1672, which was meant to appease Nonconformists and resign them to non-resistance to government policy, in particular, the war with the Protestant Dutch. Despite the fact that Julia Palmer's husband Nicholas received a licence as a Presbyterian preacher in May (for the same congregation in Windsor which wrote the letter of support to Christopher Love included in Mary's 'Life'), she was certainly not appeased or resigned.[32]

The convention within spiritual journals of refusing to name names may have had the pragmatic effect of deflecting government suspicion. However, there was a spiritual rationale for it. As Ollive Cooper scornfully declared in her spiritual diary for 1704, the 'Temporall favours' of one's own life are but 'the dark side of gods goodness', less spiritually valuable than the development of one's relationship with Christ.[33] This spiritual motivation may also have had the political advantage of acquiring spiritual capital, part of the double-voiced utterance I described earlier. The woman's holiness was attested to by the cultural form in which she chose to write, which was assumed to be private, the product of communion with God. Thereafter, as long as the appropriate biblical rhetoric were used, any expressed opinion would have the stamp of godly piety. A contemporary reader would of course have had little problem identifying the dated events to which Palmer was responding. The documents have little obvious political relevance today, but within their particular cultural context they could function effectively in the way I have reconstructed for Elizabeth Jekyll's spiritual diary in a recent article for *English Manuscript Studies*.[34] I have argued there that Jekyll's diary was transcribed and circulated in 1685, when her husband's printing press was closed down, and the danger was such that the only safe publications were 'private' manuscript transcriptions of a 'private' woman's journal. Nevertheless, to those who knew how to read the codes, these documents were politically charged.

The perceived power of such women's manuscripts is based on the belief that feminine weakness precludes the living of a holy life without the direct inspiration of the Holy Spirit. This 'proof' that a woman's writing is divinely supported and sanctioned is extremely valuable politically. One of the earliest 'exemplary lives' of a woman is *The Christian Life and Death of Mistris Katherin Brettergh,* which went into 34 editions between 1591 and 1700, and must have helped to form the feminine ideal of Christian heroism in the seventeenth century. Katherin Brettergh's exemplary life is enlisted in an anti-Catholic polemic:

> It must needs be a divine Religion and truth comming from God, that thus can fill the heart and mouth of a weake woman, with such admirable comfort. And a wretched conceit, and mere Antichristian, is that Religion, which so hateth and persecuteth this faith.[35]

Another series of manuscripts, which transcribe Rose Hickman's story of her Marian exile in Holland in the mid-sixteenth century, carry exactly this burden of interpretation.[36] After 1660, the symbolic capital accrued by a century of Protestant martyrology was exploited against the Stuart government.

The journals record an ever-present threat of martyrdom, which seems strange to a modern reader with the knowledge that the Glorious Revolution took place later in the century, assuring the future of a Protestant monarchy. There are recurrent concerns of invasion by the

French, which is assumed in the 1660s and 70s to entail martyrdom for all sincere Nonconformists.[37] Another trope often used, perhaps paradoxically, as polemic in anti-Catholic rhetoric of the first half of the seventeenth century, is the trope of the believer as Bride of Christ. Several women go through scripted 'marriages' with Christ, recorded in their journals; they describe feelings of spiritual bliss. Elizabeth Turner's journal entry for 22 January 1666 includes an 'amazinge covenant' based on the marriage service, marking her betrothal to God: 'I doe heer w*i*th all my power accept thee for my head & husband: for better for worse, for all times & conditions: to love honor & obey thee before all others ... neither life nor death shall part beetweene thee & mee'.[38]

While spiritual journals of this kind might inspire literary criticism of a psychoanalytic nature, this rhetoric is not usually assigned its historical and political significance. In the mid 1670s there was a major controversy over Nonconformists' use of the trope of the Bride of Christ, and the rhetoric of the Song of Songs. William Sherlock in 1674 had continued the attack on Dissenting beliefs and discourse started by Simon Patrick and Samuel Parker in *A Discourse Concerning the Knowledge of Jesus Christ, and our Union and Communion with him.*[39] This time his targets were the Independent John Owen and the Presbyterian Thomas Watson, who had both written spiritual treatises in 1657 which asserted the primacy of the marriage relationship between Christ and the believer. On the first page Sherlock denied that the person of Christ is anything more substantial than a metaphor: it is thus impossible to have a relationship of any sort with Him, let alone that suggested by an allegorical interpretation of the Song of Songs. He employed a patriarchal view of marriage to reinterpret the Biblical metaphor of the Bride:

> When the Scripture calls *Christ* our *Husband,* and the *Church* his *Spouse*, it means no more, but that Christ is our *Head and Governour,* who rules his Church with as great kindness, tenderness and compassion, as a Husband exerciseth towards his Wife, and that we are to pay the same love, duty and obedience to Christ, that Wives owe to their Husbands; and here we must have done with the *Metaphor,* unless we will turn Religion into a *Romance*.[40]

The 'romance' with Christ was of course a central experience of Reformation Christianity, particularly for women, as made clear by Thomas Vincent's sermon to a convention of Presbyterian women in 1672, *Christ The Best Husband.* Sherlock's treatise provoked many responses. Robert Ferguson, in *The Interest of Reason in Religion* (1675), identified a political intent in the reluctance of Church of England theologians to recognise the metaphorically encoded union of believers with Christ: 'by our *Fellowship with Christ* which the Sacred Writers so Emphatically speak of, we are told there is only meet such a Political Union, as is betwixt a Prince and his Subjects, between Superiours, and Inferiors'.[41] In fact, it was the immediate union of Christ and believer that Tory Anglicans considered 'political': it could give a beggar – or indeed a woman – unmediated access to the divine, with alarming consequences. The spiritual journals celebrate that access in a defiantly egalitarian manner.

Unfortunately, as with Katherin Brettagh and the women in Clarke's *Eminent Lives*, what looks like a spiritually democratic ideal only goes so far. Women's writing of this kind is valuable because of the perceived weakness of women: they are unable to become authors unless they are divinely inspired. This model is familiar to us through the activities of the female prophets during the Interregnum: for example, Anna Trapnel, and the early Quaker prophetesses such as Elizabeth Hincks. Although the women I have discussed in this essay mimic the same passive model for authorship, Presbyterians, of course, had no female prophets in their midst. Moreover, they were less willing than Quakers or even Baptists to abandon conventional politics, with its male networking to ensure personal influence. It is no coincidence, therefore, that every woman God chose to inspire from this Presbyterian or Independent context was connected to a prominent man: it was always important, as the titles of the martyrologies show, that the subjects were 'eminent'. The women whose spiritual journals have survived are those of Nonconformist activists. Elizabeth Jekyll's husband's radical career started with his involvement in the Christopher Love plot and continued until the Glorious Revolution; Elizabeth Turner was from the influential Independent Broadnax family of Kent: her father had been a major in Cromwell's army, her husband Thomas was a Canterbury lawyer employed by London Nonconformist leaders at times of crisis, and her brother-in-law was Thomas Papillon. Eleanor Stockton was wife of famous Independent minister Owen Stockton; and Marion Veitch, whose memoir exists in two eighteenth-century copies in the National Library of Scotland, was the wife of Argyll's co-conspirator Veitch, in the conspiracy which accompanied the similarly unsuccessful Monmouth Rebellion. All this opens up the question of whether these journals, conceivably the most private, spiritual writing by women, were in fact manipulated by men with political ambition. I am not entirely sure, for example, that Mary Love wrote 'The Life of Christopher Love'. It would have needed to exist, under that name, whoever wrote it. Most of these manuscripts exist in copies or fair copies, indicating the possibility of editing. Elizabeth Jekyll's diary cannot possibly be the private autograph document which it pretends to be because she was dead by the time it was copied. Since it extols the godliness of her husband, John Jekyll, who was in serious political trouble at the time that it was transcribed in 1685, my suspicions are that he responded to the shutting down of his illegal printing press and his imprisonment at the height of the Monmouth rebellion by circulating a document that had all the hallmarks of vindicatory Protestant rhetoric.

Suspicions that these documents were for public consumption rather than private reading are confirmed by the nature of the manuscripts themselves. Only in one case do we have what is obviously the original notebook of the journal, with differing inks and deteriorating handwriting. Eleanor Stockton's journal shows the editing of an 'eminent life' in progress. Her description of the death of her favourite daughter ends with what looks like an indictment of God, but it is not allowed to stand: many years later in a shaky hand she added the 'approved' interpretation of this terrible event that it was allowed to happen because of her own sin.[42] There is obviously an imperative to produce the rhetoric of the 'exemplary life' in the spiritual journal, a textual pressure which could impact on behaviour during the subject's life. The introduction to *Her Own Life* raised the possibility of the text writing the life, rather than the life forming the text: Jonathan Scott traces the behaviour whereby Algernon Sidney ensured he would be the subject of a powerful Whig martyrology.[43] In Eleanor Stockton's journal we see the pressure on the narrative induced by the fact that she knew that her text would be read by others. This pressure is of course partly self-induced: Mary Penington consciously wrote her manuscript to be read out to other Quaker congregations. Of course, if women did not want their writings to be read by others, they burned their papers at the onset of serious illness. Thus, there are very few documents in this cluster that can be considered 'private' in any sense, even, or perhaps especially, Katherine Austen's, which has the seventeenth-century equivalent of 'Private–Keep Out' on the cover: 'Whoso euer shal look in these papers and shal take notice of these personal occurrences: wil easily discerne it concerned none but my self: and was a private exercise directed to my self. The singularity of these Conceptions doth not aduantaige any'.[44]

More evidence that the spiritual journal is a literary form with rhetorical conventions rather than a divinely attested 'proof' of the holiness of its author – if we needed it – is in the survival of two manuscripts from

Royalist gentry contexts, which were not usually associated with the form. Their female authors clearly saw the potential of the form to achieve aims other than merely spiritual propaganda. Alice Thornton's first 'Book of Remembrances' is dated 1668, and was part of an attempt to refute scandalous accusations. The rumours were that she had fallen in love with Thomas Comber, then a young curate rather than the distinguished Dean of Durham he was to become, and had married her 14-year-old daughter off to him to cover for the fact that they all lived in the same house: 'I sent my owne Booke of my Life, the collections of God's dealings and mercys to me and all mine ... to sattisfy all my friends of my life and conversation ... that it was not such as my deadly enymyes sugested'.[45] She offered a contents index to help her readers interpret this document, and reported a successful outcome: apparently the conventions of the spiritual journal, which signified sincerity and holiness, were so powerful that the doubleness of the voice was not perceived.[46] Anne Halkett's well-known autobiography, justifying her relationship with Colonel Bamfield, was composed in a break from writing her rather more extensive spiritual journal which was probably perceived as a similarly vindicating project: her minister published extracts after her death.[47]

The political usage of the spiritual journal indicates several important aspects of the part gender played in politics in the second half of the seventeenth century. Unlike the activity of politically active women at the aristocratic level, it erases the personalities and circumstances of individual women. This is partly because ideal Nonconformist lives are expected to fulfil certain patterns, and partly a function of gender ideology. Conformity to stereotypes of femininity was crucial to the communication of any political opinion at all, and this gendering extended to choice of rhetorical form and style. The power of the manuscript, rather than residing in the political influence of the individual woman, who becomes less important both in the ideology and the practice of a more popular politics, resides in features such as the rhetoric of providential deliverance from persecution and accident, and the use of tropes such as the author as Bride of Christ. Such a move from the authorship of one real woman to a gendering of a particular document, of course, makes it less important that the writer is who the manuscript asserts her to be. I find these manuscripts rather unhelpful as a way of reconstructing individual women's lives, which is what feminist scholars have hoped for from journals, although there are times when the reader's awareness that this is a male-dominated rhetorical construct is overwhelmed by an irresistible sense of sisterly solidarity, as when Elizabeth Turner is abandoned in the middle of labour by her midwife who had had a better offer, and had to deliver the baby on her own.[48] What they do illustrate is the way in which a feminine ideal, based on Protestant proto-democratic principles, could operate politically in an oppositional politics which possessed moral and political currency in the second half of the seventeenth century.

Notes

Research for this essay was greatly assisted by a Leverhulme Fellowship awarded in 1999.

1 DWL, MS 28.58, p. 22; CKS, MS F. 27, [p. 106]: MS unpaginated (this is my own pagination).

2 Tim Harris, *London Crowds in the Reign of Charles II: Propaganda and Politics From the Restoration to the Exclusion Crisis*, Cambridge: CUP, 1987; Mark Knights, *Politics and Opinion in Crisis, 1678-81*, Cambridge: CUP, 1994.

3 Robert Boyle, *Occasional Reflections Upon Several Subjects. Whereto is Premis'd a Discourse About Such Kind of Thoughts*, London, 1665; 2nd ed., 1669, sigs A4v-A5r.

4 BL, Althorp Papers, Box 4: uncatalogued letter of 13 Apr. 1657. Quoted in Elizabeth Anne Taylor, 'Writing Women, Honour, and Ireland, 1640-1715', unpublished PhD thesis, University College, Dublin, 1999, p. 285.

5 London, Friends House Library, 'Morning Meeting Minutes Book', transcript of vols 1 & 2 (1673-1700) shows examples of women's manuscripts being rejected because they are too critical of the government: Judith Bulbye's 'Lament', for example, in January 1689 (p. 88). Elizabeth Redford was told in July 1695 that she had not been inspired by God to write her paper (p. 60). Alice Hayes, being forbidden to publish in print in July 1699, was allowed to publish in manuscript as long as she addressed her writing only to other women (p. 164). Abigail Fisher, in September 1693, was told to rewrite her poetry in prose (p. 24).

6 See Sylvia Brown, 'The Approbation of Elizabeth Jocelin', in Peter Beal and Margaret J.M. Ezell (eds), *English Manuscript Studies, 1100-1700, Volume 9: Writings by Early Modern Women*, London: British Library, 2000, pp.129-64.

7 DWL, MS 28.58; BL, Sloane MS 3945, fols 78-113.

8 See Leland H. Carlson, 'A History of the Presbyterian Party from Pride's Purge to the Dissolution of the Long Parliament', *Church History*, 11 (1942), 83-122. Faith Lanum, of St Edmund's College, Cambridge, has worked on these manuscripts for the Perdita Project.

9 DWL, MS 28.58, fol. [3r] (my foliation).

10 Ibid., fol.[1r].

11 See, for example, *The Speeches and Prayers of Some of the Late Kings Judges*, London, 1660; *The Dying Speeches, Letters and Prayers & c. of Those Eminent Protestants Who Suffered in the West of England and Elsewhere, Under the Cruel Sentence of the Late Lord Chancellor, then Lord Chief Justice Jeffreys*, London, 1689; *The Western Martyrology or Bloody Assizes*, London, 1705.

12 Keith Walker, *John Dryden: a Critical Edition of the Major Works*, Oxford: OUP, 1987, p. 77. Wild is described as 'the very Withers of the City'.

13 William L. Sachse (ed.), *The Diary of Roger Lowe of Ashton-in-Makefield, Lancashire, 1663-74*, London and New York: Longmans, Green, 1938, p. 25.

14 Chester RO, Parish Records of St Peter's Church, Chester: 'Mary wife unto Mr Edward Bradshaw mercer and Mrs Mary Davies died both the 14th day of May & were buried both in one grave 1663'.

15 DWL, MS 28.58, p.37.

[16] BL, Add. MS 10116, fol. 95.
[17] DWL, MS 28.58, [fol. 2r].
[18] *A Letter From K. Charles the Second, Third Monarch of Great Britain: to Mr Cawton, of the English Church in Roterdam, to be Communicated to the Rest of the Ministering Brothers of the Reformed Churches in Holland in Defence of Himselfe in the Matter of Religion*, London, 1660.
[19] 'Mercurius Politicus Redivivus', BL, Add. MS 10116, fols 79^{v}-81^{r}, 83^{v}.
[20] *CSPDom, Charles II, 1660-(1685),* preserved in the Public Record Office, (ed.) M.A.E. Green, *et al.*, 28 vols, London, 1860-1947, 14 (1671), p. 560.
[21] Daniel Defoe, *The Dissenters Answer to the High-Church Challenge*, London, 1704, p. 43.
[22] CKS, MS U1015 F 27, 'Elizabeth Turner's journal'; BL, Add. MS 42849, 'women's devotional journals', 1686-1752; Beinecke Library, Osborn MS b. 221, 'Elizabeth Jekyll's spiritual journal'; Chester RO, D/Basten/8, 'diary of Sarah Savage, 1686-87'; East Sussex RO, Lewes, DUN 52/10/3, 'Mary Roberts's (d. 1666) devotional diary, 1660-61'; BL, Add. MSS 27351-27358, 'diaries and meditations of Mary Rich, Lady Warwick, 1666-77'; DWL, MS 24.8, 'Occasional reflections of Mrs Elianor Stockton'; DWL, MS 24.49, 'Ollive Cooper's journal'; Bodl., Rawlinson MSS Q.e. 26-28, 'devotional MSS by a woman'; NLS, MSS Adv. 34.5.19, Adv. 32.4.4, 'copies of memoirs of Katharine Ross and Jean Collace, 17th c'; NLS, MS Adv. 34.6.22, 'copy of memoirs of Marion Veitch'; Friends House Library, Penington MS, vol. 4; William Andrewes Clark Memorial Library, UCLA, MS P1745 M1 P744 1671-3 Bound, 'The Centuries of Julia Palmer'.
[23] Sources in Clarke's volume: Elizabeth Juxon, married to a wealthy London citizen, her funeral sermon of 1619: Stephen Denison *The New Creature: a Sermon*. Jane Ratcliffe's spiritual journal is extracted in Clarke's volume, copied from her 1630s funeral sermon by John Ley, who was to become a fervent Presbyterian member of the Westminster Assembly. Richard Baxter produced, as conclusive proof of her elect condition, the spiritual diary of twenty-five year old Jane Baker, for whom he preached a funeral sermon in 1659: Richard Baxter, *A Treatise of Death*, London, 1660. For more politically engaged personages such as the earl of Warwick who died in 1658, such written proof of holiness turns the funeral sermon into political oratory. Edmund Calamy, *A Patterne for All*, London, 1658.
[24] *Memoirs of the Life and Character of Mrs Sarah Savage to which are added Memoirs of her Sister, Mrs. Hulton,* 4th ed. (London, 1829), p. 295.
[25] *Memoirs*, p. 279.
[26] Patricia Crawford, 'Katherine and Philip Henry and Their Children: a Case Study in Family Ideology', *Transactions of the Historical Study of Lancashire and Cheshire,* 134 (1984), pp. 39-74.
[27] Douglas R. Lacy, *Dissent and Parliamentary Politics in England, 1661-1689. A Study in the Perpetuation and Tempering of Parliamentarianism*, New Brunswick: Rutgers UP, 1967, p. 368.
[28] CSPDom, 14 (1671), p. 496: 'The people grow more fanatic: all the Presbyterians are going to Independents'.
[29] For a more detailed context see *The 'Centuries' of Julia Palmer*, Victoria Burke and Elizabeth Clarke (eds), Trent Editions, 2001, pp. i-ii.
[30] *The 'Centuries' of Julia Palmer*, pp. 178-79.
[31] See Stephen Pincus, 'Republicanism, Absolutism and Universal Monarchy: English Popular Sentiment During the Third Dutch War', in Gerald Maclean (ed.), *Culture and Society in the Stuart Restoration: Literature, Drama, History*, Cambridge: CUP, 1995,

pp. 241-166. I do not agree with Pincus' claim that there was no opposition to the Dutch war on its outbreak, but he is right to stress the importance of the events of June 1672.

[32] DWL, MS 24.28, pp. 45-6; *CSPDom*, 15 (1672-73), pp. 55, 196.

[33] DWL, MS 24.29, fol.19^{v}.

[34] Elizabeth Clarke, 'Elizabeth Jekyll's Spiritual Diary: Private Manuscript or Political Document?', in Beal and Ezell (eds), *Writings by Early Modern Women*, pp. 218-237.

[35] William Harrison, *The Christian Life and Death of Mistris Katherin Brettagh*, London, 1641, pp. 19-20.

[36] For a printed edition of this manuscript, see Maria Dowling and Joy Shakespeare, 'Religion and Politics in Mid Tudor England Through the Eyes of an English Protestant Woman: The Recollections of Rose Hickman', *BIHR*, 55 (1982), 94-102.

[37] See Jonathan Scott, 'England's Troubles: Exhuming the Popish Plot', in Tim Harris, Paul Seaward and Mark Goldie (eds), *The Politics of Religion in Restoration England*, Oxford: Blackwell, 1990, p. 115 on the sense of threat felt by English Nonconformists in this period.

[38] CKS, MS U1015 F 27, [pp. 58, 60] (MS unpaginated: this is my own pagination).

[39] Simon Patrick, *A Friendly Debate Between a Conformist and a Non-Conformist,* London, 1669; Samuel Parker, *A Discourse of Ecclesiastical Polity*, London, 1667, p. 158. Sherlock explicitly criticises Thomas Watson's book, *The saints delight. To which is annexed a treatise of meditation. and Christs Loveliness,* London, 1657, and John Owen's *Of Communion with God: The Father, Sonne and Holy Ghost, Each Person Distinctly; or, The Saints' Fellowship with the Father, Sonne and Holy Ghost, Unfolded*, Oxford, 1657.

[40] William Sherlock, *A Discourse Concerning the Knowledge of Jesus Christ, and Our Union and Communion With Him*, London, 1674, p. 287.

[41] Robert Ferguson, *The Interest of Reason in Religion With Reflections on Several Late Writings, Especially Mr. Sherlocks Discourse Concerning the Knowledge of Jesus Christ*, London, 1675, p. 187.

[42] DWL, MS 24.8, fol. 19.

[43] Elspeth Graham *et al.* (eds), *Her Own Life: Autobiographical Writings by Seventeenth-Century Englishwomen*, London: Routledge, 1989, p. 17; Jonathan Scott, *Algernon Sidney and the Restoration Crisis 1677-1683*, Cambridge: CUP, 1991, pp. 317-47.

[44] BL, Add. MS 4454, fol. 4^{v}.

[45] *The Autobiography of Mrs Alice Thornton*, Surtees Society, 62, Edinburgh, 1873, p. 259.

[46] Four differing manuscripts of Alice Thornton's 'Life' seem to have been extant when the late nineteenth-century edition was put together. Two of these are now in private hands, although microfilms are available for consultation at the British Library. One is on microfilm at Yale University, although the original has been lost, and it is this that I am referring to here. I am grateful to Raymond Anselment whose recent work on the manuscripts I have seen.

[47] NLS, MSS 6489-6502.

[48] CKS, MS U1015 F 27, [pp. 27, 28].

Chapter 14

Loyal and Dutiful Subjects: English Nuns and Stuart Politics

Claire Walker

> All though I need no incouragement to this duty besides yor Majesty's singular meritt and soveraigne power over yor loyall subjects, yett I cannot aproach yor Majesty with the duty of this address containing our Annuall tribute of prayers till first I have recorded my harty and gratfull thanks for the honer of yor Majesty's most obliging letter. A favour highly valued by us as witnessing a kind acceptance of our harty affection prayers and zeale for the prosperity of yor Majesty and the Royall Family, principles I hope Inherent to this Community, from which and from my self with hartiest wishes of a happy new year and of many succeeding happy yeares, wee present yor Majesty as a poore New Yeares Guift with two thousand communions, Masses, paires of Beads and acts of penance. May Heaven render our prayers and wishes as succesfull as they are offered to God and yor Majesty with harty affection and zeale of yor happiness.

(Abbess Mary Knatchbull to Queen Mary of Modena, New Year's Day, 1687)[1]

Abbess Mary Knatchbull of Ghent was one of several religious women who corresponded with James II's fervently Catholic consort. Mary of Modena received letters from numerous French, Italian and English nuns, and she graciously accepted their good wishes and prayers for her health, fecundity and the good fortune of her husband, reciprocating their spiritual patronage with promises to advance their communities' temporal fortunes. Associations between convents and royalty were not uncommon in the medieval world, nor indeed did they cease in early modern Catholic states. Kings, queens and princes maintained alliances with specific monastic establishments to which they were bound by kinship, patronage or tradition. Royal and aristocratic daughters often took the veil in prestigious cloisters which accordingly benefited from the social and political kudos conferred by their well-connected inmates. Houses without such intimate ties sought the benefits of royal patronage via associates at the court. Royal connections proved invaluable in economic terms, but they were also crucial politically when civic or ecclesiastical authorities challenged a convent's rights and privileges. Yet the patronage relationship between nuns and their distinguished patrons was by no means one-sided. Royal and elite nuns often acted in the interests of their secular kin. Indeed it became common in France for the monarch to appoint his female relatives as abbesses and prioresses *in commendam* to secure royal control over vital religious resources. Nuns and their monasteries were therefore no strangers to networks of power and governance, and in certain instances they engaged actively in the politics of both Church and State.

In England the relationship between crown and convent was seemingly ruptured irrevocably by Henry VIII's dissolution of the monasteries. The history of post-Reformation contact between monarchs and Catholic religious orders is invariably one of conflict. From the arrival of the missionary priests in Elizabethan England through fears of Elizabeth's assassination to the Gunpowder and Popish plots and the Jacobite uprisings of the eighteenth century, Catholic men who had taken religious vows were deemed enemies of the state. Although the majority of priests, friars and monks did not conspire to overthrow England's Protestant church and government, their priestly status and pastoral ministrations to the recusant minority were considered sufficiently subversive to warrant arrest, imprisonment and, occasionally, execution for treason. Conversely, English religious women enjoyed a less dangerous, albeit just as despised, relationship with the new regime. After the re-foundation of female cloisters in 1598, English nuns resided in France, the Low Countries and Portugal. Bound by strict monastic enclosure, they did not undertake missionary work in their homeland. Instead they provided spiritual and educative sanctuaries across the Channel for English Catholic women. Their existence, work and prayer was arguably as subversive as many of their confreres, but their exile abroad ensured they did not directly confront the English religious and political establishment. Hence they were most commonly derided as silly women in thrall to the Catholic clergy, rather than credited with any political import or potential. Yet nuns were much closer to both the English crown and political subversion than scholars have hitherto acknowledged. Several cloisters maintained close connections with the Stuart kings and their Catholic consorts by virtue of the fact that, at various junctures during the seventeenth century, the Stuarts were themselves in exile.

This essay seeks to explore the relationship between the nuns and the Stuarts to show that far from political inaction, the convents were engaged closely with English affairs. Recusant nuns worked hard to foster the kinship and patronage relationships with the royal family enjoyed by their medieval forebears and their contemporary continental religious sisters. They sought the patronage of queens consort, most notably Henrietta Maria and Mary of Modena, but they were by no means strangers to Charles II and James II, who bestowed financial and other favours on them. Various members of the royal family enjoyed the hospitality of several convents. Yet certain nuns moved beyond these activities which, as many of the other essays in this collection have shown, were typically within the locus of elite women's political action, to participate directly in England's political affairs. The 1687 New Year's greetings and gift bestowed upon Mary of Modena by Mary Knatchbull and her nuns were imbued with considerable political significance. The cloister's 'affection prayers and zeale' for the royal family had contributed to the restoration of Charles II, and were at that point focused upon an event that the nuns fervently believed would secure their long held goal. If James II and his queen produced an heir, the nuns were certain that Catholicism would be secure in their homeland. Thus, through their alliances with the Stuarts, they tried hard to influence affairs of state which might assist their own political and religious aims – Catholic toleration and the convents return to England.

Royal Patronage of the English Cloisters

From the outset of the post-Reformation monastic revival, the English nuns were no strangers to royal patronage. As religious exiles, they depended upon the assistance of well-connected friends, and therefore lobbied the Spanish and French courts in their quest to set up and maintain convents. The first English cloister, established at Brussels in 1598, secured an annual pension from King Philip III of Spain, and enjoyed the strong support of the Infanta Isabella and her husband, the archduke Albert, who governed the Spanish Netherlands. In addition to granting various tax exemptions and bestowing alms upon the Benedictine house, they publicly participated in the investiture and clothing ceremonies of its founders.[2] In 1634, Abbess Mary Percy fondly recalled the archduchess' subsequent visits, assistance and gifts, praising her 'singular piety, zeal and Religion' which had led to the erection of numerous male and female religious houses in her territories 'to the great consolation' and salvation of English Catholics.[3] While Isabella did not patronise other English cloisters to the same degree, she and Albert approved several foundations and aided them wherever possible. In 1608, they authorised the establishment of the Poor Clare convent at

Gravelines.[4] Isabella subsequently secured an abode in Aire for a 1629 filiation from the Gravelines mother house.[5] Twenty years earlier she had responded sympathetically to the Louvain Augustinians' distraught pleas to retain their premises which she had considered appropriating for a Flemish Carmelite foundation.[6] She also endeavoured to resolve the disputes over spiritual and temporal jurisdiction which erupted in various cloisters during the 1620s and 1630s, most notably among the Brussels Benedictines, the Antwerp and Bois-le-Duc Carmelites, and the Gravelines Poor Clares.[7] In France, King Louis XIII granted the establishment of an English Augustinian convent in Paris in letters patent of 1633. After his death, the regent, Anne of Austria, approved various houses, including the Poor Clare filiation from Gravelines to Rouen in 1644, and the Benedictine foundation at Boulogne in 1652, which she assisted after its relocation to Pontoise in 1658.[8] In Paris, the community of the Immaculate Conception, or 'Blue Nuns' as they are better known, begun in 1658, received a pension from King Louis XIV.[9] He also presented the Aire Poor Clares with annual alms of 240 florins.[10] Throughout his reign, the French monarch was the subject of numerous petitions for relief from the financial stress caused by the imposition of taxes, changes in interest rates, or new government policies.[11] The English cloisters therefore forged ties with the rulers of their adopted locales as a matter of economic and political necessity. The Spanish and French courts constituted the ultimate point of recourse for the nuns whose precarious circumstances often generated opposition from local ecclesiastical and civil bodies more concerned with limiting their own liability for the impoverished foreigners than with the wider struggle against English Protestantism which their monarchs supported.

The nuns sustained their connections with European royalty throughout the seventeenth century, but from 1625 they acquired powerful friends in their homeland. The marriage of Charles I to the French Catholic princess, Henrietta Maria, had significant repercussions for the Stuart monarchy, and it also prefaced a shift in the political aspirations and alliances of the recusant cloisters. The religious houses benefited from the fashionable court Catholicism of the 1620s and 1630s, which inspired the conversion of several prominent ladies and their families. Some courtiers, like the countess of Antrim (formerly the duchess of Buckingham), became ardent supporters of exiled monasteries. After lodging in the Ghent Benedictine cloister for fifteen months in the 1640s, she proposed funding a filiation in Ireland.[12] Others, like the daughters of Elizabeth Cary, viscountess Falkland, whose conversion estranged her husband, chose to take the veil. Lucy (Dame Magdalena), Mary (Dame Maria), Elizabeth (Dame Augustina) and Anne (Dame Clementina) Cary were professed in the Cambrai Benedictine convent in 1640.[13] Whether members or simply friends of the cloisters, these women represented a crucial link between the convents and the English royal family. Henrietta Maria became a staunch patron of several religious houses. In 1637, Abbess Mary Percy of the troubled Brussels Benedictines sought the Queen's influence in Rome to prevent the resurgence of hostilities in her community.[14] Upon Henrietta Maria's flight from England in 1644, she personally befriended the establishments on French soil, reputedly endowing the Poor Clare filiation from Gravelines to Rouen.[15] When the Cambrai Benedictines decided to send a colony to Paris in 1651, Anne Cary, who before entering the convent in 1639 had been a favourite of the Queen at Whitehall, was put in charge of the venture. Henrietta Maria did not disappoint the nuns, paying for the founders' temporary sojourn at the English Augustinian convent, and subsequently proving 'our best friend and Gratious Benefactris'.[16] The English Queen's straitened circumstances meant that she was unable to provide substantial financial aid to the cloisters which were often in dire economic need. However, her personal experience of England's religious and political upheavals made her a sympathetic intercessor on their behalf to France's ecclesiastical and ruling elites.

After 1649 the future Charles II and James II were no strangers to convent parlours. During the Interregnum they received the nuns' allegiance and hospitality, and maintained the patronage links initiated by Henrietta Maria. The Paris Augustinians entertained the Queen and her children on several occasions between 1644 and 1660.[17] In 1650 Charles visited the Ghent Benedictines and was promised their prayers. Abbess Mary Roper reputedly exhorted the prince's spiritual and moral reformation, and impressed him as so 'wise and worthy a lady' that when she was on her deathbed a month later, he sent his physician to tend her. Her successor, Mary Knatchbull, also found favour with Charles, who was a regular visitor to the cloister throughout the 1650s.[18] He likewise frequented the Bruges Augustinian establishment where the annals recorded hospitality both at the grate and inside the enclosure for Charles, the dukes of York and Gloucester, and their sister, the Princess of Orange.[19] Although the Restoration severed direct contact, the nuns nevertheless attempted to preserve their relationship with the King and the duke of York. They were more successful with the latter, whose conversion to Catholicism, and that of his duchess, Anne Hyde, strengthened the bonds of religious and patriotic friendship. Anne Hyde was acknowledged as a generous benefactor to the Ghent Benedictines, who yearly commemorated the anniversary of her 1671 death with a requiem mass.[20] James' subsequent marriage to an Italian princess, and his accession to the throne in 1685 proved another watershed in the relationship between the convents and the Stuart royal family. The nuns believed that in James and Mary Beatrice of Modena they had secured the means for Catholic toleration, and eagerly awaited their recall to English soil. The events of 1688 dashed such expectations, but the royal family's exile in France invariably strengthened their ties with the convents, particularly those in proximity to the Jacobite court at St Germain. The Paris Augustinian nuns entertained James, Mary Beatrice and their children on several occasions. In 1695, the nuns received James in their church where they performed various religious motets, before he breakfasted in the prioress's chambers. The following year, his son received similar hospitality and, in 1697, Mary Beatrice joined the convent for prayers and music after evensong, before partaking of a light supper with Prioress Eugenia Perkins.[21] Other houses, including the Benedictines of Ghent, Dunkirk, Brussels, Cambrai and Ypres, the Brussels Dominicans, and the Bruges Augustinians, maintained similar contact. All mourned James' death in 1701 and pledged their support for 'James III'.[22]

Yet despite the obvious favour shown to the nuns by James II, their closest relationship was always with his queen. Mary of Modena was extremely devout and had intended to become a nun before powerful churchmen, including the pope, insisted that her vocation lay in England.[23] In 1673, en route to her husband and new home, she gave the 'Blue Nuns' of Paris 40 pistoles 'that we might pray for her prosperity in our Nation she having some apprehentions by Reason they wer of an other Religion'.[24] As queen consort and in exile, she maintained regular correspondence not only with monastic friends in Italy, but also with religious houses in other parts of Europe. Thus, the English nuns were by no means her only religious supplicants and supporters.[25] However, like Henrietta Maria before her, the deposed Mary Beatrice had a particular concern for her religious compatriots abroad. In 1686, she had thanked the Dunkirk Benedictines for their loyalty and prayers and promised her assistance should they ever require it.[26] The following year she pledged an annual pension of 40 pounds to help the 'Blue Nuns' whose fortunes had been damaged during a decade of internal dissension. She again intervened on their behalf in 1704 when they were in danger of dissolution because their house's official documentation was not in order.[27] In 1696, the Queen approached the archbishop of Paris to resolve a problem concerning jurisdiction of the city's English Augustinian cloister.[28] She was also acutely concerned about the precarious future of the Ypres Benedictine community. James II had sponsored its relocation to Dublin in 1688 and his protégées had experienced nothing but misfortune since their forced return to the Continent in the aftermath of the Glorious Revolution. Keen to secure the house's survival, the Queen regularly lobbied the bishop of Ypres to assist the cloister. She offered financial support, and was most likely behind the generous endowments in 1699 from Pope Innocent XII and King Louis XIV which enabled the convent, numbering only two nuns, to survive into the eighteenth century.[29] Mary Beatrice's proximity to the French court, coupled with her access to high-ranking ecclesiastical officials in France and Rome, made her an obvious patron for convents like Ypres which remained on a precarious financial footing, and often required dispensations from local civil and religious obligations in order to survive. Indeed, at the height of its troubles, abbess Mary Caryll of Dunkirk suggested that without the Queen's assistance the Ypres cloister would cease to exist.[30] Given the uncertain financial footing of several other convents, and diminishing recruitment as the seventeenth century drew to a close, the same might have been said for many of the English establishments.

Yet the patronage relationship between Mary of Modena and the cloisters was by no means one-sided. As Mary Knatchbull's New Year's gift indicated, the nuns bestowed a variety of favours on their royal associates. During the Interregnum, they lobbied heaven incessantly for the Royalists' success. After Charles visited the Ghent Benedictines in 1650, the nuns instituted daily prayers for 'the good success of his bleeding affairs'.[31] Abbess Mary Knatchbull regularly reminded his ministers of her nuns' divine petitions, writing in February 1659 'all o*ur* prayers are for his Majestys prosperity and happy success to his affaires'. In January 1660, she conferred a New Year's gift of prayers for Charles' good fortune.[32] In the aftermath of the Restoration, the Brussels Benedictines continued to pray 'night and day for his Majesties felicity'.[33] James II and his queen were similarly recipients of religious devotion. Like the Ghent Benedictines, several cloisters sought divine intercession in the royal couple's quest for an heir. In May 1688, Prioress Mary Wigmore of the Antwerp Carmelites assured Mary Beatrice that 'the petitions of this Community ... are incessantly presented to the Throne of mercy beseeching the preservation of Both your Royall persons with the Benediction of the soe much wished and prayed for gift of heaven a Prince to Inherit your Crownes and vertues'.[34] After the Revolution, the cloisters resumed their pleas for a Stuart restoration in the person of James and his heirs.[35] The nuns' religious status therefore placed them in a unique position as dispensers of spiritual alms. For the Stuarts who believed in the efficacy of Catholic prayers and relics, links with the exiled cloisters were propitious as the nuns petitioned heaven for their souls, political fortunes, health and happiness. Even those who did not openly admit to Catholic leanings received similar spiritual munificence. Several convents prayed for Charles II's conversion. Others, like the Ghent and Brussels Benedictines, solicited the good fortune and religious enlightenment of his ministers.[36] In 1686, Mary Knatchbull advanced beyond 'the teares prayers and good works which Heaven hath been so oft importuned with' on the duke of Ormond's behalf to urge him to consider the veracity of Catholic salvation.[37] Whether the beneficiaries appreciated these spiritual gifts or not, the nuns persevered regardless, convinced that the prayers would eventually bear fruit.

Moreover, the Stuarts' political troubles empowered the convents to dispense favours beyond the purely spiritual. As exiles, accompanied by a retinue of loyal servants and friends, the English royal family was dependent upon the goodwill and charity of anyone who would assist them. Mary of Modena was evidently overwhelmed with pleas from Catholics whose fortunes had dissipated as a result of their Jacobite sympathies, and accordingly were unable to provide for their families. From 1688, she called upon religious houses to reciprocate her patronage by assisting her impoverished retainers. In 1689, the Queen prevailed upon prioress Barbara Boyle of the Brussels Dominican cloister to accommodate Sir Richard Bulstrode and his family for six months. Although she offered a small pension to defray the guests' expenses, the house would not earn full recompense for its compliance until James II was restored to his throne.[38] More commonly, Mary Beatrice sought places in monastic schools, guesthouses and novitiates for the daughters of destitute Jacobites. In 1691, a postulant in the Dunkirk Benedictine abbey arrived upon the Queen's recommendation. Michelle de Latte, another royal protégée, who joined the Cambrai Benedictines in 1695, was accepted with the promise of a dowry only in the event of James' restoration.[39] Without sufficient means to pay personally for accommodation or dowries, Mary Beatrice drew upon a wider circle of associates to finance her placement of impecunious gentlewomen. Given the straitened circumstances of the English cloisters in the wake of 1688, most requests were directed towards continental abbesses and prelates. In May 1697 she asked the archbishop of Vienne to find convent schools for one or two poor Irish girls. By July she was thanking him for procuring a place in the Visitation convent at Cremieux, and she rapidly despatched the daughter of a dead Jacobite colonel to the house, assuring its mother superior that the nuns would be paid once she was in a position to do so.[40] In return for the nuns' co-operation, the Queen endeavoured to further their needs by approaching ecclesiastical and civil contacts on their behalf. Thus, in 1696, she informed the Bishop of Le Mans that the Calvary nuns at Mayenne had taken two penniless Irish women into their novitiate, and thereby requested a diminution of the house's tax obligations in recognition of their charity.[41]

Although the assistance rendered by religious houses demonstrates the reciprocity of patronage, it nonetheless points to the primacy of the royal participant in the relationship. In numerous instances, convents were levered into difficult positions by their regal benefactors. An arrangement between Mary Beatrice and the Nôtre Dame sisters at Poitiers to educate Miss Wyer, a distant relation of the duke of Tyrconnel, evolved into an ongoing commitment on the convent's part. In 1697, Miss Wyer transferred (gratis) into the novitiate of the French abbey of Xaintes, and the Queen immediately sent her sister to the school at Poitiers. When this second Wyer daughter was ready to take the veil, the Nôtre Dame nuns were prevailed upon to accept charitably a third girl in her stead.[42] However, Mary Beatrice did not merely burden her monastic friends financially. She also sought favours which compromised cloisters' rules and statutes. In 1697, the highly capable and respected Dunkirk Benedictine abbess, Mary Caryll, was enlisted to supervise 'young Strickland', one of the Queen's pages. Noting that her request was highly unusual and, moreover, logistically difficult for the enclosed nun to execute, Mary Beatrice nevertheless insisted upon it, later admitting 'I presumed much upon your good inclination to serve me'.[43] For her part, Mary Caryll had no choice but to acquiesce because her cloister depended upon the Queen's ongoing advocacy. Mary Beatrice had recently engaged the bishop of Ypres to assist the Dunkirk nuns. Moreover, she was extremely influential in the protracted negotiations about the future of the Ypres Benedictine house. Abbess Caryll feared that her convent might be asked to merge with the troubled abbey, and she astutely recognised that retaining the Queen's good will was crucial if she was to avoid such an impost.[44] Other English houses were similarly compromised. In 1701, the 'Blue Nuns' reluctantly accommodated Mary Caryll, three other Dunkirk nuns and two gentlewomen, who were in Paris on business, 'by the desire of her majesty who could not well be refused'.[45] Various cloisters, particularly those near St Germain, were troubled in the 1690s by reports of lax adherence to regulations, especially with respect to strict enclosure. Mary of Modena's sway as a powerful patron was evidently partially responsible for such lapses in monastic discipline.

The relationship between Mary Beatrice and her monastic friends therefore indicated that although patronage often operated to the mutual advantage of both parties, the Queen always had the upper hand, by virtue of her social position. Yet patronage of the cloisters by members of the English royal family emanated predominantly from their joint experiences of exile. The nuns, whose expatriate existence predated that of the Stuarts, had developed considerable resources to compensate for their isolation from England. Thus, when the Royalists in the 1650s and the Jacobites in the 1690s and eighteenth century required effective channels of communication, and access to sympathetic locals who might finance and enlist indigenous support for their quest to return to England, the convents proved worthy allies. Nowhere is this more evident than in the political intrigues into which they entered on the behalf of their royal friends.

Nuns and Politics

The convents' loyalty to the Stuarts was explicit in their Royalist sympathies during the Civil War and Interregnum. At the outbreak of hostilities between Charles I and Parliament in 1642, the nuns identified closely with the King's cause. Many houses suffered financially as a consequence of the upheaval in their homeland which, in addition to the loss of annuities and potential dowries from their impoverished families, led to the failure of their English investments.[46] However, in the aftermath of the King's execution, described by Abbess Anne Neville of Pontoise as 'that horrible sacrilegious murther', the nuns were determined to do all they could to assist what they deemed to be the legitimate authority of a restored monarchy in the person of his son.[47] Those convents situated in the southern Netherlands where Charles resided during the 1650s offered the political exiles the aforementioned hospitality and spiritual support. Some, like the Bruges Augustinians and Ghent Benedictines, even provided financial help.[48]

No cloister was more staunchly Royalist during this period than that governed by the resourceful Mary Knatchbull. The Ghent Benedictines not only entertained and funded Charles and prominent Royalist leaders, including Sir Edward Hyde, the marquis of Ormond, and the earl of Bristol, but also they provided more practical assistance. Most significantly, abbess Knatchbull placed her reliable mail network at the King's service, and from late 1657 her convent was in receipt of the Royalists' correspondence to and from their allies in England. Knatchbull forwarded letters to their intended recipients, and she was fully conversant with the aliases and ciphers they used. Moreover, she channelled pamphlets, newsletters and gossip of unfolding political events to Hyde, as well as passing on information regarding the whereabouts of the King's supporters. On occasions she even ventured her interpretation of the political situation, and offered advice about the best course of action.[49] The gratitude and respect

Charles and his ministers felt towards the abbess were evident in their endeavours to reward her, both during the 1650s and after 1660. Although Knatchbull had to fight hard for the money promised by the King, which she spent founding a new cloister at Dunkirk, unlike innumerable other unsuccessful petitioners, she ultimately obtained her reward.[50] The auspicious restoration of Charles II left no doubt in the minds of the Jacobite nuns that James II would similarly regain his lost throne. Several cloisters supported the deposed monarch, and his son and grandson in turn. The Paris Augustinians, who decried William of Orange as 'perfidious' and 'detestable', instituted devotions dedicated to his overthrow, as well as providing a meeting place for Jacobite sympathisers.[51] The Pontoise Benedictine community, which included James' illegitimate daughter, Arabella (Dame Ignatia) Fitzjames, professed in 1690, was closely linked with the 1715 and 1745 Stuart uprisings.[52] In Brussels the Dominican convent was similarly dedicated to the Stuart cause. Mary Rose Howard, briefly prioress from 1721 to 1724, assumed the role for 'James III' undertaken by Mary Knatchbull in the 1650s for Charles II, acting as an intermediary between the pretender and the Jacobite party in England. Like Knatchbull she transported news and mail, and was endorsed by James as a trustworthy ally.[53] Although the efforts of these later monastic conspirators failed to evince the triumphal result enjoyed by their predecessors in 1660, the bonds between them and James II and his heirs were strengthened by the Stuarts' ongoing exile.

It is evident therefore that the recusant nuns' separation from their homeland to preserve the institution of female monasticism for future generations of English Catholics equipped them to act as political conspirators. The convents were located in France and the southern Netherlands, but they retained close ties with England from whence they drew most of their membership, revenues and sense of identity. Conversant with the difficulties of successful communication with supporters across the Channel and accordingly skilled in secretive transportation of personnel, news and funds, they proved ideal allies for the Stuarts. Their utility was strengthened by the generally dismissive attitudes of English spies and officials, who denied the religious women any capacity for political agency. The success of Mary Knatchbull's Royalist postal network testifies not only to her skill, but also to the failure of the Protectorate's intelligence services to consider a nun's mail packets politically significant. Even when the convents' discourse with government officials and military leaders was acknowledged, it was most commonly derided as 'gossip'. In 1717, a spy informed the duke of Marlborough about the Gravelines Poor Clare abbess, Catherine Dominic Bagnall's, connections with the duke of Ormonde, noting 'you can judge what secretaries nuns are, but more particularly my Lady Abbess, who can keep nothing longer than she can find an occasion to tell it'.[54] Attitudes such as this ensured that nuns were never considered to pose a serious threat to the state.

However, as this essay has demonstrated, women could participate in the ostensibly masculine domain of high politics. Indeed it might be argued that by virtue of their confessional separatism and monastic profession, the nuns were dissidents worthy of consideration. Even without their patronage of the Stuart cause, their Catholicism rendered them enemies of the Protestant establishment in a state which tied political loyalty so closely with religious conformity. Yet for most of the seventeenth century, the nuns deemed themselves loyal English subjects (even during the 1650s). Staunch supporters of the Stuarts, it was only after 1688 that their religious nonconformity was matched by a withdrawal of allegiance to the crown. The cloisters' fidelity to the royal family was nonetheless grounded in their religious ambitions. In 1637, Abbess Mary Percy of Brussels observed of Charles I, 'the king (that mirrour of goodnesse) whoe thoughe of a different religion to ours [is] inclined to wish well to all honest and well meaning people'.[55] Charles's sons were considered even more sympathetic. Indeed, the nuns' motives for befriending the royal family were most clearly articulated in Mary Knatchbull's congratulatory letter to Mary Beatrice upon the birth of her son. In June 1688 the abbess wrote

> ...the share wee have in all blessings conferd on yor Sacred Majesty makes us now completely blest and happy in yor Majestys safe delivery of so brave a prince of wales for which with hart and voice having sung our Te deum and with the whole quire of Heaven presented our greatfull thankes to the Blessed Trinity for this saving Guift to the 3 Nations imparted by yor Majesty ... I ... assure you of the longest share in all our prayers and best actions that God may continu his blessings to you in the preservation of o[u]r sacred prince with speedy addition of a Duke of York.[56]

A Catholic monarch was deemed the best bet for a return of a Catholic England, and the nuns' prayers, patronage and conspiratorial efforts on the Stuarts' behalf were all directed towards this goal. Hence, in spite of their exile and strict monastic enclosure, the nuns were arguably as subversive as their clerical missionary counterparts who operated on English soil. Employing a range of tactics commensurate with their gender and their monastic profession, they aimed to reverse or, in the very least, mitigate the negative consequences of England's Protestant Reformation for those who remained faithful to the Roman Church. Ultimately, as the events of 1688 made obvious, although the nuns correctly identified the Stuarts as sympathetic to their goals, they failed to grasp the centrality of Protestantism in English religious, political and national identity, which rendered their hopes untenable. Yet they were by no means alone in misreading the realities of the Jacobite cause. Thus, despite the derogatory observations of their contemporaries, and their virtual anonymity in the scholarship on Stuart politics, the English nuns' actions testify to the fact that not only were early modern women politically conscious, but also they often possessed the requisite contacts and skills to influence affairs of state.

Notes

1 BL, Add. MS 28225, fol. 126.

2 'Abbess Neville's Annals of Five Communities of English Benedictine Nuns in Flanders, 1598-1687', in *Miscellanea V*, Catholic Record Society, vol. 6, 1909, pp. 2-3, 5; Paul Arblaster, 'The Infanta and the English Benedictine Nuns: Mary Percy's Memories in 1634', *RH*, 23, 4 (Oct. 1997), 522-23; Downside Abbey, Hazlemere MS 1888, Letter from the Abbess and Nuns to the Deputies of the Estates of Brabant, c. 1705; *Chronicle of the First Monastery Founded at Brussels for English Benedictine Nuns*, Bergholt: St Mary's Abbey, 1898, p. 46; PRO, SP Flanders 77/6, fol. 73; SP Flanders 77/8, fol. 275.

3 Arblaster, 'Infanta and English Nuns', p. 517.

4 A. Pasture, 'Documents Concernant quelques Monastères Anglais aux Pays-Bas au XVIIe Siècle', *Bulletin de l'Institut Historique Belge de Rome*, 10 (1930), 213-14.

5 St Clare's Abbey, Darlington, MS Aire Register, [fol. 3].

6 Adam Hamilton (ed.), *The Chronicle of the English Augustinian Canonesses Regular of the Lateran, at St Monica's in Louvain (now at St Augustine's Priory, Newton Abbot, Devon) 1548-1644*, Edinburgh and London: Sands and Co., 1904, vol. 1, p. 75.

7 Arblaster, 'Infanta and English Nuns', pp. 523-24; St Clare's Abbey, MS Aire Register, [fol. 3]; Pasture, 'Documents', pp. 221-22; Peter Guilday, *The English Catholic Refugees on the Continent 1558-1795*, London: Longmans, Green and Co., 1914, pp. 257-64, 298-99, 362-68; C. Walker, *Gender and Politics in Early Modern Europe: English Nuns in France and the Low Countries*, Basingstoke and New York: Palgrave, 2003, chs 2, 5.

8 François Cédoz, *Un Couvent de Religieuses Anglaises à Paris de 1634 à 1884*, Paris: Victor Lecoffre, 1891, p. 16; Ann M. C. Forster, 'The Chronicles of the English Poor Clares of Rouen – I', *RH*, 18 (May 1986), 59-102 (pp. 59, 64); 'Abbess Neville's Annals', pp. 37, 47-50.

9 Joseph Gillow and Richard Trappes-Lomax (eds), *The Diary of the 'Blue Nuns' or Order of the Immaculate Conception of Our Lady, at Paris, 1658-1810*, Catholic Record Society, vol. 8, 1910, p. 23.

10 St Clare's Abbey, MS Aire Register, Benefactors.

11 Archives Départementales du Nord, Lille, 20 H 57, Petition, 13 Aug. 1664; Antony F. Allison, 'The English Augustinian Convent of Our Lady of Syon at Paris: its Foundation and Struggle for Survival during the First Eighty Years, 1634-1713', *RH*, 21 (Oct. 1993), 451-96 (pp. 475-76).

12 'Abbess Neville's Annals', p. 31.

[13] Joseph Gillow (ed.), 'Records of the English Benedictine Nuns at Cambrai (now Stanbrook), 1620-1793', in *Miscellanea VIII*, Catholic Record Society, vol. 13, 1913, pp. 44-45.
[14] PRO, SP Flanders 77/27, fol. 195: Mary Percy to Gerbier, 29 May 1637.
[15] Guilday, *Catholic Refugees*, p. 299; Basil Whelan, *Historic English Convents of Today: the Story of the English Cloisters in France and Flanders in Penal Times*, Burns, London: Oates and Washbourne, 1936, pp. 67-68.
[16] Joseph S. Hansom, 'The English Benedictine Nuns of the Convent of Our Blessed Lady of Good Hope in Paris, now St Benedict's Priory, Colwich, Staffordshire: Notes and Obituaries', in *Miscellanea VII*, Catholic Record Society, vol. 9, 1911, pp. 340-41.
[17] Allison, 'English Augustinian Convent', p. 466.
[18] 'Abbess Neville's Annals', pp. 31-32, 34; *Annals of the English Benedictines at Ghent, Now at St Mary's Abbey, Oulton in Staffordshire*, Oulton: St Mary's Abbey, 1894, pp. 24-25.
[19] C. S. Durrant, *A Link Between Flemish Mystics and English Martyrs*, London: Burns, Oates and Washbourne, 1925, pp. 262-63; Whelan, *Historic English Convents*, pp. 87-88.
[20] *Annals of the English Benedictines at Ghent*, pp. 43-44, 179-80.
[21] Downside Abbey, Ealing MS Journal 1695-1738, fols 8-9, 12-13, 16-17, 28, 40.
[22] *HMC, 15th Report (Stuart MSS)*, vol. 1, pp. 46, 89, 90, 107, 125, 126, 149, 155; 'Abbess, Neville's Annals', pp. 17-18; Durrant, *Flemish Mystics*, pp. 316-24; BL, Add. MS 28226, fols 127, 132; Cédoz, *Religieuses Anglaises*, pp. 187-95. The convents also remained in contact with Charles II's widow. En route to Portugal in 1692, Catherine of Braganza attended mass in the Rouen Poor Clares' church, and she subsequently spent a day with them, during which she reassured them that Charles had converted on his deathbed. Forster, 'Poor Clares of Rouen – I', p. 97.
[23] Martin Haile, *Queen Mary of Modena: her Life and Letters*, London: J.M. Dent, 1905, pp. 16-22.
[24] *Diary of the 'Blue Nuns'*, p. 23.
[25] BL, Add. MS 28225, fols 270-75, 285-86, 301-2, 306-7, 315-16; *Stuart MSS*, 1, pp. 15, 18, 21-22, 80, 113, 119-20, 127.
[26] *Stuart MSS*, 1, p. 22.
[27] *Diary of the 'Blue Nuns'*, pp. 34, 55.
[28] Allison, 'English Augustinian Convent', pp. 479-80.
[29] BL, Add. MS 28226, fols 113, 116, 119, 120; *Stuart MSS*, 1, pp. 125, 149, 155; Whelan, *Historic English Convents*, pp. 54-60.
[30] BL, Add. MS 28226, fol. 113.
[31] *Annals of the English Benedictines at Ghent*, p. 25; 'Abbess Neville's Annals', p. 39.
[32] Bodl., Clarendon MS 60, fol. 65; Carte MS 30, fol. 450. See also Clarendon MS 59, fol. 29; Clarendon MS 64, fol. 258; Clarendon MS 65, fol. 69; Carte MS 30, fol. 663.
[33] Bodl., Carte MS 214, fol. 253: Mary Vavasour to Ormond, 2 Nov. 1660.
[34] BL, Add. MS 28225, fol. 276.
[35] *Stuart MSS*, 1, p. 90; Allison, 'English Augustinian Convent', p. 484.
[36] Bodl., Carte MS 30, fols 450, 543, 663; Carte MS 31, fols 28, 157; Carte MS 214, fols 171, 253; Clarendon MS 64, fol. 258; Clarendon MS 65, fol. 147; Clarendon MS 72, fols 15, 394; CKS, U269 C324, Mary Knatchbull to Lord Fitzharding, 29 Nov. 1664.
[37] St Mary's Abbey, Oulton, Ghent MS G.16.
[38] *Stuart MSS*, 1, p. 46.
[39] Ibid., pp. 89, 107.
[40] Ibid., pp. 124-25.
[41] Ibid., p. 117.

[42] Ibid., pp. 126-27, 136.
[43] Ibid., p. 126.
[44] Ibid., p. 125; BL, Add. MS 28226, fols 113, 116, 119.
[45] *Diary of the 'Blue Nuns'*, p. 50.
[46] The financial impact is discussed in Walker, *Gender and Politics*, ch. 3.
[47] 'Abbess Neville's Annals', p. 31.
[48] Whelan, *Historic English Convents*, pp. 87-88; 'Abbess Neville's Annals', pp. 36-37.
[49] For a full discussion of Knatchbull's activities, see C. Walker, 'Prayer, Patronage, and Political Conspiracy: English Nuns and the Restoration', *HJ*, 43 (2000), 1-23, (pp. 6-11).
[50] Walker, 'English Nuns and the Restoration', pp. 14-18.
[51] Allison, 'English Augustinian Convent', pp. 479, 484.
[52] 'Registers of the English Benedictine Nuns of Pontoise, now at Teignmouth, Devonshire, 1680-1713', in *Miscellanea X*, Catholic Record Society, vol. 17, 1915, p. 311; Guilday, *Catholic Refugees*, p. 271.
[53] *Dominicana*, Catholic Record Society, vol. 25, 1925, pp. 208-9; Guilday, *Catholic Refugees*, pp. 417-18.
[54] Cited in 'Registers of the English Poor Clare Nuns at Gravelines, with Notes of Foundations at Aire, Dunkirk and Rouen, 1608-1837', in *Miscellanea IX*, Catholic Record Society, vol. 14, 1914, p. 115.
[55] PRO, SP Flanders 77/27, fol. 195.
[56] BL, Add. MS 28225, fol. 293.

Chapter 15

Assuming Gentility: Thomas Middleton, Mary Carleton and Aphra Behn

Valerie Wayne

'Let her nat be clothed with velvet, but with wollen: nor with sylke, but lynnen, and that course. ... As for the wearyng of golde, or sylver, or perle, or precious stones, I se nat what hit is good for'.[1] These words by Juan Luis Vives admonish young women to assume an identity of plainness that exhibits the 'shamefastness' he wanted them to embody. But for the early audience of the English translation of his text, they would also be inflected by social class, because it was gentlewomen and their superiors who wore velvet, silk and jewels rather than the unadorned, domestically-produced materials of wool and coarse linen. Vives's book counsels that even royal women should present themselves in a manner less opulent than their station would require,[2] and one could infer that commoners were all the more obligated to dress with simplicity. The first important Tudor sumptuary law was issued in 1533, four years after the English publication of Vives's book,[3] and it limited certain materials, decorations, or constructions in clothing to persons of higher degrees. Elizabeth later reaffirmed the sumptuary laws in many proclamations that extended through 1597.[4] Those from 1577 and 1580 specified that women below the following degrees – countesses; baronesses; wives of knights of the order and members of the Privy Council, Ladies and Gentlewomen of the Privy Chamber, Bed Chamber and Maids-of-Honour; wives of barons' sons, daughters of barons, and wives of knights or those who could dispense and be assessed £200 in land in the subsidy book – were forbidden to wear gowns or cloaks of velvet, satin or tufted taffeta, silk embroidery, silk hose and furs of leopard. The entitlements of women within these and lower degrees were specified by colour as well as fabric and type of fur. Cloth of gold or silver tissue and sable were limited to countesses or above, and purple silk was reserved for their superiors.[5]

How might these restrictions have contributed to a desire on the part of early modern women to array themselves in sumptuous materials?

The laws arose in part from recognition of that desire and the state's wish to preserve 'an organic hierarchical order in society'.[6] Although they were not always enforced, especially beyond church and the workplace,[7] the laws surely created a desire for those goods as well, precisely because they served to mark and reinscribe degree over the period when sumptuary legislation was in place. During that time the goals of social mobility for some became interlaced with the desire to wear the materials and decorations of the elite. The young woman who dreamed of becoming a princess wanted, like Amy Denver in Toni Morrison's *Beloved*, to touch and possess velvet. But unlike Amy Denver, the early modern woman also wanted to put it on in order to become a different kind of person, because the legal and social system used the language of clothing to tell her precisely what kind she was and was not. By far the most important distinction was between those who were 'gentle' and those who were 'common' or 'base'.

Frank Whigham concludes that by the time the sumptuary laws were withdrawn in 1604,

> ...the individual self-determination that such laws sought to restrict had become normative, and what many had wished to retain as differences in kind had finally become differences in degree only. At least in the realm of symbolic clothing, the chasm between ruling elite and subject classes had become permanently bridgeable.[8]

Clothing and jewellery then became a means by which commoners might imitate their social superiors through what Ann Rosalind Jones and Peter Stallybrass have characterised as the '"transnaturing" power of clothes': 'that the materials we wear work as inscriptions upon us is an insight more familiar to pre- or proto-capitalist societies than to fully capitalist ones'.[9] After 1604, it was legally permissible to imitate one's betters and in that sense to reconstitute oneself as gentle, especially in the context of the increased social mobility that developed under James I. The 'transnaturing' power of clothing and personal effects opens up the possibility that what we might read as a simple imitation or performance on the part of early modern women and men also enacts a desire to 'become' a different degree of person through altered self-presentation, and that such enactments might have been very convincing if the cultural codes were carefully followed.

In this essay I will consider three texts that focus on a woman's imitation of a gentle status that she was not born to but does have the ability to perform in such a way that others believe her and are duped into marrying her. These texts include two plays, Thomas Middleton's *A Trick to Catch the Old One* and Aphra Behn's *The City-Heiress*, as well as *The*

Case of Mary Carleton, a narrative that presents itself as the autobiography of a woman who was tried for bigamy for disguising herself as a German princess in order to entrap in marriage a man named John Carleton, who disguised himself as a lord in order to entrap her. In all of these texts, the economic and class imperatives of early modern marriage are appropriated by commoners in their own interests when they reconstitute themselves as gentle, and the codes in the sumptuary laws provide the terms by which those performances would have been read. Margreta de Grazia describes sumptuary laws as 'a system for fastening identity into materiality, persons into cloth, in stratifications ranging from "[loop'd] and window'd raggedness" (III.iv.31) to gorgeous "Robes and furr'd gowns" (IV.vi.164)'.[10] Once the restrictions were lifted, then, the opportunity for those who had the resources to 'become' socially superior opened up in new ways.

Thomas Middleton's *A Trick to Catch the Old One* was first produced in 1605, only one year after the sumptuary laws were withdrawn, and its plot might be seen as arising from, even revelling in, the disruptions to the social hierarchy made available through that statutory change. Theodorus Witgood is a young gentleman who has squandered his inheritance from his rich uncle but hopes to marry a virgin with a large dowry. To make this marriage he must regain some of his capital, get out of debt, and cast off his mistress. The 'trick' of Middleton's title is a plan to pass Witgood's former mistress off as a rich country widow with a large estate and £400 a year who is interested in marrying him. Its purpose is to entrap Witgood's uncle, Pecunius Lucre, into returning Witgood's mortgage to his property, which Lucre has assumed after paying innumerable debts for his nephew's profligate life. The ruse ends up entrapping not only Lucre, who returns the mortgage in the hope that the widow will marry his nephew, but also Lucre's archrival, Walkadine Hoard, who discovers at the end of the play that the woman whom he has pursued and won in marriage in an attempt to outdo Witgood and Lucre is not a rich widow but Witgood's 'whore'. When Hoard marries a 'whore' and promotes her to the status of a respectable wife, the thieving usurer is then caught in his own trap.

Critical tradition has given Witgood primary credit for the trick of the title, but his mistress offers him 'what lies within the power of my performance' and adds, 'though you beget, 'tis I must help to breed'.[11] The unborn child of Witgood's parthenogenic brain is bred, within and beyond that mental space, by Jane's performance as rich widow as she develops the trick by assuming a degree of breeding and wealth that she does not possess. This performance is so persuasive that Hoard thinks he entraps her into a spousal and then carries her off to Cole Harbour for a ceremony with a priest in what is made to look like an abduction. She pretends a reluctant concession to his coercions because she sees marriage to him as her best alternative since Witgood plans to marry a wealthy gentlewoman. Although the play is not specific about her social class and she is presumably a commoner, it is preoccupied with Jane's sexual status. The references to her as a 'Courtesan' in the seventeenth-century texts identify her as an unmarried, sexually experienced woman, and even Witgood refers to her as a 'whore'.[12] Yet she is not a professional prostitute, for Middleton's use of 'courtesan' here denotes a mistress or a kept woman, as it does in *A Mad World, My Masters*, and 'whore' in this context means she has had sexual relations outside of marriage.

In the play's first scene, Jane reminds Witgood of 'the jewel which I prodigally gave you: my virginity',[13] and the jewels associated with women's virginity or chastity in early modern texts signified their sexual containment as a kind of property.[14] In the last scene Witgood says she has slept only with him and objects that she is not a 'common strumpet' when Hoard assumes she is.[15] Hoard has married a 'whore', but he has not married a woman whose sexuality was commonly available. The play insists on these distinctions in part because the circulation of Jane's sexuality is important for determining her social status. In *The Creation of Patriarchy*, Gerda Lerner discusses the larger development of this principle: 'As men's class positions became consolidated and defined by the relationship to property and the means of production, the class position of women became defined by their sexual relationships'. The emphasis on chastity in conduct books from Vives through Tilney, Gouge and beyond reasserts this principle that women's social status required a consideration of gender difference and that their sexual virtue was weighed as highly as their wealth or lineage in determining their class.[16] Once her marriage to Hoard is consummated and 'sure',[17] Jane can become a respectable gentlewoman for all but a small group of people who know of her prior relation with Witgood.

All of those people are on stage in the last scene, however, and it is precisely that group that Hoard wants most to impress by marrying her: 'In this one chance shines a twice happy fate: / I both deject my foe, and raise my state'. His foe is Lucre, whom he envisions becoming so vexed at the sight of Hoard's 'ten men' riding after him 'in watchet [pale blue] liveries with orange-tawny caps'[18] that he hopes Lucre will hang himself. Since 'livery was a form of incorporation, a material mnemonic that inscribed obligations and indebtedness upon the body',[19] those ten men become extensions of Hoard's newly-elevated self. He takes twenty-three lines to describe the lifestyle he hopes to acquire with this 'wife large in possessions' and 'spacious in content', and imagines journeying to her country lands 'following my brother and other worshipful gentlemen' dressed in 'broad velvet cassocks and chains of gold twice or thrice double'.[20] When Hoard is reassured at the end that Jane 'ne'er had common use, nor common thought',[21] the repetition reinforces the intersection between a woman's sexual experience and her social status: 'common' denotes sexual availability in the first half of the phrase, and by the second its reference to reputation evokes social degree. This particularisation of Jane's sexual relations in a play replete with social distinctions is in some respects analogous to the specificity of the prohibited materials for different social levels in the sumptuary laws: both sets of signifiers denote degree with some precision.

Middleton's play exposes the motivations of self-interest, social mobility and greed that lay behind early modern marriage. Gary Taylor remarks that Jane's ability 'to outmaneuvre a greedy suitor ... surely owe[s] something to Middleton's mother', who for fifteen years was engaged in law suits to prevent her second husband from gaining control over the trust she had created to protect her children's inheritance. Like Witgood, Middleton himself was a gentleman who had lost his father and was frequently in need of money. His wife even had a rich uncle who left her very little when he died in the same year the play was probably written, so its connections to Middleton's own story are close.[22] For Jane marriage is an act less of convenience than of survival, one she engages in as a socio-economic solution within a rigidly class-conscious culture that allowed sexually experienced women very few options. It is also a promotion because 'marriage elevated women to a loftier rank in village as well as élite society'.[23] But it is an act that the audience cannot unequivocally endorse, for it presents a fairly brutal compromise between a woman's desires and a culture's requirements; Aphra Behn explored that compromise further when she adapted Middleton's play. Yet Hoard's desire to 'raise my state' is surely Jane's as well, and if she wins the promotion to a wife, Hoard earns a woman who has in a sense already become the gentlewoman required by her new position.

Fifty-eight years after Middleton's play, a woman named Mary Moders, alias Mary Steadman, perhaps alias Mary Day, and for this exploit Maria de Wolway, decked herself out with jewels and fine clothing and arrived in London claiming to be a noble German lady fleeing an unwanted marriage. Her innkeeper tipped off his father-in-law, who alerted his younger son John, who presented himself as a lord with an urgent desire to marry her.

After keeping her 'close in the nature of a Prisoner'[24] so that he alone could woo her, John and Mary were joined in a bliss that lasted only a few days before the Carletons were informed by letter of Mary's humble origins and her two previous marriages. She was charged with bigamy and became the talk of the town. Since Restoration London was busy re-establishing the primacy of birth and class after the levelling effects of the Civil War, it was fascinated by her impersonation of rank.[25] Francis Kirkman explains the city's response to her:

> She was so famous and so generally beloved and visited by all [in prison], that she fared the better, and so did those who had her in Custody. so great Novelty had not been known or seen in our age, nor in any other age as I can read of, I never heard of her Parallel in every thing, and I believe had she been exposed to publique shew, for profit, she might have raised 500 *l.* of those that would have given 6 *d.* and 12 *d.* a peece to see her; It was the only talk for all the Coffee-houses in and near *London*.[26]

Samuel Pepys went to see Mary on 29 May 1663 and later defended 'her wit and spirit' to Lady Batten, a *real* lady who 'enveighd mightily against the German princesse' after she was released.[27] These events occasioned fourteen pamphlets and a play in 1663 and another nine publications in the early 1670s, when Mary was caught stealing a silver tankard and condemned to be hanged, was instead transported to Jamaica, then returned to London and stole a piece of plate. After she answered her judges too smartly, she was hanged at Tyburn on 22 January 1673.[28]

A Trick to Catch the Old One with its female impersonation of rank and wealth was performed again between 1662 and 1665 on the London stage,[29] and its parallels with these events may have prompted its revival. If we credit the account presented in *The Case of Mary Carleton*, which purports to come from 'Mary' herself, she managed to convince people of her degree while making few direct claims about herself. They were persuaded by her dress, her comportment, her jewels, and the letters that she wrote to and appeared to receive from the continent about the money from her estate. After seeing the letters, 'Mary' says that the innkeeper 'conceived such imaginations in his Head thereupon' that he exaggerated her worth, with the estimate rising to £8000 a year.[30] These conjectures allow her to claim concerning the Carleton family that 'it is sure a greater imputation and shame to them to be found such Cheats and Lyars, than it can be the least blur to me, who never avowed any such thing, nor boasted of my Quality and Fortune'.[31] Her defence is much like Jane's reminder to Hoard at the end of *Trick*: 'Alas, you know at first, sir, / I told you I had nothing'.[32] The accomplished performance is so convincing that its disavowal is read as false modesty. Mary also says she has done nothing wrong. 'What harme have I done in pretending to great Titles? ... I think I do rather deserve commendation than reproach; if the best *things are to be imitated*; I had a good precept and warrant for my assumption of such a personage as they were willing to beleive [sic] me to be'. She objects to social distinctions and sees the imitation of one's 'betters' as a means of personal improvement, voicing a perspective that had particular appeal to some after the privileges of the elite were challenged during the Interregnum. She even admits that 'it was very difficult to personate greatness for so long a time without slips or mistakes', justifying her actions on the principle that '*to deceive the deceiver, is no deceit*'.[33]

That axiom disrupts 'Mary's' claims to gentility elsewhere in the narrative, and Hero Chalmers also reads it as an intervention in the construction of women's subject positions in patriarchal cultures:

> ...this statement draws attention to the fact that feminine duplicity is not, as patriarchal culture suggests, innate, but rather, that it is the inevitable result of the imposition on women of androcentric versions of truth. Since men set the terms of feminine identity, women may be seen to be in a perennial state of enforced disguise inside the costumes with which patriarchy has fitted them out.[34]

Characterising disguise as a performative necessity for women in patriarchy, Chalmers proposes that 'women may actively select and swap those disguises' of feminine identity as a way of negotiating their subject construction.[35] Both *Trick* and *The Case* show women acting out the cultural script of mercenary marriage by playing dumb: they know they are the prey and pretend not to know in order to entrap the men. Their convincing performance depends on men's assumptions that women are ignorant about how marriage operates within the culture. Mary knows better: she describes marriage as '*an affayr, to which there are more intrigues and perplexities of kin and alliance, and necessary dependance, than to any other thing in the world*'.[36] Early modern marriage gave husbands immediate control over their wives' property and offered little recourse through divorce, so wealthy women were at particular risk of being tricked into it by potential partners and their families.[37] When Mary pretends ignorance, she is negotiating her subject construction within the positions available to her in early modern culture, and she is contributing to a culture of deceit in which responsibility is so diffused that it becomes difficult to apply.

The means by which Mary and John entrap each other reflect the gendered determinants of class. John's deception occurs in stages: he presents himself first as a 'Noble person' and only later as a Lord with a coach attended by two footmen. He also tells Mary he has ordered 'a great Glass Coach of the new fashion ... where eleven or twelve might conveniently sit, and that he would sute it with a set of Lacquies and Pages, the neatest and handsomest of the Town for their Liveries and persons'.[38] Hoard and John both fantasise about displaying their wealth by way of their liveries as they travel through town, and Mary's finest moment occurs after her marriage when she rides through Hyde Park in Lady Bludworth's coach 'in open view of that celebrious Cavalcade and Assembly, much gazed upon by them all, the eximiousness of my fortune drawing their eyes upon me'. Since the achievement of social status depends for its confirmation on the judgement of others, these social climbers want to be the object of the gaze in a public show of wealth. John also intends to get a Knighthood by which he might 'oppose the envy of men' for having so great an estate as Mary would bring him.[39]

For her part, Mary's gentility first becomes apparent when she acquaints the innkeeper 'with charge of my Jewels, and that I was as I do justifie my self to be a person of Quality'. This conjunction of jewels and gentility is maintained throughout *The Case*: her jewels are mentioned a dozen times and valued by a goldsmith at £1500.[40] The Carletons claim that the jewels, like Mary herself, are counterfeit, and throughout this text they function as a synechdoche for her person, so the confiscation of her jewels becomes analogous to her imprisonment. After she has lost possession of her finery, she protests that she is 'not such a loose irregular leud woman as I am slandered to be'.[41] She needs her clothing to maintain her gentility, and the variations in her representations parallel the shifting constructions of her sexuality in *The Case*, which range from virginity to promiscuity. The legal case brought against her for bigamy charged that she had violated the sexual norms of her society by refusing, in Chalmers's words, 'the fixed or monogamous feminine identity which sustains the system of patriarchal ownership and control',[42] so it is the circulation of her sexuality that constitutes a possible crime. Although she cannot be punished for her class pretensions, her 'most sordid and base extraction in this Kingdom, no better than the Daughter of a Fidler at *Canterbury*'[43] is alleged at her trial, and the accusation that she is a loose woman connects her sexuality to her 'base' origins.

When Mary was released from prison and in need of money, she turned to the stage and performed her own character in a play called *The German Princess*. Kirkman reports that 'a great Confluence of People [went] to behold her, yet she did not perform so well as was expected'.[44] Pepys was one of the disappointed: he complained that 'never was anything, so well done in earnest, worse performed in Jest upon the stage', and he found the whole play 'very simple'.[45] But if clothing and jewels can have the 'transnaturing' effect that Jones and Stallybrass propose, then Mary's performance for the Carletons was a different kind of imitation from her theatrical disguise: the former was an attempt to 'become' a different kind of person, while the latter assumes that the imitation is false and temporary and may even have required her wearing a costume rather than her own garments. Unlike Moll Cutpurse in *The Roaring Girl*, Mary's performance in a play about her own life staged the disguise of her class rather than her gender. She was finally hung for committing a crime against property, and such a harsh sentence affirms how closely that culture connected property to persons and locked 'subjectivity effects into personal effects'.[46] Her life shows how attempting to 'transnature' oneself could fail dismally after its temporary success.

Aphra Behn had much in common with Mary Carleton. Janet Todd says that Mary 'was born about the same time in roughly the same place into roughly the same rank' as Behn: both were 'upwardly mobile Canterbury girls' who were 'quick, pretty and ambitious ... [and] might be taken into grand homes for long periods where ... they could acquire a patina – or more than that – of education'.[47] Behn's play *The City-Heiress, or Sir Timothy Treat-all* was performed by the Duke's company in 1682, well received by the town, published in the same year, and probably revived in 1698. It made extensive use of *A Trick to Catch the Old One*.[48] The play opens with the same conflict between an uncle and his profligate nephew, here named Tom Wilding, whose mistress, Diana, disguises herself as a rich city heiress and ends by marrying Wilding's uncle, Sir Timothy. The title character is Charlot, whom Diana pretends to be, but Charlot also appears as a character, is greatly expanded from Middleton's Joyce, and is joined by a rich city widow named Lady Galliard. All three women – a mistress, a virginal heiress, and a rich widow – desire the promiscuous Wilding, who has evolved into a Restoration rake. In the end Diana entraps Sir Timothy, the 'real' Charlot gets Wilding, and Lady Galliard marries Sir Charles Merriwell the morning after having slept with Wilding.

Diana is the only commoner among these characters. Having been Wilding's mistress for several years, she has grown accustomed to an upscale life, but Wilding has not yet made good on his promise to marry a wealthy woman, so she complains that 'things go backward with me, my Coach is vanisht, my Servants dwindled into one necessary Woman and a Boy ... my twenty Guinnies a week, into forty Shillings', and although it is summer she is forced to wear her 'embroider'd Manto, when I'm drest, lin'd with Velvet; 'twou'd give one a Feavor but to look at me'. Behn takes a long, amused look at Diana's predicament in a way that Middleton did not do with Jane's. Wilding placates Diana with gold and tells her to 'lay it on, till you shame Quality, into plain Silk and Fringe': even the elite could be humbled by displays of wealth from their social inferiors. And he coaches her on how to pass for an Alderman's heiress: 'trick and betawder your self up like a right City-Lady, rich, but ill-fashion'd; on with all your Jewels, but not a Patch, ye Gipsie, nor no Spanish Paint'. Acting the part of this gentlewoman includes looking *out* of fashion and behaving herself 'very soberly, simple, and demure': 'take heed you drink not off your Glass at Table, nor rant, nor swear; one Oath confounds our Plot, and betrays thee to be an errant Drab'. [49] The difference between an heiress and a common prostitute is as slight as one swear word. Once she has been transformed, Wilding introduces Diana to Sir Timothy as 'the richest Jewel all *London* can afford'.[50]

Sir Timothy is tricked into marriage by her performance and Diana receives her reward: 'How, Mrs. Dy Ladyfi'd! This is an excellent way of disposing an old cast-off Mistriss'. In this play she is the one who corrects Sir Timothy's charge that she is a strumpet by explaining that she has loved Wilding, 'onely him, and was true to him'.[51] Sir Timothy threatens to disinherit his nephew or hang him, but Wilding, who is now in possession of his inheritance through stealing some documents, offers his uncle the use of his own estate during his life on condition that he not undermine the King and government, for Sir Timothy is a Whig in a play that Behn proclaims is 'in every part true Tory Loyal all-over!'.[52] Yet it does sanction the rise of a commoner to the degree of a lady. Behn's allegiance to royalty and her affiliation with Tory politics were other ways of performing a social status she was not born to. As she manipulated the conjunction between playwright and 'whore' that aligns her with Diana in this play, Behn's practice affirmed that 'the proof of self ownership is self sale'.[53] Both Diana and Behn maintain their upwardly-mobile self-representations by means of their sexual exchange.

The play's 'real' Lady has the problem of preserving her reputation while she desires a man who wants to undo her, and her predicament becomes most compelling in this play. Lady Galliard has 'Fortune ... Youth ... Quality ... Fame' and is 'much govern'd by Honour'.[54] She is courted by Sir Timothy and Sir Charles as well as by Wilding, who admits that her resistance is what appeals most to him, so that every blessing from her 'seems a kind of Rape'.[55] Behn's celebration of Wilding's rampant virility rewrites Middleton's social critique of early modern lust and greed and appropriates it for Royalist politics. Lady Galliard is also threatened with rape by Sir Charles, who has been coached by his uncle to be 'impudent and sawcy, Sir; / Lewd, ruffling, mad',[56] although he has to work at it, and she concedes to marry him when she is under that threat. This marriage will preserve her reputation since she has given in to Wilding's seduction. Catherine Gallagher points out that 'to lose honor is to give away control over one's public representations':[57] Lady Galliard regains that control when she marries a man of appropriate degree, one who tries hard to be a libertine in a play where 'wenching, drinking, and spending money are "natural" manifestations of ... inherent virtue',[58] but the audience knows she has lost the man who suits her best. Angeline Goreau claims that 'everyone knew that the "lewd widow" was also Aphra, Mrs. Behn',[59] and their making the association between her and Lady Galliard suggests that Behn had managed to assume a level of gentility that she was not born to, even as she revelled in the author-whore metaphor and had much in common with Diana.[60] As Behn shifts Middleton's politics and values to write this play, she also broadens and deepens the connections in *Trick* between rape, theft, and marriage. Her text stages female desire while it directs that desire to Royalist libertines for whom marriage is a way of expanding their property without abandoning their promiscuity. For Diana, Lady Galliard, and for Charlot, who has already run away with Wilding, marriage is a way of reclaiming honour when each is threatened with its loss. The price that Diana pays becomes clear when she contemplates what it will be like 'to lie with such a Beast' as Sir Timothy:

> When I shall meet, instead of Tom's warm Kisses,
> A hollow pair of thin blue wither'd Lips,
> Trembling with Palsie, stinking with Disease.[61]

Lady Galliard's marriage to Sir Charles is satisfying neither to her nor to the audience. Charlot wins the man she desires, but since he has married her to revenge himself on Lady Galliard's scorn and his uncle's cruelty,[62] Wilding may not be hers for long.

When Behn takes up the narratives about conning one's social superiors and donning the habits of higher degrees that figure in *Trick* and *The Case of Mary Carleton*, she downplays their disruption of social hierarchies and foregrounds women's erotic desire. Her play was a timely success since it endorsed Tory loyalties, libertine values, and made fun of Sir Timothy, who was a parody of Shaftesbury and other Whig politicians, but the possibilities that *The City-Heiress* offers to women are remarkably narrow: fleeting erotic pleasure followed by an 'honourable', largely loveless marriage. All three texts convey the limited opportunities available to women in early modern England, and Behn's expansion of the female characters from *Trick* also narrows their options while it deepens their passions and predicaments. If these texts nonetheless present women – and authors – who are admirable for their energy, skill and intelligence as they manoeuvre within and sometimes outsmart a highly rigid social system, Middleton's and Carleton's stories also provide the pleasure of seeing that very system undermined through the women's success. That is a textual pleasure that Behn does not engage in her play, because she endorsed the existing structures that had accommodated her social promotion instead. The blurred boundaries between these writers and their characters suggest that the 'transnaturing' power of textual identities could be every bit as appealing as the 'transnaturing' power of clothing to writers as accomplished and aspiring as Middleton, Carleton, and Behn.

Notes

My thanks to Barbara Hodgdon for introducing me to Mary Carleton and to my students at the University of Hawai'i for their lively engagement with these texts. A version of this essay was presented to the Shakespeare Association of America in 2001.

[1] Juan Luis Vives, *The Instruction of a Christen Woman*, Virginia Walcott Beauchamp, Elizabeth H. Hageman, and Margaret Mikesell (eds), Urbana and Chicago: University of Illinois Press, 2002, p. 46.

[2] Vives's book was dedicated to Catherine of Aragon and 'is regarded as a model for the education of her daughter, the Princess Mary': 'Introduction', *The Instruction of a Christen Woman,* p. xv.

[3] The date of *The Instruction* is c. 1529. See 'Introduction', pp. lxxix, cxii, n. 2.

[4] Frank Whigham, *Ambition and Privilege: the Social Tropes of Elizabethan Courtesy Theory*, Berkeley: University of California Press, 1984, pp. 155-69 (pp. 157-58).

[5] The information on permitted materials is taken from Whigham, *Ambition and Privilege*, Fig. 2: Women's Apparel, pp. 166-67, that modernises the text from Paul L. Hughes and James F. Larkin (eds), *Tudor Royal Proclamations*, 3 vols, New Haven and London: Yale UP, 1964-69, 2, pp. 458-61: Proclamation 646 (1580), which is identical to Proclamation 623 (1577).

[6] Whigham, *Ambition and Privilege*, p. 158, citing G.R. Elton, *Reform and Reformation: England, 1509-1558*, Cambridge, MA: Harvard UP, 1977, p. 227.

[7] 'Before the repeal of the sumptuary laws in 1604, it could be a risky undertaking to wear "unsuitable" clothes, particularly in church or the workplace, where one was most liable to surveillance and arrest': Ann Rosalind Jones and Peter Stallybrass, *Renaissance Clothing and the Materials of Memory*, Cambridge: CUP, 2000, pp. 187-88.

[8] Whigham, *Ambition and Privilege,* p. 169.

[9] Jones and Stallybrass, *Renaissance Clothing*, pp. 4, 3.

[10] Margreta de Grazia, 'The Ideology of Superfluous Things: *King Lear* as Period Piece', in Margreta de Grazia, Maureen Quilligan, and Peter Stallybrass (eds), *Subject and Object in Renaissance Culture*, Cambridge: CUP, 1996, pp. 17-42 (pp. 23-24).

[11] Thomas Middleton, *A Trick to Catch the Old One*, (ed.) Valerie Wayne, *The Collected Works of Thomas Middleton*, Gary Taylor *et al.* (eds), Oxford: Clarendon Press, forthcoming, I.i.54, I.i.61.
[12] I have discussed this issue in the 'Introduction' to my edition of the play and at greater length in 'The Sexual Politics of Textual Transmission', in Laurie E. Maguire and Thomas L. Berger (eds), *Textual Formations and Reformations*, Newark: University of Delaware Press, London: Associated University Presses, 1998, pp. 179-210.
[13] Middleton, *Trick*, I.i.37-38.
[14] See, for example, *The Rape of Lucrece,* ll. 34, 1191, and *All's Well That Ends Well*, IV.iv.47 in Stephen Greenblatt *et al.* (eds), *The Norton Shakespeare*, New York and London: Norton, 1997.
[15] Middleton, *Trick*, V.ii.159-60, V.ii.125-28.
[16] Valerie Wayne, 'Introduction', in Edmund Tilney. *The Flower of Friendship: a Renaissance Dialogue Contesting Marriage,* (ed.) Valerie Wayne, Ithaca and London: Cornell UP, 1992, pp. 53-54. The quotation from Lerner is from *The Creation of Patriarchy*, New York: OUP, p. 96.
[17] Middleton, *Trick*, IV.i.18.
[18] Middleton, *Trick*, II.ii.79-80, IV.iv.31-32, IV.iv.19-23.
[19] Jones and Stallybrass, *Renaissance Clothing*, p. 20.
[20] Middleton, *Trick*, IV.iv.5-6, IV.iv.13-17.
[21] Middleton, *Trick*, V.ii.128.
[22] Gary Taylor, 'Thomas Middleton (1580-1627)', entry for the *New DNB*, forthcoming.
[23] Sara Mendelson and Patricia Crawford, *Women in Early Modern England, 1550-1720,* Oxford: Clarendon Press, 1998, p. 131.
[24] Janet Todd and Elizabeth Spearing (eds), *The Case of Mary Carleton*, in *Counterfeit Ladies: 'The Life and Death of Mal Cutpurse', 'The Case of Mary Carleton'*, New York: New York UP, 1994, p. 95.
[25] Todd and Spearing, 'Introduction', *Counterfeit Ladies*, pp. xxvi-xxxi.
[26] Francis Kirkman, *The Counterfeit Lady Unveiled*, London: Peter Parker, 1673 [Wing 152.2], pp. 91-92.
[27] Robert Latham and William Matthews (eds), *The Diary of Samuel Pepys*, 11 vols, Berkeley: University of California Press, 1971, vol. 4, p. 177.
[28] Todd and Spearing, 'Introduction', *Counterfeit Ladies*, pp. xxx-li and Appendix 2.
[29] John Downes, *Roscius Anglicanus,* Judith Milhous and Robert D. Hume (eds), London: Society for Theatre Research, 1987, pp. 59, 114.
[30] *The Case*, pp. 94, 100.
[31] Ibid., p. 129.
[32] Middleton, *Trick*, V. ii. 103-4.
[33] *The Case*, pp. 92, 94.
[34] Hero Chalmers, '"The Person I Am, or What They Made Me to Be": the Construction of the Feminine Subject in the Autobiographies of Mary Carleton', in Clare Brant and Diane Purkiss (eds), *Women, Texts and Histories, 1575-1760*, London and New York: Routledge, 1992, pp. 164-94, (p. 187).
[35] Chalmers, 'The Construction of the Feminine Subject', p. 187.
[36] *The Case*, p. 79.
[37] I discuss this issue and cite statutes on abduction in 'The Sexual Politics of Textual Transmission', pp. 200-2.
[38] *The Case*, pp. 96, 98.
[39] Ibid., pp. 101, 98.
[40] Ibid., pp. 93, 124.

[41] Ibid., p. 123.
[42] Chalmers, 'The Construction of the Feminine Subject', p. 174.
[43] *The Case*, p. 90.
[44] Kirkman, *The Counterfeit Lady Unveiled*, pp. 98-99.
[45] *The Diary of Samuel Pepys*, 5, p. 124. Entry dated 15 Apr. 1664.
[46] Margreta de Grazia, 'The Ideology of Superfluous Things', p. 21.
[47] Janet Todd, *The Secret Life of Aphra Behn*, New Brunswick, New Jersey: Rutgers UP, 1996, pp. 23-24.
[48] Behn's sources are usually said to be Massinger's *The Guardian* and Middleton's *A Mad World, My Masters*, as in the headnote to Janet Todd's edition of the play, cited in note 50; but Marston Stevens Balch has shown that she was even more indebted to *Trick*. See his book, *Thomas Middleton's 'A Trick to Catch the Old One', 'A Mad World, My Masters' and Aphra Behn's 'City Heiress'*, Salzburg: Institut für Anglistik und Amerikanistik, Universität Salzburg, 1981.
[49] Aphra Behn, *The City-Heiress*, in *The Works of Aphra Behn*, Janet Todd (ed.), Columbus: Ohio State UP, 1996, vol. 7, II.ii (pp. 27-29).
[50] Behn, *The City-Heiress*, III.i (p. 35).
[51] Ibid., V.v (pp. 74-75).
[52] Ibid., Dedication to the Right Honourable Henry, earl of Arundel, and Lord Mowbray, p. 7.
[53] See Catherine Gallagher, 'Who Was That Masked Woman?: the Prostitute and the Playwright in the Comedies of Aphra Behn', in Heidi Hutner (ed.), *Rereading Aphra Behn: History, Theory, and Criticism*, Charlottesville and London: UP of Virginia, 1993, pp. 65-85 (p. 76).
[54] Behn, *The City-Heiress*, I.i (pp. 17, 14).
[55] Ibid., I.i (p. 18).
[56] Ibid., I.i (p. 20).
[57] Gallagher, 'The Prostitute and the Playwright', p. 80.
[58] Robert Markley, '"Be Impudent, Be Saucy, Forward, Bold, Touzing, and Leud": the Politics of Masculine Sexuality and Feminine Desire in Behn's Tory Comedies', in J. Douglas Canfield and Deborah C. Payne (eds), *Cultural Readings of Restoration and Eighteenth-Century English Theater*, Athens: University of Georgia Press, 1995, pp. 114-40, (p. 117).
[59] Angeline Goreau, *Reconstructing Aphra: a Social Biography of Aphra Behn*, New York: Dial Press, 1980, p. 251.
[60] Behn's origins are murky. Todd concludes in *The Secret Life of Aphra Behn* that although the earliest account of Behn's life says she was the daughter of a gentleman from Kent, she was instead the 'daughter of a barber and a wet-nurse', Bartholomew Johnson and Elizabeth Denham (pp. 12-16). Janes Jones adds that the Johnsons were in trade and 'it would seem the family had fallen down the social scale', although she says Behn could claim to be the gentlewoman of a good family on her mother's side. 'New light on the background and early life of Aphra Behn', *Aphra Behn Studies*, Janet Todd (ed.), Cambridge: CUP, 1996, pp. 310-20, (pp. 313-14).
[61] *The City-Heiress*, V.v (p. 74).
[62] Ibid.

Index